OXFORD STUDIES IN MEDIEVAL EUROPEAN HISTORY

General Editors

CAROLINE GOODSON   AMY REMENSNYDER

and

JOHN WATTS

Stephen I, the First Christian King of Hungary

From Medieval Myth to Modern Legend

NORA BEREND

Great Clarendon Street, Oxford, OX2 6DP,
United Kingdom

Oxford University Press is a department of the University of Oxford.
It furthers the University's objective of excellence in research, scholarship,
and education by publishing worldwide. Oxford is a registered trade mark of
Oxford University Press in the UK and in certain other countries

© Nora Berend 2024

The moral rights of the author have been asserted

All rights reserved. No part of this publication may be reproduced, stored in
a retrieval system, or transmitted, in any form or by any means, without the
prior permission in writing of Oxford University Press, or as expressly permitted
by law, by licence or under terms agreed with the appropriate reprographics
rights organization. Enquiries concerning reproduction outside the scope of the
above should be sent to the Rights Department, Oxford University Press, at the
address above

You must not circulate this work in any other form
and you must impose this same condition on any acquirer

Published in the United States of America by Oxford University Press
198 Madison Avenue, New York, NY 10016, United States of America

British Library Cataloguing in Publication Data
Data available

Library of Congress Control Number: 2024930838

ISBN 9780198889342

DOI: 10.1093/9780191995439.001.0001

Printed and bound in the UK by
Clays Ltd, Elcograf S.p.A.

Links to third party websites are provided by Oxford in good faith and
for information only. Oxford disclaims any responsibility for the materials
contained in any third party website referenced in this work.

Anyám emlékére és Apámnak

Mikor mozdulok, ők ölelik egymást.
Elszomorodom néha emiatt –
ez az elmulás. Ebből vagyok.
(József Attila, A Dunánál)

Acknowledgements

Working on this book, I benefited from the help and critical comments of many people. I am immensely grateful to Ineke van't Spijker and Vedran Sulovsky for reading and commenting on the entire manuscript. To both, I owe so much; hartelijk bedankt, hvala ti! I thank all those who read parts of the text, discussed particular issues with me, drew my attention to relevant literature, and gave me invaluable advice, or helped me gain access to various items: László Veszprémy, Jonathan Shepard, Béla Zsolt Szakács, Annette Kehnel, Beatrix Romhányi, David Buckton, Paul Binski, Roman Hankeln, Nicholas Vincent, Liesbeth van Houts, Lindy Grant, Géza Pálffy, Johanna Dale, David d'Avray, Jessie Sherwood, Olenka Pevny, Carl Watkins, Miklós István Földváry, Balázs Horváth, Chris Clark, Franz-Albrecht Bornschlegel, Balázs Nagy, Sandra Schieweck. I am also grateful to the staff of the Országos Széchényi Könyvtár for facilitating my research.

I thank Géza Komoróczy for inspiring conversations; Clare Kudera for discussions that helped me formulate some inchoate thoughts; and Matthew Champion and Amy Remensnyder for encouragement to get this finally to the finish line. I am grateful to the organizers and audiences of seminars and conferences for their questions and comments at the universities of Cambridge, London, Harvard, Stockholm, Vienna, Szeged, York, Odense, and Valladolid; at the Eötvös Loránd Tudományegyetem Budapest; the Royal Danish Academy of Sciences and Letters, Copenhagen; Trinity College, Dublin; the École Normale Supérieure, Paris; and NTNU Trondheim. I also benefited from exchanges within the project 'El ejercicio del poder: espacios, agentes y escrituras', organized by Carlos Reglero de la Fuente, University of Valladolid, Spain.

Finally, I am grateful to the robin in the garden who tamed me during the pandemic and sang songs of hope.

Contents

List of Illustrations	xi
Introduction: Stephen I, from Myth to History and Back Again	1
1. Cupan	27
2. *Stephen, the King*: A Rock Opera in the Late Communist Period and Questions of National Identity	69
3. The Holy Dexter	129
4. The Hungarian Crown	156
Epilogue	237
Selected Bibliography	239
Index	251

List of Illustrations

1. Portrait of Stephen from the contemporary chasuble   xii
2. The quartering of Cupan from the fourteenth-century Illuminated Chronicle   33
3. Gyula Vikidál as Koppány   74
4. The Holy Dexter   130
5. The so-called 'Holy Crown of Hungary'   160

Figure 1. Portrait of Stephen from the contemporary chasuble
https://hu.wikipedia.org/wiki/Magyar_koron%C3%A1z%C3%A1si_pal%C3%A1st#/media/
F%C3%A1jl:Portrayal_of_Stephen_I,_King_of_Hungary_on_the_coronation_pall.jpg

Introduction

Stephen I, from Myth to History and Back Again

Stephen I (r. 997–1038) was the first Christian king of Hungary. Celebrated as the founder of state and church, he has been a fundamental figure in national history and in politics. His case is one of only nine globally where a national holiday is dedicated to a medieval personage.[1] Equally unusually, in the Middle Ages, three separate feasts were devoted to his memory: the day of his death (15 August), the translation of his body (his canonization, 20 August), and the invention of the relic of his right hand (30 May).[2]

Stephen's portrait gazes at us from an embroidered textile, made while he was still alive. We are face to face with Stephen, who is represented on the chasuble that was a present from him and his wife Gisela to the royal church dedicated to the Virgin Mary at Fehérvár in 1031.[3] It was later turned into the coronation mantle of Hungary's kings. The chasuble is undoubtedly authentic, even if repaired; an inscription on the piece itself provides its date and purpose. It features not only a portrait of the king and his wife (both as donors) but also representations of prophets, apostles, and martyrs. Yet, despite the chasuble's authenticity, the portrait gives us a mere illusion of reality, suggestive of more profound problems with our medieval sources. Medieval portraits were not true likenesses: artistic conventions, rather than a desire for life-like depiction governed them, not to mention the additional challenge of embroidering a portrait in golden and silk thread on silk fabric.[4]

---

[1] Eviatar Zerubavel, *Time Maps: Collective Memory and the Social Shape of the Past* (Chicago— London: Chicago University Press, 2003), 33.

[2] Vilmos Fraknói, 'A Szent Jobb', *Századok* (1901): 880–904, at 880; Géza Karsai, 'Szent István király tisztelete', in *Emlékkönyv Szent István király halálának kilencszázadik évfordulóján*, ed. Jusztinián Serédi, 3 vols. (Budapest: Magyar Tudományos Akadémia, 1938), vol. 3, 155–256, at 170–4, 178. The vigil of 20 August was also listed separately as a feast on 19 August. These feast-days were not always consistent, for example, a fifteenth-century breviary listed 30 July for the *inventio* of the Holy Dexter: ibid., 182.

[3] Éva Kovács—Zsuzsa Lovag, *The Hungarian Crown and Other Regalia*, 2nd rev. edn (Budapest: Corvina, 1980), 58–75; on the inscription, 58; István Bardoly, ed., *The Coronation Mantle of the Hungarian Kings* (Budapest: Hungarian National Museum, 2005), 158–9. The chasuble has been repeatedly repaired.

[4] There are no life-like portraits even two centuries later, of Louis IX (r. 1226–70): Jacques Le Goff, *Saint Louis* (Paris: Gallimard, 1996), 516–17.

2   STEPHEN I, THE FIRST CHRISTIAN KING OF HUNGARY

Did Stephen wear a short beard and moustache? He may have, but it was also the conventional image of the ruler, as attested by the depiction of Henry II, and Christ himself, in the Regensburg sacramentary (1002–14).[5] Did Stephen wear the type of crown he wears in the image? Perhaps so, but the same type of diadem crown is used on the chasuble not only for the queen but also for the various martyr saints who are represented.[6] We cannot draw any firm, historically reliable conclusion about Stephen from the portrait, beyond the knowledge of how and why it was made. The tangible presence teases us, yet yields no certainties. It is symbolic of our knowledge of the first Christian king of Hungary: we have some real, authentic traces of the past, yet there are hard limits to what we can know about that past. Some interpretations, especially if well contextualized, provide a rough sense of past developments, but many areas remain where we cannot hope to gain true knowledge.

Our historical information itself is meagre.[7] Sources are few, fragmentary, and difficult to interpret. This basic impediment determines our ignorance, extending to even the most elementary biographical data. This is easily demonstrated by means of one example, Stephen's lifespan. He is usually depicted as an old man by the time of his death. The fourteenth-century chronicles narrate that in his old age, he was afflicted by pains in his foot.[8] This may be true, or it may be a literary borrowing: limping in old age occurs in Einhard's *Life of Charlemagne* (which in turn was based on Suetonius's description of Augustus).[9] It may even be an elaboration on his saint's *Lives*, which stated that Stephen was so ill before his death that he was unable to stand.[10] In this particular case, we simply cannot know; moreover, we do not even know how old Stephen was when he died, because we have no reliable information on the date of his birth.[11] Later sources variously provide 967, 969, and 975, but none of them is trustworthy.

---

[5] Munich, Bayerische Staatsbibliothek, Clm 4456, fol. 11r, numerous online reproductions, for example, https://ff-65a4.kxcdn.com/assets/uploads/OriginalDocs_old/1229/treasures-bavarian-state-library-collection-facsimile-edition-06.jpg.

[6] Kovács—Lovag, *The Hungarian Crown*, 65.

[7] While this is often acknowledged, its implications for historical analysis is not necessarily heeded, e.g. Gyula Kristó, 'Szent István', in *Írások Szent Istvánról és koráról*, Gyula Kristó (Szeged: Szegedi Középkorász Műhely, 2000), 35–47.

[8] 'nam et pedum doloribus urgebatur', in 'Chronici Hungarici', *SRH* I, 319.

[9] László Veszprémy, 'Fikció és valóság István korában: Kós Károly, Az országépítő', *Korunk*, 26, no. 8 (2015): 13–21, at 14; O. Holder-Egger, ed., 'Einhardi Vita Karoli Magni', *MGH SS Rer. Germ.*, vol. 25 (Hanover: Hahn, 1911), 1–41, at 27 c. 22; Suetonius, *De Vita XII Caesarum*, Loeb Classical Library 31 (London: Heinemann, 1913), Divus Augustus 246, c. 80. https://penelope.uchicago.edu/Thayer/L/Roman/Texts/Suetonius/12Caesars/Augustus*.html.

[10] 'in pedibus stare nequibat', 'Legenda Minor' and Life by Hartvic, *SRH* II, 399, 430, respectively.

[11] Uncertainties bedevil his burial too; the sarcophagus that traditionally was thought to have held Stephen's remains is now thought to have been used for the canonization; it cannot even be definitively linked to Stephen. Most recently, with further bibliography: Orsolya Bubryák, 'Észrevételek a Szent István-szarkofág történetéhez', in *Szent István király bazilikájának utóélete: A középkori Romkert 1938-tól napjainkig*, ed. Petra Gärtner (Székesfehérvár: Szent István Király Múzeum, 2015), 23–8.

INTRODUCTION 3

Among the indicators for his potential birth date is a claim by the *Legenda Maior* (a hagiographical life probably written for the canonization of 1083) that his father designated him his successor when Stephen entered *adolescentia* and Stephen then gained power as a *iuvenis*. The fourteenth-century chronicles claim that Stephen fought his opponent Cupan directly after his father's death in 997 while he was *in adolescentia*. The *Legenda Minor* (probably written between 1083 and 1100) maintains that Stephen ascended the throne while he was still a child (*puer*).[12] Although scholars have attempted to reconcile the sources or opt for a logical solution, in fact again, we cannot know. It is impossible to tell if any of these sources contains historically correct information. Even if they do, different understandings of the exact age-group designated by *puer* and *adolescens* existed (thus, *pueritia* in some schemes covers the entire span that is divided between *pueritia* and *adolescentia* in others), and the age-range in accepted usage meant that *adolescens*, for example, could designate a fourteen-year old or someone in their late twenties.[13] Stephen thus could have been still in his teens or close to thirty when he took power. The date of his death in 1038 is about as certain as we can get, reported in the Annals of Altaich.[14] He could have been in his fifties or around seventy when he died. The convention representing him as an old man derives from the period when the Angevins ruled in Hungary (1301–86), when the court fostered the cult of the three 'holy kings' (actually two kings and a prince: Stephen, Ladislas, and Stephen's son Emeric); inspired by several models including the three kings who rendered homage to Jesus, the royal saints were represented as a youth (Emeric), middle-aged warrior (Ladislas), and wise old man (Stephen).[15]

Since we cannot even pinpoint his birth date, no wonder we are not able to discern his character traits. Endless and futile debates have tried to ascertain which medieval text contains an authentic description of the king: was he pious,

[12] Gyula Kristó, *Szent István király* (Budapest: Vince Kiadó, 2001), 30–1; Gyula Kristó, 'Szent István születési ideje és megkeresztelése', in *Árpád fejedelemtől Géza fejedelemig: 20 tanulmány a 10. századi magyar történelemről*, Gyula Kristó (Budapest: Akadémiai Kiadó, 2002), 225–32.

[13] Isabelle Cochelin, 'Introduction: pre-thirteenth-century definitions of the life cycle', in *Medieval Life Cycles: Continuity and Change*, ed. Isabelle Cochelin, Karen Elaine Smyth (Turnhout: Brepols, 2013), 1–54, esp. 3–5, 7–10, 12.

[14] 'Annales Altahenses maiores', ed. W. de Giesebrecht, Edmund L. B. von Oefele, in *MGH SS Rer. Germ.*, vol. 4 (Hanover: Hahn, 1890), 23. Not all sources are unanimous: the *Illuminated Chronicle*, for example, claims that he ruled for forty-six years, which does not match the usually recognized regnal dates 997–1038: *SRH* I, 321. A thorough analysis of all different datings: Zoltán Tóth, 'Szent István legrégibb életirata nyomán 2: A Szent Istvánra vonatkozó időadatok és a Szent Jobb hagyományának tanúsága', *Századok*, 123 (1989): 241–72.

[15] Tünde Wehli, 'Az 1083-ban kanonizált szentek kultusza középkori művészetünkben', in *Művelődéstörténeti tanulmányok a magyar középkorról*, ed. Erik Fügedi (Budapest: Gondolat, 1986), 54–60, at 58–9; Ernő Marosi, ed., *Magyarországi Művészet 1300–1470 körül* (Budapest: Akadémiai Kiadó, 1987), 206.

4 STEPHEN I, THE FIRST CHRISTIAN KING OF HUNGARY

cruel, or both?[16] Again, a small detail illuminates how impossible it is to give a historical answer, even though we can speculate about what seems plausible. The texts we have are shot through with *topoi* and while some of their statements may be true, nothing is innocuous enough to warrant blind trust in its authentic descriptiveness. One of the hagiographical texts that depicts the saint, the *Legenda Maior*, and another based on it, Hartvic's Life, stated that he barely ever laughed in his lifetime.[17] The famous Hungarian historian Gyula Szekfű counted this among the 'realistic characteristics' of Stephen.[18] However, since Christ does not laugh in the Bible, ecclesiastical authors have long depicted saints in a similar manner.[19]

Even most history books, let alone popularizing work, shy away from the admission of so much tenuousness and maintain or at least strive to offer much more certainty. Thus, based on plausible explanations or interpretive claims, various historians 'fixed' Stephen's birth date to 975 or c. 980 for example. Every brick in the edifice of such interpretations is held together by the mortar of hypothetical reasoning. While each hypothetical step towards a 'certainty' may be minor, their cumulative effect is to offer a narrative tale of Stephen which, in the end, is largely speculative when it comes to his character, intentions or beliefs, and several aspects of his reign.

What we can infer of his reign with the greatest plausibility from contemporary written and material sources more or less fits into the central European, Scandinavian, and Rus' trends of the period; in these regions, warrior chiefs anchored their power in novel ways by adopting Christianity and developing more stable territorial control roughly in the tenth and eleventh centuries.[20] Stephen's father had already played some role in the creation of a new religious foundation for power: he asked for baptism, invited missionaries, and successfully

---

[16] E.g. György Györffy, 'Szent István történeti kutatásunkban', in *Szent István és kora*, ed. Ferenc Glatz, József Kardos (Budapest: MTA Történettudományi Intézet, 1988), 18–22, at 20–1; György Györffy, *István király és műve* (Budapest: Gondolat, 1977; 4th rev. edn Budapest: Balassi Kiadó, 2013), 122–33.

[17] *SRH* II, 392, 429, respectively.

[18] Gyula Szekfű, 'Szent István a magyar történet századaiban', in *Emlékkönyv Szent István*, Serédi, vol. 3, 1–80, at 6; repr. *Szent István Emlékkönyv* (Budapest: Szent István Társulat, 1988), 529–606, at 532.

[19] Jacques Le Goff, 'Rire au Moyen Age', *Les Cahiers du Centre de Recherches Historiques*, 3 (1989), http://journals.openedition.org/ccrh/2918; DOI: https://doi.org/10.4000/ccrh.2918; Winfried Wilhelmly, ed., *Seliges Lächeln, höllisches Gelächter: Das Lachen in Kunst und Kultur des Mittelalters. Sonderausstellung des Bischöflichen Dom- und Diözösenmuseums Mainz* (Mainz: Dom Museum, 2012). Hagiographers of the Hungarian princess Margaret were still reluctant to represent a saint laughing much later; see Miklós Halmágyi, 'Sírás, mosoly és nevetés a Szent Margitról szóló középkori forrásokban', *Magyar Egyháztörténeti Vázlatok* (2016, nos. 1–4): 5–20.

[20] The following summary on Stephen's reign is based on: Nora Berend, József Laszlovszky, Béla Zsolt Szakács, 'The kingdom of Hungary', in *Christianization and the Rise of Christian Monarchy: Central Europe, Scandinavia and Rus' c. 950–c. 1200*, ed. Nora Berend (Cambridge: Cambridge University Press, 2007), 319–68, and Nora Berend, Przemysław Urbańczyk and Przemysław Wiszewski, *Central Europe in the High Middle Ages, c. 900–c. 1300* (Cambridge: Cambridge University Press, 2013), especially 125–37, 147–60. Further details and bibliographies can be found there.

negotiated for the hand of a German princess for his son. It is possible that a monastery and a missionary bishopric were also established during his reign. Stephen created ecclesiastical structures and founded more ecclesiastical institutions, in parallel to extending his territorial power, as other contemporary rulers did in central and northern Europe. He established dioceses, monasteries, and churches. He founded the bishoprics of Veszprém and Győr, and the archbishopric of Esztergom by the early years of the eleventh century, as well as the dioceses of Pécs (1009) and Csanád (1030). A number of other bishoprics were established by Stephen, but the dating is debated, while some others may have been established by him or by his successors: Transylvania (1003?), Eger (1009?), Kalocsa (perhaps as early as 1009, first mentioned in the middle of the eleventh century), and Vác, first mentioned in 1075, but according to some historians founded by Stephen.

Church building was also fundamental to create the infrastructure for the new religion. Cathedrals and baptismal churches were first erected in western Hungary, which was firmly under the control of the royal dynasty. None of them survives in its original form. The three-aisled basilica of Fehérvár was built to be the king's chapel and was an imposing stone building. However, many of the early churches were wooden or wattle-and-daub constructions. Stephen's father Géza is mentioned as the founder of the first monastery, that of Pannonhalma, with Stephen completing his work. Stephen also continued to establish more Benedictine monasteries, as well as Greek Orthodox ones. Monks as well as clerics came from foreign lands.

Missionary work continued, primarily with Slavic and German missionaries, but some individuals from other areas played a role as well, such as a Venetian monk. Liturgy, church dedications, artefacts, and architecture channelled influences from many areas, including German and Italian lands, although the precise origin of many architectural styles, for example, remains debated, as does the extent of Byzantine influence. The large number of Slavic words in the Hungarian ecclesiastical vocabulary can be understood as either due to borrowing from local populations or introduced by missionaries. Bruno of Querfurt and other sources mentioned the use of physical violence against some who refused to convert. Immigrant clergy were crucial in laying the foundations of Christianity, and some are known by name, including men who became bishops.

Sources refer to Stephen collecting relics, acquiring them from Otto III, perhaps from Cluny, and from Ochrid while he was on military campaign there. He was hailed by many contemporaries for opening the overland pilgrimage route to Jerusalem by making travel through Hungary safe. He was, perhaps through his wife Gisela, sister of Emperor Henry II, also linked to monasteries outside the kingdom: Stephen and his wife were remembered in the prayers of the Benedictines of Salzburg and Tegernsee. In all these, it is impossible to separate Stephen's personal piety from his fulfilling the role of a Christian king.

Stephen also issued legislation, which survives in later, interpolated copies in collections of law-books that were most probably compiled after Stephen's death. The laws place a very great emphasis on compelling people to follow basic Christian practices, such as going to church on Sundays, fasting on prescribed days, and Christian burial. Heavy punishments were prescribed both for breaching such regulations and for following practices that were deemed pagan. The legislation also decreed how basic ecclesiastical infrastructure was to be set up, with ten villages to build a church and the king and bishop to provide vestments and liturgical books; however, it is impossible to know the extent to which this was carried out. The practical impact of Christianization—that is, the speed of change during Stephen's reign itself—is impossible to measure. Archaeological excavations of cemeteries bring us the closest to the evidence for change; however, their interpretation is debated. Whether row cemeteries were pagan, Christian, or started out as pre-Christian and then at some point were converted to Christian use, has not been resolved. The overall decline in grave goods over the course of the eleventh century can be traced, but there was no decisive break during Stephen's reign. Likewise, pagan cemeteries seem to end only during the reigns of Ladislas I (1077–95) and Coloman (1095–1116), as these rulers' coins are the last that have been found in pre-Christian burials. Graveyards appeared around churches during the eleventh century, but in some areas only at the end of that century.

Géza and Stephen accelerated the change in power structures that had started after the Hungarian settlement. The system of many chieftains was being replaced by sole rulership; Stephen defeated some independent territorial lords, including his maternal uncle Gyula. He also eliminated potential opponents from his kingroup, by blinding or exile. At the start of his reign, Stephen's rule only extended to limited areas; over time, he attached the regions from local lords he defeated, and married his daughters to other chieftains, extending the sphere of his real power. However, the idea that he established the borders of the Kingdom of Hungary where they eventually lay for centuries is ahistorical, and was created by later political ideology. He also harnessed the tools and personnel provided through Christianization. The warriors who formed the entourage of his wife Gisela served as heavy cavalry. Organizational and institutional forms that accompanied Christianity provided new means to increase his power.

Géza's precise role is impossible to establish, because the written sources credit Stephen, as the first Christian king, and do not describe Géza's reign in detail. The beginnings of territorial organization, royal administration, written legislation, coinage, and taxation are thus linked to Stephen. He followed western, especially German models that were available often through immigrant ecclesiastics and warriors. Such influences are detectable, for example, in the production of written documents and coinage. Administrative literacy was introduced during Stephen's reign, although only a few, interpolated charters remain. The usage of the German

INTRODUCTION 7

imperial chancery was introduced by its former personnel. Two coin-types, both silver deniers, are known from Stephen's reign, although their exact dating is debated. The first, issued before 1006, bears the inscriptions 'Lancea regis' and 'regia civitas', the second, issued before 1025, those of 'Stephanus rex' and 'regia civitas'. Their weight and design show similarities to Bavarian coinage. The king used the lance received from the emperor as his regnal symbol. Political connections to both the Ottonian-Salian Empire and Byzantium were sustained during and after his reign.

There is evidence of the start of a territorial-administrative organization during his reign as well. Royal forts, at first often wooden and earth constructions, were built as local power-centres, the focal points of a rudimentary territorial organization that divided the territory under Stephen's control into counties. The network of strongholds is dated by some to the reign of Stephen himself, but others argue its origins go back earlier. The origins of the county system—distinct from royal lands also overseen by the same royal representative—are shrouded in the silence of the sources. Hypothetical reconstructions include the possibility of a parallel administrative and military territorial division, or one that included both functions. The counties organized during Stephen's reign were only the beginning of the later fully fledged system. Royal representatives exercised both military and judicial functions, and castle warriors provided the military force. Serving people produced the necessities for the court, complemented by the collection of royal revenues. The system of taxation was reformed in the early twelfth century.

Probably the most famous source linked to Stephen, the so-called Admonitions, is a representative of the 'King's Mirror' genre. It purports to record the words of the king to his son, preparing him for rulership. The text, however, was certainly not written by Stephen, but instead, by an ecclesiastical author.[21] Yet Stephen failed to leave behind a living male heir, and designated his sister's son Peter Orseolo, whose father was the doge of Venice, to inherit the throne. This triggered repeated revolts and civil war, until members of another branch of the dynasty established their rule.

It is also clear that Stephen did not establish the Hungarian state or church single-handedly; immigrant nobles and ecclesiastics played a crucial role during his reign, as did his successors in developing, changing, and refining political and ecclesiastical structures. The very fact of parallel developments elsewhere in the region militates against attributing the foundation of the state and church to his wisdom; similar processes took place in other Central European realms, as well as Scandinavia. Historians have debated the role of Otto III (996–1002) in the political and ecclesiastical changes of the region, while national historiographies all

---

[21] Előd Nemerkényi, 'Review of scholarship on the "Admonitions" of King Saint Stephen of Hungary', *Acta classica Universitatis scientiarum Debreceniensis*, 44 (2008): 151–8.

8   STEPHEN I, THE FIRST CHRISTIAN KING OF HUNGARY

suggested the significance of their own local rulers.[22] Clearly, however, these were interlinked processes with multiple drivers of change.

Yet the significance of Stephen in Hungarian historiography cannot be overstated.[23] Throughout the centuries, he has been recognized as the founder of the state and church, but through variations of that basic tenet, each age also created its own Stephen. Thus, there are numerous biographies of the ruler, many of them deliberately or unconsciously catering to the then prevailing regime. Not all historical work of course had an immediate political agenda, but most saw Stephen through a lens at least as focused on the present as on the past. Thus, for example, in early modernity and in the context of confessional rivalry, Protestant historians saw him as bringing a pure form of Christianity to Hungary that was closer to evangelical reformed Christianity than to Catholicism, while Catholics championing a *Regnum Marianum*, Hungary as the country of the Virgin, extolled Stephen for offering the kingdom to Mary.[24] Harnessed by the counter-reformation and by propagators of anti-Ottoman war, from the early seventeenth century, Stephen was represented, together with the Virgin Mary, as a national patron saint who liberates the country.[25] In the eighteenth century, Franz Adam Kollár wrote of St Stephen as an apostolic ruler, whose power was limited neither by the estates nor by the church, a model absolutist king for the Habsburg ruler Maria Theresa. Writing for the millennial celebrations of the foundation of the Hungarian state, Henrik Marczali depicted a Stephen independent of everyone, preaching, and baptizing his people. Morally and spiritually far above the people, he wanted to elevate them to his level, while at the same time he was a talented politician and military leader. Marczali also emphasized the creation of the realm

---

[22] Johannes Fried, *Otto III. und Boleslaw Chrobry: Das Widmungsbild des Aachener Evangeliars, der 'Akt von Gnesen' und das frühe polnische und ungarische Königtum. Eine Bildanalyse und ihre historischen Folgen*, 2nd edn (Stuttgart: Franz Steiner Verlag, 2001); Gerd Althoff, *Otto III*, tr. Phyllis G. Jestice (Philadelphia, PA: Pennsylvania University Press, 2003; Berend, ed., *Christianization*, 16–17; 110–11; Berend, Urbańczyk and Wiszewski, *Central Europe in the High Middle Ages*, 121–2.

[23] Overviews on the historiography: Szekfű, 'Szent István a magyar történet századaiban'; Györffy, 'Szent István történeti kutatásunkban'; László Veszprémy, ed., *Szent István és az államalapítás* (Budapest: Osiris, 2002).

[24] Szekfű, 'Szent István a magyar történet századaiban', 52, repr. 578 and 35, repr. 561, respectively; Gergely Tóth, *Szent István, Szent Korona, államalapítás a protestáns történetírásban (16–18. század)* (Budapest: MTA Bölcsészettudományi Kutatóközpont Történettudományi Intézet, 2016). During the sixteenth century, while some Protestant writers turned Stephen into a model king along Protestant ideas, he became especially a reference-point for Catholic constructs of the realm, disseminated by preaching, songs, and drama: István Bitskey, *Eszmék, művek, hagyományok* (Debrecen: Kossuth Egyetemi Kiadó, 1996), 269–71. Such a representation had its roots in religious images, e.g. a 1511 Missale for the diocese of Zagreb represented the Virgin with Sts. Stephen, Prince Emeric, and Ladislas I; repr. in *Szent István és kora: kiállítás az Országos Széchényi Könyvtárban 4 July–29 October 1988*, ed. Györgyné Wix [no page numbers].

[25] Éva Knapp—Gábor Tüskés, 'Szent István király és a Szent Jobb együttes ábrázolása a sokszorosított grafikában', in *Jubileumi csokor Csapodi Csaba tiszteletére: tanulmányok*, ed. Marianne Rozsondai (Budapest: Argumentum Kiadó, 2002): 103–34, at 126.

INTRODUCTION 9

by the Hungarian nation.[26] In 1904, the Roman Catholic priest and historian János Karácsonyi wrote that the quick and permanent conversion of the Hungarians was due to St. Stephen; indeed, Stephen's 'efforts, sharp mind, sublime moral conduct caused the Hungarian nation to accept willingly rather than out of compulsion legal order, Christian culture, work instead of theft, mutual neighbourly love instead of violence, soul-lifting Christian faith instead of soul-killing revelry'.[27]

In 1938, Bálint Hóman wrote of a Stephen who spent much of his life at war, and was a friend and ally of Germany and 'Italy' (Venice and the papacy) while saving national sovereignty; according to Hóman, the king also formulated Hungary's historical vocation.[28] Hóman was a favoured 'court' historian, Minister of Religion and Education in the years 1932–8 and 1939–42, and member of the House of Representatives (1932–45) during the authoritarian, limited parliamentary system of Regent Miklós Horthy, an ally of fascist Italy and Nazi Germany. In the same year (1938), Gyula Szekfű insisted that it was impossible to understand Stephen without accepting that Hungarian statehood and Christianity were inseparably one in that period.[29] For Szekfű, Christianity was the protection against the 'barbarians' of his days: communists and Nazis. In 1945, Erik Molnár relegated Christianity to an ideology in the service of power and extolled a secular Stephen who resolved the great crises of his time while fighting for power.[30] For Molnár, the communist solution to the crises of his own era compared in significance to Stephen's achievements in resolving the crises of his epoch.[31]

With Hungary moving towards a communist takeover, and then as it became part of the Soviet Bloc, Slavic influence on Stephen and the Hungarians was emphasized. Thus, Erik Molnár in 1945 suggested that more advanced agriculture was learned from the Slavic inhabitants of the country, and the Slavic origin of the word *megye*, a term that came to designate county in Hungarian, was used to argue for the Slavic origin of the county-organization itself.[32] Slavic influence on

---

[26] Henrik Marczali, *Szent István királysága* (1896, repr. Budapest: Kassák Könyv és Lapkiadó Kft, 2000), 8, 13, 62, 71.

[27] János Karácsonyi, *Szent István király élete* (Budapest: Szent István Társulat, 1904), introduction (for the quotation) and chapter 6, http://www.mek.oszk.hu/11200/11211/html/#7.

[28] Bálint Hóman, *Szent István* (1938, reprint Budapest: Szent István Társulat—Kairosz Kiadó, 1998), 263, 266, 276, 321.

[29] Szekfű, 'Szent István a magyar történet századaiban', 3–5, repr. 529–31.

[30] Erik Molnár, *Szent István* (Budapest: Szikra, 1945), 8, partial repr. in Veszprémy, *Szent István*, 551–4. Later on, the 'progressiveness' of Stephen's role was also linked to creating class society, feudal property, using religion to prop up the new social and economic system, e.g. Lajos Elekes, Emma Léderer, György Székely, ed., *Magyarország története a korai és virágzó feudalizmus korszakában (A honfoglalástól 1526-ig)* (Budapest: Tankönyvkiadó, 1957), 26–31.

[31] Ivan T. Berend, 'Szent István a magyar történet századaiban', in *Szent István és kora*, Glatz—Kardos, 9–17, at 12–14.

[32] Molnár, *Szent István*, 11, repr. in Veszprémy, *Szent István*, 552; on early Slavic linguistic traces, Gyula Kristó, 'A magyar fejedelemség a 10. században' in *Árpád fejedelemtől Géza fejedelemig*, 241–68, esp. 241–3; in 1977, Györffy argued that while the origin of the word is Slavic, both in Slavic

10   STEPHEN I, THE FIRST CHRISTIAN KING OF HUNGARY

Stephen's state was opposed to the earlier (and later) emphasis on Stephen joining western Europe through Christianization. Published in 1956, György Bónis's biography of the king argued that the Hungarian populace, under the guidance of a great man, was the true hero, able to transform their economic, social, and religious structure in order to survive; a framework of analysis derived from the then compulsory communist form of Marxism.[33] In the 1950s and 1960s, historians refuted Hóman's ideas about Stephen's German orientation, asserting that, on the contrary, his state was built on the foundations of Slavic state organization and he started to defend Hungary's independence from German attacks using 'Slav-Hungarian tactics'.[34] In the late 1980s, when Hungary started to have more economic ties to western Europe, Stephen appeared as the precursor of those bridging the divide between East and West.[35] From all these perspectives, however, Stephen, founder of the Hungarian state, realpolitician, strong in action, brave in danger, willing to abolish what was obsolete, was said to represent the noblest progressive traditions of the country.[36] Yet what those noblest traditions consisted of changed over time; even radically different meanings filled that receptacle.[37]

Recognizing and criticizing the ideological biases of previous generations, each historian writing about Stephen was certain of presenting a truer image of the 'real' Stephen. Virtually every historian has noted that the followers of the most diverse trends tried to expropriate Stephen in order to justify their own ideas; an acknowledgement usually followed by the claim to have access to the more genuine Stephen. There is not much to distinguish Hóman's claim in 1938 from Bónis's in 1956, despite the chasm that lies between the ideologies of the periods. For Hóman, 'After sending the false portraits that came to life in the rich imagination of pedantic minds back to the world of the imagination, we must now evoke and get to know the real St Stephen.'[38] For Bónis, 'It is a difficult task, involving heavy responsibility, after so many good- and bad-intentioned distortions, to draw the true face of King Stephen.'[39]

At the same time, diametrically opposite conclusions have been offered by medievalists writing biographies of Stephen. There are those who claim that

---

and originally in Hungarian the word meant boundary; it was not used to designate 'county' in Slavic and cannot be used to suggest a Slavic origin of the county organization: Györffy, *István király*, 212.

[33] György Bónis, *István király* (Budapest: 'Művelt Nép' Tudományos és Ismeretterjesztő Kiadó, 1956).

[34] Elekes et al., *Magyarország története*, 30; Erik Molnár, Ervin Pamlényi, György Székely, ed., *Magyarország története*, 2 vols. (Budapest: Gondolat Könyvkiadó, 1964), vol. 1, 54–5.

[35] György Györffy, 'Államszervezés', in *Magyarország története: Előzmények és magyar történet 1242-ig*, vol. 1, ed. György Székely (Budapest: Akadémiai Kiadó, 1984), 717–834, at 815–19.

[36] Bónis, *István király*, 156; Hóman, *Szent István*, 321.

[37] On such preservation of pre-existing structures to be 'refilled': Philippe Buc, *Holy War, Martyrdom and Terror: Christianity, Violence and the West, ca. 70 C.E. to the Iraq War* (Philadelphia, PA: Pennsylvania University Press, 2015), 4.

[38] Hóman, *Szent István*, 8.   [39] Bónis, *István király*, 5.

INTRODUCTION   11

medieval hagiography provides the key: 'Many historians qualify Christian legends as tales like the myths of antiquity or even think of them as conscious falsification of history. We should not be deceived by the legendary accretions; these works [medieval hagiography] do indeed conserve the memory of the historical personage.'[40] Yet even based on the same hagiographical sources, Stephen's alleged character varies. For one historian, the *Lives* show the grim majesty of a king who never laughed and knew no mercy, although he was great even in his mistakes.[41] For another, the historical personality of the king revealed by the hagiographical lives is one of deep piety; he saw as his main task the religious re-education of the population.[42] On the contrary, for another scholar, 'St Stephen was a great statesman who consciously followed the medieval ideal of kingship, and who only became one-sidedly religious after the loss of his son, Prince Imre [Emeric], in his illness in old age.'[43] While a fourth maintains: 'There is no reason to doubt that acquiring the entire Carpathian basin featured from the beginning in Stephen's programme.'[44]

The strong emphasis on finding the 'true' Stephen in historiography has not been unrelated to the very direct uses made of Stephen by politicians in order to legitimize their own activities and interpretations through alleged continuities with the founder figure. The history of his feast-day (20 August) is illustrative of growing political instrumentalization. Initially a purely religious event, it started to acquire the trappings of a day of national celebration in the nineteenth century. Its status as a national holiday was further elevated by the jubilee celebrations in 1938, but was then reduced to a religious event once more after the war. Soon— via becoming the 'day of the new bread'—it was transformed into the day of the Socialist Constitution between 1950 and 1989, but restored as St Stephen's feast-day, celebrated nationally, thereafter, to become in the new millennium one of the most important national holidays.[45]

In the age of mass politics and later on, populism, Stephen's prominence was cemented especially in right-wing political rhetoric. He was upheld as fundamental to secular statehood, and used to legitimize government policies in internal and external discourse in interwar Hungary. The idea that Hungarians were destined to lead other nationalities in the Carpathian Basin was attributed to St Stephen ('Szentistváni gondolat') and was used to justify irredentist territorial claims; the slogan to restore 'St Stephen's realm' lent historical justification to the contention that Hungary's inalienable territorial borders had been violated by the

---

[40] Tamás Bogyay, *Stephanus Rex* (Budapest: Ecclesia Kiadó, 1988), 9.
[41] Elemér Varjú, *Legendae Sancti Regis Stephani. Szent István király legendái* (Budapest: Singer—Wolfner, 1928), 48–9.
[42] Bogyay, *Stephanus Rex*, 45.   [43] Györffy, 'Szent István történeti kutatásunkban', 20.
[44] Zoltán Lenkey—Attila Zsoldos, *Szent István és III. András* (Budapest: Kossuth Kiadó, 2003), 33. Z. Lenkey is a pseudonym for Zsoldos, who is sole author.
[45] Gábor Gyáni, 'Kommemoratív emlékezet és történelmi igazolás', in *Szent István*, Veszprémy, 569–81, at 570–1. Law of 1938 in Veszprémy, ed. *Szent István*, 539.

12   STEPHEN I, THE FIRST CHRISTIAN KING OF HUNGARY

Treaty of Trianon (1920).[46] In 1938, St Stephen's year (the 900th anniversary of his death), Budapest also hosted the eucharistic world congress. Governmental participation in a Catholic event turned it into a national celebration; evoking St Stephen, the occasion was used as a vehicle for the regime's 'Christian national' ideology.[47] Cardinal Pacelli, the papal legate, was also involved in the celebration of the year of St Stephen, a 'neobaroque legitimation' exercise, with the Calvinist Regent Horthy participating at the mass he celebrated.[48] Horthy, in his speech on St Stephen's day in 1938, extolled the king who 'trampled all opposition under-foot' to create the Christian Hungarian kingdom, who resolved the life or death situation in which his nation found itself, and whose political thought equated to peace and justice in central Europe.[49] At the Mausoleum of St Stephen in Székesfehérvár Horthy himself was represented along with the holy dexter and the 'Holy Crown' on frescoes by Vilmos Aba-Novák. While in the socialist state Stephen had a much lesser role, he was not completely written out of the story: Stephen built his state based on Slavic state organization, and defended it against the expansionist, imperialist West, according to 1950s propagandistic work.[50] Moreover, the return of the crown long held to be 'St Stephen's crown' in 1978 from the USA was widely seen as a legitimization of the Kádár regime.

Stephen is once again a key political reference point in the early twenty-first century. The 'Basic Law of Hungary' (Magyarország Alaptörvénye, a term which also has the connotations of 'fundamental', and 'foundational'), accepted by Parliament in April 2011 and effective from 1 January 2012, that replaced the constitution, starts with a 'national creed' (nemzeti hitvallás) containing a series of propositions put forward in the name of 'members of the Hungarian nation'. The first one states: 'We are proud that our King St Stephen a thousand years ago placed the Hungarian state on stable foundations, and made our fatherland a part of Christian Europe',[51] and adds, 'We recognise the role of Christianity in con-serving the nation.'[52] Among the state-commissioned fifteen historical paintings that represent the last 150 years of Hungarian history, one (by Iván Szkok)

---

[46] The post-First World War treaty detached significant territories from the former Kingdom of Hungary in the break-up of the Austro-Hungarian Monarchy, see Chapter 4. József Kardos, 'István—és a "szentistváni gondolat"', Népszabadság, 39, no. 195 (20 August 1981): 11.

[47] Jenő Gergely, 'Az 1938-as Szent István év', in Szent István és kora, Glatz—Kardos, 231–8; Jenő Gergely, Eucharisztikus világkongresszus Budapesten, 1938 (Budapest: Kossuth Könyvkiadó, 1988).

[48] Gergely, 'Az 1938-as Szent István év', 233, 237.

[49] 'Horthy Miklós kormányzó Szent István-napi beszéde (1938)', repr. in Szent István, Veszprémy, 541–2, at 542.

[50] [no author] 'Rákosi Mátyás és a magyar történettudomány', Századok, 86, no. 14 (1952): 1–23, at 2.

[51] 'Büszkék vagyunk arra, hogy Szent István királyunk ezer évvel ezelőtt szilárd alapokra helyezte a magyar államot, és hazánkat a keresztény Európa részévé tette'. Magyar Közlöny, 43 (2011): 10656. All translations are my own unless otherwise stated. The law can also be accessed online at: http://www.kozlonyok.hu/nkonline/MKPDF/hiteles/mk11043.pdf [last accessed 14 December 2011].

[52] Ibid. 'Elismerjük a kereszténység nemzetmegtartó szerepét'.

INTRODUCTION   13

celebrated the Basic Law.[53] The legible title page of the law is in the centre, and above it is St Stephen of Hungary, wearing the 'Holy Crown'. He justifies or even sanctifies the Basic law: the image suggests that the law ultimately derives from him. This conforms to nationalist ideas often aired in the Horthy period on St Stephen having 'set the direction of the whole future life of the nation'.[54] The representation of Stephen with the 'Holy Crown' also confirms another dearly held tenet of the current government, that this object embodies and symbolizes the Hungarian state.

Despite disagreement over the 'true' character of Stephen and his heritage, there is a consensus in historiography, modern cultural memory, and commemoration about Stephen's outstanding significance. Although writers of history from medieval to modern times created the stories, Stephen's popular image was also perpetuated through preaching, drama, and other forms of literature. The image of Stephen was changed to suit the needs of different epochs in literature as well, for example, in the renaissance as a donor and builder; as a ruler who listened to preachers and reined in anarchy in sixteenth-century Protestant works, while from the late sixteenth century onwards, Catholic school plays perpetuated the image of a baroque 'athleta Christi' helped by supernatural forces. In 1845, a Hungarian preacher in Vienna, giving a sermon on Stephen, spoke of the duty of Christian subjects to honour their king and concluded that the close tie to Austria had to be preserved inviolate, as nation and king made one whole, so it was the duty of Hungarians to honour the Habsburg ruler who was St Stephen's heir.[55] Yet nineteenth-century drama, in the age of rising nationalism, presented Stephen as working for the good of the motherland, and after the defeat of the anti-Habsburg revolution (1848–9), as someone who castigated ungrateful foreigners. After the treaty of Trianon, a Stephen anxious for the survival of his people, as well as a Stephen capable of forging a nation from diverse ethnicities was in vogue. In the later twentieth century, a search for 'Hungarian identity' was expressed through Stephen.[56]

Even neo-pagan right-wing conspiracy theorists share this assessment of Stephen's centrality, albeit with a negative inflection, as they see Stephen turning Hungary away from its right path.[57] Thus, Stephen's centrality in historiography

---

[53] A photo is available at https://hvg.hu/itthon/20111207_kerenyi_festmenyek_kesz_vannak; the second image is the one discussed here [last accessed 27 February 2024].

[54] 'Horthy Miklós kormányzó Szent István-napi beszéde (1938)', repr. in Szent István, Veszprémy, 542. Even pictorially, the law-giving of Stephen is prefigured in an image by Pál C. Molnár, in his 'In memoriam s. regis Stephani' series from 1938, in which Stephen gives laws to the nation, repr. in Szent István és kora, Wix [no page numbers].

[55] Alajos Sámuel, Szent István első és apostoli magyar király mint népe szent hite- 's nemzetiségének megalapítója (Pest, 1845), 9, 18.

[56] Bitskey, Eszmék, 269–76.

[57] See Chapter 2. In nationalist discourse in popular culture now, Stephen can be a hero or a villain. On popular nationalist discourses: Margit Feischmidt, 'Nemzetdiskurzusok a mindennapokban és a nacionalizmus populáris kultúrája', in Nemzet a mindennapokban: Az újnacionalizmus populáris

14   STEPHEN I, THE FIRST CHRISTIAN KING OF HUNGARY

far surpasses his significance in history itself. How can we account for the discrepancy between the dearth of historical knowledge and historiographical lionization, apart from once outdated, now again fashionable nationalism? The legitimizing function of narratives of beginnings clearly plays an important role here (see below), but it does so through accrued tradition based on medieval sources that first started to invest Stephen with such a meaning. Crucially, we know how and why Stephen was first turned into a saint, a founder, and mythical legitimator of kings, and how various other social groups' claims were subsequently based on such a view of Stephen during the Middle Ages. This, ultimately, is where we find the root of Stephen's exaggerated importance; a heritage then perpetuated in modern historiography.

While a handful of written sources survive from the lifetime of Stephen—a few mentions in chronicles outside Hungary, three charters that are not original but survive in later, interpolated form, and legislation that was also interpolated—the texts (hagiographical lives and chronicle accounts) at our disposal from the late eleventh century onwards are much more numerous and elaborate. László Veszprémy coined the phrase the 'invented 11th century' of Hungary, demonstrating that because the main narrative sources we possess that describe Stephen's reign were written during the reigns of Ladislas (László) I (r. 1077–95) and Coloman (Kálmán) (r. 1095–1116), the figure of Stephen we have access to is the product of the late eleventh and early twelfth centuries.[58] This version of the past was linked to then-current issues, including the refutation of the claims of the Gregorian papacy for papal superiority over the Hungarian ruler, and the defence of the king's independence from the Empire.[59] It was in this period that Stephen's role as the founder of the kingdom was elaborated, and various stories were invented.[60] These narrative sources created a past that modern historians had to

---

kultúrája, ed. Margit Feischmidt, Rita Glózer, Zoltán Ilyés, Katalin Veronika Kasznár, Ildikó Zakariás (Budapest: L'Harmattan, 2014), 7–48. There were a few exceptions prior to the emergence of neopaganism, notably Protestants who reacted to restrictions under Leopold I, for example, by minimizing Stephen's importance: Szekfű, 'Szent István a magyar történet századaiban', 46, repr. 572, and Unitarians whose negative portrayal of Stephen as a Nero was linked to their grievances under Maria Theresa: Tóth, *Szent István*, 143–8.

[58] László Veszprémy, 'The invented 11th century of Hungary', in *The Neighbours of Poland in the 11th Century*, ed. Przemysław Urbańczyk (Warsaw: DIG, 2002), 137–54. He elaborated on various issues in a series of publications; for a short recent summary, see e.g. Veszprémy, 'Fikció és valóság István korában'.

[59] József Gerics, 'Über Vorbilder und Quellen der Vita Hartviciana Sancti Stephani regis Hungariae', *Acta antiqua Academiae Scientiarum Hungaricae*, 29 (1981): 425–44; Konrád Szántó, 'Pápai-magyar kapcsolatok a 12. században', in *Magyarország és a Szentszék kapcsolatának 1000 éve*, ed. István Zombori (Budapest: METEM, 1996), 21–46.

[60] 'Legenda S. Stephani regis maior et minor, atque legenda ab Hartvico episcopo conscripta', ed. Emma Bartoniek, in *SRH* II, 363–440, esp. 389–90 and 412–14; English translations with introduction: Nora Berend, trans. 'Hartvic, King Stephen of Hungary', in *Medieval Hagiography: An Anthology*, ed. Thomas Head (New York: Garland, 2000), 375–98; *The Sanctity of the Leaders: Holy Kings, Princes, Bishops, and Abbots from Central Europe (Eleventh to Thirteenth Centuries). Sanctitas principum: sancti reges duces episcopi et abbates Europae Centralis (saec. XI–XIII)*, ed. Gábor Klaniczay, Ildikó Csepregi, Central European Medieval Texts 7 (Budapest—New York—Vienna: CEU Press, 2023).

INTRODUCTION   15

work with. Because of the way the discipline developed, the focus on a national past meant reliance on medieval narrative sources for the story of Hungary's beginnings. That narrative built on ready-made elements, though inflections could always be changed. The emplotment of Stephen's role became so entrenched, such bedrock of Hungarian history, that historians have only recently started to challenge it seriously—to drill holes into that substratum, to find the edifice is built on air.

Stephen belongs to the group of royal saints canonized in the eleventh and twelfth centuries, important in the making of dynastic identities, and among them, he is one of the missionary kings who converted their realm. Yet he differs from most of these, because he was not killed and thus was not seen as a martyr.[61] Indeed, apart from some early medieval kings who were rediscovered centuries after their death as saints, Stephen was the first king to be canonized as a confessor, rather than as a martyr or monk.[62] Stephen as a founder-figure of Christianity in his realm can be compared to some other 'Christianizing kings', who came to be seen as the patron and even 'perpetual ruler' of their respective realms, and whose cults sometimes had a political significance over the *longue durée*: Olav II Haraldsson of Norway, Vladimir of Rus', Wenceslas of Bohemia.[63]

Compared to the veneration of other holy rulers, it is significant that the promotion of Stephen's cult was initially the work of a king of Hungary and the political establishment (which included the highest echelons of the ecclesiastics in the realm), as attested by the local canonization at a synod in Hungary in 1083.[64] Stephen's canonization was tied to filling the 'legitimacy deficit' of Ladislas I (r. 1077–95), who—together with his brother Géza—had wrested power from the crowned ruler, their cousin Solomon. After reigning a few years, Géza I (r. 1074–7) died, and Ladislas succeeded him, with Solomon trying to regain his throne with the help of the German ruler Henry IV. Ladislas imprisoned Solomon, and then released him when Ladislas orchestrated the canonization of Stephen

---

[61] Gábor Klaniczay, 'The paradoxes of royal sainthood as illustrated by Central European examples', in *Kings and Kingship in Medieval Europe*, ed. Anne J. Duggan (London: King's College London, 1993), 351–74.

[62] Robert Folz, *Les saints rois du Moyen Âge en Occident (VIᵉ–XIIIᵉ siècles)* (Brussels: Société des Bollandistes, 1984), 69–115. (The earlier confessor saint kings were predominantly Anglo-Saxon.)

[63] Henryk Fros, SJ, 'Le culte des saints en Europe Centrale (Bohème, Pologne, Hongrie) et son rôle socio-politique du Xe au XIIIe siècle', in *Fonctions sociales et politiques du culte des saints dans les sociétés de rite grec et latin au Moyen Âge et à l'époque moderne. Approche comparative*, ed. Marek Derwich, Michel Dmitriev (Wrocław: LARHCOR, 1999), 99–109; Gábor Klaniczay, *Holy Rulers and Blessed Princesses: Dynastic Cults in Medieval Central Europe* (Cambridge: Cambridge University Press, 2002), tr. Éva Pálmai; *Saints and Their Lives on the Periphery: Veneration of Saints in Scandinavia and Eastern Europe (c. 1000–1200)*, ed. Haki T. Antonsson, Ildar H. Garipzanov (Turnhout: Brepols, 2010).

[64] The first testimony, of the *Legenda minor*, only mentions the local initiative. Hartvic claimed papal approval by Gregory VII. Some suggest the pope may have been consulted and given his consent before the local canonization; however, it is also possible, and for me, more convincing, that Hartvic invented the papal approval. Folz, *Les saints rois*, 77–8.

16   STEPHEN I, THE FIRST CHRISTIAN KING OF HUNGARY

(together with that of his son Emeric, two hermits, and a martyred bishop) by a local synod.[65] The canonization was thus both an opportunity for political reconciliation and atonement and a way to legitimize Ladislas as a continuator, a just heir of Stephen. It also set a precedent, with Ladislas being canonized in 1192.

While Stephen is not alone in having a royal heir actively involved in his recognition as a saint, in many cases elsewhere, there was also a strong ecclesiastical initiative that was tied to ecclesiastical institutional interests.[66] For example, St Eric's cult in Sweden was fostered by the cathedral chapter of Old Uppsala; Ólafr Haraldsson's (St Olav of Norway, r. 1015–30) by the bishop he had brought with him from England, Grimkell. In Denmark, it seems King Sweyn Estridson (1047–74) tried and failed to initiate a cult of Harald Bluetooth; the successful take-off of the cult of St Canute (r. 1080–6) was due to the priests of St Alban's church in Odense (where Canute had been killed) and Canute's half-brother King Eric Ejegod (r. 1095–1103).[67] Henry II (r. 1014–24) was transformed into a ruler who spread the faith peacefully to Hungary and by war against the pagan Slavs, and his canonization was promoted by the bishopric of Bamberg he had founded.[68] In the admittedly different world of the late thirteenth century, when the papal monopoly of canonization replaced local decision making, it was Pope Gregory X who initiated the canonization of Louis IX; French prelates and the Dominicans also pressed for it, with Louis's son Philip III joining the pressure group a few years later.[69]

Personal sanctity in life was unimportant for the earlier saints (the thirteenth century was radically different in that respect); being killed in dynastic power-struggles was easily reinterpreted as martyrdom in the hagiographies, and piety and holy life were attributed retrospectively to such rulers.[70] Whoever initiated the cult, dynasties everywhere benefited from saintly forebears, with successors

---

[65] Klaniczay, *Holy Rulers*, 123–47. The strong political legitimation is also manifest in the idea of the sanctity of the whole lineage, which was not very common: Folz, *Les saints rois*, 142–8.

[66] Ibid., 114. Other examples where the ruler asked for canonization include, for example, St Wenceslas whose murderer (his own brother) and heir seems to have initiated the cult: Klaniczay, *Holy Rulers*, 101, and Knud Lavard, whose son Valdemar requested the canonization after elevating him unofficially: John Bergsagel, 'Kanute, cuius est Dacia? Knud Lavard, dux danorum: murdered or martyred?', in *Of Chronicles and Kings: National Saints and the Emergence of Nation States in the High Middle Ages*, ed. John Bergsagel, David Hiley, Thomas Riis, Danish Humanist Texts and Studies, 52 (Copenhagen: The Royal Library and Museum Tusculanum Press, 2015), 73–90, at 73–4.

[67] Tracey R. Sands, 'The cult of St Eric, king and martyr, in medieval Sweden', in *Sanctity in the North: Saints, Lives and Cults in Medieval Scandinavia*, ed. Thomas A. DuBois (Toronto: University of Toronto Press, 2008), 203–38, at 207–10; Klaniczay, *Holy Rulers*, 96–8; 150–2.

[68] Kurt Villads Jensen, 'Creating a crusader saint: Canute Lavard and others of that ilk', in *Of Chronicles and Kings*, Bergsagel et al., 51–72, at 53–6.

[69] Le Goff, *Saint Louis*, 302–4.

[70] Apart from the Scandinavian saints mentioned in this paragraph, many other examples in Klaniczay, *Holy Rulers*. The most extreme is often thought to be Eric of Sweden, because many historians identified him with the saint mentioned in a papal letter, venerated despite being killed while drunk. Others, e.g. Arne Jönsson, 'Saint Eric of Sweden—the drunken saint?', *Analecta Bollandiana*, 109 (1991): 331–46, argue against this identification. Sands, 'The cult of St Eric', 208.

INTRODUCTION   17

on the throne often quick to capitalize on incipient cults. Royal sanctity was thus at least to some extent tied to political uses in the exercise of rulership, and provided a flexible means for future rulers, as can be seen in the example of St Edmund, whose cult was embraced in succession by Viking conquerors, kings of Wessex, and the Danish conqueror Canute the Great.[71]

In Stephen's case, such dynastic legitimation was a primary motivation from the very beginning. No evidence exists of an independent popular cult even long after, let alone before, Stephen's local canonization.[72] The first incontestable trace of an independent popular cult has been dated to the late sixteenth century, when he started to feature in secular poetry.[73] Even if we consider that Latin ecclesiastical hymns were translated into the vernacular a little earlier than that, and altars dedicated to Stephen, Emeric and Ladislas used by guilds are known from the fifteenth century onwards,[74] there is no sign before the late medieval period of spontaneous pious devotion asking for the saint's intercession. (Such a lack of cult can be contrasted, for example, with the early fame of Louis IX, whose body, even as it was being transported back to France, was accredited with numerous miracles in Sicily, Italy, and France.[75])

Thus, it was the ecclesiastical feast-day, liturgy, church dedications, preaching, and drama that fostered the cult after the canonization, rather than independent earlier popular devotion. Stephen's feasts were created and promoted by the medieval church and kings; his liturgy developed gradually to include an increasing number of pieces composed specifically for his office.[76] Monastic orders also played an early role; the earliest known manuscript from the second half of the

---

[71] The distinction is modern, as no medieval ruler would have separated 'religious' and 'political'; in modern usage, however, it recognizes a particular sphere of royal sanctity that played a role in royal legitimation and the exercise of power. On Edmund's cult: Klaniczay, *Holy Rulers*, 95.

[72] Gábor Klaniczay, 'Szent István legendái a középkorban', in *Szent István és kora*, Glatz—Kardos, 185–96. Earlier claims of the existence of a popular cult from the eleventh century alleged without proof that Hartvic wrote down popular oral tradition: Karsai, 'Szent István tisztelete', 186–8, 198; from the early modern and modern periods there are traces of popular traditions, as the rest of his article shows. More recent assertion of a popular cult prior to canonization, without offering any proof, e.g. Kornél Szovák, *Szent István* (Budapest: Kossuth Kiadó, 2018), 56.

[73] Kristó, *Szent István*, 130; Béla Pomogáts, 'Szent István a magyar költészetben', *Kisebbségkutatás*, 9, no. 3 (2000): 426–31.

[74] Karsai, 'Szent István tisztelete', 200; Zoltán Magyar, *Szent István a magyar kultúrtörténetben* (Budapest: Helikon Kiadó, 1996), 46; Marie-Madeleine de Cevins, *L'Église dans les villes hongroises à la fin du Moyen Âge (vers 1320–vers 1490)* (Budapest—Paris—Szeged: Institut Hongrois de Paris—METEM, 2003), 229, 238 (this grew out of the cult of Stephen, Emeric and Ladislas promoted by the Angevins; Louis I in 1367 had a chapel built in Aachen with altars to the three saints, a site of Hungarian pilgrimage).

[75] Le Goff, *Saint Louis*, 301–2.

[76] Janka Szendrei, 'Commune pro missionariis? Die ältesten Offiziumsgesänge für König Stephan, den Heiligen', in *Political Plainchant? Music, Text and Historical Context of Medieval Saints' Offices*, ed. Roman Hankeln (Ottawa: The Institute of Mediaeval Music, 2009), 81–92; László Dobszay, *Historia Sancti Stephani Regis 1190–1270* (Ottawa: The Institute of Mediaeval Music, 2010). Sermons emphasized his legislation, piety, model kingship: András Vízkelety, 'Példaképalkotás és argumentáció a középkori Szent István prédikációkban', in *Szent István és kora*, Glatz—Kardos, 180–4.

18 STEPHEN I, THE FIRST CHRISTIAN KING OF HUNGARY

twelfth century of Stephen's legends was probably written at the Benedictine monastery of Pannonhalma.[77] His representations in art closely conformed to the ecclesiastical themes, and pale in significance compared to those of St Ladislas of Hungary.[78]

As opposed to the slow awakening of popular devotion, royal legitimacy continued to be tied ever more strongly to Stephen. Alleged continuity with Stephen became entrenched in practices and ideas about royal power. It was the archbishop of Esztergom—an archbishopric founded by Stephen—who crowned the king, in the royal church of Fehérvár, also established by Stephen, where the regalia were kept. From the thirteenth century, textual references to royal coronation oaths include indications to uphold laws and customs established by ancestors. The association of Hungarian royal power specifically with Stephen was reinforced by the papacy. This is evidenced by thirteenth-century texts heavily influenced by papal legates. In the oath of Bereg (1233), King Andrew II professes himself to have gained the throne by right of being Stephen's heir, and in 1279, King Ladislas IV (the Cuman) is made to acknowledge that all kings of Hungary bear the crown by right of having gained it from the Roman Church in Stephen.[79] By the end of the thirteenth century, this custom led to attributing the royal crown itself to Stephen and as the local dynasty died out in the early fourteenth century, legitimate rulership was made contingent on coronation with that crown, as discussed in Chapter 4.

Liturgy and manuscript illuminations give an indication of the emphasis of the ecclesiastical cult. The celebration of St Stephen in the Hungarian church naturally drew on the convention of saints' cults at the time; yet it is remarkable that even there, we find an emphasis on Stephen as a founder-figure, even if the activities highlighted are related to matters of faith. The ecclesiastic who commissioned a new Matins cycle for St Stephen's liturgical celebration may have directly polemicized against a conception of the past with more continuity between the pagan and Christian periods. The resulting late thirteenth-century additions to

---

[77] Recent overview of the manuscript tradition: Edit Madas, 'À la recherche des sources liturgiques et hagiographiques du culte des "saints rois" hongrois en Europe centrale', in Les saints et leur culte en Europe centrale au Moyen Âge (XIe–début du XVIe siècle, ed. Marie-Madeleine de Cevins, Olivier Marin (Turnhout: Brepols, 2017), 281–91, at 285.

[78] Tünde Wehli, 'Szent István kultusza a középkori magyarországi művészetben', in Doctor et apostol: Szent István tanulmányok, ed. József Török (Budapest: Márton Áron Kiadó, 1994), 107–40, revised version in Szent István, Veszprémy, 162–72, at 169.

[79] György Fejér, Codex diplomaticus Hungariae ecclesiasticus ac civilis, 11 vols. (Buda, 1829–44), III/2. 327; Imre Szentpétery and Iván Borsa, Regesta regum stirpis Arpadianae critico-diplomatica. Az Árpádházi királyok okleveleinek kritikai jegyzéke, 3 vols (Budapest: MTA, 1923–1987), 501; Fejér, Codex diplomaticus, V/2, 507–8, Szentpétery, Regesta, 2962. (These texts have been edited numerous times; all editions are listed in Szentpétery.) Cf. Szekfű, 'Szent István a magyar történet századaiban', 9, repr. 535. See Chapter 4. The papacy, however, did not accept all attempts to use St Stephen as a justification for royal power: when Béla IV asked for legatine rights in 1238, referring to St Stephen, the pope rejected this: Gábor Barabás, A pápaság és Magyarország a 13. Század első felében: pápai hatás—együttműködés—érdekellentét (Pécs: Pécsi Történettudományért Kulturális Egyesület, 2015), 144–5.

INTRODUCTION 19

the liturgy of Stephen insisted not only on a radical break with the pagan past but also on the king's role as apostle.[80] These sections, playing on the words *crudelitas* and *credulitas*, emphasized the contrast between Attila the Hun's tyrannical law resulting in savagery, and Stephen's rule that led the population to the grace of baptism and to the readiness to believe.[81] Stephen combined threats and persuasion to lead the wild lion to the sheepfold; a rebellious people needed a strong king as a preacher.[82]

In the first known illumination-cycle to depict scenes from the life of Stephen, a manuscript from 1343 commissioned by a Hungarian prelate, the four scenes shown are Géza's dream, which warned him that his son, rather than himself, is destined to convert the Hungarians; the baptism of Stephen as a child; Stephen's coronation; and the baptism of pagans in Hungary (the conversion of the Hungarians). Stephen also holds a small model of a church, signalling his status as the founder of the church, on the pictorial ribbon in the middle, used to divide the miniatures from each other. Although both Stephen's father and mother are depicted with a crown, thus implying that kingship predated Stephen, the iconographic programme clearly suggests King Stephen as foundational for Christianization in Hungary.[83] Dynastic legitimacy and a foundational role in Hungarian Christianity thus reinforced each other.

Moreover, after his canonization, Stephen quickly became a key reference point in legitimizing strategies outside the dynasty as well. Because he acquired such a crucial significance for royal legitimacy, this standing radiated out, making him a desirable touchstone and justification for rights and privileges beyond royal power. This led to a wider social acceptance that in turn reinforced his standing as the founder of the kingdom and the fount of rights. From the late eleventh century, kings referred to laws of St Stephen in their own legislation. From the beginning of the twelfth century, royal legislation stated that donations made by Stephen to monasteries and churches could not be revoked; even inheritance rules for the laity made it more advantageous to hold possessions originally given by Stephen.[84] Ecclesiastical institutions and lay people started to derive their own

---

[80] Dobszay, *Historia Sancti Stephani*, for an analysis of the third, last layer, see xxii–iv, for the edition 5–31.

[81] Ibid., 16–17. Attila and the Huns were incorporated as ancestors of the Hungarians.

[82] Ibid., 22–3.

[83] Lászlóné Gerevich, 'Vásári Miklós két kódexe', *Művészettörténeti Értesítő*, 6, nos. 2–3 (1957): 133–7. These scenes may have come from the beginning of a longer cycle: Béla Zsolt Szakács, *The Visual World of the Hungarian Angevin Legendary* (Budapest: Central European University Press, 2016), 120–1. See also: Ernő Marosi, ed., *Magyarországi Művészet 1300–1470 körül* (Budapest: Akadémiai Kiadó, 1987), 207, and image no. 12; Wehli, 'Szent István kultusza a középkori magyarországi művészetben' in *Doctor et apostol*, Török, 107–40 revised version in *Szent István*, Veszprémy, at 167.

[84] János M. Bak, György Bónis, James Ross Sweeney, ed. and tr., *The Laws of the Medieval Kingdom of Hungary 1000–1301* (Bakersfield, CA: Charles Schlacks, 1989), 21 c. 17, and 28 c. 34; 26 c. 1; 27 c. 20, respectively. (The English translations and notes in this edition are often faulty.) Nora Berend, 'Construcciones divergentes de la memoria real en el reino de Hungría: Esteban I (997–1038) en las leyes, las crónicas y la hagiografía' (tr. by J. Bronstein), in *La Construcción medieval de la memoria*

20 STEPHEN I, THE FIRST CHRISTIAN KING OF HUNGARY

legitimacy from Stephen, and even tried to prove their rights or privileges from the twelfth century onwards using forged charters allegedly issued by Stephen.[85] The more groups participated in deriving their own rights from Stephen, the more they also cemented Stephen's foundational role. In the thirteenth century, kings were promising to keep the nobles in the liberty granted them by St Stephen.[86] In 1222, the Golden Bull established the feast-day of Stephen as the yearly law-day when nobles could bring their cases to the king or, in his absence, to the count palatine (who was the highest official after the king); thus, the legal functioning of the realm itself was linked to Stephen. By that time, a rising social group that was eventually to merge into the nobility had resourcefully defined itself as the *servientes regis*, and claimed they had received their status from Stephen: a status, therefore, that must be guaranteed by the current king against the barons.[87] The Hungarian Church in the late thirteenth century also used Stephen in a polemical manner to depict a model Christian king, probably in opposition to trends at the royal court to incorporate pagan Cumans and endorse a positive pagan past.[88]

Thus, Stephen came to be entrenched as the founder of the state and the church in Hungary. Medieval myth-making served as a firm basis for centuries of further elaboration and reinterpretation, both in historiography and in legitimizing strategies.[89] Political instrumentalization did not disappear between the Middle

---

regia, ed. Pascual Martínez Sopena, Ana Rodríguez (Valencia: Publicacions de la Universitat de València, 2011), 45–58; Miklós Halmágyi, ' "boldog István törvénye szerint"—A Szent István királyra való hivatkozás példái a középkori jogi és társadalmi gondolkodásban', in *Urbs, civitas, universitas: ünnepi tanulmányok Petrovics István 65. születésnapja tiszteletére*, ed. Sándor Papp, Zoltán Kordé, László Sándor Tóth (Szeged: Szegedi tudományegyetem, 2018), 152–8. More broadly, see István Tringli, 'The liberty of the holy king: Saint Stephen and the holy kings in the Hungarian legal heritage', in *Saint Stephen and His Country: A Newborn Kingdom in Central Europe—Hungary*, ed. Attila Zsoldos (Budapest: Lucidus Kiadó, 2001), 127–79.

[85] László Solymosi, *Írásbeliség és társadalom az Árpád-korban: diplomatikai és pecséttani tanulmányok* (Budapest: Argumentum, 2006), 24–5; György Györffy, *Diplomata Hungariae antiquissima* (Budapest: Akadémiai Kiadó, 1992), 19–128 (discusses charters addressed to Stephen as well); Halmágyi, ' "boldog István törvénye szerint" '. The forged foundation charter of the abbey of Pécsvárad (between 1212 and 1228) claimed to have been issued by Stephen: Barabás, *A pápaság*, 121–2.

[86] Bak et al., *The Laws*, 34, preface, 38, preface.

[87] Ibid., 34–7; also in 1267, ibid., 42–3. On this social group, Attila Zsoldos, *A szent király szabadjai: Fejezetek a várjobbágyság történetéből* (Budapest: MTA Történettudományi Intézet, 1999).

[88] László Dobszay, 'From "crudelitas" to "credulitas": comments on Saint Stephen's Historia Rhythmica', in *Political Plainchant?*, Hankeln, 93–106; Dobszay, *Historia Sancti Stephani*, xxii–xxiii. It is usually thought that the liturgical piece was composed in response to the pagan tendencies of King Ladislas (László) IV (r. 1272–90); Dobszay, *Historia* dates the last layer of the liturgy to the second half of the thirteenth century on p. vi, and to 1270 in the title, but still links it to an ecclesiastical stance against Ladislas IV on p. xxiii. Against such an interpretation: Nora Berend, *At the Gate of Christendom: Jews, Muslims and 'Pagans' in Medieval Hungary, c. 1000–c. 1300* (Cambridge: Cambridge University Press, 2001), 2067. If the liturgy was finalized by 1270, that alone would render the interpretation linking it to the promotion of paganism at Ladislas's court impossible. The liturgy may have been a reaction to the policy of alliance with the Cumans initiated by King Béla IV (r. 1235–70), or to the thirteenth-century incorporation of the pagan past into chronicles.

[89] Éloïse Adde-Vomácka, 'Saint Venceslas de Bohême (†935). Un martyr aux multiples facettes dans les pays tchèques, entre glorification dynastique et récupération nobiliaire (Xe–XIVe siècle)', in *Martyrs politiques, Xe–XVIe siècle: du sacrifice à la récupération partisane*, ed. Maïté Billoré, Gilles

INTRODUCTION   21

Ages and the twentieth century. For example, in the seventeenth century, Stephen's cult was utilized by three political actors who were in conflict with each other: the Hungarian Catholic episcopate; the Habsburgs in their policy towards the papacy; and the Hungarian estates in their self-representation.[90] Historical work, as we have seen, gave different interpretations to Stephen's activity. Regardless of their differences, however, historians reiterated Stephen's centrality, vulgarized in the oft-repeated formula that Hungary and the Hungarians would not exist were it not for Stephen. There is no disparity in the evaluation of a historian writing in 1956 and Hungary's current prime minister. The former wrote that while many steppe peoples conquered the Carpathian basin one after another, 'only the Hungarians established a country in this region from among all the steppe peoples who had invaded it like a storm'.[91] The latter opined: 'We see how hundreds of the wandering peoples of the great steppe disappear and are lost in the dust clouds of history. We see that we, Hungarians, neither disappeared, nor were lost, but rather in the ring of Latin, German and Slav peoples, maintaining our distinctiveness, we established a homeland.'[92]

The glue that holds Stephen in his central position is the narrative of national history, in which beginnings gain a legitimizing, even sanctifying power. Stephen as the founder of the (Christian) state can occupy that position for religious or secular purposes; however, he is unsatisfactory for those who are desirous of deeper roots in earlier time periods, who therefore supplement or supplant Stephen by a pagan Hungarian ancestry. That ancestry can lead to Árpád or even Attila the Hun; it can be lionized in parallel with or instead of Stephen. One alleged pagan ancestor who gained a prominent place in alternative narratives is Koppány, supposed relative and opponent of Stephen at the start of his reign. As discussed in Chapters 1 and 2, while some heroize Koppány and vilify Stephen, others embrace both in the national narrative. The paradox of how the simultaneous cult of a Christian saint and a pagan hero who is his opponent is possible can be resolved through the lens of a national history narrative, where they can both symbolize an essence of Hungarianness: Koppány the ancient traditions, and Stephen independent statehood.

Lecuppre (Rennes: Presses Universitaires de Rennes, 2019), 33–48. Such mythologizing transformations affected all the ruler-saints who were reactualized in diverse periods, not only Christianizing kings. See, for example, Nils Holger Petersen, 'The image of St Knud Lavard in his liturgical offices and its historical impact', in *Of Chronicles and Kings*, Bergsagel et al., 129–58.

[90] Sándor Bene, 'A Szilveszter-bulla nyomában. Pázmány Péter és a Szent István-hagyomány 17. századi fordulópontja', in *Szent István*, Veszprémy, 143–62.

[91] Bónis, *István király*, 7.

[92] 'Látjuk, amint a nagy sztyeppe vándorló népeinek százai eltűnnek és odavesznek a történelem porfelhőiben. Látjuk, hogy mi, magyarok se el nem tűntünk, se oda nem vesztünk, hanem a latin, a germán és szláv népek gyűrűjében, különálló minőségünket megőrizve hazát alapítottunk.' https://2015-2019.kormany.hu/hu/a-miniszterelnok/beszedek-publikaciok-interjuk/orban-viktor-unnepi-beszede1, 6 June 2020, Sátoraljaújhely.

National history is a substantial part of the 'invention of tradition' for modern states.[93] History became an academic discipline at the time of the formation of states conceived of as 'nation-states' and therefore early academic history writing constructed narratives of a national past. Such narratives of course were not exclusively promoted through history writing: in the case of the formation of the popular image of Stephen, drama, literature, and art all contributed. Nationalism and many academic historians eventually parted ways, with the latter setting out to debunk national myths at least partly constructed by earlier historians. Yet historians also continue to contribute to myth-making—some consciously, others against their will: any historical result can be picked up in some political interpretation with more or less distortion to fit a political agenda. Myths created by earlier historians also live on through popular literature, websites and as diffuse popular 'knowledge'. Today, with the new rise of nationalism, a deep chasm has opened between scholarship and politics (including history writing that openly caters to political trends).[94] Careful historical work has dismantled many elements of the simplified idea of Stephen's greatness and foundational role, and more recent scholarship has moved away from earlier paradigms with important advances in understanding ecclesiastical organization, the building of forts, and so on. On the contrary, political use fixated on utter simplification and a conscious disregard for scholarly results, even starting to erect an alternative pseudo-scientific framework for government-sponsored history writing.

My contention is that in many ways, we cannot reach the 'real' Stephen, but we could do much more to understand the shaping of his myths. We can try to trace the origin of the stories, and contextualize the invention of early narratives. This approach has benefited from the linguistic and narrative turns in history insofar as it embraces the need to take texts more seriously as texts, literary compositions rooted in the age that produced them, rather than mere carriers of facts if only we can separate them from the chaff of fiction.[95] This book is also written in an

---

[93] Of the very extensive scholarship deconstructing nationalism, see e.g. the classic Eric Hobsbawm, *Nations and Nationalism since 1780: Programme, Myth, Reality*, 2nd edn (Cambridge: Cambridge University Press, 1992) and John Breuilly, ed., *The Oxford Handbook of the History of Nationalism* (Oxford: Oxford University Press, 2013).

[94] Benoît Grévin, 'Nationalisme et médiévalisme', in *Middle Ages without Borders: A Conversation on Medievalism. Medioevo senza frontiere: una conversazione sul medievalismo. Moyen Âge sans frontières: une conversation sur le médiévalisme*, ed. Tommaso di Carpegna Falconieri, Pierre Savy, Lila Yawn, Collection de l'École française de Rome 586 (Rome: École française de Rome, 2021), 155–83, at 159–60.

[95] I build on László Veszprémy's work on Stephen in this respect. 'Fikció és valóság István korában', 15 speaks of 'daring reconstruction' by historians when it comes to writing about Stephen. On medieval texts, Gabrielle M. Spiegel, *The Past as Text: The Theory and Practice of Medieval Historiography* (Baltimore—London: The John Hopkins University Press, 1997); Gabrielle M. Spiegel, ed., *Practicing History: New Directions in Historical Writing after the Linguistic Turn* (New York: Routledge, 2005); Elizabeth A. Clark, *History, Theory, Text: Historians and the Linguistic Turn* (Cambridge, MA: Harvard University Press, 2004); Agapitos A. Panagiotis, Lars Boje Mortensen, ed., *Medieval Narratives between History and Fiction: From the Centre to the Periphery of Europe, c. 1100–1400* (Copenhagen: Museum Tusculanum Press, 2012); Elizabeth Tyler, Ross Balzaretti, ed., *Narrative and History in the Early*

environment where scholarship has gained a growing awareness of medievalism, the uses of the medieval past in politicized ways.[96] The contribution of this book, by way of a detailed case study, is to highlight the often-seamless flow that has turned medieval myth into modern history.

A close look at how these stories were originally created and how they were used over time raises many questions. While it is easy to point out the more egregious political uses of Stephen and brand them an 'abuse' of history, the genesis of such supposed abuse is much more complex, and involves the historical profession. Clearly, there have been strong links between the historical enterprise and political designs using history, and scholarly history writing can blur into a politicized one. Moreover, and crucially, although simplifications and intentional distortions can of course be pinpointed in political usage, the real problem is the very genesis of historical analyses: medieval myths were taken as historical evidence, and used as the very basis of the scholarly enterprise. Thus, we are not merely up against an abuse of history, but its very fabric in the first instance: the sources of our history are not neutral witnesses, but were written for various purposes; on these bases, further elaborations were constructed over centuries.

Politicization was not a modern addition, but a determining factor from the start. Memorialization is not a modern phenomenon; collective memory (coined by Maurice Halbwachs) or as Jan Assmann refined it, cultural memory, determined the very nature of our source-material. The sources were created in the process of social memory work; they served the purposes of living history at the time. Thus, 'invented traditions' themselves are not linked to modernity alone, and we can trace the process of fabricating some of them in the medieval period. Originally gaining prominence in the search for royal legitimation, Stephen then became an established foundation stone for the claims of diverse social groups during the medieval period. On that basis, Stephen became a reference-point for legitimizing modern kings, but was also adopted in such a role by the estates, by a regent in a kingless kingdom in the first half of the twentieth century, and by right-wing politicians who seek to renationalize political discourse in the twenty-first century. Keeping this process in mind, we can also appreciate better why myth penetrates deeply into living history, and how the toxic use of history grows

---

Medieval West (Turnhout: Brepols, 2006), Tony Davenport, *Medieval Narrative: An Introduction* (Oxford: Oxford University Press, 2004); Tom Kindt, Hans-Harald Müller, ed., *What is Narratology? Questions and Answers Regarding the Status of a Theory* (Berlin—New York: Walter de Gruyter, 2003). On the consequences for using hagiography specifically as a source: Monique Goullet, *Écriture et réécriture hagiographiques: Essai sur les réécritures de Vies de saints dans l'Occident latin médiéval (VIIIᵉ–XIIIᵉ s.)* (Turnhout: Brepols, 2005).

[96] E.g. Patrick Geary, *The Myth of Nations: The Medieval Origins of Europe* (Princeton: Princeton University Press, 2002); Stefan Berger, ed., *Writing the Nation* series, especially R. J. W. Evans, Guy P. Marchal, ed., *The Uses of the Middle Ages in Modern European States: History, Nationhood and the Search for Origins* (Houndmills and New York: Palgrave Macmillan, 2011); Bruce Holsinger, *Neomedievalism, Neoconservatism, and the War on Terror* (Chicago: Chicago University Press, 2007); Grévin, 'Nationalisme et médiévalisme'.

24   STEPHEN I, THE FIRST CHRISTIAN KING OF HUNGARY

out of history writing itself. Generations cemented certain building blocks, and by virtue of repetition, these acquired power. While the political masquerades as historical, claiming to have access to a truer version of history, this is not a neat rupture with history *qua* academic history, but rather has deep roots in the latter.

While this book emphasizes how essential it is to consider narrativity in the building of historical tales, I am no advocate of 'vulgar postmodernism' or the 'all stories are equal with no truth-value beyond the text' approach. Historians have long struggled with the issue of truth-claims in history. We have by now given up the untenable assertion that historians can attain objectivity; yet those (myself included) who think there is a discipline called history do lay store by methodology and its scientific basis—that the value of the reasoning can be assessed by others and does not hinge on sympathies or political convictions—rather than see it as arbitrary and merely determined by personal bias. We may be comfortable with the position that we cannot reach the truth in historical reconstruction; we may even rejoice in the multicoloured variety of histories that spring up and the craftsmanship that shapes our texts. Yet the wishy-washy 'we try to approximate truth as best as we can' stance breaks down when confronted by lies. Holocaust denial of course is a principal case in point. Nationalist distortion of history is another. If all narratives are merely subjective and cannot be distinguished from each other in terms of proximity to the truth, then there could be no distorted accounts of the past or proof that the Holocaust happened. History, the sane reader may interject, should not be used for legitimation and the justification of political agendas. Yet it is used in such a way, and thus historians find themselves in a quandary.

How do we navigate between the Scylla of every historical account's positioned, relative nature, and the Charybdis of the historian's single, objective truth-claim? If we acknowledge that multiple interpretations are possible, that there is no single 'truth' we can find, this can be used to undermine the scholarly status of academic history, and assert the equal validity of all interpretations. If we claim to reconstruct a true past, we may be participating in national legend-making. We cannot depend on the scientific status of authors to distinguish between 'good' and 'bad' history: professional historians regularly contribute to the building of national myths, aptly labelled mythistory.[97] We cannot claim privileged access to truth, when so often we cannot know the answers to many questions. Maybe we cannot escape unscathed. Odysseus first sacrificed six of his men to Scylla, in order to escape Charybdis with the rest; the second time, on his own, he hung on

---

[97] Coined by William McNeill; see Chris Lorenz, 'Drawing the line: "scientific" history between myth-making and myth-breaking', in *Narrating the Nation: Representations in History, Media, and the Arts*, ed. Stefan Berger, Linas Eriksonas, Andrew Mycock (New York—Oxford: Berghahn, 2008), 35–55.

INTRODUCTION   25

to Charybdis while the latter sucked in Odysseus' boat along with the water, and dropped back in to hang onto the wreckage that was spat out.[98]

If we prefer not to think too much about possible watery graves, we may seek to engage with the old trope of the historian as detective.[99] What type of detective is the historian? Sherlock Holmes, with the penetrating intelligence that can deduce the truth from scattered traces only comprehensible to the trained investigator but easily misleading the less qualified? Bernard Nightingale from Tom Stoppard's *Arcadia*, who exults in his own reconstruction, which could not be further from the truth? Wilkie Collins's Valeria, determined to find the truth in the face of what seem to be insurmountable obstacles? Columbo, ostensibly perpetually bumbling, but with the homing instinct of a pigeon always zeroing in on the perpetrator?[100] Or Miss Marple, who declares that 'most people...are far too trusting...They believe what is told them. I never do. I'm afraid I always like to prove a thing for myself'?[101]

While our reconstructions and interpretations will always be incomplete, hypotheses and interpretations *can* be assessed in terms of how well they fit the traces of the past we have. To prove that not all narratives are equally valid, we need to show our hand more fully. Only in this way can we demonstrate the difference between the methodology of careful scholarly analysis and wilful political distortion. There is not one truth we can reach, not one true story, but that does not mean falsification cannot be detected. There are many possible interpretations, but interpretations that are based on a skewed selection of material can only be espoused from a position of ignorance or ideological dedication. My preferred solution is the clear acknowledgement of the difference between what can be known and what is hypothetical and openness about the bases of our arguments, as well as thorough contextualization of historical interpretations in the period we analyse. If we reveal in detail the way we reach our conclusions, we clearly distinguish between attempts to understand the past and instrumental uses of the past, and can perhaps facilitate better navigation in the grey zone between an educated guess and groundless speculation. Nobody can claim neutrality, but we can be both self-reflexive and have professional integrity in our methodology– consider all the sources, rather than select what suits us, avoid intentionally distorting the material, and show the lacunae.

The painstaking work of generations of scholars on early eleventh-century Hungarian history means we have gained a much better understanding in some areas, such as the early uses of literacy or coinage, while other aspects of Stephen's

---

[98] Homer, *Odyssey*, book 12.
[99] Most famously Carlo Ginsburg, 'Clues', in *Clues, Myths, and the Historical Method* (Baltimore: John Hopkins University Press, 1990), 96–125.
[100] In memoriam Simon Barton, who once in a conversation joked about this.
[101] Agatha Christie, *The Body in the Library* (London: HarperCollins, 2002), 261.

reign remain hotly contested, such as the details of early county-organization.[102] We cannot hope to gain firm knowledge of yet other facets of Stephen's reign, let alone his personality, because of the lack of reliable information. Scholars have also engaged in the deconstruction of Stephen-related myths (notably the alleged papal sending of his crown, for example) through careful analysis and the contextualization of the texts where the myths first appear. Already in 1904, János Karácsonyi argued about the need to excise the forgeries and later, uncertain material from the historical sources, but much remains to be done. Information about the context of these texts in the late eleventh and twelfth centuries onwards needs to be taken seriously; we also need to remember that the horizon of medieval authors was not national, even if they were writing for the benefit of their ruler or local community, but consisted of a European context of textual sources and stereotypes.

Medievalists regularly fight to be recognized as relevant to present-day society, and medieval history is too often relegated to being a discipline that has outlived its usefulness. The example of Stephen of Hungary reminds us that claims about medieval history can also be imposed on the present as all too relevant. One can of course point out that whatever an early eleventh-century king did or wanted is surely no guide to political action a thousand years later. It is not, but political legitimation dressed up as historical fact is flourishing. Academic historians have a choice: to turn a blind eye (or even benefit from the possibility of catering to an all-powerful regime), or to unmask myths, reveal the wildly hypothetical nature of some interpretations, demonstrate the complexity and difficulties of reconstruction, show possible alternatives and the impossibility of some claims.[103] Those who appreciate critical thinking will see the value of doubt, and the need to provide readers with the tools to be able to evaluate claims that are made, instead of a solid, polished narrative that hides the uncertainties and gives the hue of fact to mere hypotheses. In our times, we may need to oppose the deadly certainties of nationalism with the uncertainties of scholarship as well as its results.

Stephen I, the First Christian King of Hungary: From Medieval Myth to Modern Legend. Nora Berend, Oxford University Press. © Nora Berend 2024. DOI: 10.1093/9780191995439.003.0001

---

[102] It is impossible to list all the relevant more recent historical work, but two of the most important ones are: Gábor Thoroczkay, *Írások az Árpád-korról: történeti és historiográfiai tanulmányok* (Budapest: L'Harmattan, 2009); Veszprémy, *Szent István*.

[103] I agree with B. Grévin's diagnosis, 'Nationalisme et médiévalisme', 183: 'L'histoire médiévale a plus que jamais besoin d'être doublée par une histoire du médiévalisme, si nous voulons comprendre comment des discours jadis scientifiques ont pu devenir des vulgates non-scientifiques, analyser comment l'histoire peut être à la fois anthropologie et discours politique, déterminer exactement quel genre d'histoire nous voulons faire et faire passer. La permanence des nationalismes n'oblige peut-être pas toujours l'historien à se faire politique. Elle le force en tout cas à se réinventer.'

1

Cupan

It is a central tenet of Hungarian historiography that St Stephen, inheriting rulership from his father upon the latter's death (997), was challenged by an older
pagan relative (perhaps an uncle), Cupan (rendered in modern Hungarian as
Koppány[1]), duke of Somogy, who wanted to take power based on the principle of
seniority, and further tried to reinforce that claim by demanding to marry
Stephen's widowed mother. He was defeated in battle and quartered. Around this
supposed historical kernel, national rhetoric and the ever-renewed search for the
illusionary 'Hungarian identity' have woven a thick tissue of sometimes self-
contradictory narrative. The confrontation has long been seen as Hungary's foundational moment. Koppány's defeat was either the removal of the last obstacle in
the way of Hungary's joining Christian Europe, the medieval equivalent of necessary modernization for survival, or the tragic end of a noble rebel, depending on
the narrator's perspective; sometimes it is even seen as both at the same time.[2] By
the twentieth century, Koppány became the embodiment of genuine Hungarian
identity, even as Stephen was celebrated as the founder of the kingdom who laid
down its borders for all times and ensured the survival of Hungarians by bringing
them into Christian Europe; in some circles, he eclipsed Stephen as the true hero
and representative of authentic Hungarianness.

On the surface, this may seem to be a classic case of nationalist 'abuse' of history, the modern misinterpretation of medieval events. Yet the medieval events
themselves are a construct, and the historian is faced with more questions than
answers in search of the historical kernel itself. Not only modern nationalist
mythologizing has moved the historical narrative ever further from medieval
events. Medieval authors first created a story, and then modern professional historians for centuries elaborated it, while supposedly reconstructing history as it
had happened. The well-known story of Koppány's pagan rebellion and quartering is the result of historians further developing medieval myth, combining
material from divergent sources written in different centuries. Holes in the story
had to be filled through speculation, so unresolved problems triggered additional

---

[1] I shall distinguish between the Cupan of medieval sources and Koppány as a modern construct.
Koppány started to be used in late nineteenth-century historiography, and became the standard form
since the twentieth century.

[2] Recently Zoltán Magyar, *Hős vagy lázadó? Koppány alakja a folklórban és a kultúrtörténetben*
(Budapest: Magyarságkutató Intézet, 2020), 7. This is a slightly revised version of the same author's
Koppány (Budapest: Móra Ferenc Könyvkiadó, 1998).

28 STEPHEN I, THE FIRST CHRISTIAN KING OF HUNGARY

hypothetical 'solutions', such as Koppány's alleged kinship to Stephen. The tissue of hypotheses thus became so dense that it is hard to cut through it to the historical evidence. When one does, it turns out that one of the crucial 'events' in the life of Stephen, and the history of Hungary, rests on precious little foundation.

1. The Story and Its Sources

How much definite knowledge do we have, based on the primary sources? The short answer is, almost none. Cupan, Stephen's opponent may have existed, but if so, we know nothing about him; his story was certainly much embellished, and he may even be an invented figure. It is worthwhile to detail the information from the earliest sources in order to understand just how tenuous the academic historians' construct is. Hypotheses and conjectures can of course be woven around the sources, but the earliest evidence consists of a late thirteenth-century chronicle by Simon of Kéza (c. 1280), the first that mentions Cupan by name, and fourteenth-century chronicles that provide a more detailed story. Very few sources contemporary with Stephen's reign were written in Hungary, and they do not mention Cupan. Contemporary sources written outside Hungary provide evidence of some conflicts—examples include Stephen's confrontation with his uncle Procui, or Stephen compelling people to accept Christianity—but they do not reference Cupan.[3] Their silence, of course, is no proof in itself that Cupan did not exist, although it is intriguing that a supposedly major confrontation that imperilled the realm's newly established Christianity would have left no unambiguously identifiable echo, while other conflicts did.[4] Modern historians, in attempts to bridge this lacuna in the

---

[3] Thietmar of Merseburg, the *Annales Altahenses maiores*, Bruno of Querfurt, and Ademar of Chabannes are among these. A detailed analysis: Albin F. Gombos, 'Szent István a középkori külföldi történetírásban', in *Emlékkönyv Szent István király halálának kilencszázadik évfordulóján*, ed. Jusztinián Serédi, 3 vols. (Budapest: Magyar Tudományos Akadémia, 1938), vol. 3, 279–324; repr. *Szent István Emlékkönyv* (Budapest: Szent István Társulat, 1988), 629–74; on conflicts and attacks against Stephen, 318–19, repr. 668–9 (argues that a mention in a vernacular German chronicle from Austria of Stephen being killed by pagans is a reference to the Cupan story, but this text dates from the late fourteenth century and its confused account has no independent value; see http://www.geschichtsquellen.de/repOpus_01146.html). See also Nora Berend, ed., *Christianization and the Rise of Christian Monarchy: Central Europe, Scandinavia and Rus' c. 950–c. 1200* (Cambridge: Cambridge University Press, 2007), 345.

[4] An exchange of letters between Gerbert, later Pope Sylvester II, and Otto III are taken to refer to the Koppány rebellion by Mathilde Uhlirz, 'Die "Scythae" in den Briefen Gerberts von Aurillac', *Mitteilungen des Instituts für Österreichische Geschichtsforschung*, 59 (1951): 411–15; György Györffy, *István király és műve*, 4th rev. edn (Budapest: Balassi Kiadó, 2013), 121, Gyula Kristó, *Szent István király* (Budapest: Vince Kiadó, 2001), 44–5, and György Szabados, *Magyar államalapítások a IX–XI. században: Előtanulmány a korai magyar állam történelmének fordulópontjairól* (Szeged: Szegedi Középkorász Műhely, 2011), 240–79, at 265; however, both the meaning of 'Scythian' and the dating of the letters has been disputed, and others understand these letters to refer to Slavs: Julien Havet, ed., *Lettres de Gerbert (983–997)* (Paris: Alphonse Picard, 1889), 231–2, no. 219, see 232; 232–3, no. 220,

CUPAN   29

sources, have claimed that various other medieval texts refer to Cupan's uprising without naming him, and that Cupan's story originally comes from an earlier, now lost, source, a supposed first (Ur-) chronicle, which was incorporated into the fourteenth-century chronicles. Scholars also used toponyms, fifteenth- and sixteenth-century texts, and modern folk traditions, to suggest that these faithfully conserve the memory of events that took place in 997.

The earliest texts—although even they relay alleged events that took place eighty to ninety years previously—are the three hagiographical *Lives* (*vitae*) of Stephen, which give varied accounts of a pagan revolt. Although historians interpreted them as referring to Cupan's story, they never mention Cupan, nor do they write of one leader in the revolt.

According to the *Legenda Maior* (written for the canonization of 1083 or soon thereafter[5]), at the instigation of the devil—who, wishing to confuse the holy plans of Christ's servant, Stephen, stirred up civil war against him—the pagans refused to bend their neck to the yoke of Christianity, and with their leaders strove to detach themselves from Stephen's rule. This text mentions several leaders, without providing any names. Stephen finally won with the aid of the Virgin Mary and Saints Martin and George, and after their leaders were killed, the vanquished pagans were compelled to accept Christianity.[6]

The *Legenda Minor* (between 1083 and c. 1100) relates that some nobles, who did not wish to give up their traditional customs, at the instigation of the devil rejected the king's convictions, returned to their earlier pleasures, and took up arms against Stephen. They looted his lands, destroyed his towns, and besieged the royal town of Veszprém, occupying the very place where the king used to dwell, in order to humiliate Stephen. Yet Stephen finally vanquished them; some of them were killed, others were captured. The king initially gave their estates to St Martin (that is, to the abbey dedicated to the saint, now called Pannonhalma), but later altered this provision and gave St Martin a tithe instead, in order to avoid impoverishing the former rebels completely.[7] Hartvic's *Life* (c. 1100) combines

---

see 233; 236–8, Appendix II, see 237; Harriet Pratt Lattin, tr. and introduction, *The Letters of Gerbert with His Papal Privileges as Sylvester II* (New York: Columbia University Press, 1961), 285–6, no. 222; 288–9, no. 225, 297–9, no. 232 (she dates the first two letters to July and August 997, while Uhlirz dates them to November); Miklós Halmágyi, *Mi és ők: Azonosság és idegenség az első évezred fordulóján* (Szeged: Belvedere, 2014), 280–1.

  [5] Gábor Klaniczay, Edit Madas, 'La Hongrie', in *Hagiographies*, ed. Guy Philippart (Turnhout: Brepols, 1996), vol. 2, 107 suggest that it was written for the canonization. Some scholars prefer a date closer to the end of the century: Gábor Thoroczkay, 'Szent István legendái', in *Ismeretlen Árpád-kor: püspökök, legendák, krónikák*, Gábor Thoroczkay (Budapest: L'Harmattan, 2016), 90–102, at 90. Overview of the literature and debates: Tamás Körmendi, 'Szent István király nagyobb legendájának nyelvezete', *Fons*, 10, no. 1 (2003): 65–118.

  [6] 'Legenda Sancti Stephani regis maior et minor, atque legenda ab Hartvico episcopo conscripta', ed. Emma Bartoniek, in *Scriptores Rerum Hungaricarum* (hereafter *SRH*), ed. Imre Szentpétery, 2 vols. (Budapest: Magyar Tudományos Akadémia, 1938, reprint Budapest: Nap Kiadó, 1999), 2, 381–2.

  [7] Ibid., 395.

30 STEPHEN I, THE FIRST CHRISTIAN KING OF HUNGARY

the two narratives, also adding that Stephen imposed the tithe so strictly that people who had ten children had to give the tenth to the abbey.[8]

Thus according to these stories, either the pagan population under several leaders, or the nobles, rose in rebellion because they refused to convert to Christianity or give up their earlier customs, and were defeated. None of the *Lives* suggests that there was one leader in this rebellion; none mentions any of the leaders' names, nor is the rebellion localized to Somogy. Moreover, there is no question of someone trying to wrest the throne from Stephen, in order to assume power. This element as well as other basic building blocks of the modern narratives come from the chronicle families of the fourteenth century (the *Chronicle of Buda* and *Illuminated Chronicle*, 1358).[9]

According to chapter 64 of the fourteenth-century Chronicle versions, Stephen in his early youth waged a glorious war against the powerful *dux* (meaning both military leader and 'duke') Cupan of Somogy. Cupan wished to unite himself in incestuous marriage to the mother of Stephen; he wanted to kill Stephen and subjugate the latter's *ducatus* to his own power. Stephen defeated his enemy with divine aid. A German knight, Vecellinus, killed Cupan, and Stephen had Cupan's body quartered; the body-parts were sent to the gate of Esztergom, Veszprém, Győr, and Transylvania ('Erdelw').[10] Vecellinus, captain of the army, killed Cupan also according to chapter 40 in the so-called *advenae* list section—that provides stories about the ancestors of immigrant nobility in Hungary, composed in the thirteenth century—of the same chronicles.[11]

Another chapter, the 41st, in the *advenae* list, also mentions Cupan, in the context of the history of an immigrant noble family. It describes a rebellion against Stephen intertwined with the history of the services that the brothers Hunt and Paznan rendered the king. It says that Stephen converted some rebels through the

---

[8] Ibid., 408–9. On Hartvic's text: Gábor Thoroczkay, 'Még egyszer a Hartvik-féle Szent István-legenda datálásáról', *Magyar könyvszemle*, 121, no. 2 (2005): 213–18. Recent summary on dating: Éva Teiszler, 'A Hartvik-legenda XIV. századi oklevelekben fennmaradt változatai', in *Műhelyszeminariumi dolgozatok* I, ed. Szilvia Kovács, Éva Révész (Szeged: Szegedi Tudományegyetem, 2013), 131–44.
[9] Cupan's story is included in both the Chronicle of Buda and the Illuminated Chronicle families.
[10] 'Chronici Hungarici compositio saeculi XIV', ed. Sándor Domanovszky, in *SRH* I (Budapest Magyar Tudományos Akadémia, 1937, reprint Budapest: Nap Kiadó, 1999), 312–14. This account is also repeated by Thuróczy: *Johannes de Thurocz, Chronica Hungarorum*, vol. 1, *Textus*, ed. Elisabeth Galántai and Julius Kristó (Budapest: Akadémiai Kiadó, 1985), chapter 55, p. 74, chapter heading 'De bello sancti regis Stephani contra Cupan ducem Symigiensem'. According to Elemér Mályusz, Julius Kristó, *Johannes de Thurocz, Chronica Hungarorum*, vol. 2, *Commentarii*, 1, *Ab initiis usque ad annum 1301* (Budapest: Akadémiai Kiadó, 1988), 243, chapter 64 was written by the continuator of the Ur-chronicle in King Kálmán's reign.
[11] 'Chronici Hungarici', *SRH* I 296. According to some scholars, a chronicle was written in the early 1270s, which was the source of the *advenae* list which is preserved in the fourteenth-century chronicle compositions: Elemér Mályusz, *Az V. István-kori gesta* (Budapest: Akadémiai Kiadó, 1971). Alternatively, Simon of Kéza was the author of the original list. Gyula Kristó, 'Magyar öntudat és idegenellenesség az Árpád-kori Magyarországon', *Irodalomtörténeti Közlemények*, 94, no. 4 (1990): 425–43, at 439 argued that the list was composed in the 1240s. Two versions of the text exist, one that survives in Simon of Kéza's late thirteenth-century chronicle and the other in the fourteenth-century chronicles.

CUPAN 31

fear of arms. Later on, the text mentions that the nobles 'who adhered to Cupan dux, rejecting baptism and the faith' were reduced to servitude; resistance to Christianity led to the loss of freedom.[12] This is the first time Cupan is associated with pagan rebels; this association is not present in the 64th chapter, which includes the longer story of Cupan detailed above.

Cupan's name occurs in only one source before the fourteenth-century chronicle compositions: the chronicle of Simon of Kéza (c. 1280) mentions Cupan twice. The historical narrative merely states that after Stephen's coronation, 'after Duke Cupan had at last been killed' ('tandem duce Cuppan interfecto'), Stephen brought his uncle Gyula, together with the latter's family, to Hungary, and annexed Gyula's territory to Pannonia. The chronicle (similarly to the fourteenth-century chronicles) also includes a section that lists immigrant nobles and gives brief summaries of their ancestry and family history. In this section, recounting the family history of Wecelinus and his descendants (in Simon of Kéza's chronicle, the Ják kindred), Simon mentions that Wecelinus killed Cupan *dux* in the county of Somogy.[13] The implied chronology in Simon of Kéza's account differs from that of the fourteenth-century chronicle compositions, since it places Cupan's death after Stephen's coronation (1000/1001) rather than directly after Géza's death (997). Who Cupan was, what his relationship to Somogy had been, and why he was killed are not explained at all in the text.[14]

Some scholars refer to one more, allegedly early source, the charter of privileges granted to the abbey of Pannonhalma, dated to 1001/2, but interpolated in the early thirteenth century.[15] The privileges mention a war that took place in Stephen's youth between Germans and Hungarians, because the county of Somogy wished to oust Stephen from his father's throne. The story here is linked to the military leaders Poznan, Cunt, and Orzi. The charter does not mention Cupan. One scholar, Géza Érszegi, even interpreted the story as referring not to

---

[12] 'Chronici Hungarici', *SRH* I, 297, 'Pluresque nobiles Hungari duci Cupan adherentes, baptismum fidemque respuentes.'

[13] *Simonis de Kéza, Gesta Hungarorum Simon of Kéza, the Deeds of the Hungarians*, ed. László Veszprémy (Budapest: CEU Press, 1999), 102, 162. Some scholars maintain that the basis of Simon's account was a Magister Ákos' rewriting of the Ur-gesta in the thirteenth century. Thus, the list of *advenae* found in the fourteenth-century chronicle would be earlier than Simon's. There is no proof for this, and the relationship between the two lists may be the reverse. György Rácz, 'A Ják nemzetség és monostoralapításai', parts 1–2, *Vasi Szemle*, 54, nos. 1–2 (2000): 7–26; 159–81, at 19–24 summarizes the reasons for refuting the descent of the Ják from Vecellinus, and the invention of their family tradition.

[14] György Györffy, 'Koppány lázadása', *Somogy megye múltjából. Levéltári évkönyv* 1 (Kaposvár, 1970), 5–30, at 12 assumes that Simon of Kéza's version changed the original (now lost) chronicle account, yet the terse and difficult-to-interpret mention hardly qualifies as an elaboration. Had Simon wanted to embellish the account to make it more suitable for his own period as Györffy suggests, this would be a strange result.

[15] György Györffy, *Diplomata Hungariae Antiquissima*, vol. 1, *1000–1131* (Budapest: Akadémiai Kiadó, 1992), 26–41. A facsimile: Imre Szentpétery, 'Szent István király oklevelei', in *Emlékkönyv*, Serédi, vol. 2, 133–202, repr. 325–94, between 146–7 and in repr. between 338–9.

32 STEPHEN I, THE FIRST CHRISTIAN KING OF HUNGARY

the Koppány episode, but to Bavarian–Hungarian battles in the 990s.[16] However, the main problem with trying to use the charter of privileges as independent proof of authentic events underlying the Cupan story (even though the charter does not name him) is this text's own history: since the eighteenth century, scholars have repeatedly disputed its authenticity.[17]

Consensus has been reached on one issue alone: the charter is interpolated. Most scholars argue that the text as we possess it was written in the early thirteenth century.[18] What parts of the charter are original from Stephen's reign, and, in particular, when the description of the war (written in the first person singular) dates from, is debated. Some see it as part of the original privileges issued by Stephen, while others see it as part of the thirteenth-century interpolation.[19] Its early origin cannot be proven, and the later dating, advocated among others by the doyen of Hungarian diplomatic Imre Szentpétery, seems more likely, for three main reasons. First, it was only in the thirteenth century that the charter in its present form was transcribed.[20] Second, the style of the section on the war, written as if by the king himself in the first person singular, is completely different from all early charters in Hungary, and also diverges from their model, the charters of the German empire's chancery.[21] Third, the section justifies the abbey of Pannonhalma's right to the tithes from Somogy, which was the object of litigation between the bishop of Veszprém and the abbey of St Martin (Pannonhalma) in the early thirteenth century; Pannonhalma won the case in 1215, using the charter attributed to St Stephen in a transcript by Andrew II.[22] This raises the strong suspicion that the section was added in the early thirteenth century, in order to justify Pannonhalma's claim by deriving it from the holy king's donation. Given all the problems and the lack of any mention of Cupan, the charter cannot be used as evidence proving the authenticity of his story.

---

[16] Géza Érszegi, 'Szent István pannonhalmi oklevele (Oklevéltani-filológiai tanulmány)', in *Mons Sacer, 996–1996, Pannonhalma ezer éve*, ed. Imre Takács, 3 vols. (Pannonhalma: Pannonhalmi Bencés Apátság, 1996), 47–89.

[17] Gábor Thoroczkay, 'Szent István pannonhalmi oklevelének kutatástörténete', in *Szent István és az államalapítás*, ed. László Veszprémy (Budapest: Osiris Kiadó, 2002), 237–63. For more details on the early debates up to 1938: Szentpétery, 'Szent István király oklevelei', 145–84, repr. 337–76.

[18] Ibid., 168, repr. 360, dates to between 1209 and 1212.

[19] Different opinions in scholarship are presented in Thoroczkay, 'Szent István pannonhalmi oklevelének', 252, 254–5.

[20] Published by Györffy, *Diplomata*, 29–31. Szentpétery, 'Szent István király oklevelei', 162, repr. 354; Thoroczkay, 'Szent István pannonhalmi oklevelének', 255.

[21] Szentpétery, 'Szent István király oklevelei', 161–2, 165, repr. 353–4, 357. While there are a few charters where emperors drafted part of the text, these are not historical narratives and are in the first person plural: Hartmut Hoffmann, 'Eigendiktat in den Urkunden Ottos III. und Heinrichs II', *Deutsches Archiv für Erforschung des Mittelalters*, 44 (1988): 390–423.

[22] Szentpétery, 'Szent István király oklevelei', 166–8, repr. 358–60 argues that this is an interpolation; the section takes up almost eleven lines of the eighteen-line document and occurs at the beginning of the charter; an earlier papal transcript dedicated one line at the end of the charter to tithes, listing estates first. Szentpétery also lists palaeographic arguments (the writer was trying to copy an unfamiliar script, that of Heribert C, who wrote later charters of Stephen), as well as problems with the dating in the charter: ibid., 172–84, repr. 364–76.

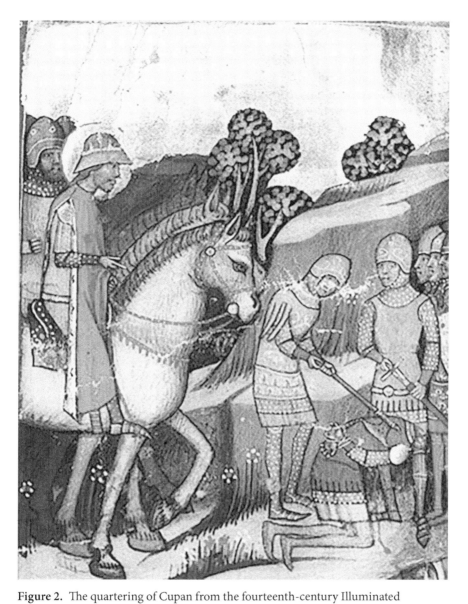

Figure 2. The quartering of Cupan from the fourteenth-century Illuminated Chronicle
https://hu.wikipedia.org/wiki/Kopp%C3%A1ny_vez%C3%A9r#/media/F%C3%A1jl:Koppany.jpg

34 STEPHEN I, THE FIRST CHRISTIAN KING OF HUNGARY

2. Tradition? Invention?

If one accepts that the fourteenth-century chronicle compositions incorporate and transmit a much earlier, eleventh- or twelfth-century text, then of course the chronicle account would be the earliest testimony to Cupan's story. This contention, however, is so problematic as to be untenable.

It is generally assumed that the fourteenth-century chronicle accounts preserve the text of a much earlier version of the chronicle, a twelfth- or even eleventh-century now lost alleged Ur-chronicle.[23] According to such a line of argument, while the chronicle was rewritten multiple times to suit each era, it continued to transmit early stories (including Cupan's), that are reliable because they were recorded close to the events. Naturally, even chronological proximity to events is no guarantee of the veracity of accounts. Yet the issue is more complicated here, because of the entanglement of questions of veracity with the idea of an early, now lost, chronicle. To clarify my point that we cannot take the fourteenth-century text as proof of the authenticity of Cupan's story, a short detour is necessary to tackle the issue of the chronicle's 'reliability' and its alleged transmission of early texts.

While scholars have researched the Hungarian chronicles for generations, hypotheses about the existence of the alleged early Ur-chronicle, and if such a chronicle ever existed, the parts of the fourteenth-century text that derive from it, lack firm foundation.[24] The tenuousness of scholarship on the alleged early chronicle is indicated even by the lack of consensus on the period when it was first composed—during the reign of Andrew I (1046-60),[25] Solomon (1063-74),[26] Ladislas I (1077-95),[27] or Coloman (1095-1116).[28] Dating was attempted, for example, based on the supposition that memory can reach back seventy years, and thus parts containing serious factual errors must have been written more than seventy years after the events.[29] Other arguments pointed to the intellectual effervescence of King Coloman's reign (1095-1116) and the composition of many

---

[23] According to Mályusz—Kristó, *Johannes de Thurocz, Chronica*, II. *Commentarii*, vol. 1, 243, the chapter was written by a continuator in King Coloman's reign.

[24] The enormous bibliography on the issue cannot be listed here; see Gyula Kristó, 'Krónikakompozíció', in *Korai Magyar Történeti Lexikon (9–14. század)*, ed. Gyula Kristó (Budapest: Akadémiai Kiadó, 1994), 381–2; Gyula Kristó, *A történeti irodalom Magyarországon a kezdetektől 1241-ig* (Budapest: Argumentum Kiadó, 1994); László Veszprémy, 'Megjegyzések korai elbeszélő forrásaink történetéhez', *Századok*, 138 (2004): 325–47; Thoroczkay, *Ismeretlen Árpád-kor*.

[25] Sándor Domanovszky, 'A Budai Krónika', *Századok* (1902): 828–9.

[26] József Gerics, *Legkorábbi Gesta-szerkesztéseink keletkezésrendjének problémái* (Budapest: Akadémiai Kiadó, 1961).

[27] Bálint Hóman, *A Szent-László kori Gesta Ungarorum és XII–XIII. századi leszármazói (Forrástanulmány)* (Budapest: Magyar Tudományos Akadémia, 1925).

[28] Kristó, *A történeti irodalom*, 105–25. He also provides an overview of dating in all previous scholarship: 11–20.

[29] György Györffy, *Krónikáink és a magyar őstörténet. Régi kérdések—új válaszok* (Budapest: Balassi Kiadó, 1993), 185–6.

known texts at that time, leading to the conjecture that the first chronicle was also written then.[30] A similar debate concerns the work's original form: whether it was a more elaborate narrative *gesta* or a chronicle that only included short notices.[31]

In addition, scholars disagree about the number of times and the periods when the supposed Ur-chronicle was rewritten (during the twelfth and early thirteenth century).[32] While most scholars who worked on the fourteenth-century chronicles maintain that at least some sections incorporate early texts, there is no agreement about which sections these may be. Lexical, grammatical and stylistic studies can sometimes show that parts of the text as they now exist cannot be dated earlier than the early thirteenth century; even features that could be seen to characterize eleventh-century texts, such as classicizing participle constructions, continued to be used at least until the early thirteenth century.[33] Such studies have not been able to produce incontestable proof of the eleventh- or twelfth-century provenance of parts of the chronicle; it has even been argued that all previous versions were thoroughly reworked in the thirteenth century, thus eliminating the possibility of recovering earlier layers of the text.[34] In some instances, modern scholarship suggested borrowings from authors such as Cosmas of Prague (d. 1125).[35] Attempts to prove the supposed eleventh-century origin of various sections rely on hypothetical reasoning that cannot be substantiated.

A key example is chapter 82 in the fourteenth-century compositions that is supposed to be the section most securely datable to an early author: it has been argued that the description of a return to paganism in the mid-eleventh century in the entourage of Ianus, son of Vatha, must be the work of an author close to the

---

[30] Cited in Kristó, *A történeti irodalom*, 17.   [31] Ibid., 21, 123–4, 130.

[32] Recent summary and bibliography: Gábor Thoroczkay, 'A magyarországi legendairodalom és történetírás a 14. század közepéig', in *Ismeretlen Árpád-kor*, Thoroczkay, 184–208, at 196–9.

[33] On classicizing usage, still found in twelfth- and thirteenth-century texts: Bernadett Benei, 'Egyes igeneves szerkezetek használata a magyar krónika 11–12. századi szövegegységeiben', in *Micae Mediaevales IV. Fiatal történészek dolgozatai a középkori Magyarországról és Európáról*, ed. Judit Gál, István Kádas, Márton Rózsa, Eszter Tarján (Budapest: ELTE BTK Történelemtudományok Doktori Iskola, 2015), 33–42; Bernadett Benei, 'Contributions to the study of the 11–12th century texts of the Hungarian Chronicle', in *Hungaro-Polonica: Young Scholars on Medieval Polish-Hungarian Relations*, ed. Dániel Bagi, Gábor Barabás, Zsolt Máté (Pécs: Történészcéh Egyesület, 2016), 49–68; Lajos J. Csóka, *A latin nyelvű történeti irodalom kialakulása Magyarországon a XI–XIV. században* (Budapest: Akadémiai Kiadó, 1967), 527–61 offers various arguments for a chronicle written in the 1210s; Kornél Szovák, 'Szent László alakja a korai elbeszélő forrásokban (A László legenda és a Képes Krónika 139. fejezete forrásproblémái)', *Századok*, 134 (2000): 117–45, at 134–8 argues that chapter 139 of the chronicle in its existing form comes from the early thirteenth century; Kristó, *A történeti irodalom*, esp. 72–3, 97, 132–4. Bernadett Benei, *A magyar krónika Árpád-kori szakaszának latin nyelve* (Budapest: Bölcsészettudományi Kutatóközpont Történettudományi Intézet, 2022), based on linguistic analysis, argued that the text concerning the Árpád period within the chronicle we have is from the end of the twelfth/early thirteenth century, and no earlier layer can be demonstrated.

[34] Arguments based on style that claimed early provenance of parts of the text, e.g. János Horváth, *Árpád-kori latin nyelvű irodalmunk stílusproblémái* (Budapest: Akadémiai Kiadó, 1954), 290–2, were criticized and rejected by other scholars, e.g. Kristó, *A történeti irodalom*, 113.

[35] Veszprémy, 'Megjegyzések', 334.

36   STEPHEN I, THE FIRST CHRISTIAN KING OF HUNGARY

events, and thus the text conserves a part of the Ur-chronicle, partly because it includes 'archaic' information, an 'unparalleled wealth of the terminology of the soothsayers and diviners of the pagan world'.[36] The medieval author used the terms *magus, aruspex, dea,* and *phitonissa*. These, however, are far from being precise terms used to denote pre-Christian Hungarian diviners and seers; they do not demonstrate any deep knowledge of eleventh-century pre-Christian practices or terminology. Instead, they reflect medieval literary culture. *Magus* was a widely used term for magician, connected to the biblical Simon Magus.[37] The rest is borrowed and reinterpreted terminology from classical antiquity: originally, *haruspex* denoted a diviner who used animal entrails, *dea* meant goddess and *pythonissa* was derived from a priestess of Apollo, Pythia. These terms entered medieval usage unrelated to Hungarian paganism. For example, *pythonissa* came to mean sorceress, and can be found in Isidore of Seville's *Etymologies*; it was even used by Chaucer.[38]

The use of this terminology indicates that the text is the work of a writer with knowledge of classical texts, instead of someone close to eleventh-century events. The text is more likely to be a literary composition than a true account of early history. Another part of the same story, where King Béla I (1060–3) had the pagan 'dea' Rasdi imprisoned, who then ate her own feet, also seems to indicate familiarity with mythology and texts from classical antiquity. The author may have drawn on the classical notion that cannibalism was the hallmark of the non-civilized, or on geographers such as Strabo and Pliny, who described Scythians as cannibals,[39] at a time when Hungarians were equated with Scythians. The story may also potentially be an echo of an episode in Ovid's *Metamorphoses*, about Erysichthon who offends Ceres, and is therefore punished by perpetual hunger (the personified Hunger is called on to issue forth from Scythia); in the end, he dies by trying to consume his own body.[40] Finally, there is also a parallel with King Agrestes in

---

[36]   Kristó, *A történeti irodalom*, 115.

[37]   For a list of Christian terms for pagan practitioners, e.g. Albrecht Classen, ed., *Magic and Magicians in the Middle Ages and the Early Modern Time: The Occult in Premodern Sciences, Medicine, Literature, Religion and Astrology* (Berlin—Boston: Walter de Gruyter, 2017), 238, note 24; *Isidori Hispalensis Episcopi Etymologiarum sive Originum Libri XX*, ed. W. M. Lindsay (Oxford: Clarendon Press, 1911), VIII.ix.1 and 25.

[38]   *Isidori Hispalensis episcopi Etymologiarum*, VIII.ix.3 (*aruspicium*), 17 (*haruspices*), 7, and 21 (*pythonissae*). R. E. Latham, *Revised Medieval Latin Word List from British and Irish Sources* (London: published for the British Academy by Oxford University Press, 1980), 385; *Dictionary of Medieval Latin from British Sources (DMLBS)*, https://logeion.uchicago.edu/pythonissa.

[39]   On cannibalism in classical texts: Rhiannon Evans, 'The discourse of Flavian empire', in *Flavian Rome: Culture, Image, Text*, ed. Anthony Boyle, William J. Dominik (Leiden: Brill, 2002), 255–76, at 271.

[40]   Ovid, *Metamorphoses*, book VIII, lines 738–878. Ovid's *Metamorphoses* was widely known in medieval European cathedral schools starting in the eleventh century: James G. Clark, Frank T. Coulson, Kathryn L. McKinley, ed., *Ovid in the Middle Ages* (Cambridge: Cambridge University Press, 2011), 7–8. On the earliest Hungarian connections to institutions where Ovid manuscripts were held: Előd Nemerkényi, *Latin Classics in Medieval Hungary: Eleventh Century* (Debrecen—Budapest: CEU Press, 2004), 20. There is evidence of an Ovidian distich from his

the Old French prose Arthurian cycle's *Estoire del Saint Graal*, written around 1230–5. Agrestes kills the Christian disciples of Joseph of Arimathea, and quickly receives divine punishment: he starts to eat his own hands before killing himself.[41] Thus, the story of the pagan diviners is no proof of the early provenance of the text in the fourteenth-century Chronicles.

It is impossible to review all the arguments and counter-arguments about other parts of the chronicles, but claims made by one scholar are often refuted by another.[42] The extremely hypothetical nature of chronicle research is also revealed by the fact that several cases exist where the same historian would reach directly opposite conclusions about the same question in two different works.[43] Since we lack real evidence, there are almost as many proposed solutions to the development of the chronicle texts as there are historians who tackle the question: 'in the swampy field of the study of early Hungarian historical work, we have few firm pointers.'[44]

Early historical work certainly existed in Hungary; the annals of one ecclesiastical institution between 997 and 1203 are still extant, and other such works may have been written.[45] In the early thirteenth century, Dominicans were reading about the old homeland of the Hungarians 'in gestis Ungarorum christianorum,'[46] and a chapter of the fourteenth-century chronicles refers to what was written 'in

Epistulae ex Ponto in a Hungarian charter from 1217: Balázs Déri, '"...tenui pendentia filo..." Ovidius-distichon egy Árpád-kori oklevélben', *Levéltári Közlemények*, 76, no. 2 (2005): 5–12.

[41] Eugène Hucher, ed., *Le Saint-Graal ou Le Joseph d'Arimathie*, vol. 3 (Le Mans: Monnoyer, 1878), 196–8, 'commença à mangier ses mains' (198).

[42] E.g. the argument whether the *Vita Maior* of Stephen borrows from the early chronicle, or the chronicle borrows from the *vita*: József Gerics, 'Domanovszky Sándor, az Árpád-kori krónikakutatás úttörője', in *Egyház, állam és gondolkodás Magyarországon a középkorban*, József Gerics (Budapest: METEM, 1995), 8–22, at 16–19; László Veszprémy, 'Korhűség és forrásérték a magyar krónika egyes fejezeteiben', in *Arcana tabularii: Tanulmányok Solymosi László tiszteletére*, ed. Attila Bárány, Gábor Dreska, Kornél Szovák, 2 vols. (Budapest—Debrecen: Kapitális Kft, 2014), vol. 2, 809–21, at 814. Also whether in chapter 80, the names 'Lodomeria' (Vladimir in the principality of Volhynia) and 'Ruscia' (Kievan Rus') are proof of an early author or a late twelfth- or thirteenth-century one: Gábor Thoroczkay, 'A magyar krónikairodalom kezdeteiről', in *Ismeretlen Árpád-kor*, Thoroczkay, 103–14, at 108.

[43] Examples include János Horváth first asserting that almost no part of the eleventh-century chronicle survived later rewriting, and later claiming that large chunks of the eleventh-century chronicle remain almost verbatim. On this and other examples of self-contradictions: Kristó, *A történeti irodalom*, 20–2.

[44] Thoroczkay, 'A magyar krónikairodalom', 114. See also Kristó, *A történeti irodalom*, 113, 122 on the impossibility of determining what was transmitted from the Ur-chronicle.

[45] 'Annales Posonienses', ed. Imre Madzsar, *SRH* I, 119–27, at 125–7; see Veszprémy, 'Megjegyzések', 341–6; and on the scholarship with bibliography: Thoroczkay, 'A magyarországi legendairodalom', 186. On possible early historical works: Thoroczkay, 'A magyar krónikairodalom', 113. On history writing with further bibliography, László Veszprémy, *Történetírás és történetírók az Árpád-kori Magyarországon (XI–XIII. század közepe)* (Budapest: Rerum Fides, 2019).

[46] 'De facto Ungarie Magne a fratre Ricardo invento', ed. Iosephus Deér, *SRH* II, 529–542, at 535. Rather fantastic conclusions have been drawn from these few words: that a now lost chronicle, perhaps the Ur-chronicle, was the 'deeds of the Christian Hungarians', covering events from the reign of St Stephen; paradoxically, this would be the source of information on the location of the pagan Hungarians who did not migrate to Hungary but had remained in the old homeland, and therefore remained unchristianized: Kristó, *A történeti irodalom*, 42. It is much more likely that the Dominican

38   STEPHEN I, THE FIRST CHRISTIAN KING OF HUNGARY

antiquis libris de gestis Hungarorum'.[47] Whether these denoted one or more chronicles written in Hungary, but now lost, is unclear; they could even refer to descriptions of the deeds of the Hungarians in works by authors such as Regino of Prüm and others. Hungarian chroniclers certainly used material from texts such as the Annals of Niederaltaich and Regino of Prüm.[48]

Even if these medieval texts do refer to now lost chronicles, they provide no evidence for the content and merely a *terminus ante quem* date of composition of those earlier works. Even hypothesizing the existence of a now lost Hungarian chronicle read by the Dominicans in the early thirteenth century offers no proof of an Ur-chronicle written in the eleventh century, or even most of the twelfth. In addition, still extant chronicles show that a later Hungarian chronicle is not necessarily the reworking of an earlier one (for example, Simon of Kéza did not rework the *gesta* of the Hungarian Anonymous), and even if we assume that early chronicle(s) existed, we know nothing about their content and relationship to the extant fourteenth-century texts. Available data does not prove that parts of the fourteenth-century text are eleventh-century compositions. Even if an earlier chronicle existed, hypothetical arguments about early origins cannot prove the reliability of the extant chronicle accounts.[49] The authors of the fourteenth-century chronicles could draw on earlier sources, and sometimes independent confirmation of events recounted in the Hungarian chronicles exists from German chronicles or other early texts; however, without such corroborating evidence, we cannot accept the fourteenth-century texts as a source of reliable historical data for tenth and early eleventh-century events.

Historians have maintained that there is such proof of the early provenance of the Cupan material now embedded in the fourteenth-century chronicles. According to one argument, the 41st chapter, containing the story of Hunt and Paznan and a brief mention of Cupan, goes back to the Ur-chronicle, or another eleventh-century text. Because this chapter contains material that fits together uneasily, and repeats some information in slightly different ways, it may have been derived from two different sources; part of the chapter is about Hunt and Paznan, while another part consists of the story of the revolt and enslavement of defeated rebels. The latter part, it has been argued, shares a common source with the *Legenda minor* of Stephen: an alleged eleventh-century now lost *vita* of St Stephen. In this way, the chapter would conserve information about Cupan's rebellion from the eleventh century. This is supposedly part of a polemic against the view (incorporated into the chapter itself) that Stephen could only curb

---

author referred to a work that described the story of those Hungarians who migrated and eventually became Christians; this may even refer to the work of the Hungarian Anonymous.

[47] *SRH* I, 338.   [48] Thoroczkay, 'A magyarországi legendairodalom', with bibliography, 197–8.

[49] The chronicle accounts' reliability if there is no corroborating evidence has recently been more systematically discounted: Veszprémy, 'Korhűség és forrásérték'.

CUPAN   39

paganism with the help of German knights; instead, the author emphasized both divine help and the voluntary conversion of some Hungarians.[50]

Yet the assertion that this story goes back to an eleventh-century source is undermined by several considerations. The hypothetical existence of an earlier *vita* of Stephen has been refuted.[51] The main polemic in the chapter is linked to the origin of servitude of former nobles, and this concern with servitude was different from the one in the *Legenda Minor*: rather than the inhabitants of a particular region being reduced to servitude and given to a monastery (as related in the *vita*), this text talks about how <u>nobles</u> could be reduced to servitude, a concern markedly similar to Simon of Kéza's in the late thirteenth century (although the reasons given differ in the two texts).[52] Other historians think that the 41st chapter is later than the 64th and includes thirteenth-century interpolations on *advenae*.[53] A later author could draw on Stephen's *Life* as well as thirteenth-century texts and recast them, and thus combine the brief mention of a Cupan in Simon of Kéza's chronicle with the *Life*'s more elaborate story of the pagan uprising.

Those who argue for the chronological primacy of chapter 64 advance different ideas. It used to be claimed that the chapter goes back to the late eleventh century, composed by Bishop Cupan (Koppány), the descendant of Vecellinus.[54] The three generations of Vecellinus's descendants listed in the chapter may indicate a late eleventh-century date (counting the average twenty-five years for one generation), but the list has also been dated to the mid- and later twelfth century.[55] The tacked-on list in any case does not say anything about the composition of the rest of the chapter, given that it is widely acknowledged that the chronicle-text merged material from a variety of sources. While both chapters may in some form incorporate diverse earlier material, no part can be proven to derive from authentic accounts contemporary or at least close to the events.

---

[50] Gerics, *Legkorábbi Gesta-szerkesztéseink*, 7–19. Cf. Mályusz—Kristó, *Johannes de Thurocz, Chronica*, II. *Commentarii*, 1, 182, 184. The argument maintained that chapter 41 does not draw directly on the extant *vita*, because it does not mention the commutation of the enslavement to a tithe, whereas both are incorporated in the *vita*. The enslavement is supposedly the original, eleventh-century depiction of the fate of the rebels by a contemporary of Stephen, while the tithe is a subsequent addition.

[51] Thoroczkay, 'Szent István legendái', 100–1.

[52] Jenő Szűcs, 'Társadalomelmélet, politikai teória és történetszemlélet Kézai Simon Gesta Hungarorumában', *Századok*, 107, nos. 3–4 (1973): 569–643 and 823–78, shorter English version, 'Theoretical elements in Master Simon of Kéza's Gesta Hungarorum (1282–1285)', in *Simonis de Kéza, Gesta Hungarorum*, Veszprémy, xxix–cii. Late medieval myths to explain the servitude of originally free nobles were not unique to Hungary: Paul Freedman, 'The evolution of servile peasants in Hungary and in Catalonia: a comparison', *Anuario de Estudios Medievales*, 26 (1996): 909–32.

[53] Györffy, 'Koppány lázadása', 12.

[54] Cf. summary and references in Mályusz—Kristó, *Johannes de Thurocz, Chronica*, II. *Commentarii* 1, 250.

[55] Györffy, 'Koppány lázadása', 8; Mályusz—Kristó, *Johannes de Thurocz, Chronica*, II. *Commentarii* 1, 250.

40 STEPHEN I, THE FIRST CHRISTIAN KING OF HUNGARY

Much has also been made of the child tithe, first mentioned by Hartvic, as a potential marker that dates the composition of the Cupan section of the fourteenth-century chronicles. Whether it was a real practice of communities (rather than families) to give every tenth child to monastic institutions as work-force, misunderstood by Hartvic, or a completely invented story, is debated.[56] Since the fourteenth-century account resonates with Hartvic and the interpolated Pannonhalma charter on the child tithe, and since a thirteenth-century charter mentions someone who had been given in tithe in the early twelfth century, it has been suggested that this verifies the Cupan story's authenticity as a whole, and dates the account to a much earlier period than the fourteenth-century chronicles in which it is included.[57] Yet several historians see the child tithe as part of the later interpolation in the Pannonhalma charter; further, the fourteenth-century chronicles drew on Hartvic's text and may have taken the child tithe from there.[58] Thus, the mention of the child tithe is no guarantee of the story's authenticity.

Cupan's quartering and the display of his body-parts on forts are also usually accepted in historiography as proof of the faithful account of real events.[59] Only László Erdélyi considered this a fourteenth-century invention; according to him, the assassination attempt by Felicián Zá-ch against King Charles Robert's wife in 1330, and his punishment, inspired the chronicler to invent the quartering of Cupan.[60] Gyula Kristó argued against this interpretation, suggesting that the opposite was the case: the fourteenth-century punishment was modelled on Cupan's quartering at the end of the tenth century.[61] The four locations where the body-parts were sent are seen as proof of the early, trustworthy recording of the story, because from early on Stephen established his power over them. According to this argument, only a contemporary would have known that, whereas a later author would have included Fehérvár, which became an important royal centre for Stephen, but did not yet have that status in 997.[62] The aim of the public display of the body-parts according to one explanation was the deterrence of would-be

---

[56] Recent summary of previous opinions and possibilities of interpretation: Tamás Lados, 'Megjegyzések a pannonhalmi gyermektized történetéhez', in *Magister Historiae II. Válogatott tanulmányok a 2014-ben és 2015-ben megrendezett középkorral foglalkozó, mesterszakos hallgatói konferenciák előadásaiból*, ed. Csaba Farkas, Tamás Lados, András Ribi, Dorottya Uhrin, ELTE BTK Történelemtudományok Doktori Iskola 10 (Budapest: ELTE BTK Történelemtudományok Doktori Iskola, 2016), 73–98.

[57] Györffy, 'Koppány lázadása', 8; on the charter: Lados, 'Megjegyzések', 79.

[58] László Solymosi, 'Szent István és a pannonhalmi apátság somogyi tizedjoga', in *Episcopus, archiabbas bendictus, historicus ecclesiae*, ed. Ádám Somorjai, István Zombori (Budapest: METEM, 2016), 11–23.

[59] Gyula Kristó, 'Koppány felnégyelése', *Századok*, 116 (1982): 959–68 (repr. in Gyula Kristó, *Írások Szent Istvánról és koráról* (Szeged: Szegedi Középkorász Műhely, 2000, 49–61); Szabados, *Magyar államalapítások*, 269–73.

[60] Cited by Kristó, 'Koppány felnégyelése', 959.   [61] Ibid., 959–60.

[62] Gyula Pauler, *A magyar nemzet története az Árpádházi királyok alatt*, 2nd edn (Budapest: Athenaeum, 1899, repr. Budapest: Állami Könyvterjesztő Vállalat, 1985), vol. 1, 389; Kristó, 'Koppány felnégyelése', 960–1.

CUPAN 41

rebels, while according to another, such display was arranged to reassure the population subject to Stephen, demonstrating the successful suppression of the rebellion.[63] Western-European examples of such display always served the purpose of deterrence; therefore displaying the body-parts in places that were securely under Stephen's power actually undermines the basis of the reasoning.[64]

There exists, however, a possible alternative explanation: Esztergom, Veszprém, Győr and Transylvania were all centres of early bishoprics,[65] and a later ecclesiastical author could well be aware of that, since in the Middle Ages ecclesiastical memory probably had the longest reach. This would also explain why later royal centres do not appear in the list, and why one of the places of display is named as Transylvania. Fehérvár was not the centre of an early bishopric; Transylvania—while not a fort with a gate where one could display body-parts—was. It was a rare case where a bishopric initially was not named after a town; perhaps because at first it was a missionary bishopric, it bore the name of a territory.[66] 'Transylvania' did not have a gate; however, a later author using the names of early bishoprics as suitable places for the public display of body-parts to deter wrongdoers may have included it in the list. Why Transylvania would feature on this list otherwise remains a mystery, which early modern authors tried to solve by adding the name of a city in Transylvania, which indeed would have a gate, but which is not what the chronicle account contains.[67]

György Győrffy claimed that the reality of Cupan's quartering could be substantiated by an account of the Arab traveller Ibn Fadlan, who travelled to the Volga Bulghars in 922.[68] Ibn Fadlan recounted that the Bulghars punished adultery by tying down the guilty between four stakes, cutting their body in half with an axe, and hanging the two parts from a tree.[69] Győrffy initially asserted that the quartering of Cupan was the result of a pre-Christian legal custom still in force,

[63] Győrffy, *István király*, 119–21; Kristó, 'Koppány felnégyelése', 961–3. Szabados, *Magyar államalapítások*, 272 suggests that it was both. See also Magyar, *Hős vagy lázadó?*, 58–60. Zoltán Lenkey, Attila Zsoldos, *Szent István és III. András* (Budapest: Kossuth Kiadó, 2003), 25 claims it was proof of victory, and perhaps a show of strength towards Transylvania. Kornél Szovák, *Szent István* (Budapest: Kossuth Kiadó, 2018), 30 sees it as both deterrence and proof that Stephen can defend family interests. See also Mályusz—Kristó, *Johannes de Thurocz, Chronica*, II. *Commentarii* 1, 248.

[64] J. G. Bellamy, *The Law of Treason in England in the Later Middle Ages* (Cambridge: Cambridge University Press, 1970), 52.

[65] Kristó, 'Koppány felnégyelése', 963–4 mentions the link to early ecclesiastical organization.

[66] János Karácsonyi, 'Az erdélyi püspökség története 1526-ig', in *Ódon Erdély. Művelődéstörténeti tanulmányok*, ed. Péter Sas (Budapest: Magvető, 2004), http://mek.niif.hu/04900/04920/html/mhodonerdely0034.html. László Koszta, *Fejezetek a korai magyar egyházszervezet történetéből. Doktori disszertáció (MTA doktora)*, Dissertation of Academic Doctor (Szeged, 2012), 35–6, 44–5, 89, 259.

[67] Modern historians followed suit: Mályusz—Kristó, *Johannes de Thurocz, Chronica*, II. *Commentarii* 1, 248 also supply Alba Julia.

[68] Győrffy, 'Koppány lázadása', 21.

[69] A. Zeki Validi Togan, *Ibn Faḍlān's Reisebericht* (Leipzig: F. A. Brockhaus, 1939), 66; Richard Frye, tr., *Ibn Fadlan's Journey to Russia: A Tenth-Century Traveler from Baghdad to the Volga River* (Princeton: Markus Wiener Publishers, 2005), 57. He also related that the oghuz (Ghuzz) tied adulterers to the branches of two trees, bent down, and, as the branches sprang back, the guilty were torn in two.

42 STEPHEN I, THE FIRST CHRISTIAN KING OF HUNGARY

rather than of Stephen's personal judgement; later he claimed that a truly Christian king like Stephen could not be responsible for such a cruel punishment, which therefore must have been meted out on the orders of Stephen's mother Sarolt, who was only superficially a Christian and had closer ties to the world of the steppe where a similar culture of punishment reigned.[70] Therefore, according to this explanation, a punishment from the steppe days for adultery was adopted by Stephen or Sarolt to punish a new Christian crime, incest. Sometimes historians mention fornication instead of incest,[71] confusing the issue even further, because fornication refers to sexual relations outside marriage, whereas incest refers to sexual relations within the prohibited degrees of kinship; the medieval chronicle quite clearly mentions (proposed) incest: 'per incestuosum connubium'. The Ibn Fadlan analogy to Cupan's quartering has been widely accepted.[72] This logic is problematic even because of its internal inconsistencies. Ibn Fadlan wrote of cutting people in two, not quartering. There is no proof at all that (if such a punishment existed among the Volga Bulghars), Hungarians before Christianization practised the same customs as the Volga Bulghars. Even more importantly, however, Ibn Fadlan's account is not the real analogy for the quartering of a rebel.

The real analogy is the punishment for treason against the king (lèse-majesté), such as attempted assassination. The judicial punishment of executing those convicted of such a crime by quartering was introduced in the mid-thirteenth century, first in England, then from the fourteenth century increasingly regularly in the various countries of Europe.[73] (By contrast, in Stephen's laws conspiracy against the king is punished by capital punishment and in another canon by anathema.[74]) The body-parts of those who had rebelled against royal authority were sometimes hung on public display after their execution. Therefore, a fourteenth-century author at the Hungarian Angevin court, relying on judicial practice then current in France and elsewhere, could well deem quartering to be a

[70] Györffy, 'Koppány lázadása', 21; Györffy, István király, 119–20. That Stephen's mother was called Sarolt comes from the fourteenth-century chronicles, and there is no way to tell if it is correct. SRH I, 312.

[71] E.g. Györffy, István király, 119 claims that the levirate was seen as fornication.

[72] Kristó, 'Koppány felnégyelése', 960; Tamás Bogyay, Stephanus Rex (Budapest: Ecclesia Kiadó, 1988), 40; Szabados, Magyar államalapítások, 271 (with some caveats).

[73] Bellamy, The Law of Treason, 13, 21, 23–6, 38–9, 46–7, 94; Alan Harding, England in the Thirteenth Century (Cambridge: Cambridge University Press, 1993, repr. 1997), 308; S. H. Cuttler, The Law of Treason and Treason Trials in Later Medieval France (Cambridge: Cambridge University Press, 1982), 116–18, 152, 171–2, 206; Claude Gauvard, «De Grace Especial» Crime, État et Société en France à la fin du Moyen Âge (Paris: Publications de la Sorbonne, 1991), vol. 2, 924. The introduction of the punishment in England is usually dated to the late thirteenth century; two episodes recounted by Matthew Paris would give a more precise and slightly earlier date, as he describes the division of the body into three parts in 1238, while depicting quartering in 1242 for treason. Matthew Paris, Chronica Majora, ed. Henry R. Luard, iii, 498 and iv, 196, respectively. I am grateful to Nicholas Vincent for this reference. The 1242 case of William de Marisco is an exact parallel to the Cupan story: 'miserum cadauer in quatuor partes est diuisum, et ad quatuor principales regni ciuitates eaedem partes, ut miserabile spectaculum illud singulos intuentes exterreret, sunt transmisse'.

[74] János M. Bak, György Bónis, James Ross Sweeney, ed., The Laws of the Medieval Kingdom of Hungary, vol. 1 (Bakersfield, CA: Charles Schlacks, 1989), 9, c. 2 and 11, c. 19, respectively.

CUPAN   43

fitting punishment for Cupan's crime: this crime was not his intended incestuous marriage, but his desire to kill Stephen and appropriate his power.

In the *Illuminated Chronicle*, an image also accompanies Cupan's story, representing Cupan's death. Strikingly, despite the textual narrative, Cupan is not depicted as being killed in battle, but beheaded in what looks like an execution. Cupan is kneeling, with his hands tied behind his back, his decapitated head lies on the ground, while a soldier, wielding an axe, proceeds to dismember the body. King Stephen, on horseback and wearing his crown over his helmet, looks on; his gesture orders the execution.[75] The visual vocabulary of quartering varied to some extent in medieval representations, but the later medieval and early modern imagery of quartering differs radically from this illumination. That may indicate the unfamiliarity of the illuminator with the practice of quartering, although he clearly rendered Cupan's quartering as a Christian judicial punishment, rather than a throwback to ancient Hungarian customs.

*   *   *

Whereas researchers have been looking for the lost Ur-text that contained the full story originally, leaving scattered remnants in now extant texts, one should be alert to the possibility of medieval literary construction, the imaginative elaboration of stories that can be based on a very limited, or no historical kernel. The medieval sources that have been used by modern historians to 'reconstruct' the story of Cupan are not independent of each other. Therefore, we cannot treat them as if they had conserved the memory of the same event with varying amounts of detail. The author of a later text could draw on earlier written sources and embellish the stories they found; therefore, it may be that medieval intertextuality gave birth to the Cupan story.[76] Did Simon of Kéza abridge a now lost chronicle that included the full Cupan story that is now only transmitted in the fourteenth-century chronicles?[77] Alternatively, did a later author take Simon's terse text and elaborate on it, also drawing on the hagiographical *Lives* of Stephen?[78] It is, for example, possible that Cupan became *dux* of Somogy because the fourteenth-century author took the mere mention of Cupan being killed in Somogy from the thirteenth-century chronicle of Simon of Kéza (where Somogy could have featured as part of a noble family's claim to territorial rights from an alleged ancestor, see below), embroidered it further and wove it into his story.

Rather than the fourteenth-century chronicler having more detailed knowledge on Cupan than Simon of Kéza, from a now-lost more authentic eleventh-century

---

[75] Reproduction: László Veszprémy, Tünde Wehli, József Hapák, *The Book of the Illuminated Chronicle* (Budapest: Kossuth Publishing House, 2009), 90.

[76] This possibility is mentioned briefly in Thoroczkay, 'A magyar krónikairodalom', 113.

[77] Claim that Simon abridged an existing chronicle: e.g. Gyula Kristó, *Magyar Historiográfia I. Történetírás a középkori Magyarországon* (Budapest: Osiris Kiadó, 2002), 74.

[78] Chroniclers drew on existing *vitae*: Thoroczkay, 'A magyarországi legendairodalom', 197.

44 STEPHEN I, THE FIRST CHRISTIAN KING OF HUNGARY

text or oral tradition, we need to consider the possibility of the fourteenth-century author reworking and embellishing mentions found in Simon of Kéza's (or a similar) text as well as drawing on Hartvic's *vita* of Stephen. There are many parallels to such literary elaborations of stories in medieval narrative sources.[79] Literary borrowing from other sources, including common European stock, and fanciful literary creations were not alien to medieval chronicles and narratives, and since the work of Hayden White and the 'literary turn', medievalists are increasingly alert to the literary, constructed nature of medieval historical sources such as chronicles, and the need to contextualize them in the period of their composition.[80] Yet an approach to medieval Hungarian narrative sources that considers such literary creation is rather recent.[81] A national 'system of relevance' traditionally underpinned Hungarian chronicle research, automatically elevating literary stories to the status of evidence that contain some form of historical truth.[82] Research formulated based on 'national canons' has also restricted comparative approaches, further creating the illusion of unique textual problems.[83]

It is also possible to account for the origins of the Cupan story in family traditions. Perhaps the interpolation of the charter of Pannonhalma and the entry for the Hunt-Paznan (modern Hont-Pázmány) kindred in chapter 41 of the fourteenth-century chronicles, in the list of immigrant nobles (*advenae*), are not independent of each other. It is possible that the Hunt-Paznan kindred's evolving ancestor cult influenced both the thirteenth-century interpolation of the charter and the development of the Cupan story in the *advenae* section of the chronicle. The interpolated section of the charter of Pannonhalma emphasized the importance and heroism of the founding ancestors of the kindred.[84] The family's endeavour to exalt their ancestors may have led to linking Cupan with the story of the pagan rebels. In these traditions, the Hunt-Paznan family's ancestors were given credit for helping Stephen early on in his reign. Thus, the family history of the Hunt-Paznan kindred may have drawn on and combined various stories associated with the turbulent start of Stephen's rule: the pagan uprising in the *Lives*, and

---

[79] E.g. Scott Waugh, 'The Lives of Edward the Confessor and the meaning of history in the Middle Ages', in *The Medieval Chronicle* III, ed. Erik Kooper (Amsterdam—New York: Rodopi, 2004), 200–18. On the methods of compilation: Bernard Guenée, *Histoire et culture historique dans l'Occident médiéval* (Paris: Aubier-Montaigne, 1980), 211–16.

[80] Examples include, but are not limited to: Gabrielle M. Spiegel, 'History, historicism, and the social logic of the text in the Middle Ages', *Speculum*, 65, no. 1 (1990): 59–86; Werner Verbeke, Ludo Milis, Jean Goossens, ed., *Medieval Narrative Sources: A Gateway into the Medieval Mind* (Leuven: Leuven University Press, 2005); Chris Given-Wilson, *Chronicles: The Writing of History in Medieval England* (London: Hambledon Continuum, 2007).

[81] Veszprémy, 'Korhűség és forrásérték'.

[82] Ann Rigney, *Imperfect Histories: The Elusive Past and the Legacy of Romantic Historicism* (Ithaca—London: Cornell University Press, 2001), 69–70.

[83] Lars Boje Mortensen, 'The canons of medieval literature from the Middle Ages to the twenty-first century', *Analecta Romana Instituti Danici*, 42 (2017): 47–63.

[84] Szentpétery, 'Szent István király oklevelei', 161, repr. 353, note 2 suggests that there is no proof that these names occurred in the original charter.

CUPAN   45

Cupan in the family tradition of those claiming descent from Vecellinus (the Ják kindred).

There seem to be dialogue and borrowing between the stories of the Ják kindred and the Hont-Pázmány (Hunt-Paznan) kindred, whose entry immediately follows that of the Ják in the list of immigrant nobles. The embryonic Cupan story thus migrated. This may have been linked to noble rivalry expressed through at least partly invented family traditions. In the list of *advenae* recorded in the late thirteenth-century chronicle of Simon of Kéza, the killing of Cupan is only linked to Vecellinus (using the form Wecelinus).[85] In contrast, the list of immigrant nobles in the fourteenth-century chronicle compositions includes the mention of Cupan not only when recounting the deeds of Vecellinus, but also when relating those of the brothers Hunt and Paznan: their help and counsel ensured Stephen was victorious.[86] (It seems the Vecellinus story appealed to several families, as the Gut-Keled kindred tried to claim Vecellinus as their ancestor in the fourteenth century.[87])

The tale of Cupan perhaps started to be developed in the context of the rivalry of noble families in the thirteenth century, with the Hunt-Paznan family playing a role in its embellishment.[88] The idea that family traditions transmitted information that ended up in the chronicles has been widely accepted.[89] Those who mention family tradition as a vehicle of transmitting Cupan's story, however, give credence to that tradition, suggesting that it conveyed the memory of real events, or at best take a haphazard approach, trying to detect 'family bias' and exaggeration in some details, while accepting the veracity of the basic story.[90]

We need to question the reliability of noble family tradition much more radically, as has been done in some contexts. In fact, many noble families claimed made-up military and other heroic deeds for their ancestors; many erroneously

---

[85] *SRH* I, 189. Simon of Kéza uses the form Wecelinus; the fourteenth-century chronicles Vecellinus, Vecelinus, and Vencellinus in chapter 40, *SRH* I, 296, and Vencilinus, Welinus, Wecellinus, Vencellinus, and several other forms in chapter 64, *SRH* I, 313. I use Vecellinus.

[86] 'Chronici Hungarici', *SRH* I, 296–7. Gerics, who argued that the tale in chapter 41 of the fourteenth-century chronicles is earlier, also suggested that the section on the Hunt-Paznan in that chapter merges two accounts in the thirteenth century, an earlier one aggrandizing their role, and a polemic against that. Gerics, *Legkorábbi Gesta-szerkesztéseink*, 17–19. The chronological primacy of chapter 41 would imply that Vecellinus was connected to Cupan later than the Hunt-Paznan. This would mean the Hunt-Paznan possibly inventing Cupan. To me this seems less likely, because of the descendant list with a Cupan included in the Vecellinus story. While both chapters may well incorporate material from diverse sources, thirteenth-century noble rivalry provides the context for the heightened interest in ancestors' deeds.

[87] János Karácsonyi, *A magyar nemzetségek a XIV. század közepéig* (Budapest, 1900, repr. Budapest: Nap Kiadó, 1995), 470.

[88] Csóka, *A latin nyelvű történeti irodalom*, 537–40 argued that the story of Vecelin's family, including the victory over Cupan, was composed in the early thirteenth century.

[89] Györffy, 'Koppány lázadása', 8; László Veszprémy, 'Szent István felövezéséről', *Hadtörténelmi Közlemények*, 102 (1989): 3–13; László Veszprémy, *Lovagvilág Magyarországon* (Budapest: Argumentum Kiadó, 2008), 67–77.

[90] Györffy, 'Koppány lázadása', 13; Györffy, *István király*, 117; Csóka, *A latin nyelvű történeti irodalom*, 541–2.

46   STEPHEN I, THE FIRST CHRISTIAN KING OF HUNGARY

projected people who lived and events that happened later back into the period of St Stephen's reign; many, at least partly invented traditions about immigrant noble families' ancestors were incorporated into the *advenae* list.[91] The extent to which such inventions could diverge from reality can be demonstrated by a few examples from the same passages where we find the Cupan story. First, although in the list of *advenae* in Simon of Kéza's chronicle, Vecellinus's descendants are the Ják kindred, according to several historians the newly powerful Ják merely claimed Vecellinus as their ancestor in the thirteenth century from the Rád who were his genuine descendants, but whose fortunes were declining.[92] Second, the Hunt-Paznan family tradition incorporated into the fourteenth-century chronicles included the story of the brothers girding Stephen with a sword; according to the chronicle, this took place at the river Garam. It had been argued that the event itself was true, but because the story was transmitted by Vecellinus to his descendants in German, when he referred to 'Gran' (the German name of Esztergom), this was subsequently erroneously turned into the river 'Garam'.[93] Yet research has shown that the custom of girding did not yet exist at the end of the tenth century, and thus the narrative is not a trustworthy account of events.[94] As these examples of the potential complete unreliability of family tradition show, we should not assume that family traditions about Cupan incorporated in the *advenae* stories reflect real events.

* * *

Allegedly, the memory of real events was transmitted in other ways as well, through toponyms, and through oral or early (but now lost) written tradition encapsulated in fifteenth- and sixteenth-century sources and modern folklore. Toponyms have been used in hypotheses about the veracity of the fourteenth-century chronicle texts, as supposedly the memory of events was preserved in the place names at the scenes of Cupan's activity.[95] Historians working on toponyms warned about the need to exercise caution; some place names may seem to be connected to the name Cupan, but may derive from a Slavic root for 'ditch' instead, for example.[96] Further, as has been demonstrated, it is impossible to date

---

[91] Karácsonyi, *A magyar nemzetségek*, 235–8; Kristó, 'Magyar öntudat és idegenellenesség', 439; Mályusz, *Az V. István-kori gesta*, 64–83; Nora Berend, 'Noms et origines des immigrants nobles en Hongrie (XIIIe siècles): la liste des advenae entre mythe et réalités', in *Anthroponymie et migrations dans la Chrétienté médiévale*, ed. Monique Bourin, Pascual Martínez Sopena (Madrid: Casa de Velázquez, 2010), 247–64. Rácz, 'A Ják nemzetség', 21–4.

[92] Györffy, 'Koppány lázadása', 14; Rácz, 'A Ják nemzetség', 20.

[93] Györffy, 'Koppány lázadása', 13; Györffy, *István király*, 116.

[94] Veszprémy, 'Szent István felövezéséről', 5–8; Veszprémy, *Lovagvilág Magyarországon*, 66–77.

[95] Györffy, *István király*, 111.

[96] Györffy, 'Koppány lázadása', 16. Gyula Kristó, Ferenc Makk, László Szegfű, 'Adatok korai helyneveink ismeretéhez [part 1]', *Acta Universitatis Szegediensis de Attila József Nominatae: Acta Historica*, 44 (1973): 1–96, see 47–8 (some derive from the name of the Katapan kindred, others may come from Slavic kopan, 'ditch'); the toponym Törökkoppány is unrelated to Cupan, Stephen's opponent, according to Gyula Kristó, 'Szempontok korai helyneveink történeti tipológiájához', *Acta Universitatis Szegediensis de Attila József Nominatae: Acta Historica*, 55 (1976): 1–101, at 36.

CUPAN 47

the emergence of toponyms accurately.[97] The earliest toponyms attested in the sources that could be linked to Cupan date from 1086 and 1138.[98] Even if these are tied to the personal name Cupan, it is impossible to determine which historical person they are named after, because several late eleventh-century Cupans are attested in charters, as well as a Koppán family probably originating in the early twelfth century: none of them are related to the supposed rebel, and any of them could have been the basis for the formation of toponyms (which occurred in several different ways, including from the name of an estate's owner).[99] Later on, ever more colourful popular legends were woven around Koppány, resulting in popular etymologies connecting a variety of places to chief Koppány.[100] On the one hand, in none of these cases is it possible to prove that the place was named after Stephen's opponent in a period close to the supposed events. On the other hand, it is possible at least partially to show folkloric myth-making with no basis in historical facts, as the same stories were attached to several different locations.[101] Toponyms, therefore, are useless in proving that a chief Cupan, Stephen's adversary, lived at the end of the tenth century.

A similar conclusion must be drawn about an attempt to authenticate the Koppány story with the hypothesis of early county-organization.[102] According to this, giant counties (later subdivided into smaller counties) were created from the territories of Stephen's defeated opponents, and one of these giant counties incorporated the later counties of Somogy, Zala, and others. Thus, the existence of the early giant county would prove the veracity of Koppány's revolt. Yet the hypothesis of a giant county's existence in the area itself comes from the supposition that the Koppány story is true. There is no evidence to prove its existence and other historians disagree with this thesis.[103] Little factual basis exists for the early counties and much is speculative. We do not know when and how counties

---

[97] Summary of issues in Szabados, *Magyar államalapítások*, 257–9. On problems of determining whose name was given to a place: Kristó, 'Szempontok korai helyneveink', 18–19.

[98] See a list, for example, in Magyar, *Hős vagy lázadó?*, 30–4; the map on 32 shows that such toponyms were spread out over most of the kingdom.

[99] Toponyms from owner's name: Kristó, 'Szempontok korai helyneveink', 10. On toponyms that include the name Koppány: György Györffy, 'A honfoglaló magyarok települési rendjéről', *Archaeológiai Értesítő*, 97 (1970): 191–242, at 203; Kristó et al., 'Adatok korai helyneveink', 47–8; Katalin Fehértói, *Árpád-kori személynévtár (1000–1301)* (Budapest: Akadémiai Kiadó, 2004), 229–30; Karácsonyi, *A magyar nemzetségek*, 784–93; Szabados, *Magyar államalapítások*, 257–8. Toponyms were formed from personal names until the thirteenth century according to some scholars, and throughout the Middle Ages according to others: Kristó et al., 'Adatok korai helyneveink', 3; Kristó, 'Szempontok korai helyneveink', 15–17.

[100] On folk memory first linking Bény fort to the Ottomans and then to the confrontation of Stephen with pagans: Vilmos Voigt, 'Ezeréves-e a magyar folklór?', *Ethnica*, 2, no. 4 (2000): 97–9, at 98–9.

[101] Zoltán Magyar, 'Koppány alakja a néphagyományban', in *Szent István és az államalapítás*, Veszprémy, 95–104, at 99 (this is a reprint of the article from *Valóság*, 41, no. 3 (1998): 29–38).

[102] Attila Zsoldos, 'Somogy vármegye kialakulásáról', in *Szent István és az államalapítás*, Veszprémy, 431–9.

[103] E.g. Gyula Kristó, 'Néhány vármegye kialakulásának kérdéséhez', in *Szent István és az államalapítás*, Veszprémy, 468–71.

48   STEPHEN I, THE FIRST CHRISTIAN KING OF HUNGARY

developed in many other parts of the kingdom either, unconnected to rebels against Stephen. Thus, the existence of early giant counties is not certain, nor can it be localized exclusively to former territories of rebels.

It has also been suggested that details only found in late medieval texts such as a sermon on St Stephen by the Franciscan Osvát Laskai (d. 1511) conserve authentic early history and reinforce the veracity of the Cupan story (a claim refuted by others).[104] Laskai used Hartvic's story of a pagan rebellion against Stephen (without naming Cupan), but added that nobles from Zala as well as Somogy rose up against him.[105] Moreover, according to the anonymous Carthusian author who wrote between 1524 and 1527, Kupán ruled in Somogy and Zala.[106] It has been claimed that these authors drew information from now lost eleventh-century written work.[107] This cannot be substantiated; the Carthusian author perhaps merely reinterpreted Laskai's text, and Laskai may have drawn on local tradition or a text written in the late medieval period.[108] Since the Ják kindred, who had creatively acquired Vecellinus as their ancestor in the thirteenth century, had estates in Zala county, it could be the development of Ják family traditions (rather than authentic early sources) that eventually left its trace in fifteenth-century sources.[109] Such local (family) tradition, as shown above, is no guarantee of authenticity. Additions to the Cupan story are much more likely to be due to later imaginative elaborations, rather than to a more authentic tradition surviving underground for centuries, only to be expressed openly so much later.

Oral folk traditions supposedly go back to a medieval kernel, even if they were embellished by later additions.[110] Yet such traditions cannot be used as proof of the historical authenticity of the Koppány story, as some of the most basic elements of this folklore can be shown to derive from later periods. These traditions usually refer to the protagonist's name as Kupa, allegedly proving continuity with the original

---

[104] Zsoldos, 'Somogy vármegye kialakulásáról', 433–4. The large amount of clearly ahistorical information in Laskai has already been pointed out, e.g. Kristó, 'Néhány vármegye', 469; Balázs Kertész, 'Laskai Osvát és a Karthauzi Névtelen magyarországi forrásairól. Feltételezett elbeszélő művek használatának problémája', Századok, 142, no. 2 (2008): 474–90.

[105] Osualdus de Lasco, Sermones de sanctis Biga salutis intitulati (Hagenau: Heinrich Gran für Johann Rynman, 1499), Zentralbibliothek Zürich Ra 39, http://www.e-rara.ch/zuz/content/pageview/12786040; Oswaldus de Lasko, 'Sermones de Sanctis Biga Salutis intitulati, Sermo LXXVI. De sancto Stephano, rege Hungarorum, I', in Domus sermonum compilatorium, ed. Balázs Kertész, Eötvös Loránd Tudományegyetem Régi Magyar Irodalomtudományi Intézet, http://sermones.elte.hu/szoveg-kiadasok/latinul/laskaiosvat/index.php?file=os/os076.

[106] J. Budenz, G. Szarvas, Á. Szilády, ed., Nyelvemléktár: Régi magyar codexek és nyomtatványok, vol. 5 (Budapest: Magyar Tudományos Akadémia, 1876), 239.

[107] Zsoldos, 'Somogy vármegye kialakulásáról', 434.

[108] Kertész, 'Laskai Osvát és a Karthauzi Névtelen magyarországi forrásairól'. One of the sources of Osvát Laskai seems to be a recently discovered fifteenth-century chronicle: Gábor Mikó, 'Élt-e valaha Szent István fia, Ottó herceg?', Történelmi Szemle, 55 (2013): 1–22.

[109] On their estates: Karácsonyi, A magyar nemzetségek, 717; Rácz, 'A Ják nemzetség', 7.

[110] Magyar, 'Koppány alakja', 95; a collection of such tales from the late nineteenth and twentieth centuries: Magyar, Hős vagy lázadó?, 85–112.

medieval name.[111] This form of the name, however, goes back to early modern authors such as Bonfini; it was the form widely used in nineteenth-century historiography, and was broadly disseminated, for example, through a leaflet issued for St Stephen's feast day in 1860 detailing the sequence of festivities.[112] The form Kupa, therefore, was probably borrowed from such sources, rather than representing an unbroken oral folk tradition since the Middle Ages. Archaeological excavation also contradicts folk memory: the most widely known folk tradition is the identification of Somogyvár as Koppány's seat,[113] but the fort was dated to the mid-eleventh century. The complete excavation demonstrated that an eleventh-century layer was directly superimposed on the Bronze Age settlement, with no objects or pottery from the tenth century; the earliest coin found dated to the reign of Andrew I (1046–60).[114] Thus, Somogyvár could not have been Koppány's seat.

It is impossible to date the emergence of the folk traditions; they were written down in the nineteenth and twentieth centuries. It can, however, be proven that the folk stories about Koppány include motifs from other legends, for example, those of St Ladislas (ruled 1077–91) and King Matthias (ruled 1458–90), and also borrow myths relating to the Ottoman period (sixteenth-seventeenth century) and associate them with Koppány.[115] They also show literary influences. The folk story that Koppány escaped with his wife, and then stabbed her to death to avoid having the enemy capture her,[116] shows the influence of the story of Mihály Dobozi fleeing the Ottomans, which originates in late sixteenth-century sources and was popularized in literature and historical paintings of the nineteenth century.[117] Further, stories learned in school can be recognized.[118] Finally, the unreliability of oral traditions is obvious in the very different tales attached to the same place, explaining its name through folk etymology: for example, the village of Kötcse has been linked to Koppány as 'köt-seb' (dress-wound) because that is

[111] Magyar, 'Koppány alakja', 95.
[112] On Bonfini and others, see below; István Sándor, Sokféle írás egybeszedése, 1. darab (Győr, 1791), 41 uses both forms, 'a somogyi Koppányt (Kupát)'; anonymous author, Sz. István király ünnepe az ünnepélyes menetrenddel, A nagy király életrajzával és ereklyéinek, s a Szt. Korona történetével (Pest: Werfer Károly nyomda, 1860), 11 (Kupa); Henrik Marczali, Szent István királysága (1896, repr. Budapest: Kassák Könyv és Lapkiadó Kft, 2000), 6–7 also used the form Kupa.
[113] Magyar, 'Koppány alakja', 95.
[114] István Bóna, Az Árpádok korai várai (Debrecen: Ethnica, 1998), 40.
[115] László Lukács, 'Szent István király a néphagyományban', in Szent István és Székesfehérvár, ed. Gyula Fülöp (Székesfehérvár: Szent István király múzeum, 1996), 30–9, at 31–3. Magyar, 'Koppány alakja', 96, 100, 102. The author assumes but cannot prove the authenticity of some of the traditions he records. In one instance, Koppány is even turned into an Ottoman chieftain: Magyar, Hős vagy lázadó?, 109. On borrowings from later legends in St Stephen folktales more generally, see Zoltán Magyar, Szent István a magyar kultúrtörténetben (Budapest: Helikon Kiadó, 1996), 119–22.
[116] Magyar, 'Koppány alakja', 98.
[117] Ironically, the elaboration of the Dobozi story may have been influenced by Tacitus: István Borzsák, 'A Dobozi-legenda', in Jubileumi csokor Csapodi Csaba tiszteletére: tanulmányok, ed. Marianne Rozsondai (Budapest: Argumentum Kiadó, 2002), 65–9.
[118] Magyar, 'Koppány alakja', 95–104; Rózsa Ignácz, 'Hagyományok földjén', Vigilia, 18, no. 4 (April 1953): 190–7, at 191–3. Also evident in a story linking the pagan revolt against Stephen to Bény: Ildikó Landgraf, ed., 'Beszéli a világ, hogy mi magyarok...' Magyar történeti mondák (Budapest: Magyar Néprajzi Társaság—Európai Folklór Központ, 1998), 68.

50 STEPHEN I, THE FIRST CHRISTIAN KING OF HUNGARY

where Koppány's wounds after a battle were dressed, and as 'költség' (expense) because of Koppány's expensive travels in the area.[119] It is entirely impossible to prove that there are independent, authentic oral traditions about a historical chief Koppány, going back to the end of the tenth century, and then written down in the nineteenth and twentieth centuries. Analyses of folk memory on St Stephen show that they do not go back to the early eleventh century; many folk stories reflect nineteenth-century historical tradition and are unreliable as a historical source.[120] Indeed, a few examples show how such folk tales lack even the faintest trace of historical knowledge. Thus, the Holy Dexter is accounted for by Stephen cutting off his own hand after striking his mother in anger, and the crooked cross on the 'Holy Crown' by a battle against pagans when Stephen had to flee in haste so the cross was damaged;[121] why would 'memories' about Koppány be more reliable? The fourteenth-century chronicles, and the later literary reworkings of the Cupan story in subsequent chronicles became the basis of the most diverse and colourful folk legends, which were linked to local identity creation and to folk etymologies of local toponyms attached to natural features and villages.

The historical sources we possess about Cupan are late and self-contradictory. They consist of a late thirteenth-century chronicle's two brief notices of a Cupan killed early in Stephen's reign, according to one of these in Somogy county; a fourteenth-century mention of the enslavement of nobles who adhered to Cupan and rejected baptism; and the fourteenth-century longer story. No proof exists that Cupan led a pagan revolt, or that the two stories—the pagan rebellion in the *Lives* and Cupan's revolt in the chronicle—narrate the same event. The first fourteenth-century remark connecting the two may be the outcome of literary combination, perhaps in the service of family myths. There is no independent confirmation that these events took place. No contemporary texts describe Cupan's revolt, and while a later provenance for at least parts of the story can be proven, nothing substantiates the claim that an early, now lost description transmitted a reliable account of genuine events from the end of the tenth century. Are the fragments we have disparate and self-contradictory traces of past events, or the evidence of literary elaboration over time? Was there a historical Cupan, Stephen's opponent, or was he born in family myth woven over time about the glorious deeds of ancestors, based on the name Cupan that occurred in a noble family? Was that story then further borrowed and elaborated in the rivalry with other noble families, and did stories merge, with later authors reading, borrowing from, and associating originally different stories to create new composite narratives? Did the hagiographical stories of a pagan rebellion and Cupan become associated in thirteenth- or fourteenth-century family traditions?

---

[119] Magyar, *Hős vagy lázadó?*, 97, 109, respectively.

[120] Voigt, 'Ezeréves-e a magyar folklór?'; Zoltán Ujváry, 'Kis adalék Voigt Vilmos cikkéhez: Ezeréves-e a magyar folklór?', *Ethnica*, 2, no. 4 (2000): 116–17.

[121] Lukács, 'Szent István király a néphagyományban', 38; Magyar, *Hős vagy lázadó?*, 109–10.

3. Historiography: Completing the Story

The modern constructed story lacks even tenuous foundations in the sources on some crucial points. The severe poverty of the source material, and the problems of interpretation related to the few existing sources spurred historians working on the period to resort to a wide range of hypotheses in order to fill the holes, and these hypotheses slowly acquired the status of fact through repetition. One can create chains of conjectures about anything, but this at most proves the wealth of the historian's imagination. Nothing demonstrates better the futility of such guesswork than the diametrically opposed 'explanations' historians have arrived at, based on the same available source material. For instance, one historian claimed Stephen's mother Sarolt would have liked to wed Cupan, while another alleged Sarolt was fighting for her son's right to the throne against Cupan.[122]

The fanciful modern 'reconstructions' in some respects have a prototype in the late fifteenth-century humanist writer Antonio Bonfini. While the slightly earlier chronicler Thuróczy's text (1488) followed closely the fourteenth-century chronicles, Bonfini, court historian of King Matthias, significantly added to the story. His historical work (1497) combined the account of the *vita* by Hartvic with that of the chronicle and further embellished the story. Bonfini includes both the pagan revolt led by many nobles from hagiography, and Cupa's (as he calls the protagonist) rebellion from the chronicles, reconciling the two by stating that a pagan rebellion led by nobles broke out, fostered by Scythian savagery, and then Cupa elevated himself to be its leader (although Bonfini also mentions that the chronicles call Cupa the rebellion's initiator). Cupa's desire to marry Stephen's widowed mother is called adultery rather than incest, presumably because incest made no sense to Bonfini, who does not see Cupa as Stephen's relative. In this elaborated account, Cupa wants to deprive Stephen of his life and power through trickery. He incites hatred against Stephen in the pagan population; among other accusations, he claims Stephen had the statues of Mars, Hercules, and other gods destroyed. This is clearly the humanist author's effort to model paganism on antiquity and has nothing to do with the beliefs of a pre-Christian population. Bonfini also provides a lengthy description of the battle, adding that the outcome was doubtful. This is an inflation of earlier chronicle accounts, which mentioned a long battle. He emphasized that Stephen's prayer to God turned the tide. When relating Cupa's quartering, Bonfini adds that the body-part sent to Transylvania was sent to Alba Iulia to frighten the Dacians; the addition of the name of the city provided an explanation of what otherwise would have seemed to be a mistake,

---

[122] Szabolcs Vajay, 'Géza nagyfejedelem és családja', in *Székesfehérvár évszázadai*, vol. 1, *Az államalapítás kora*, ed. Alán Kralovánszky (Székesfehérvár: István király Múzeum, 1967), 63–100, at 75–6; similarly György Szabados, 'Rokonok rivalizálása: Árpád-házi Koppány és István ellentétéről', *Korunk* (2018, no. 2): 3–10, at 8 (Sarolt wanted to wed Koppány); Györffy, *István király*, 119–20 (Sarolt fought for her son Stephen). For a summary of views, see Szabados, *Magyar államalapítások*, 262–3.

52 STEPHEN I, THE FIRST CHRISTIAN KING OF HUNGARY

since Transylvania had no gate to which one could affix a body-part.[123] Bonfini's text provides clear proof of combining various earlier sources, and fanciful additions either to complete the story, to reconcile contradictory parts coming from different sources, or to explain problematic issues.[124]

If Cupan wanted power based on seniority, he must have been Stephen's relative in the male line.[125] Yet no medieval source states that the two were related, and no evidence of their kinship exists. The contention of modern historians on the two being related rests on tautological arguments. The fourteenth-century chronicles designate both Cupan and Stephen using exactly the same title, *dux* (military leader, chief, 'duke'), and call their respective territories *ducatus*. For both Cupan and Stephen, this terminology is clearly used to signal a ruler who is not crowned, and therefore has no royal title, as well as the territory under his rule, thus distinguishing *dux* from *rex*, a crowned king.[126] Cupan wanted to attach Stephen's territory to his own; however, with his defeat, Cupan's lands became Stephen's instead.

Historians, claiming that only a member of the same dynasty could have attempted to seize the throne, made Cupan a member of the ruling Árpád dynasty, despite the fact that such a relationship has been impossible to prove, and not for lack of trying. The most ingenious hypothetical constructions were created by generations of historians (started by chroniclers in the fifteenth century) to define Cupan's place in the dynasty, with at least four different identifications suggested, but none of them is more than speculation without a shred of proof.[127] Indeed, György Györffy, for example, changed his mind over the years, first arguing for one ancestor (Fajsz), then later for another (Tarhos).[128]

For the time being shelving the possibility that Cupan, the self-appointed claimant to the throne, may be a mere literary creation, supposing a historical

---

[123] Antonio Bonfini, *Rerum ungaricarum decades* (Basileae, 1543), Munich, Bayerische Staatsbibliothek 2 Austr. 21, 172–3 (decadis 2, chapter 1), https://reader.digitale-sammlungen.de/de/fs1/object/display/bsb10141205_00188.html.

[124] Other early writers also added their interpretations, trying to make sense of the text they copied, paraphrased, or used in some way. E.g. Ransanus, *Epithoma rerum Hungarorum* (1490), OSZK Cod. Lat. 249, http://ransanus.atw.hu/pdf/Ransanus.pdf f. 98 wrote of Cupa's consanguinity with Sarolt, Stephen's mother.

[125] E.g. Györffy, *István király*, 110 explicitly states that Cupan wanting the throne and marriage to Sarolt means that he must have been a member of the dynasty.

[126] *Dux* has been interpreted as a synonym of *comes* (ispán) by Pál Engel, *Szent István birodalma* (Budapest: História, 2001), 39–40 and as a member of the Árpád dynasty holding a specific territory (*ducatus*) by Györffy, 'Koppány lázadása', 15; both refuted: Gábor Thoroczkay, 'Ellenszegülő ispán vagy független törzsfő? Megjegyzések Ajtony történetéhez', in *Ismeretlen Árpád-kor*, Thoroczkay, 29–44, at 38–9. The institution of the early Hungarian *ducatus* was probably a power-sharing mechanism, with specified territories within the kingdom given to a relative of the king. The chronicle account, however, speaks of both Stephen and Cupan having a *ducatus*.

[127] Ransanus speculated on the relationship; historians claimed that Koppány was Sarolt's relative or Géza's, tried to identify Koppány's father named in the fourteenth-century chronicles with various other people named in other sources, and tried to place Koppány within the genealogy provided by Emperor Constantine VII's account; summaries: Mályusz—Kristó, *Johannes de Thurocz, Chronica*, II. *Commentarii* 1, 244–5; Szabados, *Magyar államalapítások*, 243–52; Magyar, *Hős vagy lázadó?*, 27–8.

[128] Györffy, *István király*, 111.

CUPAN   53

Cupan existed, the historical sources do not justify the assumption that he would necessarily have had to be a member of the Árpád dynasty.[129] Constantine VII Porphyrogenitus, who wrote of a confederation of clans in the mid-tenth century, mentioned that overall leadership was passed down in one family, that of Árpád, but did not claim that the heads of the various clans were from the same (Árpád) dynasty.[130] Further, although the lack of sources means that we may not know about other challengers to the rule of the Árpáds, at least the brief mention of a *comes* Bors and Iván elected kings by rebels during the reign of Stephen II contradicts the idea that the Árpád dynasty was understood to have an absolute monopoly on rulership.[131] Some scholars also emphasized the novelty of creating firm central power by Géza and especially Stephen in the face of the earlier independence of the various 'tribes' in the Hungarian confederation of the conquest period.[132] Nothing precludes the possibility of an independent, non-dynastic challenge to Stephen's rule early on.

The narrative that the foundation of Cupan's aspiration to power was seniority within the lineage, which he wished to reinforce with the attempt to marry Stephen's widowed mother therefore rests on modern hypotheses. The chronicle does not mention the system of seniority, which was the basis, according to modern historians, of Cupan's bid for power, and at the same time the guarantee of his dynastic membership. The idea that power had originally rotated to different branches of the dynasty, with the eldest male member of that branch (rather than the son of the ruler) succeeding upon the ruler's death is a hypothetical construct. It is modelled on Constantine Porphyrogenitus's account about the succession pattern of the Pechenegs, one of the nomadic people of the steppe, and his mention of the then-current ruler of the Hungarians who descended from one of the younger sons of Árpád.[133] Its general validity for Hungarian succession patterns

---

[129] Marczali, *Szent István királysága*, 6 suggested that it was more likely that he was a relative of another former chieftain, not of the Árpád dynasty.

[130] Constantine Porphyrogenitus, *De administrando imperio*, ed. Gyula Moravcsik, tr. R. J. H. Jenkins, rev. edn (Washington, DC: Dumbarton Oaks Center for Byzantine Studies, 1967), 172–3, 178–9. The translation of *genea* has been debated, traditionally in Hungarian scholarship it was 'tribes', but is more correctly 'kindreds'.

[131] 'Chronici Hungarici', *SRH* I 444. While some historians claim that one or both were members of the dynasty, e.g. Szabolcs Vajay, 'I. Géza király családja', *Turul*, 79 (2006): 32–9, at 33–4, there is no proof of this, and in the case of Iván, even circumstantial evidence of such an identification is missing. The latest thorough analysis of the story and discussion of possible identifications of the protagonists: Tamás Kádár, 'Saul herceg, Bors ispán és Iván úr: megjegyzések, észrevételek a II. István király uralkodása vége körüli trónutódlási küzdelmek történetéhez', *Századok*, 151, no. 4 (2017): 787–808.

[132] Péter Váczy, 'A királyság központi szervezete Szent István korában', in *Emlékkönyv*, Serédi, vol. 2, 33–69, repr. 261–97, at 36–8, repr. 264–6.

[133] On the Pechenegs: 'For law and ancient principle have prevailed among them, depriving them of authority to transmit their ranks to their sons or their brothers, it being sufficient for those in power to rule for their own life-time only, and when they die, either their cousin or sons of their cousins must be appointed, so that the rank may not run exclusively in one branch of the family, but the collaterals also inherit and succeed to the honour; but no one from a stranger family intrudes and becomes a prince.' Constantine Porphyrogenitus, *De administrando imperio*, 167; Szabados, *Magyar*

54 STEPHEN I, THE FIRST CHRISTIAN KING OF HUNGARY

is undermined not only by a lack of data on how power was passed down in most cases before Géza, but also by both Constantine's explicit remark that Árpád's son inherited the rule over the 'Turks' (Hungarians) and the account that Géza (Stephen's father) had taken power as the son of the previous ruler.[134]

The hypothesis that the principle of seniority clashed with that of primogeniture when Cupan confronted Stephen is complemented by another assumption, suggesting that Cupan's planned 'incestuous' marriage was a remnant of nomadic pagan custom to gain power among the Hungarians. Supposedly, according to pagan Hungarian convention, marriage to a widow secured the dead man's power and wealth for the new husband; this is called a steppe tradition by some scholars and the biblical levirate by others.[135] No independent evidence of such a custom among the Hungarians exists. In fact, it is a speculation merely built on the reference to the 'incestuous' nature of the proposed marriage to Stephen's widowed mother in the chronicle text.

In medieval canon law, however, marriage was branded as incestuous in a wide range of cases: not only with the relative of a former spouse, but also within seven (from 1215, four) degrees of kinship. That is, based on this reference, Cupan could have been a relative of Stephen's mother (and therefore without a claim to power based on seniority), rather than his father; moreover, marriage between godparents also fell in the incest category.[136] The reference to incest, therefore, is no guide to Cupan's identification or to the basis of his claim. Moreover, the motif of proposed incest could originate from a variety of literary roots: the accusation of incestuous desire may serve to sling mud at the enemy of the hero, alluding to the story of Herod.[137] Bede's *Ecclesiastical History* reviled Eadbald, who refused to receive the faith of Christ, by adding that 'he was polluted with such fornication' as to be unknown even among gentiles: he took his dead father's second wife.[138]

Államalapítások, 249. Hypothetical reconstruction of succession among Hungarians: Lenkey [Zsoldos], *Szent István*, 15.

[134] Constantine Porphyrogenitus, *De administrando imperio*, 176–7; 'Chronici Hungarici', *SRH* I, 311. This is disregarded by historians who argued that primogeniture was entirely new when Géza passed his power to Stephen: e.g. Kornél Bakay, *A magyar államalapítás* (Budapest: Gondolat, 1978), 46.

[135] Bálint Hóman, Gyula Szekfű, *Magyar Történet* (Budapest: Királyi Magyar Egyetemi Nyomda, 1928), vol. 1, 177; Lenkey [Zsoldos], *Szent István*, 24. Györffy, 'Koppány lázadása', 15, and his *István király*, 111 combines succession through seniority and marriage plans through levirate. Mályusz—Kristó, *Johannes de Thurocz, Chronica*, II. *Commentarii* 1, 244–5 suggest a pagan Hungarian version of the levirate, called incest by the chronicler because the marriage would have been illicit from an ecclesiastical point of view.

[136] Pierre J. Payer, 'Confession and the study of sex in the Middle Ages', in *Handbook of Medieval Sexuality*, ed. Vern L. Bullough, James A. Brundage (New York—London: Garland, 1996), 6–7; James A. Brundage, *Law, Sex and Christian Society in Medieval Europe* (Chicago—London: University of Chicago Press, 1987), 140–1, 163–4, 355–6, 434–5.

[137] Flavius Josephus, *The Antiquities of the Jews*, tr. William Whiston, 18.5.1, https://gutenberg.org/files/2848/2848-h/2848-h.htm#link182HCH0005; Matthew 14:1–12; Mark 6:17–29.

[138] Venerabilis Beda, *Historiam ecclesiasticam gentis Anglorum*, II.5, http://www.thelatinlibrary.com/bede/bede2.shtml#5: 'At uero post mortem Aedilbercti, cum filius eius Eadbald regni gubernacula suscepisset, magno tenellis ibi adhuc ecclesiae crementis detrimento fuit. Siquidem non solum fidem Christi

The victorious military leader demanding the hand of the defeated king's widow in marriage was also a literary motif.[139]

Only one of the sources that name Cupan creates a link between him and those who reject Christianity; the fourteenth-century chronicles' Hunt and Paznan story, which states that rebel nobles adhering to Cupan rejected baptism and the Christian faith. Neither the longer story of Cupan in the chronicles nor thirteenth-century references to him state that he was a pagan. The tale about the brothers Hunt and Paznan may have started to conflate the story of the *vitae's* pagan uprising with the brief mention of Cupan as Stephen's opponent that is conserved in the late thirteenth-century chronicle of Simon of Kéza, because both are related to the troubled early years of Stephen's reign. Modern historians followed the lead of the late fifteenth-century humanist author Bonfini and worked out the more systematic conflation of the fourteenth-century chronicle story with the story of the pagan uprising in the *Lives*. Supplementing that with the 'evidence' of Cupan's alleged behaviour—he was ready to use pagan inheritance strategies, so he cannot have been too far removed from pagan practices—historians arrived at the conclusion that Cupan was to all intents and purposes a pagan (whether or not he had been formally baptized), the leader of the pagan revolt.[140] Such arguments begin to resemble an Ouroboros, the snake that is eating its own tail.

Further 'proof' of Cupan's paganism is based on the chronicle mentioning that his father's sobriquet was 'szár' in the vernacular, 'Calvus' in Latin—that is, bald.[141] Since texts mention that pagans shaved their hair,[142] the reasoning goes, such a sobriquet must denote someone who adhered to pre-Christian customs.[143] This seemingly logical hypothesis, however, does not get us any closer to revealing Cupan's religious adherence, since in the same vein, King Béla I, whose piety is recorded, and who is granted the epithet 'rex clementissimus', would also have to be a pagan, since he too is styled 'calvus' and 'szár' by the same chronicler; 'calvus' obviously (also) designated those who were not sporting a shaven head according to pagan custom, but were simply bald.[144]

The idea that Cupan was a pagan became entrenched, as shown by the choice of illustration in the volume produced for the commemorative St Stephen year (1938). An image from the fourteenth-century *Illuminated Chronicle* features with the inscription 'Stephen defeats Koppány'.[145] 'Koppány' wears the

---

recipere noluerat, sed et fornicatione pollutus est tali, qualem nec inter gentes auditam apostolus testatur, ita ut uxorem patris haberet.' I thank Alban Gautier for drawing this story to my attention.

[139] Stith Thompson, *Motif-Index of Folk Literature* (Bloomington, IN: Indiana University Press, 1955–8), T104.2.

[140] Lenkey [Zsoldos], *Szent István*, 24.

[141] Szabados, *Magyar államalapítások*, 244–5, 264; Magyar, *Hős vagy lázadó?*, 27.

[142] 'Theotmarus archiepiscopus Iuvaviensis, epistola', in *Catalogus Fontium Historiae Hungaricae*, ed. Albinus Franciscus Gombos, vol. 3 (Budapest, 1938, repr. Budapest: Nap Kiadó, 2011), 2198–201, see 2200; 'Chronici Hungarici', *SRH* I, 338.

[143] Szabados, *Magyar államalapítások*, 245.

[144] *SRH* I, 359–60.   [145] Serédi, ed., *Emlékkönyv*, vol. 1, 7, repr. 13.

56   STEPHEN I, THE FIRST CHRISTIAN KING OF HUNGARY

Cuman-style clothing and holds a bow associated with pagan steppe nomads. This miniature, however, in the original Chronicle accompanies the text that described Stephen's defeat of Kean, whom the Chronicle calls 'duke of the Bulgarians and Slavs'.[146] Thus, the association of Koppány with paganism led to the appropriation of an image that had nothing to do with the Cupan story, but seemed to 'fit' because of its pictorial representation of a pagan adversary. There was a visual precedent for this 'paganizing' of the Cupan imagery: the Chronicle of John Thuróczy illustrates the battle between the forces of Stephen and Koppány with a woodcut (the same woodcut serves as illustration for more than one battle scene throughout the chronicle) that represents Cupan's forces as wild barbarians, reminiscent of some representations of natives of the New World, fighting against knights in heavy armour.[147]

The supposed Turkic origin of his name reinforces the idea of Cupan's paganism and his high status in the pre-Christian hierarchy. Unquestioned acceptance of this alleged Turkic origin (from the Turkic title of a dignitary, 'qapan'[148]) as well as its correspondent modernization as Koppány concealed the name's original context in the medieval sources: there are more Cupans in the chronicles as well as in the charter evidence. Two more Cupans appear in the chronicle text. After the story of *dux* Cupan's defeat and quartering, the chronicler listed the descendants of the alleged vanquisher of Cupan, Vecellinus (in the textual variations of the chronicles, the name appears in many different ways, from Welinus to Ucelinus). According to this, his son was Radi, his grandson Misca, and his great-grandsons Cupan and Martin.[149] The narrative section does not refer to Vecellinus's origins, but in the list of *advenae* (immigrant nobles), he appears as Bavarian. (Simon of Kéza gives the place of origin as Wazurbuirc/Wasurburc, which is usually interpreted as Wasserburg.)

Cupan, son of Misca and supposed descendant of Vecellinus, is much more likely to have been a historical person than Cupan, Stephen's alleged opponent. He is identified by some historians with a bishop named Cupan who accompanied King Coloman and was killed in battle in Rus' in 1099,[150] and who, according to some historians, authored the early chronicle. The identification is based on the chronological coincidence: the late eleventh century is the likely period for the great-grandson of a man who had been active at the end of the previous

---

[146] *SRH* I, 315.

[147] Johannes de Thurocz, *Chronica Hungarorum* (Augsburg, 1488), Cambridge University Library Inc.5.A.6.18, f35v, De bello sancti regis Stephani contra Cupan ducem Symigiensem.

[148] Gyula Németh, 'Géza', *Magyar Nyelv*, 24 (1928): 147–51, at 149; cf. Mályusz—Kristó, *Johannes de Thurocz, Chronica*, II. Commentarii 1, 244.

[149] Karácsonyi, *A magyar nemzetségek*, 697; Fehértói, *Árpád-kori személynévtár*, 796 ('Vecelinus').

[150] 'Annales Posonienses', *SRH* I, 126; 'Chronici Hungarici', *SRH* I, 424. Samuel Hazzard Cross, Olgerd P. Sherbowitz-Wetzor, ed. and tr., *The Russian Primary Chronicle* (Cambridge, MA: The Mediaeval Academy of America, 1953), 196 (using the form Kupan and dating the event to 6605 [1097]); Karácsonyi, *A magyar nemzetségek*, 697 suggested this identification.

century. There is no proof that the two Cupans—Cupan son of Misca, and the bishop—are identical; indeed, several historical persons called Cupan lived during the second half of the eleventh century and later; they are attested by charter evidence.[151] Was a member of an allegedly Bavarian and certainly Christian family named in the late eleventh century after someone his great-grandfather had killed, Stephen's defeated, quartered and potentially pagan enemy?[152] Alternatively, do we encounter here an example of family mythology—that is, members of the family attributing heroic deeds to their (alleged) ancestor? The family held lands in Somogy county;[153] members of the family called Cupan may have given their name to villages there in the eleventh century, and that may have been the basis for the birth of the story about the alleged defeated enemy later on.

One more Cupan appears in the fourteenth-century chronicles; one of the sons of Cund, the fourth captain of the conquering Hungarians, is called Cupan, but in the Hungarian translation of the text he is called Kaplony and thus the identity of the names is not widely recognized.[154] It is important to point out that thirteenth- and fourteenth-century narrative sources included more than one Cupan, and the name did not carry a sense of uniqueness, unlike Koppány in modern national historiography. Moreover, it could not have been seen as the name of Stephen's greatest enemy or a specifically pagan name in the eleventh century, because the people called Cupan who appear in the charters are Christians, several of them ecclesiastics. The chaplain of Ladislas I, the king who had Stephen canonized, was called Cupan.[155] The fact that the name Cupan was fairly widespread during the Árpád age, including among ecclesiastics, completely contradicts the hypothesis that we only have the transmission of Cupan/Koppány's name from a later source, and not earlier ones such as Stephen's *vitae* because contemporary authors tried to eradicate the story and the name from memory through a *damnatio memoriae*.[156] Finally, linguists should revisit the origin of the name: Misca, Radi, and Cupan may be Slavic names.[157]

4. The Birth of Koppány, the Pagan National Hero

Whether or not there was a historical Cupan, Stephen's opponent was portrayed in a negative light in the medieval sources. Cupan's transformation from

---

[151] Fehértói, *Árpád-kori személynévtár*, 229–30.

[152] Csóka, *A latin nyelvű történeti irodalom*, 542–3 suggested that the aim was to demonstrate the resolution of past conflict, but this is unconvincing.

[153] The descendants of Vecellinus listed in the chronicle were the Rád, who held possessions in Somogy county, according to ibid., 537–46.

[154] *SRH* I, 291.

[155] György Fejér, *Codex diplomaticus Hungariae ecclesiasticus ac civilis* (Buda, 1829), vol. 1, 484; Fehértói, *Árpád-kori személynévtár*, 229. He is thought to be identical to Bishop Cupan killed in 1099.

[156] Szabados, *Magyar államalapítások*, 246.

[157] The name exists today in Slavonia, for example.

58 STEPHEN I, THE FIRST CHRISTIAN KING OF HUNGARY

treacherous anti-hero to an embodiment of Hungarian identity may seem even more surprising than the elaboration of his story in the first place. How and why did Cupan come to symbolize true Hungarian identity? If we follow the Cupan story in the work of major Hungarian historians over the centuries, we can see that in narratives written between the fifteenth and nineteenth centuries, whether Cupan played a minor role, or whether the story of the fourteenth-century chronicles was further elaborated, he remained a negative figure. This started to change in the nineteenth century, with the beginnings of the positive re-evaluation of Hungary's pagan past; and a major transformation followed in the early twentieth century, with Koppány recast from villain to the representative of authentic Hungarian values, a counterpoint to the decadent and treacherous West.

Bonfini represented Cupa negatively, as we have seen above. In 1574, Gáspár Heltai, an influential Protestant historian, published a vernacular Hungarian history of Hungary, in which he transformed Kupa, as he calls him, into the main traitor who turned people away from Christianity. He wants to marry Stephen's mother and oust Stephen. Heltai followed Bonfini in several details, such as including the name of Alba Iulia as one of the places where Kupa's quartered body-parts were sent.[158] Fighting against enemies of Christianity was also crucial in János Sommer's (1540–74) verse history of the kings of Hungary.[159] Haugen's *Chronica* in German (1534) is based on Thuróczy and contrasts King Stephen and Herzog (duke) Cupan.[160] In a university publication under Jesuit leadership, the likes of which proliferated for the education of the elite, Kupa represents a series of sins (including error, licentiousness, anger, self-love, discord, envy), in contrast to Stephen epitomizing virtues.[161]

István Katona's *Historia critica regum Hungariae* only fleetingly mentioned Cupa, the war between him and Stephen, and the latter's victory, in the context of donations to the Abbey of St Martin (Pannonhalma).[162] Mihály Horváth, one of the most important nineteenth-century historians, claimed that both the existence of Christianity in Hungary and the fate of the nation depended on Stephen squashing Koppány's revolt.[163] Thus, these texts, whether in a short abridged form or in a longer narrative, upheld the fundamentally negative image of Cupan.

Koppány as martyr and the true model for Hungarians started to emerge in the wake of a more positive re-evaluation of paganism, which was nourished by multiple roots. Those who espoused enlightened anti-Catholicism in the eighteenth

---

[158] http://mek.oszk.hu/06400/06417/html/heltaiga0070001.html, 'Szt István hadai' chapter.
[159] Gyula Szekfű, 'Szent István a magyar történet századaiban', in *Emlékkönyv*, Serédi, vol. 3, 1–80, at 33, repr. 529–606, at 559.
[160] Hans Hauge zum Freystein, *Der Hungern Chronica* (Vienna, 1534), 16v–17, chapter 20, 'Von der Schlacht des heiligen Königs Steffan wider Cupan den herzogen Symichensem'.
[161] Duo fulmina belli, under the leadership of Fr Bilecki S. J. (Lőcse, 1703), quoted in Szekfű, 'Szent István', 44, repr. 570.
[162] István Katona, *Historia critica regum Hungariae*, 42 vols. (Pest, 1779–1817), vol. 1, 93, 143.
[163] Mihály Horváth, *A kereszténység első százada Magyarországon* (Budapest: Ráth Mór, 1878), 108.

century also presented pagan ancestors in a more positive light: pagan Hungarians were neither polytheists, nor barbarians.[164] Such an opinion, however, belonged to a minority, and Catholic preaching in the early nineteenth century still upheld the traditional view that pagan Hungarian ancestors were anathema and castigated them as barbarians. By the middle of the century, however, even Catholic priests started to present Hungarian ancestors as simply lacking in knowledge rather than being malicious, or even as having some kind of respectable religion before Christianity.[165] Such a shift was brought about by the wave of romantic nationalism connected to the Ossian craze, whose proponents searched for and invented pre-Christian national myths, gods, and heroes. In 1822, Sándor Székely Aranyosrákosi (1797–1854), from a Unitarian Transylvanian family who was studying in Vienna, wrote an epic poem, *The Seklers in Transylvania*, which was published the following year. It featured the invented ancestral Hungarian god, Hadúr.[166] Hadúr was immediately accepted and adopted by poets and historians; by 1845, he appeared in a sermon.[167]

In this period, the traditional cult of Stephen and the nationalist authors' desire for a more positive reincorporation of the Hungarians' pagan past clashed; tradition held many back from criticizing Stephen too openly.[168] The solution initially was to emphasize Stephen's feebleness in his old age, and thus the first pagan to be openly praised was Vazul (in 1838), Stephen's pagan relative, whom the king, near the end of his reign had condemned to be blinded in order to prevent his rise to power.[169] By the late nineteenth century, nationalism increasingly espoused the openly positive portrayal of pagan Hungarians, part of a trend to re-evaluate the pagan past that was widespread in Europe.[170]

This had an impact during the nineteenth century on the reinterpretation of Koppány himself. The poet and writer Ádám Pálóczi Horváth in his book on the pagan Hungarian nation (1817) wanted to provide an ancient and distinguished past, and stressed the good morals and positive contributions of the pagan

[164] István Sándor, *Sokféle írás egybeszedése*, 41.   [165] Szekfű, 'Szent István', 65, repr. 591–2.

[166] Géza Hegedüs, *A magyar irodalom arcképcsarnoka* (Budapest: Trezor Kiadó, 1995), http://mek. oszk.hu/01100/01149/html/index.htm.

[167] Alajos Sámuel, *Szent István első és apostoli magyar király mint népe szent hite- 's nemzetiségének megalapítója* (Pest, 1845), 4 (sermon delivered in Vienna, 24 August 1845); Szekfű, 'Szent István', 65, repr. 591.

[168] Ibid., 75, repr. 601: the first criticisms were expressed in plays for the stage. A play by József Katona in 1813 about Stephen portrayed Koppány somewhat more sympathetically, as a tragic hero trying to uphold ancient customs, who, nonetheless, must fail because his ideas endanger the future of the country: Magyar, *Hős vagy lázadó?*, 117–20.

[169] Szekfű, 'Szent István', 75, repr. 601.

[170] Ibid., 73–4, repr. 599–600; from the 1890s, Árpád became a positive reference point in political legitimization: Sinkó Katalin, 'Árpád versus Saint István. Competing heroes and competing interests in the figurative representation of Hungarian history', in *Hungary between 'East' and 'West'. Three Essays on National Myths and Symbols*, ed. Tamás Hofer (Budapest: Néprajzi Múzeum, 1994), 9–26. On Romantic nationalism and paganism: Michael F. Strmiska, 'Modern paganism in world cultures: comparative perspectives', in *Modern Paganism in World Cultures: Comparative Perspectives*, ed. Michael F. Strmiska (Santa Barbara, CA: ABC Clio, 2005), 1–53, esp. 7–8.

60   STEPHEN I, THE FIRST CHRISTIAN KING OF HUNGARY

Hungarians. He turned Kupa into Géza's younger brother, and quoted from Bonfini the accusations that Kupa levelled against Stephen, 'an even more dangerous enemy of his nation than his father', preferring foreigners, destroying the old gods, and forcing the Hungarians to become slothful in peace. Those hating the new religion sided with Kupa. Horváth stated he wished to avoid giving judgement as to the rightness of either Stephen's or Kupa's cause. Horváth dates the battle to 1000, and, while citing Kupa's ultimate fate in a footnote in Latin, he does not mention the quartering in the text, presumably not to dwell on the humiliating end to a man with whom he clearly sympathizes.[171]

With Stephen entrenched as the fount of order and useful regulations, the quartering of Koppány started to pose a problem for other authors too. How could the good Christian king order such a barbaric punishment?[172] Despite the logic of 'national awakening', nineteenth-century authors struggled fully to embrace Kupa/Koppány, as exemplified by the case of the famous poet Dániel Berzsenyi, who, in the first half of the century, started to write a play turning Kupa into the leader of a national resistance movement who represents tradition and national freedom, but left it unfinished because he could not solve the problem of glorifying Kupa without denigrating the foundational role of Stephen.[173] Literary depictions of Koppány continued at the end of the nineteenth and during the first half of the twentieth century, with some condemning him, while others presented him in a more positive light, as someone who tried to save Hungary from foreign influence, or specifically from servitude to Germans, a tragic rebel.[174] Rarely, his quartering was even evoked as a parallel to Hungary's fate at the Treaty of Trianon (1920), and thus as a symbol of the country.[175]

Mainstream historiography diverged here from the beginnings of a literary rehabilitation. A few key examples suffice to show that mainstream historiography continued to draw on the *vitae* and chronicles to depict Stephen as acting for the 'good of the nation'. The representative *History of the Hungarian Nation* produced for the millennial celebrations of the state contrasted Kupa, the pagan pretender who commits treason, with Stephen, who fights not simply to retain his

---

[171] Ádám Horváth, *A' magyar Magóg pátriarkhától fogva I. István királyig* (Pest, 1817), 311–13, 'A maga Nemzetének még veszedelmesebb ellensége lessz, mint az Atyja' (311).

[172] The piarist Glycér Spányik, *Historia pragmatica regni Hungariae* (Pest, 1820), 44–5 suggests that Stephen, merciful to those defeated, would have been even more so to an enemy already killed in battle and invokes Hartvic's silence on the quartering to call it into doubt. Similarly, the Calvinist József Péczely, *A magyarok történetei*, vol. 1 (Debrecen, 1837), 36–57; quoted by Szekfű, 'Szent István', 69, repr. 595.

[173] Dániel Berzsenyi, 'Kupa támadása', in *Berzsenyi Dániel Költői művei—Régi Magyar Könyvtár 39*, ed. Oszkár Merényi (Budapest: A Magyar Tudományos Akadémia, 1936), 279–306; quotation from a letter by Berzsenyi on the reason he stopped writing the play: ibid., 412–13.

[174] Magyar, *Hős vagy lázadó?*, 121–7.

[175] 'The great historical symbol of Hungarians as a race is not the right hand of St Stephen, husband of the German woman; its tragic, forever bleeding symbol is the quartered Koppány.' Dezső Szabó, 'Vádlók és vádlottak' (1922), repr. *Hunnia füzetek*, 1–2 (1989): 7–17, at 8.

power, but to uphold the religion of the nation as well as its place in Europe.[176] Gyula Pauler's fundamental book on Árpád-age Hungarian history largely follows the fourteenth-century chronicles; Stephen defends himself and Christianity against Koppány.[177] The best known medievalist of the interwar regime, Bálint Hóman, who also had a political role in government, characterized the confrontation as one between ancestral pagan law and the new Christian legal system, and saw the western—Christian turn as essential for the preservation of the nation.[178]

Koppány, however, found staunch supporters and a wholesale rewriting of his role in a new wave of Hungarian nationalism after the First World War, namely a branch of the Turanian movement that propagated a 'return' to ancient forms of Hungarian beliefs, which they equated with embracing Hungarian destiny and throwing off the western yoke.[179] Koppány thus became central to new paganism. The Turanian movement grew out of scholarly, economic, and political interests in the nineteenth and early twentieth centuries.[180] 'Turanism' as an idea was so vague that from orientalists to politicians all could fit under its umbrella. The Turan Society, founded in 1910, which included leading politicians and aristocrats as well as scholars in its presidium, expressed the increasing interest in eastern origin-myths, supposed kinship with Sumerian, Japanese and other 'Turanian races', and propagated cultural and economic ties to 'kindred' populations of the 'Turanian race'.[181] Its president, Pál Teleki, later prime minister of Hungary, expressed the society's aims in encouraging scientific interest in and economic expansion to the east. During and especially after the First World War, the more amorphous Turanism was channelled into various organizations, and its political and anti-western aspects gained prominence. The Turanist Alliance of Hungary was founded in 1920. Some of its representatives invested Turanism with pronounced political aspirations. One branch of the society wanted to rejuvenate European culture and politics with notions borrowed from 'unadulterated' eastern 'relatives'.[182]

---

[176] Henrik Marczali, 'Magyarország története az Árpádok korában (1038–1301)', in *A magyar nemzet története*, vol. 1, book 4, chapter 3, 2nd edn, ed. Sándor Szilágyi (Budapest: Athenaeum, 1895), http://mek.oszk.hu/00800/00893/html.

[177] Pauler, *A magyar nemzet története*, vol. 1, 26–7.

[178] Hóman—Szekfű, *Magyar Történet*, vol. 1, 177.

[179] It is no accident that a later film, *Hannibál Tanár Úr*, featuring a fictional Hungarian fascist movement, called it the 'Koppány tribe of Töhötöm'.

[180] On the beginnings of Turanian ideas: Balázs Ablonczy, *Keletre, magyar! A magyar turanizmus története* (Budapest: Jaffa Kiadó, 2016), 7–91.

[181] On the history of the Turan Society: Éva Kincses-Nagy, 'A turáni gondolat', in *Őstörténet és nemzettudat 1919–1931: Az 1988. áprilisában Szegeden rendezett egynapos ülésszak előadásai*, Magyar őstörténeti könyvtár 1, ed. Éva Kincses-Nagy (Szeged: JATE Magyar Őstörténeti Kutatócsoport, 1991), 44–9; Ablonczy, *Keletre, magyar!*, 47–70.

[182] Selected quotations by various members of the Turanian movement (not including Bencsi) on their purpose, and contemporary criticism: László Szendrei, *Turanizmus: Definíciók és értelmezések 1910-től a II. Világháborúig* (Máriabesnyő—Gödöllő: Attraktor, 2010). Also János Gyurgyák, *Ezzé lett magyar hazátok: a magyar nemzeteszme és nacionalizmus története* (Budapest: Osiris Kiadó, 2007), 229–32; Ablonczy, *Keletre, magyar!*, 92–112; Kincses-Nagy, 'A turáni gondolat'.

62   STEPHEN I, THE FIRST CHRISTIAN KING OF HUNGARY

While many different groups defined themselves based on their version of Turanism, some started to promote what they saw as the 'original' religion, morals, and lifestyle of the Hungarians.[183] They condemned Stephen who called in foreigners to squash the pagan Hungarians.[184] Anti-western sentiment, fostered by governmental policies of blaming the West for the Treaty of Trianon (1920) which reassigned large parts of the territory of the previous Kingdom of Hungary to neighbouring states, was expressed in a rejection of everything western, and sought Hungary's salvation in the east based on the common 'Turanian race'.[185] 'Decadent' and 'ungrateful' Europe was to be abandoned. Other currents valorizing some aspect of supposed pre-Christian Hungarian customs flourished as well—for example, the belief among many lawyers at the time in an ancient 'pagan Hungarian constitution'.[186] In 1930, a lawyer, Zoltán Bencsi, founded the 'Turanian Monotheists' Camp'. They saw Koppány as a martyr for 'our ancestral God and race', and defined themselves as descendants of Koppány. The group had a tower ('Pagan tower') built in 1934 to honour Attila, Árpád and Koppány on a hill in Buda.[187]

Turanian Monotheists emphasized the sins of the Hungarians for abandoning their ancestral God, Hadúr ('Lord of hosts') and the seer-leaders he had sent, in favour of following western ways; yet liberation from western dominion was foretold.[188]

The group's founder Bencsi stated that Koppány not only was a champion of Hungarian faith, but also fought against foreigners, who were, and continue to be, the root of all problems in Hungary.[189] Bencsi also wrote a historical novel entitled *Koppány or Stephen?*, with a publication date of 'the year 1504 of our lord Attila'.[190] This provided the most detailed positive re-evaluation of Koppány, and an accompanying romanticizing rewriting of early history. Through invented pagan ancestors, who are virtuous, generous, proud, and victorious all over Europe, Bencsi criticized western hypocrisy, pointed to flaws in Christianity, and lionized

---

[183] The authorities tried to suppress such expressions; for example, a pamphlet on 'ancestral faith' was confiscated: *Nyírvidék Szabolcsi Hírlap* (15 June 1938), 7. https://library.hungaricana.hu/en/view/Nyirvidek_1938_01-02/?query=Bencsi&pg=76&layout=s.

[184] Szekfű, 'Szent István', 75, repr. 601.   [185] Examples: Szendrei, *Turanizmus*, 35–6, 66–7.

[186] Elemér Mályusz, 'Az Eckhart-vita', *Századok* (1931): 406–19, at 419; Szekfű, 'Szent István', 4–5, repr. 530–1.

[187] *Délmagyarország* (17 July 1938): 10–11, https://library.hungaricana.hu/en/view/Delmagyarorsz ag_1938_07/?query=kopp%C3%A1ny-torony&pg=161&layout=s; *Zalamegyei újság* (20 May 1937): 2, https://library.hungaricana.hu/en/view/ZalamegyeiUjsag_1937_2/?query=kopp%C3%A1ny%20 torony&pg=189&layout=s; contemporary post-card of the tower, https://gallery.hungaricana.hu/en/OSZKKepeslap/896/?list=eyJxdWVyeSI6ICJrb3BwXHUwMGUxbnkgdG9yb255In0&img=0. Overview on Bencsi and his group: Ablonczy, *Keletre, magyar!*, 154–9.

[188] *A turáni egyistenhívők egyszerű istentiszteletének szertartása*, composed and partly written by Batu (Budapest: Turáni Roham Kiadóhivatal, 1936), 7–8. This was written by a co-founder who was, as a result of this publication, expelled from the movement by Bencsi: Ablonczy, *Keletre, magyar!*, 157.

[189] Dr Zoltán Bencsi, 'Koppány és Vattha nyomában…', *Turáni roham*, 1, no. 4 (7 February 1935): 1.

[190] Zoltán Bencsi, *Koppány-e vagy István (Történelmi korrajz)* (Budapest: author's edition, Gyarmati Ferenc könyvnyomda [1938]).

representatives of supposed traditional Hungarian religion, customs, and tolerance: Hungarians had acknowledged everyone's right to worship their own god, and did not want to force people to accept theirs.

In Bencsi's book, Attila is a positive figure, and the ancestor of the Hungarians. Stephen fell under the spell of westerners, symbolized by the rejection of his Hungarian name (Vajk), and welcomed all western newcomers at his court, which resulted in the oppression of Hungarians by Germans. The free Hungarians still following their ancient faith hoped to persuade Stephen to return to his nation and refuted the idea that only conversion to the western faith would ensure the survival of the Hungarians. The westerners Stephen relied on, however, stoked enmity in the hope of a fight from which they could profit. Stephen is a well-meaning but weak figure in the novel. He does not realize that papal coronation means the end of Hungarian independence, and servitude to both Rome and Germany. 'Stephen believed he was doing good when he foisted the West on us. A holy fire burnt in him, a sense of vocation lived in him. He felt himself to be an apostle.'[191] The true ruler, however, is Gisela, his wife, whose will dominates. The adoption of western beliefs made Hungarians lose themselves, and the West mocked rather than feared them. 'The nation falls into servitude.'[192]

Koppány is the true positive hero of the novel.[193] He is brave, clear-sighted, a born leader who opposes western servitude, but equally wants to avoid the shedding of blood. According to him, Hungarians should rule the West rather than be ruled by it, and he upholds the superiority of the Hungarian religion. The clean morals of Asia are to be imported into the depraved West. Koppány does not want to take power although it would be his right, and he rejects the idea advanced by his followers that he should marry Géza's widow. He wants to make peace with Stephen, although many Hungarians urge war. Koppány, the rightful heir to power over the Hungarians and backed by all true Hungarians, falls victim to German intrigues. As Koppány prepares to meet Stephen, Táltos (the soothsayer) looking into the future sees renewed danger from the West and the rejection of help from eastern relatives of the Hungarians.[194] When Koppány rides to Stephen's camp, he is assassinated by westerners, who then falsely claim that Koppány had wanted to kill Stephen and was killed in a duel.

Such ideas did not go unchallenged. In 1938, the same year that Bencsi wrote his novel, the historian Gyula Szekfű condemned Turanism as neo-paganism linked to its German counterpart, threatening Christianity.[195] He lashed out against the growing cult of Koppány, Turanism's first martyr, which he branded detrimental to Hungarian interests, and saw Stephen's cult as essential for the

---

[191] Ibid., 23: 'István azt hitte, jót cselekszik, mikor nyakunkra ültette Nyugatot. Benne szent tűz lobogott. Benne hivatásérzet élt. Apostolnak érezte magát.'
[192] Ibid., 56.   [193] Ibid., 31–5.
[194] Ibid., 57–8.   [195] Szekfű, 'Szent István', 76–7, repr. 602–3.

64 STEPHEN I, THE FIRST CHRISTIAN KING OF HUNGARY

preservation of the Hungarian nation.[196] The Catholic Church and politicians also condemned Turanism linked to paganism.[197]

Yet positive ideas about Koppány (Kupa) were also developed in local traditions in Somogy county, where people passed on stories about their 'father' Koppány (written down in the mid-twentieth century). In these, Koppány is the leader of free Hungarians, he is not a pagan; he is generous to the poor, and allows the fishermen to keep a particularly large fish they caught instead of giving it up to him in tax. Moreover, he acts in self-defence; it is Stephen who attacks.[198]

The traditional communist interpretation in this respect rewrote an older nationalist approach. Stephen was still the positive hero, and Koppány a negative figure, with the survival of the country itself at stake in their fight. But while prewar historiography emphasized Stephen's saintliness and Christianity as the right choice, the early communist reformulation by Rákosi himself insisted this did not mean turning to the 'civilized' West against a 'barbarian' East. Instead, Stephen's positive role consisted of creating a more advanced class society, and establishing the country through decades of fighting against German would-be conquerors, against western imperialism.[199] This is a curious antecedent (but without embracing paganism) to later right-wing ideas that reject western identity.

During the socialist period, there was an emphasis on the clash between a western orientation that included both feudalism and Christianity on the one hand, and a pagan tribal aristocracy attempting to stop progress on the other hand.[200] In the late socialist period, and since then, academic historians, based on their interpretation of the sources as well as ideological commitment, took diverse positions on Koppány's role. Some claim that Koppány had converted to Christianity; the medieval sources say nothing about this, unless we want to extrapolate from the 41st chronicle chapter's brief mention of his followers 'rejecting baptism'.[201] There are also ideas he was a convert to Byzantine Christianity,[202] which is mere speculation or at best built on a parallel to other tenth-century military leaders, including opponents of Stephen, who converted to eastern

---

[196] Ibid., especially 77–80, repr. 603–6.   [197] Ablonczy, *Keletre, magyar!*, 160–2.

[198] Ignácz, 'Hagyományok földjén', 191–3.

[199] [no author] 'Rákosi Mátyás és a magyar történettudomány', *Századok*, 86, no. 14 (1952): 1–23, at 2.

[200] Gyula Kristó, *Levedi törzsszövetségétől Szent István államáig* (Budapest: Magvető Könyvkiadó, 1980), 483–7. Later (2001), he emphasized that Koppány represented a tribal, pagan route, while Stephen represented a new type of state and Christianity: Kristó, *Szent István*, 47.

[201] Györffy, *István király*, 112; Kornél Bakay interview in Gábor Koltay, *István, a király* (Budapest: Ifjúsági Lap- és Könyvkiadó Vállalat, 1984), 121. As early as in 1808, Benedek Virág pointed out that there was no proof that Kupa was pagan: Márta Mezei, Éva Wimmer, ed., *Virág Benedek, Magyar Századok* (Budapest: Neumann, 2004), http://mek.niif.hu/04900/04919/html/mhmszaza-dok0010.html.

[202] Kálmán Magyar, *Szent István államszervezésének régészeti emlékei* (Kaposvár—Segesd: Segesd Önkormányzat Kiadása, 2001), 129, 233–5. György Györffy, 'Szent István történeti kutatásunkban', in *Szent István és kora*, ed. Ferenc Glatz, József Kardos (Budapest: MTA Történettudományi Intézet, 1988), 18–22, at 20 claimed that a victorious Koppány would have created a Hungary similar to Bulgaria, Poland, and Rus'.

Christianity. Koppány's (nominal) conversion is reconciled in some work with his reliance on pagan ideology for his ambitions.[203] This allowed the co-optation of Koppány into the mythical pre-histories of the Hungarians, as either a pagan or a Christian.

There has recently been an explosion of writings on Koppány, both as a pagan and as a 'true Hungarian Christian'. While the Turanian monotheists were a fringe movement affecting few people, belief in a fictive 'ancient history' and Koppány as the representative of traditional Hungarian values have by now penetrated society at large, and are here to stay. Popularizing Koppány for a modern audience by literally embodying him was the contribution of a rock opera, 'Stephen the king', the subject of my next chapter. As explored there, Hungarian emigrants after the Second World War and family traditions formed the chain between an interwar and a post-1989 public.[204] Christianity, imported and imposed, was an unsatisfactory base for national identity for some. Others claim both Stephen and Koppány as central for Hungarian identity; the logical contradiction is no barrier to emotional identification.[205] Cupan under the modernized name Koppány came to enjoy a central place for many Hungarian nationalists, along with other invented traditions, such as the use of runic script. Koppány also features in literature, from being a symbol of rebelliousness to being a sympathetic, wise ancestor.[206] In the first decade of the twenty-first century, Koppány was among the one hundred most common names given to new-borns.[207]

Some might wish to argue that even if all the pieces of evidence traditionally used to prove the veracity of the Koppány story can be shown to be inconclusive or outright wrong, surely, there would not be so many scraps of Koppány-related material in modern popular tradition if, at bottom, the story were not true; a sort of 'no smoke without fire' principle. This line of argument, however commonsensical it may seem, is false. Indeed, the 'envy' of pre-Christian pasts was common in nineteenth-century national enterprises, with corresponding inventions.[208] It

---

[203] Györffy, *István király*, 112.

[204] Ablonczy, *Keletre, magyar!*, 208–58; for more details and similar trends elsewhere, see the following chapter, '*Stephen, the King*: A Rock Opera in the Late Communist Period and Questions of National Identity'.

[205] An early proponent of such a synthesis: Mihály Ferdinandy, 'A lázadó Koppány mítosza', in *Az Árpád-ház mítoszai*, Mihály Ferdinandy (Budapest: Attraktor, 2005), 69–83, originally published in 1938. John A. Armstrong, *Nations before Nationalism* (Chapel Hill, NC: University of North Carolina Press, 1982), 47–51 pointed to two identity myths, a pagan and a Christian one, in Hungary, although he did not write of Koppány and there are many factual errors.

[206] E.g. Endre Ady, 'A civódó magyar', in *A Minden-titkok versei* (1910), Endre Ady, https://www.arcanum.hu/hu/online-kiadvanyok/Verstar-verstar-otven-kolto-osszes-verse-2/ady-endre-13441/a-minden-titkok-versei-13DBB/a-magyarsag-titkai-13EB8/a-civodo-magyar-13ECB; Sándor Cs. Szabó, *Koppány a lázadó vezér* ([no location]: Gold Book Kft, 2019); Cey-Bert Róbert Gyula, *Koppány a Fény Harcosa* (Budapest: Püski, 2014).

[207] http://www.nyilvantarto.hu/archiv_honlap/kozos/index.php?k=statisztikai_adatok_lakossagi_legujsznevek_hu_archiv.

[208] Mortensen, 'The canons of medieval literature', 55–6.

66   STEPHEN I, THE FIRST CHRISTIAN KING OF HUNGARY

may seem counterintuitive that a pagan hero is invented—rather than a historical person being merely reinterpreted—in the modern period, yet that is exactly what happened in Finland. A brief consideration of a case that is very comparable to the development of the Koppány story warns us not to jump to conclusions about the historicity of pagan figures.

According to his Latin *vita*, written at the end of the thirteenth century, Henry, supposedly bishop of Uppsala, accompanied King Eric of Sweden, and then stayed with the recently converted Finns. (According to later stories, he became the first bishop of Turku.) He tried to give penance to a murderer, who, enraged, killed Henry.[209] When the murderer put on the bishop's mitre, he lost his scalp.[210] Historically, even Bishop Henry's existence is questionable,[211] let alone the murderer's; the original story neither names Henry's killer, nor gives other information about him, but implies that he is a Christian, since the bishop gave him penance. A Finnish ballad, Pyhän Henrikin Surmavirsi (The Slaying of Bishop Henry), that originally dates probably from the late sixteenth century or the seventeenth, and is known from a seventeenth-century manuscript, gave Henry's killer the name Lalli (thought to be from Laurentius), as did a hymn in the same period.[212]

The ballad further developed the story: the reason for the killing is the mendacious account by Lalli's wife Kerttu. She tells him that Bishop Henry took food from them without payment while Lalli was away. Lalli removing his scalp when he takes the mitre off is the prelude to his descent into Hell. Since the poem represents the country as not yet converted, this implies that Lalli is a pagan, which builds on a late medieval (fifteenth-century) version of the *Life*, that represents Henry as the one who introduced Christianity to Finland.[213] Subsequently Lalli, Bishop Henry's killer was explicitly called a pagan; the cleric Hemminki of Masku (1550–1619) referred to Lalli as an 'evil pagan', and in the early eighteenth century, Daniel Juslenius described Bishop Henry's murderer as a pagan Finnish nobleman.[214] While the pairing of Bishop Henry and Lalli initially served the

---

[209] Tuomas Heikkilä, *Pyhän Henrikin Legenda* (Helsinki: Suomalaisen Kirjallisuuden Seura, 2005). I thank Kirsi Salonen for drawing my attention to Lalli, Christian Krötzl and Kurt Villads Jensen for suggesting further literature, and Otso Kortekangas for translations from Finnish.

[210] This is also represented in the missal of the diocese of Åbo (Turku), 1488; see Tuomas M. S. Lehtonen, ed., *Europe's Northern Frontier: Perspectives on Finland's Western Identity* (Jyväskylä: PS Kustannus, 1999), 21.

[211] No earlier sources mention him, the *vita* is thought to have been written in the 1280s or 1290s, in preparation for the consecration of the cathedral of Turku, and it is possible that he was an invented character: Heikkilä, *Pyhän Henrikin Legenda*, 8–9, 16, 54–5, 78, 234.

[212] Lehtonen, *Europe's Northern Frontier*, 22; Pertti J. Anttonen, 'The Finns party and the killing of a 12th century bishop: the heritage of a political myth', *Traditiones*, 41, no. 2 (2012): 137–49, at 139–40.

[213] Heikkilä, *Pyhän Henrikin Legenda*, 208–11.

[214] Mikko K. Heikkilä, *Kuka oli herra Heinäricki?—piispa Henrikin arvoitus* (Tampere: Tampere University Press, 2016), 157; Derek Fewster, *Visions of Past Glory: Nationalism and the Construction of Early Finnish History*, Studia Fennica Historica 11, 2nd edn (Helsinki: Finnish Literature Society, 2006), 55.

purposes of the Church, in modernity, the story became foundational for Finnish identity.[215]

As with the story of Stephen and Koppány, the legend has been used in multiple ways. It is a foundation story of Finnish Christianity, and Bishop Henry's cult continues to be central.[216] Yet Lalli was also transformed from a killer, merely significant as the tool for Henry's martyrdom, to a positive figure: the legend and the ballad were combined and further transformed in the nineteenth century, turning Lalli into a defender of traditional values against a foreigner importing an alien religion and values.[217] Lalli started to enjoy a great popularity as a Finnish hero, the embodiment of the true spirit of Finns. In the early nineteenth century (1813–16), Lalli featured in a sculpted representation of the arrival of Christianity in Finland as a representative of pagan resistance, signalled by the ethnic marker of Finnishness, a skullcap (*patalakki*).[218] From around the mid-nineteenth century, Finnish proto-history became the domain of nationalists.[219] Around the same time, pagan Finnish beliefs were rehabilitated and even presented as monotheistic to make pagan ancestors acceptable.[220] It was then that Lalli was 'elevated to a heroic status' by nationalists.[221] Catholicism, a foreign religion, was now part of foreign domination that Finns had to reject.[222]

Probably the first painting of Lalli killing Bishop Henry was created in 1854 by Carl Andreas Ekman; in 1873, a play was written about the story, which turned Lalli into the leader of the Finns in their tragic battle against the conquering Swedes.[223] Axel Gallén (Akseli Gallen-Kallela), an artist who was central in 'rediscovering' pre-Christian Finnishness, renowned for his illustrations of the Kalevala, worked between 1891 and 1911 on a triptych entitled Bishop Henry and Lalli. He saw Lalli's action of killing the bishop as justified resistance to foreign invaders. In 1924, he published a short story about an invented thirteenth-century pagan chieftain who rebels against the Christian order and is condemned to being buried alive.[224] He also continued to contrast pagan Finnish heritage with the introduction of foreign Christianity. Finnish nationalism and the embrace of supposed original pagan traditions were intertwined.[225] Paganism became the bearer of original Finnish spirituality, and was associated with former independence.[226] At

---

[215] Anttonen, 'The Finns party', 140–1.   [216] Ibid., 141.
[217] Heikkilä, *Pyhän Henrikin Legenda*, 22–3.   [218] Fewster, *Visions of Past Glory*, 107.
[219] Ibid., 172.
[220] Johan Fredrik Cajan, *Suomen historia* (1846), quoted in Fewster, *Visions of Past Glory*, 102–3.
[221] First in G. Z. Forsman's *Pohjanpiltti* (1859), a historical novel, then in Evald Ferd Jahnsson's play *Lalli* (1873): Fewster, *Visions of Past Glory*, 123. Such developments were linked to celebrations of 700 years of Christianity in Finland (1857), when the Swedish conquest started to be criticized by nationalists, therefore conversion became a contentious topic and Finnish pagan spirituality was glorified: ibid., 124, 139; Anttonen, 'The Finns party', 142.
[222] Ibid., 142.
[223] Fewster, *Visions of Past Glory*, 171, painting reproduced 172; 168 (on play). Another play featured Lalli in 1907: ibid., 276.
[224] Ibid., 422.   [225] Ibid., 225–6.   [226] Ibid., 229.

68 STEPHEN I, THE FIRST CHRISTIAN KING OF HUNGARY

the end of the nineteenth century, the Lalli story was recast in a popular novel, centred on the confrontation of a priest and a pagan who is finally burnt at the stake.[227] It continued to be depicted in images and plays, popularized, and taught in school: Lalli, the pagan hero, the first freedom fighter against foreign intruders, became part of national history in the early twentieth century.[228] There are also local Lalli 'traditions' at the supposed site of Henry's killing, and even a town of that name exists (unconnected to the mythical figure), none of them proof of the fictional Lalli's existence.[229] Therefore, a pagan hero can indeed be invented in modern times, and folk 'memory' and popularity is no proof of historical existence.

*   *   *

If the thirteenth-century references to Cupan designate a historical person, he may have been killed during Stephen's reign as the king's enemy, but if so, we know next to nothing about him. In eleventh-century sources written inside and outside Hungary, we find mentions of Stephen's opponents, and one or more rebellions against the centralization of power and Christianization probably took place, but Cupan's name does not appear. It is also possible that Cupan is an invented figure. Perhaps Cupan, Stephen's vanquished opponent, was born through thirteenth-century noble family myth-making about founding ancestors. In that case, a Cupan who lived in the later eleventh century may be the only real historical figure, lending his name to an invented opponent of Stephen, allegedly killed by the family's ancestor; a myth created in order to glorify the kindred. Different stories about the difficult start of Stephen's reign could then be further combined, and Cupan's story embellished because it suited not just noble family prestige, but also the needs of the then relatively newly established Angevins in Hungary. The fourteenth-century story, including Cupan's quartering, can be contextualized in the establishment of Angevin power in Hungary: it was a message about the fate of traitors to anyone intending to be disobedient to new royal power, a warning against treason. Even if there was a historical Cupan in the early part of Stephen's reign, the well-known story that is now firmly entrenched in national history is merely the figment of the imagination of a fourteenth-century chronicler, elaborated around at most a very small historical kernel.

In the early twentieth century, Koppány was picked up as a hero by a fringe movement. However, the nationalist interpretation of Koppány as a representative of traditional Hungarian values, resisting western influence, made him attractive beyond the fringe. Embodied by a popular rock musician in 1983, himself seen as a dissident in communist Hungary, the popularity of Koppány has flourished ever since. This, however, is no mere abuse or misinterpretation of history; generations of medieval and early modern writers, as well as modern historians, actively participated in constructing the myth of Koppány.

Stephen I, the First Christian King of Hungary: From Medieval Myth to Modern Legend. Nora Berend, Oxford University Press. © Nora Berend 2024. DOI: 10.1093/9780191995439.003.0002

---

[227] Ibid., 279.
[228] Ibid., 282, 295, 327, 334, 352, 396, 397; Anttonen, 'The Finns party', 142.   [229] Ibid., 141.

2

Stephen, the King: A Rock Opera in the Late Communist Period and Questions of National Identity

Over the medieval period, myth, like ivy, covered the historical traces of the first king of Hungary. By the time professional history writing developed as a discipline, the climber gained more visibility and seeming historicity than the authentic fragments, which were unsatisfactorily patchy and buried deep underneath. Academic historians turned the medieval myths into historical sources: used them as raw material for their own work, incorporated them as facts and converted them into bases for arguments about medieval events. Myth became the stuff of history. Popularizing academic history entrenched widely held ideas about the past that were even further removed from the original sources. The survival of the Hungarians became Stephen's achievement; he was made the cornerstone of the state, of the Hungarian church, and of alleged Hungarian identity. The myth of Stephen was thus invested with explanatory power as a key determinant of Hungarian history. The narrative's emotional power could only be challenged by counter-myths, rather than the cold clarity of deconstruction and the admission of the inevitable, massive limitations to our knowledge. Contestation crystallized into the issue of pagan or Christian Hungarianness, of Stephen as saviour or traitor. (In an even more complicated twist, some pit an invented 'original Hungarian Christianity' against Catholicism.) Nor did the assessment of Stephen merely centre on the (a)historical role of the king; he became part of a paradigm for the entire course of Hungarian history. In the late communist period, a rock opera embodying Stephen and Koppány burst onto the scene, offering audiences the possibility of identifying with rival mythic protagonists. It quickly became the focal point for contested meaning, not only of the beginnings of the Hungarian state but also of more recent history, and national identity.

1. The Rock Opera

In August 1983, *István, a király* (Stephen, the king) was performed on the 'sleigh hill' of Városliget (City Park), in central Budapest. Based on Miklós Boldizsár's

70   STEPHEN I, THE FIRST CHRISTIAN KING OF HUNGARY

play, *Turn of the Millennium* (Ezredforduló),[1] it represented the confrontation between Stephen and Koppány upon the death of Stephen's father. Two claimants to the throne and, embodied in them, two value-systems clash in the rock opera. Stephen accepts the inevitability of following 'Rome', along with the new Christian customs and a German wife, while Koppány upholds Hungarian traditions.

Both in strength of character and as the subject of viewers' emotional identification, Koppány far surpasses Stephen. Stephen is pushed around by his domineering mother and is tormented by doubts, while Koppány is a strong virile presence, surrounded by three adoring wives, and certain of his cause. The two opponents are also distinguished by musical styles and dance, strengthening the imbalance expressed in the storyline: Stephen sings pop songs and protagonists on the Christian side are characterized by monumental immobility, while Koppány and the pagan rebels sing hard rock, and move in vigorous, sometimes improvised dance.[2] Despite Stephen's attempts to persuade Koppány to change course, even offering him supreme power if he embraces Rome, confrontation cannot be avoided. Koppány cannot abandon his vision of upholding tradition and freedom, while Stephen cannot turn away from the choices he believes ensure Hungary's survival. Set on a 'forced trajectory', the collision of the two main protagonists is unavoidable and ends in Koppány's defeat, death, and quartering.

The rock opera was an immediate huge popular success.[3] Around 100,000 spectators saw the first seven live performances in August 1983,[4] c. 1 per cent of the entire population of Hungary. The location of the performance in Városliget, informally renamed 'king's hill' for the occasion, has been known by that name ever since.[5] By November 1983, more than 100,000 copies of the music on LP had been sold; by May 1984, this number had risen to more than a quarter of a

---

[1] *Ezredforduló: Opera prózában, két részben*, in Miklós Boldizsár, *Királyok és alattvalók: színművek* (Budapest: Magvető, 1982), 151–277, republished *Ezredforduló: Opera prózában, két részben, 1972–1974* (Budapest: Szabad Tér, 1990). The drama differs significantly from the rock opera; notably, Koppány's death is engineered by a priest and he is killed by the frenzied mob. Stephen vows to restore and defend Koppány's truths, while helping people to move on.

[2] On music: Gábor Koltay, *István, a király* (Budapest: Ifjúsági Lap- és Könyvkiadó Vállalat, 1984), 36; Tamás Falus, 'István, a király', *Mozgó Világ*, 10, no. 7 (1984): 124–8, at 126; János István Németh, 'István, a király', *Alföld. Irodalmi, művelődési és kritikai folyóirat*, 35 (1984): 92–5, at 92–3. Gregorian music for ecclesiastics and Hungarian folk-music for Réka and the traditional *regösök* (singers) are also used. On dance: Márta Péter in Koltay, *István*, 68, 71. On the creation of the rock opera: András Stumpf, *Szörényi. Rohan az idő* (Budapest: Trubadúr-Helikon, 2015), 149–58 (the book is based on Szörényi's account of his life).

[3] Tamás Ligeti Nagy, 'István, a király', *Képes Újság*, 24, no. 37 (10 September 1983): 16. A selection of contemporary reviews of the live performances: Koltay, *István*, 40–9. 'The largest cultural mass demonstration of the Kádár regime': János Sebők, *Rock a vasfüggöny mögött: hatalom és ifjúsági zene a Kádár korszakban* (Budapest: GM & Társai Kiadó, 2002), 366.

[4] Falus, 'István', 124; Koltay, *István*, 5, 31–2, 41, 48, 58, 69, 96; Gábor Koltay, ed., *István, a király 1983–2008: Emlékkönyv az ősbemutató 25. évfordulójára* (Budapest: Szabad Tér, 2008), 7, 152. The number of spectators is based on the tickets sold, plus a hypothetical calculation of people entering the open-air performances without a ticket. Erroneous numbers (six performances, 120,000 spectators) posted at http://cultura.hu/kultura/istvan-a-kiraly-30-eve.

[5] Koltay, *István, a király 1983–2008*, 159.

STEPHEN, THE KING   71

million.[6] In 1984, a filmed version of the live performance—directed, as the open-air production, by Gábor Koltay—was released. The basis of the film was a recording of the live performance, but retakes of some scenes were substituted, with live action re-performed for the cameras at night after the audience left; cinematic effects such as stills, slow motion (further stylizing movement), and about 5,000 dissolves were then added.[7] Despite some critical voices in the newspapers,[8] it was a massive box office hit, with 1,412,000 viewers during that first year; in comparison, the second most popular film of that year only drew just over half that many spectators.[9]

Politics—the suggestion of dissidence –, music, and ambiguous meaning were inseparably intertwined in generating such popularity.[10] Many saw *Stephen, the king* as making a stand for Hungarian national identity after a long period when open expressions of nationalism were suppressed by declared official socialist ('proletarian') internationalism.[11] It offered a vision about the country's birth and used the national anthem and flag. Key elements of the pre-1945 Hungarian identity discourse on supposed national characteristics (some of which survived in official discourse, while others were only transmitted in families after Hungary was incorporated into the Soviet sphere) were also manifest: internal division, perpetual victimhood, and tragic defeat.[12] Insistence on national identity in itself was associated with dissidence, but the rock opera also had other features to suggest antagonism to the regime. Rock music had long been an element of

---

[6] The LP was made before the premiere, and playback was used at the performance. Koltay, *István*, 40; Falus, 'István', 124. Later also on tape and CD: Koltay, *István, a király 1983–2008*, 7.

[7] Koltay, *István*, 30; 76 (György Ónodi, production manager), 78–9, 81 (Péter Tímár cameraman); *Népszabadság*, 68, no. 194 (21 August 2010), http://nol.hu/kultura/20100821-istvan__az_elso_es_utolso-779481.

[8] Criticisms of clumsy slow-motion and cutting, clichés, and ahistorical approach, e.g. László Bernáth in *Esti Hírlap*, 18 April 1984, p. 2 (repr. Koltay, *István*, 166); Ilona Gantner in *Népszava*, 26 April 1984 (repr. Koltay, *István*, 168). Criticism of similarities to the musical *Jesus Christ Superstar*, and of borrowings from film director Miklós Jancsó: Koltay, *István*, 139, 146, respectively.

[9] József Gombár, ed., *A magyar játékfilmek nézőszáma és forgalmazási adatai 1948–1987* (Budapest: Magyar Filmtudományi Intézet és Filmarchivum and MOKÉP, 1987), 101 http://mandarchiv.hu/dokumentum/6538/Gombar_Jozsef_A_magyar_jatekfilmek_nezoszama_es_forg_adatai_48_87_compressed.pdf.

[10] Interviewees named various reasons for success, e.g. music: Koltay, *István*, 107; thinking rock opera would be banned: 117; it was 'about more than Stephen and Koppány, this caused fear but also drew people in': 124–5.

[11] Béla Szilárd Jávorszky, 'István a király—Koppány a szupersztár', *Népszabadság*, 60, no. 193 (19 August 2002), 9, http://www.jbsz.hu/interjuk/regmult-/463-istvan-a-kiraly-koppany-a-szupersztar.html; István Povedák, 'Mitizált Történelem. Szent István dekonstruált—rekonstruált legendáriuma' in *Már a múlt sem a régi... Az új magyar mitológia multidiszciplináris elemzése*, ed. László Hubbes, István Povedák (Szeged: MTA-SZTE: Vallási Kultúrakutató Csoport, 2015), 100–21, at 102–9 (English tr. 'Mythicised history: the deconstructed—reconstructed legend of Saint Stephen', in *Religion, Culture, Society*, 2, Yearbook of the MTA-SZTE Research Group for the Study of Religious Culture (Szeged, 2015), 100–16.

[12] On victimhood narratives Aleida Assmann, *Der lange Schatten der Vergangenheit. Erinnerungskultur und Geschichtspolitik* (Munich: C.H. Beck, 2006).

72   STEPHEN I, THE FIRST CHRISTIAN KING OF HUNGARY

counterculture in Hungary,[13] and the singers performing the parts of the leading pagan rebels (Koppány, Laborc, Torda) were played by rock musicians widely known to be in opposition to the regime (Gyula Vikidál, Feró Nagy, Gyula 'Bill' Deák[14]). Feró Nagy's rock band was banned in 1981, and his passport confiscated.[15] The composer Szörényi and the lyricist Bródy were no strangers to clashes with the regime either, although their standing had fluctuated widely. Seen as the 'state beat orchestra' in 1968, subsequently their rock band had been proscribed for a time, a number of political scandals broke out around their music, several of their songs were banned, and Bródy had even been placed under house arrest (and thus prevented from performing) and investigated on suspicion of incitement against the state in 1973, although by the early 1980s they were back in favour.[16] In addition, many saw the rock opera as a coded message about the 1956 uprising, with Stephen representing János Kádár (General Secretary of the Hungarian Socialist Workers' Party, de facto leader of Hungary), and Koppány, the executed Imre Nagy.[17] Many viewers felt liberated by a whiff of dissidence: spectators later on reminisced that they 'felt free'.[18] Construed by many as

---

[13]   Bence Csatári, *A Kádár rendszer könnyűzenei politikája*, PhD dissertation, Budapest ELTE, 2008, http://doktori.btk.elte.hu/hist/csatari/disszert.pdf; Tamás Szőnyei, *Nyilván tartottak: titkos szolgák a magyar rock körül 1960–1990* (Budapest: Magyar Narancs and Tihany-Rév Kiadó, 2005). In the early 1980s, rebellious rock bands were persecuted, while some rock musicians were co-opted by the regime: Sebők, *Rock a vasfüggöny mögött*, 287–360. See also Alexander Vari, 'Nocturnal entertainments, five-star hotels and youth counterculture: reinventing Budapest's nightlife under socialism', in *Socialist Escapes: Breaking Away from Ideology and Everyday Routine in Eastern Europe, 1945–1989*, ed. Cathleen M. Giustino, Catherine J. Plum, Alexander Vari (New York—Oxford: Berghahn Books, 2015), 187–209.

[14]   '[T]heir role in the rock opera corresponded to their public image': Endre Varjas, *ÉS*, 26 August 1983, repr. Koltay, *István*, 51. On the more weighty presence of the rock musicians: Tamás Mészáros, *Magyar Hírlap*, 16, no. 202 (27 August 1983), 7; Judit Máriássy on Hungarian Radio [Magyar Rádió], 'Láttuk, hallottuk', 22 August 1983, both repr. Koltay, *István*, 50–2; Erzsi Sándor, 'Megérteni a konfliktust—Beszélgetés Rényi Andrással az István, a királyról', *Mozgó Világ*, 39, no. 10 (2013): 120–8, at 122.

[15]   Feró Nagy, *'Boldog szép napok'* (Nagy Feró Produkció Kft., 2005), cited in Koltay, *István, a király 1983–2008*, 82, 85; Csatári, *A Kádár rendszer könnyűzenei politikája*, 253 (Nagy's passport had been confiscated; in 1983, he was encouraged to emigrate), 277–8 (on financial difficulties, police harassment); Sebők, *Rock a vasfüggöny mögött* on Nagy and his band 'Beatrice' 256–64.

[16]   Interview with J. Bródy and L. Szörényi, *Magyar Nemzet*, 71, no. 161 (14 June 2008), 30. On Szörényi and Bródy's numerous clashes with the regime from 1968: Sebők, *Rock a vasfüggöny mögött*, 120–30, 154–66; Stumpf, *Szörényi*, 90–3, 97, 100–3, 164–5; Gábor Koltay, *Szörényi Bródy. Az első 15 év*, 2nd edn (Budapest: Zeneműkiadó, 1980), 245–54.

[17]   Expressed openly by emigrants, e.g. István Filippi, *Katolikus Magyarok Vasárnapja*, 91, no. 7 (19 February 1984), 8; Zsuzsánna Kesserű Haynalné, 'Utazás egy Rock-Opera körül', *Chicago és Környéke*, 21 (26 May 1984), 9 (both published in the USA). In Hungary, this was only alluded to (and refuted), e.g. 'to see Koppány as a fighter for national independence and Stephen as a lackey of foreign powers is not a historical approach', one 'should not claim relevance in such a vulgar way;' 'ill-intentioned made-up appropriation': Koltay, *István*, 122 (K. Bakay); 'arbitrary arrogation': ibid., 157 (politician L. Maróthy).

[18]   *Népszabadság*, 68, no. 194 (21 August 2010), http://nol.hu/kultura/20100821-istvan__az_elso_es_utolso-779481.

STEPHEN, THE KING 73

dissident at the time,[19] after 1989, with retrospective prescience and a great deal of exaggeration, the rock opera was even labelled emotional preparation for regime change.[20] According to the most extreme *ex post facto* assertion, it was a conscious contribution towards toppling communism.[21]

The contention that the rock opera offered national pride, hinting at an alternative view of history, contributed greatly to both its appeal and its controversial status. The rock opera claimed professional historical credentials: its historical advisor was the medievalist György Györffy, who had written a voluminous and celebrated monograph on Stephen I. This strengthened the argument that the rock opera presented 'true' history and therefore unlocked access to a supposed 'genuine' national identity. However, defining national identity is in fact a political project, rather than a historical one. While national identity is not an objectively existing reality, attempts to demarcate one certainly constitute a social practice, and wars, metaphorical or real, have broken out over such endeavours.[22] The debate, in deceptive historical garb, revolved around a political meaning. It tapped into a long-standing tendency to conceptualize Hungarian identity through two opposing figures, one that stands for 'national self-determination' and the other for cooperation; such a duality has been pervasive in approaches to defining 'Hungarianness'.[23] Such a framework allows the two main protagonists, Stephen and Koppány to become a paradigm fit for every historical age, and a channel for the sterile debate concerning the supposed genuine representative of true Hungarian identity.[24] The rock opera facilitates such an interpretation: from its creators to audience members, many have emphasized that both main characters

[19] On fear that the rock opera would be banned: Koltay, *István*, 117, 124. Writer György G. Kardos at a public jury session said that 'some leading circles are paying close attention to who likes it and who doesn't', *Filmvilág*, March 1984, repr. Koltay, *István*, 164. Treated a topic that seemed to be taboo: ibid., 182 (György Gémes). Feró Nagy on his suspicions because a rock opera was so foreign to the socialist emotional world: Nagy, '*Boldog szép napok*', cited in Koltay, *István, a király 1983–2008*, 83–4. After 1989, Koltay claimed he had worried the production would be banned during the first performance as it reached 'we don't want a god who speaks no Hungarian' and 'fly free bird': ibid., 158.

[20] E.g. Gabriella Lőcsei, *Magyar Nemzet*, 61, no. 218 (17 September 1998), 11. The authors reacted more cautiously to such retrospective claims. For Koltay, 'it is perhaps an exaggeration to say that it was the wind of approaching regime change': Koltay, *István, a király 1983–2008*, 8. Bródy repeatedly commented that, attuned to popular feelings, they reflected the shift of the population's mood, rather than causing regime change: *Magyar Nemzet*, 71, no. 161 (14 June 2008), 31; *Magyar Nemzet*, 78, no. 193 (18 August 2015), 6; *Népszabadság*, 68, no. 194 (21 August 2010), http://nol.hu/kultura/20100821-istvan__az_elso_es_utolso-779481; Bródy, Szörényi, and Miklós Boldizsár all rejected such an interpretation: *Népszabadság*, 56, no. 194 (19 August 1998), 33; https://zene.hu/cikkek/cikk.php?id=13351 &currentPage=3. Szörényi rejected the view in 1995, repr. Sebők, *Rock a vasfüggöny mögött*, 369, but later said, 'I heard regime change started with the first performance, this is a strong exaggeration, but it did really trigger something [self-esteem and national identity]': Stumpf, *Szörényi*, 154.

[21] István Nemeskürty, *Elrepült a gyors idő* (Budapest: Szabad Tér Kiadó, 1998), 101.

[22] Rogers Brubaker, *Nationalism Reframed: Nationhood and the National Question in the New Europe* (Cambridge: Cambridge University Press, 1996).

[23] A recurrent theme in nineteenth- and twentieth-century literature and history, e.g. Gyula Szekfű, ed., *Mi a magyar?* (Budapest: Magyar Szemle Társaság, 1939).

[24] J. Bródy, https://zene.hu/cikkek/cikk.php?id=13351&currentPage=3.

Figure 3. Gyula Vikidál as Koppány
https://i.ytimg.com/vi/2eyfodDJI5M/hqdefault.jpg

represent their own truths and values, rather than a positive hero opposing an evil villain.[25]

2. Resurgent Nationalism

István, a király triggered the open discussion of national identity and feelings. Numerous people objected to the socialist devaluation of patriotism and national identity; many clamoured for a reawakening of 'national consciousness'.[26] The rock opera was even said to be a source of historical knowledge with the potential to correct the shortcomings of the educational system that failed to inculcate patriotism.[27] (After 1989, Szörényi claimed that the rock opera had provided

---

[25] Péter Fábri, 'Mítosz az egész nemzethez szólóan', *Magyar Ifjúság*, 27, no. 35 (2 September 1983), 29; letter by István Feitl, *Magyar Ifjúság*, 27, no. 42 (21 October 1983), 41; also see below.

[26] Koltay himself: Koltay, *István*, 186–7 and in a later interview, *Új Magyarország*, 7 August 1992, 2, no. 186, p. 9. Similar sentiments in *Olvasó Nép*, winter 1983, cited in Jávorszky, 'István a király— Koppány a szupersztár'; Sándor Hári, *Zalai Hírlap*, 13 December 1983, p. 5. 'We should rejoice if a rock opera raises... the consciousness of national belonging': Koltay, *István*, 95. It 'awakens Hungarian consciousness in everyone': Márta Barna, *Magyar Ifjúság*, 28, no. 13 (30 March 1984), 37. 'Triggering national feelings is good': Tamás Donát, *Napló*, 13 December 1983, repr. Koltay, *István*, 96; also ibid., 100; 117–18 (Kornél Bakay, archaeologist and historian).

[27] Sándor Hári, *Zalai Hírlap*, 13 December 1983, p. 5, repr. Koltay, *István*, 95; ibid., 123 (K. Bakay), 129–30; 144 (university students). 'Every Hungarian teenager can hear the voices of the past': László Domonkos, *Délmagyarország*, 19 April 1984, 5, repr. Koltay, *István*, 171–2. Ibid., 176 (Ferenc Pallagi

STEPHEN, THE KING   75

self-esteem and national identity at a time when the Party state was trying to breed a 'socialist type of person'.[28]) Nevertheless, the rock opera was criticized by some for painting a negative picture of Stephen: if the young 'who lack a Hungarian identity' 'cannot even love Stephen who founded the state and was canonized by the church, who can they love?'[29] On the contrary, another critic suggested that all the rock opera's many flaws could be forgiven for its whole-hearted missionary stance towards the 'burningly important' issue of historical and national consciousness.[30] As one reviewer suggested, almost unanimously, viewers distilled one issue, that of 'Hungarian consciousness' (*magyarságtudat*), as the rock opera's crux, and their ethical position in relation to that determined their evaluation of the piece.[31] The two poles in this identity war were 'those who do not like it cannot be good Hungarians' and 'those who like it are pub-level nationalists'.[32]

In fact, those who claimed that the rock opera allowed them to experience a previously suppressed joy of being Hungarian could not conceptualize very clearly what they were celebrating, and they expressed inchoate feelings. For example, they were 'celebrating Hungary'; 'the Hungarian nation will exist for a long time if we see many plays like this'; 'it is wonderful to be Hungarian'.[33] As one analyst remarked, despite their claims, they did not find national pride because of the rock opera, which only facilitated a diminished identification and emotional reaction.[34] A few voices, professional critics and audience members alike, found fault with the schematic representation and near-kitsch clichés, and suggested that realistic historical models were needed for a genuine debate on

---

Szabó, A Magyar Rádió Láttuk, hallottuk műsora, 13 March 1984); Gabriella Lőcsei's conversation with Miklós Boldizsár, *Magyar Nemzet*, 47, no. 53 (3 March 1984), 9. On the historical consciousness taught in schools, critically rejecting the alternative offered by *István*: Koltay, *István*, 116 (Ferencné Bíró, history teacher). In 1987, a high school student said his generation's ideas about Stephen were formed by the rock opera: 'Ünnepi körkérdés', *Magyar Ifjúság*, 31, no. 34 (21 August 1987), 10 (János Kiss). Historian Győrffy claimed the rock opera brought Stephen, otherwise little known, close to young people: Sándor Tóth interview with György Győrffy, *Új Ember*, 19 August 1984, p. 3.

[28] Stumpf, *Szörényi*, 154.

[29] Koltay, *István*, 127 (Mihály Sárdi, assistant to the director). Also critical of Stephen's 'weakness' was György Fejti, First Secretary of the Central Committee of the Communist Youth League (KISZ), ibid., 152; Falus, 'István', 127; József Ballai, 'István, a gyönge', *Petőfi népe*, 19 April 1984, p. 5.

[30] László Domonkos, *Délmagyarország*, 19 April 1984, 5 repr. Koltay, *István*, 171. Koltay retrospectively lauded the 'more than usual honesty about our history' and 'the use of national symbols': Koltay, *István, a király 1983–2008*, 158.

[31] Győző Mátyás in *Filmkultúra*, 1984/2, repr. Koltay, *István*, 174. Similarly the rock opera being about national consciousness: Falus, 'István', 128; on polarized opinion: Sebők, *Rock a vasfüggöny mögött*, 366–9.

[32] Statement of György G. Kardos, writer, member of the jury, *Filmvilág*, March 1984, repr. Koltay, *István*, 164. On the rock opera's greater success in nationalist circles: Sebők, *Rock a vasfüggöny mögött*, 367.

[33] Koltay, *István*, 90–1 (audience responses to a reporter); similar in a roundtable debate, ibid., 128–9, and by high school students, 134–7. In retrospect, the director claimed that the rock opera offered the possibility of community-building: Koltay, *István, a király 1983–2008*, 9.

[34] Péter Rényi, 'Identitás-értelmezés', *Népszabadság*, 41, no. 303 (24 December 1983), 10.

76 STEPHEN I, THE FIRST CHRISTIAN KING OF HUNGARY

patriotism.[35] Yet the warning of a few analysts—that while a search for identity is natural, self-imposed isolation through a flight into the past, and politically charged fiction could release the genie of xenophobic nationalism from the bottle—fell mainly on deaf ears.[36] Even a sociologist claimed that while 'one should not expect the solution to the debated questions of our approach to history' from a rock opera, 'it is sufficient...that these questions were raised, and honestly'.[37]

Instead of constructive discussion about the past and present, however, a polarizing national identity discourse resurfaced. The communist regime, which had indeed banished open nationalism from public discourse, was covertly blamed for substituting a demeaning, falsified version of history for reality, trying to indoctrinate Hungarians to forget their past. Reality was more complex: the government had attempted to erase the toxic interwar nationalist narrative, which had blamed the Habsburgs, ethnic minorities, communists (the 1919 Republic of Councils), Jews (often equated with communists), and the West (the Treaty of Trianon, 1920) for all the ills that befell Hungary. However, merely aiming to suppress the false narrative, instead of a concerted effort to face the reality of the past, ultimately led to an equally toxic mix of real grievance caused by political oppression and anger at the supposed communist suppression of national identity.[38] That the traditional narrative was in fact far from eradicated was shown when a question on the trauma of the Treaty of Trianon was first included in a 1983 poll; 64 per cent of respondents said it was the deepest trauma for Hungary.[39] For many ordinary people, the national feeling they saw expressed in the rock opera was embedded in obliquely expressed conspiracy theories: 'once in a lifetime we experience our own history; it should not be others who explain it to us' and 'for very many people, it would not come in handy if we spoke about our common concerns, our history candidly, because they like to fish in troubled waters'.[40]

---

[35] Imre D. Magyari, *Magyar Ifjúság*, 27, no. 45 (11 November 1983), 20–1, partly repr. Koltay, *István*, 85, similar ibid., 140 (university students); Letter by László Dezső, *Magyar Ifjúság*, 27, no. 45 (11 November 1983), 39.

[36] Rényi, 'Identitás-értelmezés', 10; Koltay, *István*, 110–11 (Gábor Bányai).

[37] Ibid., 100 (Iván Vitányi). Similarly, Antal Dobozy, a salesman, at a roundtable discussion: 'the rock opera cannot be the solution to Hungarian historical or cultural problems,...but it can open eyes', ibid., 131.

[38] Communists combined the eradication of the earlier nationalist narrative with the replacement of Hungarian symbols; compelled by Soviet demands, the coat-of-arms, military uniform, art and fashion followed Soviet models: Tamás Aczél—Tibor Méray, *Tisztító vihar* (Szeged: JATE Kiadó, 1989), 126–34.

[39] By 1989, this rose to 78 per cent, György Csepeli, 'Competing patterns of national identity in post-communist Hungary', *Media, Culture and Society*, 13, no. 3 (1991): 325–39, https://doi-org.ezp. lib.cam.ac.uk/10.1177/016344391013003004, at 334–5. About two-thirds of intellectuals polled also thought Hungary was among the countries with a history of misfortunes: György Csepeli, *National Identity in Contemporary Hungary*, tr. Mario D. Fenyo (Boulder, Co: Social Science Monographs—Highland Lakes, NJ : Atlantic Research and Publications, Inc, 1997), 168–9; 194–8 on Trianon.

[40] Koltay, *István*, 129–30 (Vikidál, who linked the view that the rock opera was nationalist manipulation to hidden agendas: ibid., 130).

Many more felt what only some people expressed explicitly: 'it was good, because young people did not think the thoughts they had been indoctrinated into during the years. That Hungary [was] the last satellite [i.e. of Hitler], a rotten nation. I always felt it very clearly that I am not that, and that I am proud to be Hungarian.'[41] The merit of *István* was to have presented to the broad masses an image of the past 'finally not suggestive of feelings of guilt, but of "proud people of the wide plains", "soar free bird from the ring of the Carpathians", "beautiful Hungary, our sweet homeland".'[42] These lines from songs of the rock opera all hit the buttons of amorphous national pride. Many saw it as 'finally providing a normal sense of [Hungarian] history.'[43] The director Koltay said: 'in a country where one must creep along the wall in shame, it would be time to talk about the issues we have in common.'[44]

What surfaced was a twisted victim-complex, a refusal to process the past. Echoes of the Trianon complex (the idea of undeserved punishment at the conclusion of the First World War through the machinations of jealous neighbours and an ungrateful western Europe, see below), were combined both with the rejection of responsibility for the Holocaust of the Hungarian Jews during the Second World War, and with blaming communists for undermining Hungarians' self-respect (which easily acquired antisemitic overtones, by equating communists with 'Jews'). These were all conflated, resulting in inchoate grievance, which, thanks to the rock opera, could now be expressed. Not just the older generations with possible personal experience, but the young were also affected by the distorted victim complex, as reflected in the opinions of high-school students: 'Hungary still exists, and this should be a cause for joy', 'we shouldn't always feel ashamed', 'Hungarian people should not have a distorted consciousness, to feel ashamed for something they did not commit.'[45] These people rejected what they thought was the official socialist view: the collective guilt of Hungarians expressed in the oft-repeated dictum that Hungary was Hitler's last satellite. In fact, the official line was that Hungary's ruling class allied with Hitler, while the common people were victims of the ruling class.[46]

---

[41] Ibid., 145.

[42] László Domonkos, *Délmagyarország*, 19 April 1984, 5, repr. Koltay, *István*, 172.

[43] Ibid., 127 (by a Catholic priest); similar ibid., 130.

[44] Ibid., 189. In 1991, István Nemeskürty claimed that all other films made in the 1980s depicted Hungary in a bitter light, focusing on the fathers' sins, while, as the only exception, the rock opera expressed faith in Hungary's future: *Távlatok*, 1991, no. 1, repr. Koltay, *István, a király 1983–2008*, 166.

[45] Koltay, *István*, 136.

[46] Examples: 'The regime of aristocrats, landowners, factory owners and bankers left a sad inheritance to the liberated Hungarian people.... half a million Hungarian lives criminally sacrificed on the altar of the predatory Hitler-fascist war, a country in ruins.' Speech on 15th anniversary of liberation, 3 April 1960, in János Kádár, *Tovább a lenini úton* (Budapest: Kossuth Könyvkiadó, 1964), 24. 'The Hungarian capitalist and landowning class fell, because it was unable to do anything but exploit, lead to destruction, betray and sell the people, the homeland, independence. The last quarter of a century of their rule was born in blood, counterrevolution and white terror; continued with the alliance with the most reactionary forces, Hitlerian German fascists, and then predatory war on their side, and

78 STEPHEN I, THE FIRST CHRISTIAN KING OF HUNGARY

The rock opera's finale—in the presence of a gigantic Hungarian flag, the performers sang the Hungarian national anthem (Himnusz, Hymn)—was seen by many in the Party as a sign of dangerous nationalism. Thus, state security services reported on opinions about playing the national anthem at the end of the rock opera, and on statements that one should not be afraid to play it.[47] (The anthem was played at the end of the live performances, but was not included on the LP and in the filmed version.[48]) The desire for national pride that surfaced in the 1980s had been seething under the surface in post-war Hungary, and exploded fully after the fall of communism. The communist ban on the nationalist narrative, however, was not the origin of the neuralgic problem of national identity. Rather, its roots lay in the nineteenth-century birth of nationalism in the region, when competing nation-building projects emerged. In the linguistically mixed areas of the old Kingdom of Hungary, once groups started to construe themselves along the lines of ethnic nationalism, the fight for political power, independent statehood, and territory began. Hungarians were embroiled in all this on two fronts: vindicating independence from the Habsburgs in the Austro-Hungarian monarchy, they also wanted to retain their dominant position over the Slovak, Romanian, and other minorities within the kingdom. The emerging minority nationalisms within the Kingdom of Hungary, however, joined cause with neighbouring states conceptualized as sharing a common ethnicity.

On the losing side of the First World War, the monarchy was dismantled; about two-thirds of the area of the former Kingdom of Hungary—also containing 31 per cent of the Hungarian population—was detached and granted to the

inevitably led to ignominy, German occupation and the Arrow Cross' reign of terror.' Speech on 19th anniversary of liberation, 3 April 1964, in ibid., 321. 'Populaces are not responsible for the former deeds of the old class of exploiters and their representatives, kings, landowners, big capitalists, the Horthy- and Piłsudski-type fascists. They are especially not responsible in our countries, where we did away with the power of the old privileged classes.' Undated speech, 1964/5, in János Kádár, *Hazafiság és internacionalizmus* (Budapest: Kossuth Könyvkiadó, 1968), 51. 'The reactionary then-rulers of Hungary attached the fate of our country...to Hitler-fascism. Hungary's then-rulers embroiled our people in the second world war on the side of the so-called third Reich, sacrificed hundreds of thousands of the population in the interest of their criminal goals, and reduced the country to a heap of ruins.' Speech at a dinner in the Elysée palace, November 1978, in János Kádár, *Szövetségi politika— nemzeti egység: beszédek és cikkek, 1978–1981* (Budapest: Kossuth Könyvkiadó, 1981), 66. 'The landowner and capitalist class, which was the loyal servant of the Habsburgs, then the first and last satellite of the Hitler-fascists...drove millions of our people to the slaughterhouse...took the country...into the abyss of final destruction.' Speech at the celebratory meeting of the Central Committee on the 60th anniversary of the formation of the Communist Party of Hungary, November 1978, in Kádár, *Szövetségi politika*, 90. Kádár specifically stated (contrary to Soviet statements at the end of the war) that the Soviet Union did not identify the Hungarian people with the ruling class that was Hitler's last satellite: Speech at Parliament, 25th anniversary of liberation, April 1970, in János Kádár, *Válogatott beszédek és cikkek 1957–1973* (Budapest: Kossuth Könyvkiadó, 1974), 308.

[47] On 8 December 1983, Koltay, *István, a király 1983–2008*, 160.

[48] A critic claimed that his opinion led to this omission, while Koltay said he had made the decision earlier: Koltay, *István*, 87, 89, respectively. Omitting the anthem from the film was in turn criticized by Ballai, 'István, a gyönge', 5, partly repr. Koltay, *István*, 167.

STEPHEN, THE KING 79

neighbouring countries at the treaty of Trianon (1920).[49] With internal upheavals between 1918 and 1920 (first a liberal democratic, then a communist revolution, finally the takeover by the right-wing autocratic Horthy), successive Hungarian governments were in no position to influence the victorious powers, and Horthy was forced to accept the dictates of the peace treaty. His regime lacked diplomatic competence to change opinion abroad, and consecrated most of its efforts in the interwar period to fomenting revisionism against the 'injustice of the Treaty of Trianon' at home. Ultimately leading to an alliance with Mussolini and Hitler, who granted some of the lost territories to Hungary again, such policies spectacularly failed not only because the territories were detached again after the end of the Second World War but also because they brought about the complete moral collapse of Hungarian society. Blaming all ills on Trianon, the interwar political elite failed to modernize, hanging on to aristocratic privilege and outmoded ways. Hungarian atrocities against local non-Hungarian populations on temporarily regained lands, the despoliation and murder of most of Hungary's Jewish population in the last months of the war, and Hungary's position as Hitler's last ally deprived the Hungarian political establishment of moral authority to speak for Hungarian minorities in the neighbouring countries.[50] Recent experiences as well as their own nationalism and the fear of losing territory again ensured that policies by the neighbouring states towards the Hungarian minorities on their soil would not be sympathetic.

During the communist era, official policy denied the existence of minority issues in the Socialist Bloc, while the open rhetoric of Trianon grievance was taboo, even though not entirely forgotten.[51] The prohibition of open discussion exacerbated the problem.[52] A compound of real injustice (the mistreatment of Hungarian minorities in neighbouring countries, the lack of freedom and

---

[49] An area of 232,338 km² was detached, leaving the state of Hungary with 93,073 km², and of the 20.9 million population of the former Kingdom of Hungary, 7.6 million remained in the new state of Hungary. A total of 3.3 million Hungarians became minorities in the neighbouring countries.

[50] For details, Krisztián Ungváry, *A Horthy-rendszer mérlege: diszkrimináció, szociálpolitika és antiszemitizmus Magyarországon, 1919–1944*, 2nd rev. edn (Pécs: Jelenkor, Budapest: OSZK, 2013); Miklós Zeidler, *Ideas on Territorial Revision in Hungary: 1920–1945* (Boulder, CO: Social Science Monographs, 2007).

[51] Even Kádár talked about Trianon as 'the imperialist dictate that mutilated Hungary's territory' to sow discord among peoples: response to Henry Shapiro of UPI, 27 July 1966, published in *Népszabadság*, 24, no. 181 (2 August 1966), repr. in Kádár, *Hazafiság és internacionalizmus*, 222. To a question by an ARD TV reporter on tensions within the bloc due to national issues, Kádár responded that 'an interview is not the right medium to answer', and that tensions and a clash of interests were always resolved. Interview September 1979, in Kádár, *Szövetségi politika*, 135–6. On the stance towards Hungarian minorities in neighbouring countries, especially Romania, during the Kádár era: Roger Gough, *A Good Comrade: János Kádár, Communism and Hungary* (London—New York: I.B. Tauris, 2006), 155–6, 203; György Földes, 'Kádár János és az erdélyi magyarság', in *Nemzetiség-felelősség: Írások Gáll Ernő emlékére*, ed. György Földes, Zsolt Gálfalvi (Budapest: Napvilág, 2005), 55–107.

[52] Communist doctrine maintained that communism would resolve national tensions; the Hungarian government was unable to negotiate any improvement for Hungarian minorities. On Kádár's limited sphere of movement, cautious approach and futile endeavours regarding Hungarians in Romania: Földes, 'Kádár János és az erdélyi magyarság'.

80   STEPHEN I, THE FIRST CHRISTIAN KING OF HUNGARY

political say in Hungary) and underground forms of the ugly interwar Hungarian nationalism fomented anger. Suppressed, rather than eradicated, nationalism was passed on in families, the discontent it encapsulated mingling with dissatisfaction with the communist regime. The rock opera thus provided a possible vector for the expression of diffuse discontent and officially suppressed national pride.

István and the public debate about it contributed to the reincorporation of expressions of national feeling into the permissible sphere.[53] The ground for this, however, had started to be prepared: the regime itself was already experimenting with such a reincorporation to harness national sentiment for its own legitimization.[54] Indeed, some commentators pointed out that the creators took no risks while providing the illusion of criticizing the regime: they used the conspicuously nationalistic panels that were 'still seen as daring' by many, but which were no longer seen as dissident by the authorities.[55] The rock opera's example led to the reintroduction of the Hungarian national anthem at unofficial events; its use soon became widespread at festivals and celebrations.[56] Some of the Party leadership started to emphasize the importance of 'socialist patriotism', and *István* as one of its building blocks.[57] Thus, Béla Köpeczi, minister of culture praised *Stephen the king* in 1986.[58]

3. The Rock Opera and the Kádár Regime

The rock opera's meaning, however, was so malleable that ironically, *István* ended up gaining not only popular applause for defiantly breaking the regime's taboos

---

[53] Contemporary viewers on experiencing identification with the national community: Povedák, 'Mitizált Történelem', 102; Koltay, *István*, 33, 64 (Gyula Vikidál), 82, 83. Many commented that the rock opera started something new, opened until then closed doors: e.g. ibid., 131–2. Retrospective claim of opportunity to talk through 'emotional knots': Koltay, *István, a király 1983–2008*, 159. On *István* creating national feelings: Sebők, *Rock a vasfüggöny mögött*, 268–9.

[54] On the Kádár period and nationalism, János Gyurgyák, *Ezzé lett magyar hazátok: a magyar nemzeteszme és nacionalizmus története* (Budapest: Osiris Kiadó, 2007), 521–6; on the role of nationalism during the communist period: John Connelly, *From Peoples into Nations: A History of Eastern Europe* (Princeton, NJ: Princeton University Press, 2020), 590–621. Outside the Party, there was also renewed interest in peasant folklore and dance from the 1970s: Koltay, *István*, 101, 141. An earlier play represented Stephen as a negative figure ultimately hated by his own father Géza, because of his ruthless oppression of pre-Christian Hungarian tradition: Magda Szabó, *Az a szép, fényes nap* (1980, repr. Budapest: Európa Könyvkiadó, 2004).

[55] Gábor Klaniczay, *Filmvilág*, May 1984, repr. Koltay, *István*, 170–1. Ferenc Marin accused Koltay of careerism through seeming dissidence: 'Popszínház', *Valóság*, March 1987, 69–81, at 72–5, partly repr. Koltay, *István, a király 1983–2008*, 167.

[56] Csatári, *A Kádár rendszer könnyűzenei politikája*, 296; on the Rákosi era's attempt to eliminate the Hymn, and its rehabilitation under Kádár: http://deba.unideb.hu/deba/emlekezethely/eh.php?id=7.

[57] Koltay, *István*, 158 (László Maróthy, member of Politbureau and First Secretary of the Budapest Party Committee). On the differing opinions within the Party leadership, from condemning the ascendant nationalism in *István, a király* to trying to capture it for its own ends: Jávorszky, 'István a király—Koppány a szupersztár'.

[58] Csatári, *A Kádár rendszer könnyűzenei politikája*, 261.

but also the same regime's approval. In fact, the performance of the rock opera would not have been possible without official toleration, as was indeed true of much of counterculture at the time.[59] Some suggested more active agency: that the Party leadership consciously chose to 'open the safety valve of nationalism' to release tensions, and gave permission for the performance to proceed with that express intention.[60] It has even been claimed (and vociferously denied after 1989) that the piece was commissioned from above.[61] That a few high-ranking party members helped to realize the production was acknowledged even after the fall of communism.[62]

Giving a green light to *István* fits into the politics of the late Kádár period. After the severe repression of the earlier Kádár regime, when retribution targeted dissident musicians, actors, and intellectuals, a selective thaw started. Economic imperatives led to a greater opening to the West from the mid-1970s, which also entailed trying to keep a positive profile abroad. At the same time, maintaining relatively high living standards, including the possibility for Hungarians to travel to the West, were crucial to keep the regime's popular support at home.[63] Networks of informants, pressure, and harassment replaced more severe measures such as imprisonment to keep intellectuals in check.[64] Sanctions were used against persistent, open critics, but the Party no longer tried to wipe out all intellectual dissidence, and many intellectuals accommodated to the regime.[65] From the early 1980s, the government gradually started to acknowledge pop and rock music as accepted cultural forms and became more permissive towards some of their practitioners. In 1982, for example, the filmed 1969 London Rolling Stones concert was projected in Hungarian cinemas; foreign stars appeared in concert in Budapest and Hungarian bands were allowed to give concerts abroad.[66]

Further, nationalism, condemned as an imperialist tool in the Soviet Bloc, was making a comeback. Officially, the regime continued to censure nationalism, but

---

[59] Similar point Povedák, 'Mitizált Történelem', 101–2; Marin, 'Popszínház', 73–4. On Kádár era cultural policies: Gough, *Good Comrade*, 130, 141, 154–5, 187–8, 196.

[60] Emericus [Zoltán Krasznai], 'János a király, avagy árad a kegyelem fénye reánk', in *Samizdat Hírmondó*, 1984, repr. *Rendszerváltó archívum*, 2, no. 2 (June 2017), 87–91, see 90. See also Jávorszky, 'István a király—Koppány a szupersztár'; Povedák, 'Mitizált Történelem', 102; Erzsi Sándor, 'Megérteni a konfliktust', 125.

[61] Koltay, *István*, 189. In samizdat, see e.g. Gábor Demszky, ed., *Hírmondó*, repr. Koltay, *István, a király 1983–2008*, 150–1.

[62] Szörényi (15 June 2008), https://zene.hu/cikkek/cikk.php?id=13351&currentPage=3; Koltay, *István, a király 1983–2008*, 148, 151, claiming there was no political connection. In 1990, Koltay claimed that 'popular will' had forced the authorities to grant a last-minute permission for the premiere against political opposition, a presentation at odds with all other testimony: 'Koltay Gábor levele Keglevich István atyának', *Zászlónk* (1990): 2, repr. Koltay, *István, a király 1983–2008*, 222.

[63] Gough, *Good Comrade*, 195–7.   [64] Ibid., 201 (late 1970s).

[65] On intellectuals in the Kádár regime, Éva Standeisky, 'Kádár és az értelmiség', and László Lengyel, 'A hatalom hálójában. Az értelmiség és a kádárizmus', in *Ki volt Kádár? Harag és részrehajlás nélkül a Kádár-életútról*, ed. Árpád Rácz (Budapest: Rubicon-Aquila, 2001), 136–40, 141–5, respectively. On the early 1980s, Gough, *Good Comrade*, 212–13.

[66] Csatári, *A Kádár rendszer könnyűzenei politikája*, 295–6.

82 STEPHEN I, THE FIRST CHRISTIAN KING OF HUNGARY

started to harness 'patriotism' and 'national feeling' to strengthen popular support. In 1957, Kádár declared that nationalism is a tool for imperialists in their fight against the socialist world, and Hungary must follow proletarian internationalism coupled to patriotism.[67] In 1965, Kádár stated: 'In the Horthy era, the red-white-and-green flag was carried by the members of the ruling class, it represented their state, we had the red flag in our hand. Now we profess that we should go forward with the red flag in one hand, the national colours in the other. We say: let's have national cooperation to build a socialist society.'[68] In 1977, he emphasized that the Party was both patriotic and internationalist; proletarian internationalism had to coordinate national and international interests.[69] In 1979, Kádár declared at the meeting of Party activists in Budapest that the People's Republic of Hungary represents 'national interests' within and outside the socialist alliance.[70] The following year, Kádár was cautiously alluding to some traditional grievances, while refusing to condone them. 'The history of our people turned out in such a way that about a third of Hungarians live outside the borders of the country: Hungarians live in almost every part of the globe.... We expect them to cultivate their national culture and be decent citizens of their country, help to advance social progress and the friendship of peoples.'[71] Kádár blurred the difference between the Hungarian minorities in neighbouring Socialist Bloc countries (the result of the treaty of Trianon) and emigrants to 'every part of the globe', but he started to invoke national culture and feeling. 'There is a natural national feeling, which also means that we observe the fate of Hungarians in neighbouring countries with empathy and sympathy. But this natural feeling cannot be coupled to nationalism;' he reiterated that only socialism can resolve nationality problems.[72] Alluding to growing tensions and the situation of Hungarian minorities in thinly veiled terms, Kádár refused 'irresponsible' action that would harm socialism and the country and help 'the enemy'.[73] While the regime cautiously dabbled in invoking national interests to prop up its legitimacy, would-be successors of the aging Kádár started to envision different futures; some Party members espoused nationalism more vocally.

---

[67] Speech at the Party executive committee, 23 August 1957, in János Kádár, *Szilárd népi hatalom: független Magyarország* (Budapest: Kossuth Könyvkiadó, 1959), 249–50; this echoed Gerő's speech of 23 October 1956: Tamás G. Korányi, ed., *Egy népfelkelés dokumentumai 1956* (Budapest: Tudósítások Kiadó, 1989), 53, no. 22.

[68] Speech at Békéscsaba on the day of the constitution, 20 August 1965, in Kádár, *Hazafiság és internacionalizmus*, 129.

[69] January 1977, in Kádár, *A szocializmus megújulása*, 259.

[70] Kádár, *Szövetségi politika*, 143.

[71] Report of the Central Committee for the XII. Congress, March 1980, in ibid., 177.

[72] Report of the Central Committee for the XII. Congress, March 1980, in ibid., 177. See also Földes, 'Kádár János és az erdélyi magyarság'.

[73] Both quotes: speech at the Central Committee, April 1983, in János Kádár, *A szocializmus megújulása Magyarországon: Válogatott beszédek és cikkek 1957–1986* (Budapest: Kossuth Könyvkiadó, 1986), 338.

The rock opera would not have been realized were it not for this context. Potential censorship and prohibitions were at the discretion of the party state. With the help of László Maróthy (member of the Politburo of the Hungarian Socialist Workers' Party), the Politburo authorized the rock opera prior to the premiere: while at the time, it was claimed the Politburo approved the script, after the fall of communism the director maintained he had only sent a synopsis to Maróthy.[74] It was not merely a question of gaining authorization: financing would also have been impossible without state involvement. How it was secured is indicative of behind-the-scenes conflicts within the regime, since both obstacles and money were raised by people or organizations associated to the state. Originally, a film was commissioned for Budapest Studio, and the Ministry of Culture's Film directorate did not give its approval; therefore, an alternative means of financing was needed. This gave rise to the plan of a live performance that would be filmed. Half the amount originally calculated for the cost of the production was available through Budapest Studio.[75] Hungaroton (the only record company in Hungary at the time), which issued the LP, gave 800,000 Forints.[76] After the live performance, the director of MOKÉP ('Moving Picture Distribution Company', a state enterprise that held the monopoly of film distribution) offered the remaining amount needed (6 million Ft) to finance the film.[77]

Those in power understood *István* as a justification of Kádár, although the rock opera may have appealed to the nationalists within the Party exactly because it could also be read as a covert condemnation of him.[78] An article written by a supporter and beneficiary of the regime's cultural politics explicitly interpreted the rock opera as justifying Kádár: Koppány is seen as a 'rebellious dissident', who is a backward force and is unable to grasp the true nature of the situation; Stephen alone understands that Rome will not tolerate a pagan Hungary, and because Rome is powerful, this must be accepted to ensure the country's survival. However, Stephen is no opportunist or weakling: he also truly believes that

---

[74] Compare Koltay, *István*, 154–5, with Koltay, *István, a király 1983–2008*, 151. On help from the Party, Levente Szörényi in interview: *Magyar Nemzet*, 71, no. 161 (14 June 2008), 31. Cf. Sebők, *Rock a vasfüggöny mögött*, 366.

[75] Csatári, *A Kádár rendszer könnyűzenei politikája*, 297; Koltay, *István*, 185–6 (interview with director G. Koltay); Koltay, *István, a király 1983–2008*, 146–7.

[76] Falus, 'István', 125; Koltay, *István, a király 1983–2008*, 306.

[77] On financing, *Magyar Ifjúság*, 28, no. 12 (23 March 1984), 28; Koltay, *István, a király 1983–2008*, 158.

[78] Retrospectively on possible interpretations in the Party: Jávorszky 'István a király—Koppány a szupersztár'. Politicians at the time openly merely said the rock opera was 'unusual' (Koltay, *István*, 150, by Imre Pozsgay, Secretary General of the National Council of the Patriotic People's Front), and that its topic contributed to its success (ibid., 152, by György Fejti, First Secretary of the Central Committee of the Communist Youth League [KISZ]), or spoke of a growing interest in history (ibid., 156, by László Maróthy, member of the Politburo of the Hungarian Socialist Workers' Party and First Secretary of its Budapest Committee). Levente Szörényi on alleged Party interpretation: Stumpf, *Szörényi*, 154–5.

84 STEPHEN I, THE FIRST CHRISTIAN KING OF HUNGARY

Rome's path is the path of progress and the future.[79] Could one write a more beautiful exoneration for Kádár's role in 1956? The director at the time—contrary to his later pronouncements—claimed that the figure of Stephen represented *realpolitik* and a readiness to compromise; he also stated that he aspired to stimulate young people to bond more closely with the social system and politics: a declaration of political loyalty.[80] György Aczél, the Central Committee's Secretary of Cultural Affairs, and, for most of the Kádár period, the decisive figure in cultural policy, watched a live performance in Szeged in 1984, and offered his congratulations.[81] Party recognition abounded: the director was among the nine recipients of the Communist Youth League's (KISZ) prize in March 1984, which was awarded for 'contributions to the building of an advanced socialist society through outstanding work in youth education'; the Film Directorate General of the Ministry of Culture (Művelődési Minisztérium Filmfőigazgatósága) offered its recognition to the makers of the film, which premiered in Moscow and was shown at the Cannes film festival later that year.[82] Opposition intellectuals shared the Party's interpretation of the rock opera as an apotheosis of Kádár (expressed explicitly in samizdat publications), even suggesting it was officially commissioned, and condemned it.[83]

Whether *István* represented dissidence or servility to the regime continued to divide opinion in subsequent decades. In retrospect, the distinction itself is less unambiguous. Not only was some dissidence allowed, perhaps even as a safety valve, but, as shown by a typical Hungarian (and more generally, Eastern Bloc) story that unfolded after the fall of communism, dissidence and servility could go hand in hand. In 2004, the dissident rock musician Gyula Vikidál, long admired as the rock opera's Koppány, admitted to having been an informer code-named 'Singer' (Dalos) between 1981 and 1986.[84]

István, a király has been the site of contestation not merely in terms of its status in undermining or propping up the regime, but also in relation to every aspect of its meaning. In 1983–4, lyricist, composer, and director all suggested that the rock opera was at once about the particular historical situation at the beginning of Stephen I's reign, and about Hungarian history more generally. In the specific

---

[79] Péter Erdős, responsible for pop music at the Hungarian record company (Magyar Hanglemezgyártó Vállalat), quoted in Sebők, *Rock a vasfüggöny mögött*, 367–8.

[80] Koltay, *István*, 187. On Stephen embodying realpolitik also: István Hirtling in *Esti Hírlap*, 30, no. 300 (23 December 1985) [p. 17].

[81] Koltay, *István, a király 1983–2008*, 179; on Aczél's initial hostility changing to support: Levente Szörényi in interview with Gabriella Lőcsei, *Magyar Nemzet*, 61, no. 218 (17 September 1998), 11; Stumpf, *Szörényi*, 162. On Aczél: Gough, *Good Comrade*, 129–31, 189–90. K. Berek, actress, said that the interior minister also liked the live performance: Koltay, *István*, 60.

[82] *Pest Megyei Hírlap*, 28, no. 68 (21 March 1984), 1; Koltay, *István*, 165, 178–9.

[83] Emericus, 'János a király, avagy árad a kegyelem fénye reánk', 87–91; Koltay, *István, a király 1983–2008*, 150–1; Erzsi Sándor, 'Megérteni a konfliktust', 126–7; Stumpf, *Szörényi*, 155.

[84] *Magyar Hírlap*, 23 April 2004, 10; *Origo*, 22 April 2004, http://www.origo.hu/itthon/20040422vikidal.html.

STEPHEN, THE KING   85

moment, Stephen's far-sighted wisdom made him realize what he needed to do to ensure the survival of his people, while the questions raised by this concrete situation are equally valid for other periods, and serve to prompt 'an analysis of historical processes'.[85] As Bródy put it, 'We tried to hold a mirror up to this country...to help our self-knowledge...and to realize that the problems that existed at the time of the country's establishment are still very severe problems to this day'.[86] According to Szörényi, the rock opera was to provide moral lessons to audiences.[87] What the problems (and possible solutions) were, however, intensely divided the population.

As early as in 1983–4, contrasting interpretations were voiced, and not necessarily along existing social divides.[88] There were those who objected to the nationalist veneer[89] or even 'red-white-and-green kitsch',[90] and those who welcomed the expression of 'healthy national feelings'.[91] There were those who saw the rock opera as depicting the historical choices in Stephen's lifetime,[92] those who diagnosed the archetypal historical conflict that is repeatedly manifest throughout Hungarian history,[93] and those who saw a piece about 'the problems

---

[85] Koltay, *István*, 27–30. See also Gábor Kapuvári's interview with Gábor Koltay, *Ifjúsági Magazin*, 19, no. 8 (1 August 1983), 31.

[86] At a meeting with the audience, 17 November 1983, Koltay, *István*, 94. Although Bródy also said that they had no clear goal: ibid., 91.

[87] Ferenc Török's interview with Levente Szörényi, *Magyar Ifjúság*, 32, no. 31 (29 July 1988), 42.

[88] For example, history teachers and young intellectuals were divided in their judgement: Koltay, *István*, 112–23, 144–8. See also Jávorszky, 'István a király—Koppány a szupersztár'; Sebők, *Rock a vasfüggöny mögött*, 367.

[89] E.g. Koltay, *István*, 144–5; especially concerning the finale: János Péter Sós, 'Sztár lett István király?', *Magyar Ifjúság*, 27, no. 35 (2 September 1983), 28–9, at 29, partly repr. Koltay, *István*, 44; János Péter Sós, 'Sztár lett-e István király? Egy kritika utóélete', *Magyar Ifjúság*, 27, no. 49 (9 December 1983), 27; Endre Varjas, *ÉS*, 26 August 1983, repr. Koltay, *István*, 45; Gábor Bányai, 'Minek tapsolunk', *Népszava*, 10 September 1983, 9 on 'nationalism fitted with a valve', repr. Koltay, *István*, 47–8; Bányai further elaborated in an interview in ibid., 109–10; Magyari, *Magyar Ifjúság*, 11 November 1983, 20–1, repr. Koltay, *István*, 84; ibid., 113–14 (Ferencné Bíró, history teacher); ibid., 141 (university students), ibid., 146 (young intellectuals); ibid., 152 (politician Imre Pozsgay). Some of the actors attributed criticism to envy or the fact that Hungarians have grown unaccustomed to the anthem: ibid., 57. Against critical views e.g. Tamás Mészáros, *Magyar Hírlap*, 16, no. 202 (27 August 1983), 7, repr. Koltay, *István*, 46. Similar controversy among high-school and university students: ibid., 134–5, 141–2.

[90] Erzsi Sándor, 'Megérteni a konfliktust', 126–7.

[91] Koltay, *István*, 57 (László Pelsőczy, actor playing Stephen). See also ibid., 34 (György Szomory, *Új Tükör*, 11 September 1983), 38 (Tibor Fábián, *Pesti Műsor*, 19–26 October 1983); ibid., 92–3 (audience meeting, 17 November 1983); ibid., 102 (Péter Korniss photographer); ibid., 112–13 (Béla Hódsági, history teacher); ibid., 146, 148 (young intellectuals), ibid., 174–75 (*Zalai Hírlap*, 30 April 1984); Tamás Kipke, *Új Ember*, 39, no. 37 (11 September 1983) [p. 4]. It 'gave the feeling of belonging to a national community': Feitl, *Magyar Ifjúság*, 27, no. 42 (21 October 1983), 41. It motivates to love the homeland: Koltay, *István, a király 1983–2008*, 24 (István Nemeskürty, Hungarian Radio programme *Táskarádió*, 28 August 1983). According to Koltay, politicians after seeing *István* said that 'national feeling, a healthy patriotism has to be developed': *Olvasó Nép*, 1983–4 winter, repr. Sebők, *Rock a vasfüggöny mögött*, 369.

[92] Fábri, 'Mítosz az egész nemzethez szólóan', 29, partly repr. Koltay, *István*, 32–3; ibid., 33 (Zsolt Kádár, *Reformátusok Lapja*, 11 September 1983); ibid., 34–5 (Zoltán Bóna, *Confessio*, 1983/4); ibid., 91–2 (audience meeting, 17 November 1983); ibid., 122.

[93] Tamás Mészáros, *Magyar Hírlap*, 16, no. 202 (27 August 1983), 7 (repr. Koltay, *István*, 33); Bányai, 'Minek tapsolunk', and in more detail in an interview: Koltay, *István*, 105–6; ibid., 100 (Iván Vitányi, who defined the conflict as progress and compromise vs. adhesion to traditions); 125

86   STEPHEN I, THE FIRST CHRISTIAN KING OF HUNGARY

of our own age'[94] (although two or more of these interpretations were often combined[95]). Those who enthused about finally encountering 'a normal historical perspective',[96] and those who objected to the clichéd historical approach to both the past and present.[97] There were those who claimed that the rock opera was essentially historically authentic, and those who maintained it was ahistorical and anachronistic.[98] There were those who applauded Stephen's wisdom, even if the choice was difficult and entailed sacrifices,[99] and those who mused about the 'what if', and the possible positive consequences of Koppány's victory.[100] Some saw the use of the national flag and anthem in the finale as a daring challenge to the regime, while others thought it an anachronistic misuse of national symbols, calculated to arouse an emotional response in the audience, unconnected to and undermining the rock opera, forcing the audience into identifying with and celebrating Stephen, overriding any other meaning.[101]

After the fall of communism, the divergence of opinions only grew. It is symptomatic that the two creators of the rock opera, Levente Szörényi (music) and János Bródy (lyrics), clashed politically after the fall of the party state in 1989. Szörényi sided with MDF, tending to the political right, Bródy with SZDSZ on the

(G. Koltay); 147 (young intellectuals, who drew a parallel with Kossuth and Széchenyi); 152 (György Fejti, KISZ); 175 (Ferenc Pallagi Szabó, Hungarian Radio programme *Láttuk, hallottuk*, 13 March 1984); János István Németh, 'István, a király', *Alföld: Irodalmi, művelődési és kritikai folyóirat*, 35 (1984): 92–5 (recurrent historical conflict between romantics who want independence and realists).

[94] Koltay, *István*, 57 (Kati Berek, actress playing Sarolt). See also ibid., 92 (parallel with 1945, audience meeting, 17 November 1983); 102 (Péter Korniss photographer, adding 'one should not learn history' from *István*); Péter Gál Molnár, 'István, a király', *Kritika*, 13, no. 5 (1984), 29.

[95] 'To speak to today by depicting a historical turning point': Koltay, *István*, 150 (politician Imre Pozsgay); see also 156–7 (politician L. Maróthy); 121–2 (K. Bakay); László Zöldi, *Népszabadság*, 42, no. 92 (19 April 1984), 7. Director Koltay suggested the rock opera was both about the historical Stephen and other turning points in Hungarian history: Koltay, *István*, 187, 189.

[96] Ibid., 127–8 (Béla Balás, Catholic priest); ibid., 174–5 (*Zalai Hírlap*, 30 April 1984).

[97] Klaniczay, *Filmvilág*, May 1984, repr. Koltay, *István*, 170.

[98] E.g. authentic: ibid., 118–19, 121 (K. Bakay archaeologist, historian, stating that two historical advisors, István Nemeskürty and György Györffy, ensured that); 156–8 (politician László Maróthy); emphasis on two historical advisors by director Koltay, ibid., 189. M. Boldizsár asserted that historical authenticity did not matter for the rock opera, but also that it called attention to works of historical scholarship not normally read by people: Gabriella Lőcsei interview with Miklós Boldizsár, *Magyar Nemzet*, 47, no. 53 (3 March 1984), repr. Koltay, *István*, 178. Anachronistic: László Bernáth, *Esti Hírlap*, 29, no. 92 (18 April 1984), [p. 2], partly repr. Koltay, *István*, 166. Ibid., 105–6 model-situation, therefore no attempt at historical authenticity.

[99] Fábri, 'Mítosz az egész nemzethez szólóan', 29 draws a parallel between Stephen and Christ. Koltay, *István*, 61 (interview with Nemeskürty, who claimed the fact that 'we can speak Hungarian in a Hungarian state today is thanks to Stephen'); ibid., 175 (*Zalai Hírlap*, 30 April 1984).

[100] Kipke, *Új Ember*, 11 September 1983; mentioned in Sós, 'Sztár lett', 28, repr. Koltay, *István*, 33, 34, respectively. University students' disagreement over the meaning of Torda's song: ibid., 140.

[101] Ibid., 44, 45, 47–8, 84, 104–11, 113–14, 141, 146, 152; Sándor, 'Megérteni a konfliktust', 126–7; Bányai, 'Minek tapsolunk'. Much later, Koltay stated that spectators were overjoyed to see the Hungarian flag without the communist red flag, it represented love of the homeland, and only detractors labelled it hidden nationalism: Koltay, *István, a király 1983-2008*, 8. Even some who welcomed the revival of national feeling objected to the clichéd use of the Hymn and flag: Letter by László Dezső, *Magyar Ifjúság*, 27, no. 45 (11 November 1983), 39.

STEPHEN, THE KING   87

political left.[102] They both continued to see the rock opera as an expression of a basic paradigm of Hungarian history and identity, but defined the latter in increasingly different ways.[103] Szörényi, seeking authenticity in pre-Christian times, talked about recovering the real Koppány.[104]

Such diverse interpretations signal the malleability of meaning.[105] This flexibility equally applies to the historical referent of the protagonists. The contested alleged national identity embodied in them can be made to fit a very wide range of characters from Hungary's past and present. Bródy stated: '*Stephen, the king* represents a social model that can be called general, whose characters can be allotted even to the present day among the public figures.'[106] This was indicated at the film's beginning, through the rapidly changing historical paintings depicting Péter Zrínyi, Ferenc Rákóczi II, István Széchenyi, and Lajos Kossuth: historical figures at decisive turning points in the traditional narrative of Hungarian history. Hungarian national myths surrounding these historical figures strongly evoke victimhood and defeat, as well as tragic infighting over the right course for the country, which depletes the nation.[107]

At the time of its premiere, however, the most resonant interpretation related the rock opera's hidden message to one particular defeated uprising and associated internal strife: 1956.[108] Some had no inkling of such an interpretation, and others rejected it (then or since).[109] Yet, while some interpreted Koppány's primacy in the audience's emotional identification as an accidental imbalance in the piece, many saw it as the authors' deliberate way of expressing their true feelings, condemning the regime. The year 1956, as the foundation of the Kádár regime, was inseparable from its real or supposed criticism. Koppány, understood as Imre Nagy, would therefore garner sympathy for political reasons. That *István, a király* could be read as a parable about the uprising of 1956 may seem to be an impossible assertion at first glance. Yet we should not forget that audiences in socialist Hungary were strongly attuned to hidden political messages; from Shakespeare plays to historical Hungarian pieces, cultural products were no mere entertainment, but carried actualized political references.[110] With open criticism prohibited, ingenious ways

---

[102] Miklós Győrffy interview with Bródy: 'Bródy János másfajta igazsága', *168óra*, 4, no. 30 (28 July 1992), 24–5; Koltay, *István, a király 1983–2008*, 10; Stumpf, *Szörényi*, 180–2, 192–3.

[103] János Bródy in *Magyar Nemzet*, 78, no. 193 (18 August 2015), 6; Szörényi on the constantly repeating pattern of tragic tensions in Hungarian history: Sebők, *Rock a vasfüggöny mögött*, 369.

[104] Levente Szörényi, 'Színház és történelem', *Szabad Föld*, 59, no. 33 (15 August 2003), 3.

[105] Everyone having their own interpretation: Jávorszky, cited in Povedák, 'Mitizált Történelem', 103.

[106] https://zene.hu/cikkek/cikk.php?id=13351&currentPage=3.

[107] Koltay, *István*, 147. Paul Lendvai, *The Hungarians: A Thousand Years of Victory in Defeat* (Princeton: Princeton University Press, 2004).

[108] Some commented that 'this should not frighten us': Koltay, *István*, 147. Sándor, 'Megérteni a konfliktust', 121–4, 126. Cf. note 17 above.

[109] Balázs Urbán, 'Szörényi-Bródy, István, a király', *Kritika*, 29, no. 9 (2000), 43–4, at 44.

[110] E.g. Sándor, 'Megérteni a konfliktust', 120. Another example: Shakespeare's Richard III was understood as targetting Rákosi in 1955: Aczél—Méray, *Tisztító vihar*, 379–80. Miklós Haraszti, 'Korai bevezetés a kádárizmusba. Ellenzéki látlelet 1981-ből', in Rácz, *Ki volt Kádár?*, 146–50.

88   STEPHEN I, THE FIRST CHRISTIAN KING OF HUNGARY

were found to express disagreement with official politics. The lyricist Bródy himself was adept at hiding political meaning in his songs.[111]

Contradictory opinions have been expressed on whether the creators of the rock opera meant to encode such a hidden political message. The origin of the assertion that they did has also been debated. In a contemporary interview, the author of the original play, Boldizsár, explicitly refuted the idea that any current political reference was included; this, however, was probably a mere nod to political taboos, since in the same interview he also said that the fate of those who failed at Hungarian historical turning points also had lessons to teach.[112] In various later interviews, János Bródy suggested that the echo of modern political events was embedded in the original play on which the rock opera was based, but was not particularly present in the rock opera itself, while Levente Szörényi explicitly rejected the idea that they had even ever considered to imply such a message.[113] It was Szörényi, however, who also stated that before the premiere, gossip from Party headquarters was seeping out that they understood Stephen to be Kádár and identified Koppány as Imre Nagy, who made a wrong decision at a historical turning point; and that the Party interpreted the piece as justifying Kádár. Szörényi added that this almost backfired, as the population understood the essence of the conflict.[114] Whether an intentional message or not, elements of the 1956 uprising can be certainly recognized in the rock opera, with the two key protagonists of 1956 easily substituted for the two main characters: János Kádár for Stephen, and Imre Nagy for Koppány.

In order to understand how Stephen and Koppány could be doubles for Kádár and Nagy, and why this would matter in 1983, when the uprising was still a taboo subject, as it was in the entire Kádár period, we need to go back to the history of the uprising and the subsequent establishment of the Kádár regime. The details matter, because understanding the rock opera's allusions depends on them.

4. 1956

In 1956, pent-up discontent broke out after nearly a decade-long oppression in the Stalinist mould under Mátyás Rákosi.[115] One of its protagonists, Imre Nagy,

---

[111] András Veres, 'Bródy János ürügyén', *Kritika*, 23, no. 6 (1994), 2; my interview with János Bródy, 10 August 2020.

[112] Repr. Koltay, *István*, 177–8.

[113] https://www.nlcafe.hu/sztarok/20170206/szorenyi-levente-brody-janos-cia-megfigyeles; in interview on 10 August 2020, Bródy said that he felt the resonances of 1956 when writing the lyrics, but it was not the key issue. Stumpf, *Szörényi*, 155, although he said that the 'Our sun has risen' song was modelled on those sung to greet Rákosi, ibid., p. 154.

[114] *Népszabadság*, 56, no. 194 (19 August 1998), cited in Jávorszky, 'István a király—Koppány a szupersztár'. Similar in Stumpf, *Szörényi*, 154–5. See also *Rendszerváltó archívum*, 2, no. 2 (June 2017), 86.

[115] Analyses are too numerous to list; classics and recent analyses include: Tibor Méray, *Thirteen days that shook the Kremlin*, tr. Howard L. Katzander (New York: Frederick A. Praeger, 1959); György Litván, ed. János M. Bak, tr. Lyman Howard Legters, *The Hungarian Revolution of 1956: Reform, Revolt*

STEPHEN, THE KING 89

before becoming the martyred hero of the revolution, had represented the hope of reformed socialism.[116] Nagy attempted to change the system a few years previously. On Soviet orders, he became Prime Minister on 4 July 1953.[117] The Soviet aim was to stabilize the system, and Nagy initiated the improvement of living standards, with revised industrial and agricultural policies, implemented greater religious tolerance, and ended the reign of terror, closing internment camps and discontinuing forced relocations.[118] Soon, he demanded the rehabilitation of those condemned at show trials.[119] In 1954, the stories of people released from prison opened the eyes of even many loyal communists to the true nature of the regime.[120] Nagy also tried to enable non-Party members to have at least a limited political activity.

Rákosi, who remained the General Secretary of the Party, and many of the old guard continued to hinder reforms and intrigued to have Nagy removed, portraying him in Moscow as undermining socialism. These intrigues, combined with changes in the balance of power within the Soviet Union, as well as a reappraisal of Soviet priorities, led to Nagy's removal from power. In 1955, condemned first as a 'right-wing deviationist', then as hostile to the Party (*párt-ellenes*), Nagy was deprived of his functions and offices.[121] With the return of collectivization and

---

and Repression, 1953–1963 (London and New York: Longman, 1996); Csaba Békés, Malcolm Byrne, János M. Rainer, ed., *The 1956 Hungarian Revolution: A History in Documents* (Budapest: CEU Press, 2002); Johanna Granville, *The First Domino: International Decision Making during the Hungarian Crisis of 1956* (College Station: Texas A & M University Press, 2004); Lee Congdon, Béla K. Király, Károly Nagy, ed., *1956: The Hungarian Revolution and War for Independence* (Boulder, CO—Highland Lakes, NJ: Social Science Monographs—Atlantic Research and Publications Inc, 2006); Charles Gati, *Failed Illusions: Moscow, Washington, Budapest, and the 1956 Hungarian Revolt* (Stanford: Stanford University Press, 2006), and Paul Lendvai, *Der Ungarnaufstand 1956: Die Revolution und ihre Folgen* (Munich: C. Bertelsmann Verlag, 2006). A selection of documents and analytic work: Attila Szakolczai, ed., *1956* (Budapest: Osiris Kiadó, 2006). Publications of the 1956-os Intézet (now suppressed by the government), provide detailed analyses, and László Eörsi's books treat especially the various armed rebel groups, see https://eorsilaszlo.hu/landing.php?target=el. Analytic bibliography in János M. Rainer, *Az 1956-os magyar forradalom* (Budapest: Osiris, 2016), 175–83.

[116] On Nagy: János M. Rainer, *Nagy Imre*, 2nd corr. enlarged edn (Budapest: Nagy Imre Alapítvány, 2016); in English, Rainer, *Imre Nagy. A biography*, tr. Lyman H. Legters (London–New York: Tauris, 2009). Of peasant origins, Nagy had been prisoner of war in Russia, where he joined the Communist Party, returned to Hungary in the 1920s, then spent fifteen years in the Soviet Union, returning to Hungary at the very end of 1944. After the war, he became minister of agriculture, overseeing land distribution to the peasantry, then Minister of the Interior until his resignation in March 1946. He opposed the quick transition to communism dictated in 1947–8, and was excluded from the Politburo in September 1949; Rainer, *Nagy*, 57–9.

[117] Rainer, *Nagy*, 70–4. Combination memoir and overview, Aczél—Méray, *Tisztító vihar* gives an excellent account of the contemporary impact of events; on Nagy's ascent, 147–59.

[118] Rainer, *Nagy*, 74–87.

[119] On 20 October 1954, he demanded the rehabilitation of Rajk and others: Vjacseszlav Szereda, János M. Rainer, ed., *Döntés a Kremlben, 1956. A szovjet pártelnökség vitái Magyarországról* (Budapest: 1956-os intézet, 1996), 165 (a translated document collection of the records of the Presidium meetings of the Soviet Communist Party's Central Committee). Rainer, *Nagy*, 87.

[120] Aczél—Méray, *Tisztító vihar*, 238–62.

[121] János M. Rainer, 'Döntés a Kremlben, 1956. Kísérlet a feljegyzések értelmezésére', in Szereda—Rainer, *Döntés*, 111–54, at 112. Rainer, *Nagy*, 77–8, 80–105. Aczél—Méray, *Tisztító vihar*, 160–79 on Rákosi's and 181–4, 263–6, 277–84, 315–20 on Party functionaries' activity against Nagy. Nagy protested and upheld the need to reform socialism: Rainer, *Nagy*, 107–15.

90 STEPHEN I, THE FIRST CHRISTIAN KING OF HUNGARY

heavy industrialization, hopes of reform were dashed, yet the rule of terror that had ensured compliance earlier had been relaxed, and anger and discontent intensified.[122]

Khrushchev's speech at a closed session of the 20th Congress of the Soviet Communist Party in February 1956, condemning Stalinism, while not made public officially, was a blow to the Rákosi regime. The Hungarian delegation reported on it in March to the Politburo; its main theses also became widely known from western media, and Radio Free Europe; the open criticism of Stalinist tenets was reported in the newspapers.[123] The rectification of errors and the question of leadership were at the centre of political machinations in Hungary for months, though Rákosi dodged acknowledging his personal role in the show trials.[124] Intellectual debates, especially in the Petőfi Kör (formed in March 1955, banned at the end of June 1956),[125] signalled the growing unwillingness to accept the political regime, while disagreement within the Party between the old guard and the reformers played out in tortuous ways.

Unexpectedly, a Soviet envoy oversaw the resignation of Rákosi ('at his own request') in July 1956; however, Ernő Gerő, who had been in the leadership along with Rákosi, replaced him.[126] Despite statements condemning earlier errors, and the removal of Mihály Farkas, another member of the Rákosi leadership, from the Party, the Politburo mainly tried to play for time and real change was far behind social expectations. The final spark came with the rehabilitation of László Rajk. Rajk and his co-defendants were the Hungarian victims of the show-trials conducted in the aftermath of Tito's Yugoslavia breaking with Stalin.[127] They were

---

[122] Aczél—Méray, *Tisztító vihar*, 232–4; account by the Soviet ambassador, Yuri Andropov, of conversation with Gerő on Nagy's influence and the danger (12 October 1956): Szereda—Rainer, *Döntés*, 164–70, at 165–6.

[123] Tibor Huszár, *Kádár János politikai életrajza 1912–1956*, vol. 1 (Budapest: Szabad Tér Kiadó—Kossuth Kiadó, 2001), 241–2; Aczél—Méray, *Tisztító vihar*, 373–8. The speech circulated in Poland, whence it also entered Hungary: Attila Pók, 'The year 1956—a watershed in Central European history', in *Remembering and Forgetting Communism in Hungary: Studies on Collective Memory and Memory Politics in Context* (Kőszeg-Budapest: iASK, 2017), 208–13, at 208.

[124] Huszár, *Kádár*, vol. 1, 232–73, especially 232–3, 241, 249. Rákosi released the information on Kádár's role in the Rajk trial: ibid., vol. 1, 250. Aczél—Méray, *Tisztító vihar*, 379–83.

[125] On young communist writers who turned against Stalinism (written in 1958): ibid. Examples of the problems ibid., 267–76, rebellion of the writers, 320–67, the role of the Petőfi Kör, 387–98.

[126] Soviet aims to renew relations with Tito, not just internal Hungarian intrigues, played a role. On the shock effect in Hungary, ibid., 399–406. Kádár was one of the possibilities, but was finally not chosen: Huszár, *Kádár*, vol. 1, 269–74.

[127] Tibor Zinner, *'A nagy politikai affér': a Rajk-Brankov ügy*, 2 vols. (Budapest: Saxum Kiadó, 2013–14); Tibor Hajdu, 'A Rajk-per háttere és fázisai', *Társadalmi Szemle*, 11 (1992), 17–36. According to the official charge, Rajk was a police, Gestapo, and American agent, his arrest and imprisonment in Vichy France's concentration camps was an elaborate ploy: *Vádirat Rajk László és társai elleni bűnügyben*, published by Miniszterelnökség sajtóosztálya (Budapest: Szikra Nyomda, 1949). The indictment and 'full confessions' of all the accused, including the reiterations that they confessed voluntarily, not under duress, and the verdicts were published in Hungarian and in translations in various languages: *Rajk László és társai a népbíróság előtt* (Budapest, Szikra Nyomda, 1949), see Zinner, *'A nagy politikai affér'*, vol. 2, 279–82. Reprint, with an introductory essay: Tibor Zinner: *Rajk László és társai a népbíróság előtt 40 év távlatából…Az ún. 'Kék könyv' hasonmás kiadása* (Budapest: Magyar

STEPHEN, THE KING   91

condemned to death in 1949 in order to 'prove' that Tito's spies had infiltrated the Party, trying to overthrow socialism.[128] Rajk had been a member of the then illegal Communist Party in the 1930s; fought in the Spanish civil war and was Minister of the Interior from March 1946 to August 1948, and Minister of Foreign Affairs thereafter until his arrest on 30 May 1949. Rajk and the others were publicly rehabilitated and reburied on 6 October 1956 in Budapest.[129]

University student demonstrations took place on the day, and students continued to organize throughout the country, creating the Alliance of Hungarian University and Polytechnic Students (MEFESZ). On 22 October, the Budapest Technical University's student assembly demanded the withdrawal of Soviet troops from Hungary, the reinstatement of national symbols and the restoration of a multi-party political system.[130] On 23 October, students issued their demands for immediate political and economic change (somewhat different versions were in circulation), and a student demonstration was announced. First prohibiting it around noon, the Minister of the Interior about two hours later authorized street assemblies. Mass demonstrations demanded the return of Nagy. Within the Party, those opposed to change spoke of a fascist counter-revolutionary attack the following day,[131] while various social groups declared programmes for national independence and democracy.[132] Imre Nagy, who had been reinstated as a Party member ten days earlier, gave a speech from a balcony of Parliament in the evening of 23 October, and accepted the role of prime minister on 24 October.[133] Initially he merely wanted to continue his 1953 programme to reform socialism, yet this was no longer enough to meet mass demand. Each day, he moved further towards multi-party democracy and independence.[134]

Demonstration mutated into uprising, with fighting on the streets by the night of 23 October; the army had been sent to protect parts of the city, for example, the Radio building, but switched sides. Khrushchev ordered Soviet tanks stationed in Hungary to restore order;[135] they were to act as a deterrent, but the uprising took

---

Eszperantó Szövetség, 1989). Sensationalizing accounts accepted the made-up story; see, for example, Derek Kartun, *Tito's Plot against Europe: The Story of the Rajk Conspiracy* (London: Lawrence & Wishart Ltd., 1949).

[128] George H. Hodos, *Show Trials: Stalinist Purges in Eastern Europe, 1948–1954* (New York, Westport Conn., and London: Praeger, 1987); Balázs Szalontai, 'Show trials', in *Encyclopedia of the Cold War*, ed. Ruud van Dijk et al. (London and New York: Routledge, 2008), 783–86.

[129] On Rákosi's and Soviet efforts to obstruct rehabilitation: Rainer 'Döntés', in Szereda—Rainer, *Döntés*, 116, on closed retrial at the end of 1955: Huszár, *Kádár*, vol. 1, 214.

[130] Reprint in Korányi, *Egy népfelkelés*, 43–4, no. 12.

[131] Cabinet statement on 24 October, reprint ibid., 56, no. 24; Kádár on 'counter-revolutionary elements', 24–5 October, reprint ibid., 58, no. 27, 60, no. 30. Even Nagy still used the term on 25 October, ibid., 61, no. 31.

[132] E.g. the Alliance of Hungarian Writers, reprint ibid., 59, no. 28.   [133] Rainer, *Nagy*, 120–8.

[134] Rainer, *Nagy*, 116–17, 123–63. Nagy's own account of the uprising and his policies: Imre Nagy, *Snagovi jegyzetek: Gondolatok, emlékezések 1956–1957*, ed. István Vida (Budapest: Gondolat Kiadó—Nagy Imre Alapitvány, 2006).

[135] Rainer, 'Döntés', in Szereda—Rainer, *Döntés*, 120–3.

92   STEPHEN I, THE FIRST CHRISTIAN KING OF HUNGARY

on the aspect of national liberation. Budapest was the centre of this, where armed insurgent groups formed spontaneously, but demonstrations and strikes spread around the country. Soviet armed forces fired on demonstrators in front of Parliament (25 October), killing about a hundred civilians.[136] Hard-liners wanted a military solution to put down the uprising, which, they feared, would sweep away the socialist system entirely, while reformers wanted to take the lead, seeing the uprising as a national democratic revolution that would trigger a positive transformation.

During the short-lived 1956 uprising, time accelerated. While Nagy, over the space of a few days, shifted from reform communism to declaring neutrality and democracy, János Kádár was first propelled to be a member of Nagy's revolutionary government, and then to betray it.[137] Kádár had joined the then illegal Communist Party in 1931, was a member of the Politburo from May 1945, and one of Rákosi's two deputies from September 1946. He took part in engineering the forced merger with the Social Democratic Party in 1948, and the same year he was appointed Deputy General Secretary of the Hungarian Workers' Party (MDP), and member of the State Security Committee; by the end of October 1948, Kádár together with Rákosi and Farkas were in charge of the State Security Bureau, that coordinated secret police operations.[138] Kádár had been Minister of the Interior at the time of Rajk's trial.[139] He was present at the meeting that decided Rajk's arrest, and was actively involved in creating the show-trial, whether out of fear or conviction, knowing the 'case' consisted of lies: he devised questions for Rajk, oversaw his interrogation, and personally told Rajk that the Party unanimously considered him to be an enemy, in order to convince him to confess to the trumped-up charges.[140] Not long after Rajk's execution, Kádár himself fell victim

[136] On events in the countryside: Attila Szakolczai—László Á. Varga, *A vidék forradalma, 1956*, 2 vols. (Budapest: 1956-os Intézet—Budapest Főváros Levéltára, 2003, 2006).

[137] Kádár was an illegitimate child and lived in deep poverty in his youth. Huszár, *Kádár*, vol. 1, 11–12 (joining Communist Party); 12–14 (imprisonments in 1930s); 28 (PB 1945); 31 (deputy); 33–4 (merger and deputy GS); 37 (activity in destroying other political parties); 37 (in State Security Committee and operative directing committee); 72, 75–7, 80–111, 116–36 (roles 1945–9, up to Rajk's arrest). In English, Gough, *Good Comrade*.

[138] State Security Committee: Államvédelmi Bizottság. State Security Bureau: Államvédelmi Hivatal (the secret police, ÁVH was part of this Bureau).

[139] Kádár took over the role from Rajk himself, who was moved to the Foreign Ministry in August 1948: Huszár, *Kádár*, vol. 1, 125–8; Gough, *Good Comrade*, 36. On Kádár's insincere manipulations for power: Huszár, *Kádár*, vol. 1, 121.

[140] Huszár, *Kádár*, vol. 1, 141–53 (from July 1949, a Soviet Lieutenant General directed the case and Kádár had no further role: 151); Zinner, 'A nagy politikai affér', vol. 1, 323–4, 341–2, 348–53; on Kádár personally questioning Rajk: 335–6, 338–9; on Kádár's presence at execution: vol. 2, 286 (also Huszár, *Kádár*, vol. 1, 152–3). Later myth that Kádár was a mere puppet of Rákosi, denying his active involvement: Zinner, 'A nagy politikai affér', vol. 1, 355, cf. Huszár, *Kádár*, vol. 1, 148. László Varga, *Kádár János bírái előtt. Egyszer fent, egyszer lent. 1949–1956* (Budapest: Osiris—Budapest Főváros Levéltára, 2001), 16–23, 58–63, suggests his rivalry with Rajk and desire for power motivated Kádár: 672, 675–7. The transcript of the tape recording Kádár's interrogation of Rajk (the tape does not survive) is controversial. With evidence supporting its authenticity: Tibor Hajdú, 'Farkas és Kádár Rajknál. Az 1949. június 7-i beszélgetés hiteles szövege', *Társadalmi Szemle*, 47 (1992, no. 4): 76–89;

to the continued repression: first replaced as Minister of the Interior in June 1950, then arrested in 1951, condemned to life imprisonment in a secret trial the following year, he was released in 1954 during the rehabilitations under Nagy's first premiership.[141] Cautiously, and according to some, deviously, navigating between Rákosi and those wanting reform, he rose to become a member of the Politburo in July 1956.[142] Party functionaries wanting reform saw their leader in Kádár, while intellectuals coalesced around Imre Nagy. Some of the latter tried to create an alliance between Kádár and Nagy; Kádár was unwilling.[143] Although he pushed for speedier rehabilitations and more permissiveness, he failed to realize the depth of popular discontent.[144] He was mostly abroad on Party business, and returned from a trip with a Party delegation to Yugoslavia on 23 October.

As a member of the Politburo, Kádár did not oppose Soviet intervention on 23 October.[145] Subsequently, trying to occupy the middle ground and to gauge the wishes of the 'working class', he modified his message each day, from the need to crush the counter-revolutionaries to the necessity for a political solution. He remained hesitant over many of the details and defined the uprising as part justified demonstration, part counter-revolutionary activity.[146] On 25 October, Kádár became First Secretary with Soviet acquiescence as Ernő Gerő was forced out.[147] From 30 October, he was a member of the Nagy government as Minister of State.

Kádár's ascent could not obscure the fact that the Party lost all influence over the unfolding revolt. It scrambled to address that problem, but its reactions were belated and unsatisfactory. On 28 October, a new Presidium was formed to take over the

Eng. tr. Tibor Hajdú, 'The Party did everything for you. Preparing the show trial: Farkas and Kádár visit Rajk', *The Hungarian Quarterly*, 37, no. 141 (1996): 82–99. Nagy, *Snagovi jegyzetek*, 90 mentioned the recording; according to him, Kádár spoke to Rajk in a despicable, rude, provocative way (Nagy also discusses Kádár's role in other arrests, and his cowardice in blaming others to disculpate himself: 89–91). Varga, *Kádár János bírái előtt*, 157–70 reprint of transcript, which is 'truncated' according to a committee reviewing the case of Kádár and Farkas in 1956: ibid., 23. See also Gough, *Good Comrade*, 41–5. In 1954, still in prison, Kádár was asked to write down his opinion on the Rajk case; he probably guessed that the case was under review and wrote it was 'without real foundation', 'provocation by an imperialist spy association through Gábor Péter': 'Kádár János Rajk Lászlóról. Kádár János sajátkezű feljegyzése Budapest, 1954. július hó 20', in Rácz, *Ki volt Kádár?*, 47–8, quotation at 47.

[141] Huszár, *Kádár*, vol. 1, 154–220; Varga, *Kádár János bírái előtt*, 58–122 (the volume contains the edition of the trial materials, including Kádár's interrogation and rehabilitation); Gough, *Good Comrade*, 48–61, 63–6. Whether Kádár was tortured is debated: he initially said he had been (Aczél— Méray, *Tisztító vihar*, 244–5), but once in power, denied it (Huszár, *Kádár*, vol. 1, 175–6). Torture was a routine part of forcing confessions from those arrested. On this and myths about Kádár during his lifetime: Bihari, 'Kádár és rendszere', 153.

[142] Varga, *Kádár János bírái előtt*, 677; Huszár, *Kádár*, vol. 1, 248–55, 270–6; Gough, *Good Comrade*, 74. Directly after his release, Kádár sided with Rákosi, rather than Nagy: Huszár, *Kádár*, vol. 1, 221–30; Varga, *Kádár János bírái előtt*, 127–8; Gough, *Good Comrade*, 67–9. After his release, he was initially Party District Secretary for Budapest's 13th district.

[143] Huszár, *Kádár*, vol. 1, 248–9, 256–60.   [144] Ibid., 281–97.   [145] Ibid., 299–300.

[146] Ibid., 300–10, 316–28. Summary on Kádár's role between 23 October and 1 November: Gough, *Good Comrade*, 77–91.

[147] Rainer, 'Döntés', in Szereda—Rainer, *Döntés*, 123; Huszár, *Kádár*, vol. 1, 300–1. The MDP's leader was called General Secretary until 1953, and First Secretary thereafter.

94   STEPHEN I, THE FIRST CHRISTIAN KING OF HUNGARY

functions of the Party's Central Committee and the Politburo.[148] The same day the government's radio broadcast announced a ceasefire and reforms, including disbanding the feared State Security Police and the creation of a socialist democracy. The broadcast also relayed the Soviet promise to withdraw from Budapest, and indicated that the government initiated talks on the complete withdrawal of Soviet troops from Hungary; the uprising was now called a 'national democratic movement'.[149] Hardliners in the Party leadership left for the Soviet Union. Popular demand, however, called for far more than the reform of Stalinist communism. The rebels refused to put down arms, demanding the immediate withdrawal of Soviet troops, and the reintroduction of a multi-party system; strikes continued.

On 30 October, Nagy announced on radio the abolition of the one-party system.[150] Previously banned political parties such as the Social Democrats and Peasants' Party started to re-form. A new seven-member inner cabinet was established, comprising three communists including Kádár. Kádár declared a renewal of the Party; retrospectively, he stated that he had believed significant communist influence could be retained within the multi-party system; he warned against military intervention, as it would transform the uprising into a national war against the Soviet Union.[151] After sporadic lynchings in previous days of people accused of having worked for the State Security forces, the headquarters of the Party in Budapest, defended by police who until a few days before had been members of the State Security, were besieged and many of its defenders killed. Some of the armed rebels tried to establish an alternative government. On 31 October, the Hungarian Workers' Party (MDP) was dissolved, and the Hungarian Socialist Workers' Party (MSZMP) established with Kádár as General Secretary, to signal a break with the past.[152]

Matching the quickly unfolding events in Hungary, the Soviet position changed rapidly as well. After a show of force, the Soviet leadership postponed the final decision.[153] From 26 October, the Soviet Central Committee debated possible alternatives; some members wanted the withdrawal of Soviet troops from Hungary.[154] On 30 October, the Soviet government issued a statement suggestive

---

[148]   Ibid., 321–4.

[149]   Text in László Varga, ed., *A forradalom hangja. Magyarországi rádióadások 1956 október 23.–november 9.* (Budapest: Századvég Kiadó—Nyilvánosság Klub, 1989), 131–2; national democratic movement on 131. State Security Police: ÁVH, Államvédelmi Hatóság; prior to September 1948, called ÁVO.

[150]   Varga, *A forradalom hangja*, 226.

[151]   Huszár, *Kádár*, vol. 1, 318–20 (11 November 1956, the first meeting of the Temporary Central Committee of MSZMP).

[152]   Ibid., 321–4; Szereda—Rainer, *Döntés*, 79.

[153]   Soviet envoys' positive assessment on ease of military solution, 24 October: ibid., 181–5. On 26 October, they reported on Soviet successes and berated the effectiveness of Hungarian police and civil forces used against the counterrevolution: ibid., 186–8.

[154]   On 28 October, Soviet envoys reported that if the revolt continued, the USA might demand UN intervention: ibid., 197. On the Soviet debates and decisions, discussing military intervention on 28 October, Rainer, 'Döntés', in Szereda—Rainer, *Döntés*, 125–33. János M. Rainer, 'A Szovjetunió', in

STEPHEN, THE KING   95

of a peaceful solution. Promising to develop friendship and cooperation with socialist countries, it declared that while the Hungarian workers had been justified in demanding the eradication of serious problems, reactionary and counter-revolutionary forces had tried to take advantage of the workers' discontent to restore the old landholding and capitalist system. Therefore, at the demand of the Hungarian government, the Soviet government had agreed to send troops to Budapest to help the Hungarian army to restore order (a reference to 23 October); however, aware that the continued presence of Soviet troops in Hungary may serve as a pretext for further escalation, the Soviet government was ready to withdraw its troops from Budapest at Hungarian demand, and to negotiate about the presence of Soviet troops in Hungary.[155] This decision was predicated on the idea that Nagy would stabilize the situation, and the Communist Party would retain its leading political position. The following day (31 October) Khrushchev at the meeting of the Presidium of the Central Committee of the Communist Party of the Soviet Union decided on military intervention, sending further troops from the Soviet Union. He seems to have been motivated by the fear that not doing so would undermine the Soviet Bloc, and he received reassurance from the USA that they would not intervene.[156] Details were discussed the following day,[157] and plans for the intervention completed on 2 November.[158]

Nagy was apprised of Soviet troop movements into Hungary that started on 31 October. He demanded an explanation several times on 1 November from the Soviet ambassador, Yuri Andropov (future General Secretary of the Soviet Union, 1982–4), who responded by a series of farcical lies.[159] While it became obvious that a military intervention had started, no official declaration was issued by the Soviets. Nagy, hoping for western help, declared Hungary's withdrawal from the Warsaw Pact (the 1955 military alliance of Soviet Bloc countries), and declared

Evolúció és revolúció: Magyarország és a nemzetközi politika 1956-ban, ed. Csaba Békés (Budapest: 1956-os Intézet—Gondolat Kiadó, 2007), 31–54, at 48–9.

[155] Szereda—Rainer, *Döntés*, 202 (entire document 200–2). On Soviet decision-making on 30 October, Rainer, 'Döntés', in Szereda—Rainer, *Döntés*, 134–40. On 30 October, A. Mikoyan and M. Suslov reported worrying deterioration, open revolt, and the occupation of Party buildings: ibid., 198–9.

[156] Ibid., 64, 73, on debates 62–73. Although not confronting Nagy openly, the opinion in Moscow on 30 October was that he betrayed the Party and was playing a 'double game': ibid., 51, 55, 56, 57. On Soviet decision-making on 31 October, Rainer, 'Döntés', in Szereda—Rainer, *Döntés*, 140–3.

[157] Ibid., 69–73. On Soviet decision-making on 1 November, Rainer 'Döntés', in Szereda—Rainer, *Döntés*, 144–5.

[158] Ibid., 86–7. On Soviet decision-making on 2 November, Rainer 'Döntés', in Szereda—Rainer, *Döntés*, 145. Over these two days, the consent of other Soviet Bloc countries' leaders was secured.

[159] Kádár's account on 2 November in Moscow: 'we were told that Soviet troops in motor cars crossed the border' and the question was raised whether the Hungarian army should shoot at them; Andropov was called in, who 'said these are railwaymen. From the Hungarian border they sent a telegram that they are not railwaymen. Then came the notification that Soviet tanks are approaching Szolnok. This was at noon. There was a nervous mood in the government. We called in Andropov. He responded it was due to regrouping. Then came the new report: the airport was surrounded by Soviet tanks. Again we called in Andropov. He responded: wounded soldiers are being transported. Nagy was convinced that an attack was being prepared against Budapest.' Ibid., 78.

96   STEPHEN I, THE FIRST CHRISTIAN KING OF HUNGARY

Hungary's neutrality.[160] János Kádár participated in this decision,[161] but soon ended up on a separate path. At the demand of the Soviets, on 1 November late at night, Ferenc Münnich (Interior Minister in Nagy's government), misleading Kádár as to their purpose, took him to the Soviet embassy; they were secretly flown to Moscow without the knowledge of other members of the government.[162] On 2–3 November, they took part in the meetings of the Presidium of the Central Committee of the Communist Party of the Soviet Union.[163]

The reality of the international situation did not match the hopes of the rebels.[164] The Soviets were afraid that non-intervention would be construed as weakness by the West and Hungary would be lost. Leaders of Soviet Bloc countries were worried about the unrest spreading. The Suez crisis preoccupied the Security Council of the United Nations, which only started seriously to take stock of the Hungarian events after the start of the Soviet attack. The USA decided against military aid to Hungary, avoiding direct confrontation with the Soviet Union; the Soviets were thus reassured that a (nuclear) world war would not break out if they quashed the revolt.[165] An independent, neutral Hungary with a multi-party system was not on the cards, although the rebels did not know that.

For a couple of days, an ambiguous situation reigned in Hungary. Fighting ceased, although the rebels kept their arms. Nagy still thought it was possible to negotiate with the Soviets, who were actively misleading him, while it must have dawned on Kádár in Moscow that he was faced with a stark choice: accept the irrevocable Soviet decision to intervene, become head of state in Hungary, and try to salvage the situation, or stay loyal to Nagy and fall with him.[166] Initially, he

---

[160] Announcement on radio: Varga, *A forradalom hangja*, 357–8, 361. On 2–3 November, Nagy also asked G. Gheorghiu-Dej, the First Secretary of the Romanian Workers' Party for advice and to mediate: ibid., 91, 95.

[161] Huszár, *Kádár*, vol. 1, 325–7. Kádár's testimony in Moscow the following day concerning this unanimous government decision: Szereda—Rainer, *Döntés*, 79.

[162] Nagy initially thought Kádár and Münnich had been abducted by the Soviets: ibid., 82–3; Nagy, *Snagovi jegyzetek*, 69–70; Rainer, *Nagy*, 157–9. Kádár was unaware of the plan to fly him to Moscow (he made a radio speech on the formation of the new Party on 1 November, in which he called the events a glorious revolution against the Rákosi regime, and backed the demand for Soviet troop withdrawal), and was initially reluctant; it is unknown how he was persuaded: Vida, 'Bevezető', 41–2; Huszár, *Kádár*, vol. 1, 329–35. On Kádár's activities on 1–7 November, see also Gough, *Good Comrade*, 93–102.

[163] Szereda—Rainer, *Döntés*, 75–90.

[164] On various countries' reaction, Békés, *Evolúció és revolúció*.

[165] An early analysis on international constraints, covering the aftermath to 1963: János Radványi, *Hungary and the Superpowers: The 1956 Revolution and Realpolitik* (Stanford, CA: Hoover Institution Press, 1972). Gati, *Failed Illusions* argues that a more restrained Hungarian demand (along the lines of the 30 October first resolution) could have succeeded.

[166] Nagy's own fate was not decided yet in Moscow; on 1 November, there were different opinions on whether Nagy's name was merely used by the rebels or whether he was backing them: Szereda—Rainer, *Döntés*, 70. On 3 November, according to a Hungarian report written at the meeting, Khrushchev said Nagy was a traitor, and if he did not resign, it was in the service of the enemy: ibid., 93.

presented himself as a member of the Nagy government, albeit pointing out some of the dangers and 'counter-revolutionary aspects' of Nagy's policy, and argued that military intervention would destroy the moral position of the communists completely. By 3 November, however, he agreed with the necessity of Soviet military intervention against the counter-revolution, and accepted the Soviet decision that he would be Prime Minister, at the head of a new government.[167] He was, however, able to refuse the inclusion of earlier hard-liners now in exile in the Soviet Union and to insist on condemning the mistakes of the Rákosi leadership in the declaration to be read out on radio after his return to Hungary.[168]

The seeming ambiguity evaporated in Hungary on 4 November with the start of the Soviet military attack.[169] Nagy's last speech broadcast on radio at 5.20 a.m. informed 'the population of the country and the public opinion of the world' about the Soviet attack 'to overthrow the legal, democratic Hungarian government'.[170] Later the same day, the establishment and programme of Kádár's 'Hungarian revolutionary workers' and peasants' government' (including his break with Nagy) was announced on radio and via leaflets.[171] According to this, a justified mass movement to rectify the sins of Rákosi and his associates was infiltrated by counter-revolutionaries; members of the former Arrow Cross Party (the Hungarian Nazi party) and other reactionaries started to murder democrats and patriots, due to the weakness of Nagy's government, endangering socialist achievements. Therefore, the new government was formed, and it called on the High Command of the Soviet army to help restore order. The Yugoslavs, after secret negotiations with the Soviets, offered refuge to Nagy and other members of his government at the Yugoslav embassy; including family members, forty-two

---

[167] On these two days, see Huszár, *Kádár*, vol. 1, 336–48; Gough, *Good Comrade*, 93–9. Kaganovitsch at the Presidium of the Soviet Communist Party's Central Committee on 28 October wanted to demand more firmness from Kádár to neutralize the counter-revolution: Szereda—Rainer, *Döntés*, 36–7, although many still wondered whether Nagy will turn against the Soviets: 37–45. On 31 October, Khrushchev hesitated between Kádár and Münnich to lead the new government: ibid., 62–4; Huszár, *Kádár*, vol. 1, 314–15; the ousted Rákosi, Hegedüs and Gerő backed Münnich: Rainer, 'Döntés', in Szereda—Rainer, *Döntés*, 143. On Yugoslav influence on Khrushchev to choose Kádár: Huszár, *Kádár*, vol. 1, 335–6. On 28 January 1958, in Parliament, Kádár claimed that Münnich almost became Prime Minister, but asked that Kádár be appointed, as he had been away from Hungary for so long: Kádár, *Szilárd népi hatalom*, 368. Münnich was named Deputy Prime Minister.

[168] Szereda—Rainer, *Döntés*, 88–90. Refuting the idea that Khrushchev was ready to reinstall Rákosi: Huszár, *Kádár*, vol. 1, 341–2.

[169] On 4 November, Marshal I. Konev's order to attack stated that former Horthyists were restoring fascism in Hungary, so at the demand of the Hungarian government (no names are mentioned) the Soviet army is carrying out its duty of protection according to the Warsaw Pact: Szereda—Rainer, *Döntés*, 203–4. Imre Nagy later wrote that by 4 November, order had been restored in Hungary, but the Soviet military attack led to an armed fight: Nagy, *Snagovi jegyzetek*, 66–7.

[170] Korányi, *Egy népfelkelés*, 112, no. 77; Varga, *A forradalom hangja*, 487. Between 4 and 9 November, radio stations repeatedly called for external help against the Soviet attack: ibid., 490–506.

[171] This was largely composed in Moscow before Kádár was chosen to head the new government: Huszár, *Kádár*, vol. 1, 339, finalized with Kádár's corrections ibid., 347–8. Radio: Varga, *A forradalom hangja*, 489. Text of leaflets in Korányi, *Egy népfelkelés*, 113–16, nos. 79–80. Cf. Gough, *Good Comrade*, 100–2.

98   STEPHEN I, THE FIRST CHRISTIAN KING OF HUNGARY

people proceeded to seek asylum there.[172] The Yugoslav ambassador asked Nagy for a written statement that he would accept Kádár's new government; Nagy, however, refused.[173] Kádár flew back to Hungary on the same day; and was taken to Budapest by Soviet tanks on the night of 6–7 November.[174]

After days of fighting, a significant Soviet military force crushed resistance by 11 November. Nagy stayed at the Yugoslav embassy, while the Kádár government took power.[175] Yet Kádár lacked effective authority and legitimacy. Economic production and the administrative system were near-collapse; the armed forces were not loyal to the new government. Within the Party, Kádár was faced by reformers who wanted to continue Nagy's programme and hard-liners who wanted to return to the policies of pre-1953 days. This was compounded by dictates from the Soviet leadership. Neither Hungarian popular nor international opinion regarded his government as legitimate. Antagonism and the lack of popular support were manifest at home, through strikes and the opposition at workers' councils, as well as abroad, where the UN put the 'Hungarian question' on its agenda, condemning cruel repression and Soviet intervention. Crucially, nobody was able to persuade Nagy to resign, and open the route to legitimacy for the Kádár government. The latter was seen as the heir of the regime the uprising had rejected.[176]

The ambiguity of Kádár's position was acute. In Moscow on 2 November, he had not known what to expect and was cautious, while also trying to justify his own actions. He insisted that it had been a mistake to brand the rebels counter-revolutionaries, as it alienated people who were fighting to remove the Rákosi clique, rather than to overthrow the 'people's democracy'. He also emphasized that masses in the countryside demonstrated for social change and democratization, and that workers and Party members led the rebels and armed resistance.[177] He claimed that counter-revolutionary bands subsequently formed within those armed groups, although he acknowledged everyone wanted the withdrawal of Soviet troops. Kádár also alleged that Nagy resorted to counter-revolutionary measures, that every passing hour increased the shift to the right, and the Austrians supported a Hungarian fascist (Horthyist) organization.[178] He

---

[172] György Litván, 'A Nagy Imre-per politikai háttere', in A per: Nagy Imre és társai, ed. Alajos Dornbach, Péter Kende, János M. Rainer, Katalin Somlai (Budapest: 1956-os Intézet—Nagy Imre Alapítvány, 2008), 41–62, here 45–6; Rainer, Nagy, 163–6.

[173] Message by Edvard Kardelj, vice-president of the Yugoslav government, on 4 November, transmitted by the Soviet ambassador: Szereda—Rainer, Döntés, 209. The Soviet ambassador was instructed to respond that, while earlier a public statement from Nagy—at the time prime minister—would have facilitated defeating the counter-revolution, it was no longer needed; Nagy and his group should be handed over to the Soviet troops who would then transfer them to the Hungarian government: ibid., 99.

[174] Tibor Huszár, Kádár János politikai életrajza 1957. November–1989. június, vol. 2 (Budapest: Szabad Tér Kiadó—Kossuth Kiadó, 2003), 5.

[175] Kádár was both General Secretary and Prime Minister until January 1958, and again between 1961 and 1965, when he resigned from the latter position.

[176] Zoltán Ripp, 'Az MSZMP legitimációja a Kádár-korszak kezdetén', in Restauráció vagy kiigazítás: A kádári represszió intézményesülése 1956-1962, ed. Tibor Huszár, János Szabó (Budapest: Zrínyi Kiadó, 1999), 43–65, at 43.

[177] Szereda—Rainer, Döntés, 75.   [178] Ibid., 76–7.

equivocated on the issue of Soviet military intervention and cautiously expressed support for a peaceful solution, including the withdrawal of Soviet troops, although he said he feared such a peaceful approach might not succeed; however, he stated more firmly that a military solution would ruin the moral position of communists and harm socialist countries.[179] On 3 November, after a meeting with Khrushchev,[180] and as the newly selected head of government, he was already more categorical: while condemning the long-time Soviet support of Rákosi and Gerő (Khrushchev had backed Gerő to replace Rákosi in July 1956[181]), he also stated that communists were being murdered in Hungary and Nagy's government lacked both the power and the will to crush the counter-revolutionaries. Therefore, a revolutionary government had to be formed. Yet he still reiterated that the entire population had risen up, that Soviet troops should be withdrawn, and he also mentioned how national feelings were hurt, for example, by having to imitate Soviet military uniform and name streets after Soviet citizens in Hungary.[182] He asserted: 'This government should not be a puppet government, and the support of the workers is necessary for its activities.'[183]

As the new head of government he was bound by Soviet decisions, indeed, was under direct Soviet supervision,[184] but he also tried to gain popular legitimacy, claiming to occupy the middle ground.[185] The declaration of the new Kádár government on 4 November to the Hungarian people, while justifying taking power and Soviet intervention, also tried to appease the population. It asserted that while the Rákosi-Gerő clique had done grave harm to the legal order, and much needed to be rectified, the reactionaries were only pursuing their own interests to restore feudal-capitalist oppression, and misled many honest patriots; the latter should not be condemned. The rule of workers and peasants must be upheld and the ravages of counter-revolutionaries ended. Promises of material goods, more apartments, increased

---

[179] Ibid., 80–1.   [180] Rainer, 'Döntés', in Szereda—Rainer, *Döntés*, 148.

[181] According to a Hungarian report of the meeting on 3 November, Khrushchev said it had been a mistake to support Gerő, incapable of standing up to Rákosi, instead of Kádár: ibid., 92.

[182] Both a Soviet and an independent Hungarian record was made, consisting of notes jotted down during the meeting. Soviet record of Kádár's statements: ibid., 88–90; Hungarian record: ibid., 92–5, at 94. The substance is the same, except when Kádár says that Nagy provides cover for the killing of communists, the Hungarian note says that is just a false impression; the Soviet version omitted this, thereby lending a different meaning to Kádár's words. The Hungarian note is also more detailed on the Soviets offending national feelings, mentioning the coat-of-arms, Transylvania, and Upper Hungary (the areas of the Kingdom of Hungary that became part of Romania and Slovakia, respectively).

[183] Ibid., 90. On Kádár's interventions on 2–3 November, cf. also Rainer, 'Döntés', in Szereda—Rainer, *Döntés*, 146–50. The title of Kádár's collected speeches published in 1959 also reflected this: 'Stable people's power: independent Hungary'.

[184] Initially, the Soviet army and three members of the Soviet Central Committee—G. M. Malenkov, M. A. Suslov, and A. B. Aristov—were in Hungary to oversee the establishment of the new regime; in early December, the three CC members left, but open and covert Soviet methods to control Kádár continued even in 1957: Huszár, *Kádár*, vol. 2, 8–26. Tibor Huszár, 'A hatalmi gépezet újjáépítése, a represszió túlsúlya, a kiigazítás esélye; 1956–1960', in Huszár—Szabó, *Restauráció vagy kiigazítás*, 67–146; Gough, *Good Comrade*, 104–5. Litván, 'A Nagy Imre-per politikai háttere', 46.

[185] Ripp, 'Az MSZMP legitimációja', 48. Gough, *Good Comrade*, 103–7, on the early days (to the end of November).

100 STEPHEN I, THE FIRST CHRISTIAN KING OF HUNGARY

democracy, and an end to the compulsory agricultural quotas were included. Furthermore, the government promised to start negotiations about the withdrawal of Soviet troops after the Soviet army helped to restore order.[186] Kádár also sent a telegram to the UN, dated 4 November, branding Nagy's request to the UN to discuss the Hungarian situation unlawful and categorically objecting to any such discussion.[187]

5. The Early Kádár Regime: Reprisals and the Judicial Murder of Nagy

As Kádár struggled to establish himself in Hungary, even continued Soviet backing was not a foregone conclusion. On 6 November, the Presidium of the Central Committee of the Communist Party of the Soviet Union discussed whether to pressure Kádár to restore the Party's name to Hungarian Workers' Party (Magyar Dolgozók Pártja), and demand removing the designation 'Rákosi clique', or whether to influence Kádár in a 'tactical manner', finally deciding to communicate the desired changes to Kádár 'tactfully'.[188]

Although initially arrests in reprisal were carried out by the Soviets, even ignoring Kádár's protests, and some of those arrested were secretly taken to the USSR, soon the Soviets left retaliation to the Kádár government.[189] From that point, the Party leadership decided on what to brand 'counter-revolutionary crimes'.[190] At the end of November, a declaration that the counter-revolution would be suppressed by firm action signalled the start of years of repression and reprisals by the Hungarian authorities, breaking Kádár's earlier promise not to punish participants of the uprising.[191] Special army units and special forces were established under government control. People criticizing the new regime were dismissed from their job, and any glorification of the October revolt was suppressed. From December, mass arrests and imprisonment terrorized the population, and attempts at mass demonstration were met by the military forces opening fire.[192] Martial law with the death sentence was introduced at Soviet initiative,[193]

---

[186] Korányi, *Egy népfelkelés*, 114–16, no. 80; Szereda—Rainer, *Döntés*, 205–8.

[187] Ibid., 99. Similarly Kádár's speech to Party's executive committee, 23 August 1957, in Kádár, *Szilárd népi hatalom*, 257–8; 'a Hungarian issue exists only in the dictionary of imperialists, the statement on Hungary consists only of lies, and serves the interests of American imperialists', speech for visiting Mongolian party functionaries, 11 September 1957, ibid., 286.

[188] Szereda—Rainer, *Döntés*, 101–7.

[189] Tibor Zinner, *A kádári megtorlás rendszere* (Budapest: Hamvas Intézet, 2001), 11–37.

[190] On decisions about who to punish, ibid., 197–213, 428; on Party directing reprisals, ibid., 215–335.

[191] Huszár, *Kádár*, vol. 2, 7–8.

[192] On repression, Huszár, 'A hatalmi gépezet újjáépítése'; Zinner, *A kádári megtorlás*; Gough, *Good Comrade*, 108.

[193] Huszár, 'A hatalmi gépezet újjáépítése', 80; 1 December 1956, government decree on martial law: Korányi, *Egy népfelkelés*, 174–7, no. 111; extension of martial law on 11 December: ibid., 186–7, no. 115.

and internment camps were re-established. Military courts condemned some of the leaders of the revolt, henceforth officially called counter-revolution.[194] From January, calling for strikes was punishable under martial law. A 'workers' militia' was organized in February 1957, creating a loyal paramilitary corps.

Reprisals escalated over time. On 26 November 1956, Kádár, together with the Soviets, decided that five to seven people who had led the armed rebellion should be executed to facilitate the pacification of the country; military tribunals were to judge the accused.[195] From early 1957, the day-to-day organization of retaliation was left to the Kádár government and the Party in Hungary.[196] At first, judgements were pronounced through court martial and fast-track procedures; eventually, people's courts were created, and participation in 1956 was now treated as criminal, rather than as political activity. At the same time, resignations in protest and removals significantly affected the judiciary, judges, and prosecutors.[197] Retaliation was extended to ever-broader circles, and attempts to restart protests in March were suppressed.[198] Kádár's rhetoric suggested the government had been too lenient and the population rightly called for harsher punishments.[199] He backed the use of force and death sentences against 'class enemies' who threatened the People's Republic, and escalated reprisals in April and May 1957, which lasted several years.[200] In December 1957, he spoke at the Central Committee of seventy to eighty more people to be punished, yet in October 1958, he mentioned around 600 more.[201] As late as 1961, people were condemned to death and executed for their role in the uprising. More than 20,000 people were condemned to prison and internment camps, with even more dismissed from their job, and at least 225 people were executed between 1957 and 1961, among them István Angyal, a survivor of Auschwitz.[202]

---

[194] See below. [195] Zinner, *A kádári megtorlás*, 30–1.
[196] Ibid., 39–55. The Soviets followed events and the possibility of interference did not cease: Huszár, *Kádár*, vol. 2, 25–6.
[197] On the judicial framework, laws and personnel: Zinner, *A kádári megtorlás*, 105–95.
[198] Detailed analysis in Huszár, 'A hatalmi gépezet újjáépítése'.
[199] Kádár, *Szilárd népi hatalom*, 35–6 (2 February 1957, MSZMP conference, Salgótarján). He also spoke of continued lurking danger, need for alertness and repression: e.g. speech on the return of a Party delegation from a visit to the Soviet Union, 31 March 1957, ibid., 55. In an interview given to Unità, 18 April 1957, ibid., 68 he emphasized the government's lenience with only forty death sentences. In his 1 May 1957 speech, he claimed that contrary to 'imperialist' allegations of terror in Hungary, in fact 'our people rightly objects to the fact that those guilty have not been sufficiently punished;' 'our institutions only satisfy the demands of humanitarianism and democracy if they proceed against the guilty as firmly as possible': ibid., 80. Kádár demanded serious punishments, rejecting appeals for leniency in his closing speech to Parliament, 11 May 1957, ibid., 141–2.
[200] Huszár, 'A hatalmi gépezet újjáépítése', 92–8. Huszár, *Kádár*, vol. 2, 46, 49, 50, 53, 79, especially on Kádár's active role.
[201] https://adatbazisokonline.mnl.gov.hu/pdfview2?file=static/documents/mszmp_mdp/HU_MNL_OL_M-KS_288_04_00141.pdf#search=&page=1, p. 6; https://adatbazisokonline.mnl.gov.hu/pdfview2?file=static/documents/mszmp_mdp/HU_MNL_OL_M-KS_288_04_00190.pdf#search=&page=1, p. 21.
[202] An early, samizdat calculation put executions between 350 and 400: Elek Fényes [János M. Rainer], 'Adatok az 1956-os forradalmat követő megtorláshoz', *Beszélő*, 19 (1987/1); http://beszelo.c3.hu/cikkek/adatok-az-1956-os-forradalmat-koveto-megtorlashoz. Based on UN data, 453 executed:

102   STEPHEN I, THE FIRST CHRISTIAN KING OF HUNGARY

Kádár coupled repression with efforts to shape opinion and gain public support.[203] His interpretation of 1956 evolved in parallel with the reprisals, although not independent of Soviet pressure, in a manner strongly reminiscent of *Animal Farm*. At least some of this shift can be chalked up to his vulnerability due to his role in the Nagy government; a chameleon-like transformation was needed to tackle Soviet pressure to label the entire uprising a counter-revolution from its very beginning on 23 October. Initially protecting himself by emphasizing that real grievances led to justified demands in October, he conceptualized two phases, only considering the second, from 30 October, a counter-revolution; however, he finally reframed 1956 and buried his own role as a member of the Nagy government, who had participated in its decisions.[204] He acknowledged that even 'grave mistakes' had been committed earlier that 'infringed socialist principles', which had to be corrected; yet, he claimed, these were used by counter-revolutionaries in order to mislead workers and undermine the 'people's democracy'.[205] 'Fascist terror' had nearly caused a 'national tragedy' before he formed a government and called on Soviet help.[206]

Péter Gosztonyi, *Föltámadott a tenger...1956*, 3rd rev. edn (Budapest: Népszava Kiadó Vállalat, [1990]), 206, with a partial list of the condemned and dates of execution, 220–38. These calculations include the effect of martial law on common crimes. László Eörsi calculated 225 executed, not counting common criminals, now widely accepted: Rainer, *Az 1956-os magyar forradalom*, 56. Detailed statistics and mechanisms of retribution, with slightly different numbers: Zsuzsanna Mikó, *A terror hétköznapjai. A kádári megtorlás, 1956–1963* (Budapest: Libri Kiadó—Magyar Nemzeti Levéltár, 2016), 144 (1963 amnesty gave clemency to 4,123 imprisoned, 4,629 doing community work, 4,094 sentenced to fines, and a further 10,044 prior to the conclusion of their case); 151 (1957–63 process against more than 26,000 people, of whom close to 13,000 charged, 228 executed). Huszár, 'A hatalmi gépezet újjáépítése', especially 80–116, on the first year of reprisals (4 November 1956–1 November 1957, 180 death sentences) on 105–6. Alajos Dornbach, 'A pártállami igazságszolgáltatás és a Nagy Imre-per', in Dornbach et al., *A per*, 17–40, at 23: 229 cases of capital punishment, more than 22,000 imprisoned, more interned or held without trial; overall, around 0.5 per cent of the population; many others fired from their job, and more than 200,000 emigrated. Zinner, *A kádári megtorlás*, 421: between 4 November 1956—end of 1963, 26,621 juridical sentences, 12,900 interned, until 31 December 1962, 367 condemned to death, of whom 229 definitely because of their role in 1956; according to data that is not final, 341 executed. Cf. Gough, *Good Comrade*, 113–14, 117–18. The philosopher George Lukács was dismissed from his university post in October 1958; among other 'mistakes', he maintained that Soviet intervention and harsh reprisals had been unnecessary: Tibor Huszár, ed., *Kedves, jó Kádár elvtárs! Válogatás Kádár János levelezéséből* (Budapest: Osiris, 2002), 117–19.

[203]   Gough, *Good Comrade*, 112 on trying to win public support from 1957.

[204]   Huszár, *Kádár*, vol. 2, 20–9; Ripp, 'Az MSZMP legitimációja', 51–6. In June 1957, he spoke of his own mistakes, but then ceased to do so: Huszár, *Kádár*, vol. 2, 62. On Soviet pressure changing Kádár's initial two-phase assessment: Rainer, *Az 1956-os magyar forradalom*, 51–2. The uneasy merging of these imperatives is clear in the decisions of the Temporary Central Committee of the Hungarian Socialist Workers' Party (2, 3, 5 December 1956), which referred to these two phases, but also branded the entire uprising a counter-revolution: Korányi, *Egy népfelkelés*, 177–82, no. 112. Nagy rejected the label 'counter-revolution': Nagy, *Snagovi jegyzetek*, 62–3. The Central Committee of the Party defined the events as counter-revolution in December 1956, as mentioned in the Report of the Central Committee to the VII. Congress of MSZMP, November 1959 in Kádár, *Válogatott 1957–1973*, 130.

[205]   Kádár, *Szilárd népi hatalom*, 22, 25 (27 January 1957, MSZMP conference, Csepel). Similar ibid., 28–30, though he said the Party started rectifying mistakes in July 1956: ibid., 28 (2 February 1957, MSZMP conference, Salgótarján); similar ibid., 96 (9 May 1957 report to Parliament).

[206]   Huszár, *Kedves, jó Kádár elvtárs!*, 24–6 (30 November 1956 to Javaharlal Nehru).

STEPHEN, THE KING   103

He set out the new official version of events in a speech a few months after the uprising was crushed: international imperialism tried to undermine the Hungarian People's Republic, taking advantage of the real mistakes that had been made during the last years of Stalin, but the Soviet Union, in the name of proletarian internationalism, came to Hungary's aid.[207] A well-rehearsed version in Moscow at a Soviet-Hungarian meeting on 27 March 1957 stressed that the Soviet Union helped against the counter-revolution at the express request of the Hungarian government.[208] This narrative then accommodated other novel elements in sync with changing political needs. Thus, the bourgeoisie had not only tried to retake power, it continued plotting to harm the workers,[209] which suggested a present danger rather than a past event. Betrayal within the Party made 23 October possible.[210] Kádár also explicitly denied that 1956 was a revolt for national independence.[211] In an interview given to L'Unità, the Italian Communist Party's newspaper, on 18 April 1957, Kádár added that the counter-revolutionaries would have triggered a war with the neighbouring countries to regain territories.[212] On 9 May 1957, in a report to Parliament on the government's activity over the preceding six months, Kádár claimed that the counter-revolution had wanted to erect a fascist dictatorship and turn Hungary into a colony.[213] Eventually, this adaptation of the rhetoric allowed shifting the blame definitively: Kádár claimed he realized Nagy was a traitor, and thus the new government was formed and asked for Soviet help.[214]

Above all, Imre Nagy posed a continued problem of legitimacy for Kádár. In a speech in early 1957, Kádár intimated that on 3 November he had known he would 'not be welcomed with flowers', but 'the people would understand and approve' of 'saving the Hungarian proletarian dictatorship'.[215] The reality was quite different. On 5 November, the remaining independent radio station branded Kádár a traitor, a 'new Rákosi', who wants to continue the latter's work and relies on the 'services of the bloody-handed terrorist Russian government'.[216] The Yugoslavs had promised, and attempted, to persuade Nagy to resign and declare his support for the Kádár government, but were met by Nagy's principled

---

[207] Speech at a meeting of activists during the visit of a Chinese Communist Party delegation, 16 January 1957, in Kádár, *Szilárd népi hatalom*, 13. Similar ibid., 32–4 (2 February 1957, MSZMP conference, Salgótarján).

[208] 27 March 1957: ibid., 41–3, at 42.

[209] Ibid., 22 (27 January 1957, MSZMP conference, Csepel), similar ibid., 28–31 (2 February 1957, MSZMP conference, Salgótarján).

[210] Ibid., 24 (27 January 1957, MSZMP conference, Csepel).

[211] Ibid., 32–4, see 32 (2 February 1957, MSZMP conference, Salgótarján).   [212] Ibid., 60–1.

[213] Ibid., 89, 'organized, institutional pursuit' against socialists, thousands were to be executed, ibid., 90. Similar in closing speech in Parliament, 11 May 1957, ibid., 135–6.

[214] Report of the Central Committee to the VII. Congress of MSZMP, November 1959 in Kádár, *Válogatott 1957–1973*, 131.

[215] Kádár, *Szilárd népi hatalom*, 19 (26 January 1957, speech to the National Council of the Unions).

[216] Varga, *A forradalom hangja*, 497. Similar on 8 November, 'traitor Kádár'; turned Hungary into a colony of the Soviets, holds power from the foreign conqueror: ibid., 505.

104 STEPHEN I, THE FIRST CHRISTIAN KING OF HUNGARY

refusal.[217] The Soviets declined to allow either the departure of Nagy and the others to Yugoslavia, being afraid of a counter-government forming there, or their return home; Kádár soon concurred. Initially, Kádár in his public pronouncements claimed, because of Nagy's popularity in Hungary, that it was up to Nagy whether he wanted to return to government and be a minister; yet at the same time in his negotiations with the Yugoslavs he spoke very differently, demanding Nagy's resignation and acceptance of the Kádár government.[218] On 6 November the Soviets demanded that the Kádár government's statement to members of the Communist Party in Hungary condemn Imre Nagy, his minister Géza Losonczy, and Ferenc Donáth (member of the temporary committee of the new Hungarian Socialist Workers' Party in 1956) as having opened the road to reaction and betrayed the cause of socialism; this, with the exception of Donáth's name, was incorporated into the statement issued on 7 November by the temporary Central Committee of the Hungarian Socialist Workers' Party. Kádár emphasized the condemnation of Nagy and Losonczy, adding that their group 'with a call for open anti-Soviet combat took a nationalist-chauvinist position, opened the road to counter-revolutionary forces and thus de facto betrayed the cause of socialism'.[219] On the same day, the Presidential Council (Elnöki Tanács) dismissed the government of Imre Nagy, so the Kádár government could be sworn in.[220]

Soviet agents devised a plan to take Nagy and those who had taken refuge at the Yugoslav embassy with him to Romania, and advised Kádár at a secret meeting on 16 November.[221] On 21 November, Kádár gave a written guarantee to Edvard Kardelj, vice president of Yugoslavia, that Nagy and his associates would not be subject to any legal proceedings,[222] thus ending the asylum; both parties knew they participated in a cover-up. After Nagy and the others left the embassy

---

[217] István Vida, 'Bevezető' in *Imre Nagy, Snagovi jegyzetek: Gondolatok, emlékezések 1956-1957*, ed. István Vida (Budapest: Gondolat Kiadó—Nagy Imre Alapítvány, 2006), 8–11; Litván, 'A Nagy Imre-per politikai háttere', 45 on plan that by the time of the Soviet intervention Nagy would resign, and Yugoslav initiative to offer asylum. Rainer, *Nagy*, 166. Szereda—Rainer, *Döntés*, 209. Nagy's account of Yugoslav requests for him to resign, approve the Kádár government and withdraw the political decisions of the last few days of his government, and comments on Kádár's behaviour: *Snagovi jegyzetek*, 102–3. Rainer, *Nagy*, 169–71.

[218] Nagy, *Snagovi jegyzetek*, 103–4; cf. Judit Ember, *Menedékjog 1956: A Nagy Imre csoport elrablása* (Budapest: Szabad Tér Kiadó, 1989), 109–10 (Kádár ready to negotiate with him if Nagy leaves the embassy).

[219] Szereda—Rainer, *Döntés*, 105–6, 210.

[220] Dated back to 4 November, published *Magyar Közlöny*, 12 November 1956. The Presidential Council (or Presidium) replaced the office of President from 1949; it was the highest governmental body next to Parliament, consisting of members of Parliament who were selected by Parliament; its legal decrees were binding. The PC, however, was incomplete, with many members abroad; however, this move tried to legitimize the Kádár government, which also took its oath on 7 November to the president of the PC in Parliament: Huszár, *Kádár*, vol. 2, 5.

[221] Vida, 'Bevezető', 11.

[222] 'The Hungarian government does not wish to retaliate against Imre Nagy and members of his group because of their past deeds': letter reproduced in Nagy, *Snagovi jegyzetek*, 390–2, here 392. Kádár also acknowledged the Yugoslav efforts to persuade Nagy to 'issue a statement desirable for us' (ibid.). Nagy's account of the negotiations and written guarantee: *Snagovi jegyzetek*, 104.

on 22 November, supposedly to be driven home, Soviet armed vehicles surrounded their bus; Soviet officers boarded it, and took them to a military school where the Soviet KGB guarded them. There, Münnich still tried to persuade Nagy to declare his support for the Kádár government.[223] They were then flown to Romania; the Yugoslavs called foul play, complaining that their agreement with the Hungarian government was disregarded.[224] Kádár followed the Soviet dictate and even repeatedly lied to the Central Committee concerning the circumstances of Nagy's departure.[225] On 27 November, Khrushchev at the meeting of the Presidium of the Central Committee of the Communist Party of the Soviet Union condemned Soviet participation in the abduction as a mistake, and said Nagy was a 'Hungarian matter', although the same meeting decided on gathering information to discredit Nagy.[226] Khrushchev's statement may well have been Soviet double-speak, since they routinely pretended that responsibility for Soviet decisions lay with local actors; witness the claim that the military intervention in November 1956 was at the request of the Hungarian government.

Kádár's rhetoric against Nagy grew ever fiercer, attributing to him an increasingly negative role.[227] At the end of November 1956, he blamed Nagy for having been 'helpless' and 'idle' in the face of the counter-revolution from 30 October, a few days later accusing the 'weak', 'powerless', 'yielding' Nagy government of allowing the mingling of counter-revolutionary, fascist and criminal elements with the justified democratic movement from the beginning.[228] As he shifted the blame to Nagy, Kádár finally equated him with fascists. In early 1957, he called Nagy a 'class traitor'[229] and counter-revolutionary.[230] By May, he asserted that 'the

---

[223] Nagy's account of the abduction: *Snagovi jegyzetek*, 104–7. Huszár, *Kádár*, vol. 2, 12; Szereda—Rainer, *Döntés*, 109; Gough, *Good Comrade*, 106. Ember, *Menedékjog* contains interviews with survivors who had been at the Yugoslav embassy with Nagy. Nagy, as well as others (ibid., 6–7, 28, 43–4, 109–10), recounted that Nagy refused to leave because of the presence of a Russian soldier; he was reassured that an agreement had been signed between the Yugoslavs and the Kádár government that they would go home unharmed. Two Yugoslav attachés also accompanying them, they finally got on the bus. The Yugoslavs were soon made to leave.

[224] Szereda—Rainer, *Döntés*, 212–13. Documents on the agreement between the Hungarian and Romanian governments to take Nagy and his associates to Romania, 'for their personal safety' and because they expressed the desire to leave Hungary: Nagy, *Snagovi jegyzetek*, 392–5 (22 November 1956).

[225] Huszár, *Kádár*, vol. 2, 10–13.

[226] Szereda—Rainer, *Döntés*, 108–9 (Khrushchev said it was a mistake that a Soviet army officer got on the bus that took Nagy and the others from the Yugoslav embassy).

[227] Ripp, 'Az MSZMP legitimációja' 51–6. On Kádár's turncoat behaviour earlier: Nagy, *Snagovi jegyzetek*, 92. On rapidity of recasting the role of Nagy: Litván, 'A Nagy Imre-per politikai háttere', 49–52. On Rákosi's activity in the Soviet Union against Kádár as motivating Kádár's behaviour (January–February 1957), and finally Kádár's victory avoiding the return of Rákosi: Huszár, *Kádár*, vol. 2, 29, 38–44.

[228] Radio speech, 26 November 1956, in Korányi, *Egy népfelkelés*, 171, no. 109; 30 November 1956, in Huszár, *Kedves, jó Kádár elvtárs!*, 24–6.

[229] Kádár, *Szilárd népi hatalom*, 25 (27 January 1957, MSZMP conference, Csepel); also ibid., 35 (2 February 1957, MSZMP conference, Salgótarján).

[230] Ibid., 32 (2 February 1957, MSZMP conference, Salgótarján). This was developed further in a speech in Moscow at a Soviet-Hungarian meeting, 27 March 1957: the Nagy-Losonczy group under the guise of fighting against mistakes internally disrupted the Party, allied with reactionary forces and

106   STEPHEN I, THE FIRST CHRISTIAN KING OF HUNGARY

Nagy-Losonczy group fought in the same line with the Horthy-fascist bourgeois counter-revolution' from the beginning and 'led the incitement against the Party'.[231] Nagy and his group were far worse than the Stalinists had been: the latter made mistakes, but the former were traitors to socialism who were intent on 'throwing Hungary prey to imperialist predators'.[232] Kádár's speech to the assembled crowd at the state celebrations of 1 May 1957 emphasized the 'special significance' of the occasion; the fascist Hungarian bourgeoisie allied with the traitorous Nagy group and international imperialism had wanted to destroy the social order of the Hungarian People's Republic, but the working class triumphed with international help.[233] Grave mistakes of the previous years were exploited by the counter-revolution; yet it would not have been able to reach such successes 'without the treason of Imre Nagy and his associates, who paralysed the country's leadership' and 'misled' people. Because of this, counter-revolutionary terror raged, masses of communists were murdered, and thousands were imprisoned, destined to be killed. True communists asked for the help of the Soviet Union, 'the truest friend' of the Hungarian people.[234] Retrospectively, Kádár whitewashed his own role, claiming that he had been misled by Nagy, until, upon realizing the truth, he broke with Nagy.[235]

In April 1957, Nagy and other members of his government were stealthily arrested in Romania,[236] taken to Hungary, and tried in secret for leading the counter-revolution.[237] Nagy, along with several others were condemned to death

---

provided the ideology for the counter-revolution: ibid., 42. Nagy and companions labelled enemies of the People's Republic: Huszár, 'A hatalmi gépezet újjáépítése', 86.

[231] Report to Parliament, 9 May 1957, in Kádár, *Szilárd népi hatalom*, 92–3, and quote on 95.

[232] Ibid., 96. Kádár emphasized Nagy's role as a traitor even in speeches abroad; in China during his visit, 28 September 1957: ibid., 299, and on 3 October 1957, ibid., 302. In Romania, 27 February 1958, ibid., 373.

[233] On the pressure to attend, see https://index.hu/belfold/maj156070430/.

[234] Kádár, *Szilárd népi hatalom*, 69–83, quotations from 70–1. By 1960, he claimed the only terror had been 'white terror' at the end of October 1956 until 4 November: Speech on 15th anniversary of liberation, 3 April 1960 in Kádár, *Tovább a lenini úton*, 29.

[235] Kádár, *Szilárd népi hatalom*, 134–5 (11 May 1957, closing speech in Parliament).

[236] On related discussions with Soviet Bloc countries between December 1956 and April 1957: Gough, *Good Comrade*, 108–10. Only Soviet and Romanian political leaders knew: Dornbach et al., *A per*, 13. On preparations and the arrest, Rainer, *Nagy*, 172–3. Who initiated the arrest remains undocumented; a series of talks took place in January 1957 between party delegations of the Soviet Bloc; on 25 January 1957, the MSZMP sent Gyula Kállai to Nagy; he returned with the news that Nagy was unrepentant: Vida, 'Bevezető', 43–6.

[237] Documents of Hungarian—Soviet secret consultations show that the Hungarian government gained Soviet approval on the charges, and an agreement on the death penalty in the summer of 1957, although the Soviets asked for some tweaking of the charges and for postponements of the trial because of other considerations: Békés et al., *The 1956 Hungarian Revolution*, 532–42. Some members of the Nagy government who had not been at the Yugoslav embassy were arrested separately: Dornbach, 'A pártállami igazságszolgáltatás', 30. The trial was held in the prison without access; no verbatim record was produced about the testimonies during interrogation; the trial exists on tape. Even family members only found out about the trial after the executions; the charges and verdict were not made public until 1989: Dornbach et al., *A per*, 7, 9. No witnesses for the defence were called, and defence attorneys were given a few hours to read the thousands of pages of trial material: János M. Rainer, 'A kihallgatószobától a vesztőhelyig', in Dornbach et al., *A per*, 63–112. Indictment in ibid.,

STEPHEN, THE KING 107

for treason and the attempt to overthrow the Hungarian People's Republic in alliance with foreign imperialists—the verdict matched the rhetoric of Kádár's speeches on Nagy's premeditated activity hidden by lies—, without the right to appeal; they were executed the following day, on 16 June 1958.[238] Initially buried in the prison courtyard, one night in 1961 the coffins were reburied without a tombstone or other sign, in the furthest, untended corner of the largest public cemetery (plot 301 of Rákoskeresztúr cemetery), with fictive names entered in the register (Piroska Borbíró for Imre Nagy). Personal writings, such as diaries and farewell letters were suppressed.[239]

After this judicial murder, Kádár lashed out at those who said he had broken his word not to prosecute Imre Nagy: Nagy broke his oath to the constitution, withdrawing from the Warsaw Treaty and wanting to restore multi-party government; had he acknowledged this as his aim, he would not have gained power in October 1956; he lied about fighting against the counter-revolution. 'What sort of justice is it that punishes someone who commits something, but does not make accountable the person who thought out, decided, organised, and directed it all?'[240] While Kádár clearly saw the trial and verdicts as necessary for legitimizing his own power internally, the international reaction was shock and condemnation by politicians and the media. Nagy and his associates had supposedly been under Romanian diplomatic protection, and the parallel with earlier show trials was drawn.[241]

Historians debate the extent of Kádár's own responsibility, because the sources offer no definitive proof; a great deal of the business was conducted orally and reminiscences from much later vary. Yet even those attributing a significant influence to Soviet decisions and pressure concede that the Soviets did not demand Nagy's execution; yet Kádár spoke of the need for death sentences even before the trial. He tried to hasten the proceedings and had a key role in steering them, kept

---

136–63. Details on autocratic justice system in Dornbach, 'A pártállami igazságszolgáltatás', in Dornbach et al., *A per*, 22–7, 29–36, 39–40. In English, see Alajos Dornbach, ed., *The Secret Trial of Imre Nagy* (London: Praeger, 1994). Rainer, *Nagy*, 174–96.

[238] Dornbach et al., *A per*, 223–30. Two others were executed with Nagy, another died during the process, and five were imprisoned. József Szilágyi had been tried earlier and executed on 24 April 1958. See also Gough, *Good Comrade*, 114–16. Nagy refused to admit the charges, and in his last speech he refused to demand clemency: Rainer, 'A kihallgatószobától', in Dornbach et al., *A per*, 122–8, 173, 222. Rainer, *Nagy*, 193–6.

[239] Dornbach et al., *A per*, 9, 110–11; Dornbach, 'A pártállami igazságszolgáltatás', 28–9; Rainer, *Nagy*, 226–33.

[240] Speech of 29 June 1958 in Kádár, *Szilárd népi hatalom*, 421. Kádár's written guarantee prior to Nagy leaving the asylum of the Yugoslav embassy had promised immunity from prosecution; he also confirmed this immunity in his radio speech on 26 November 1956, in Korányi, *Egy népfelkelés*, 171, no. 109. On a German visit on 12 July 1958, published the following day in the daily *Népszabadság*, Kádár stated that while the lords of the West disapproved of the punishment of Nagy and his fellow-criminals, the approval of Hungarian workers was more important; they had demanded Nagy's punishment, ibid., 424.

[241] Dornbach at al., *A per*, 14–16; 327–90 (collection of international reactions in translation); Radványi, *Hungary*, 37–9 on Hungarian communiqué to embassies and reactions. Kádár represented Nagy's behaviour at the trial as mendacious; Hungarian PR to justify capital punishment: Rainer, *Nagy*, 214. Opinion among emigrants: ibid., 215–17.

108 STEPHEN I, THE FIRST CHRISTIAN KING OF HUNGARY

significant parts secret even from the Party leadership, and refuted those who raised the possibility of clemency following a death sentence.[242] That Kádár's scope of decision-making was substantial is also suggested by the fact that he was able to mitigate the sentence for some of the accused.[243] Finally, it was Kádár who had most to gain: at stake was his legitimacy, which required silencing those who knew Kádár's actions as a member of the Nagy government.[244] Kádár, however, never admitted his responsibility, clinging to the fiction of a juridical verdict,[245] in a similar vein to the whitewashing of his role in the Rajk trial.[246]

After the capital punishment was carried out, Kádár 'informed' the Party's Central Committee in a speech full of lies, even making fun of Nagy.[247] Later, he obliquely alluded to 'having had to do what was necessary' when Hungary was in trouble.[248] Prior to the trial, he denied that Nagy had a role in trying to rectify the 'mistakes' committed during the Stalinist era, alleging that he only had destructive political aims.[249] He maintained that the Party had set out to remedy the earlier problems in July 1956, and 'the enemy' was confused by this, so imperialists and fascists triggered the counter-revolution; they were helped by traitors, Nagy and his associates, who initially camouflaged their connection to the enemy camp.[250] On 10 May 1958, Kádár talked to a Polish Party delegation about the

[242] Huszár, *Kádár*, vol. 2, 30–45, 58–78. Soviet pressure still in January 1957: ibid., 26–7. Chinese hard-line stance but no demand for a death sentence, ibid., 28.

[243] Dornbach et al., *A per*, 9; Litván, 'A Nagy Imre-per politikai háttere', 49–60; Varga, *Kádár János bírái előtt*, 678–9; Miklós Molnár, 'Kádár János—avagy a történelem visszavág', *Világosság* (1993, no. 10), 29–36, at 29–31. On the Hungarian leadership deciding who would be charged apart from Nagy: Litván, 'A Nagy Imre-per politikai háttere', 55, though Soviet agents were present during interrogations: János M. Rainer, 'A kihallgatószobától a vesztőhelyig', in Dornbach et al., *A per*, 63–112, see 71. Mitigation: Huszár, *Kádár*, vol. 2, 75–6. On 4 November, the Soviet position was Nagy's ultimate transfer to the Hungarian government: Szereda—Rainer, *Döntés*, 99. Soviets intervened to postpone the trial more than once, fearing its negative impact on international negotiations: Litván, 'A Nagy Imre-per politikai háttere' 53, 55–6, 58; Huszár, *Kádár*, vol. 2, 70; Gough, *Good Comrade*, 114.

[244] On Kádár saying that Nagy's execution hinged on one sentence, Litván, 'A Nagy Imre-per politikai háttere', 46–7. On the need to silence Szilágyi and Nagy: Huszár, *Kádár*, vol. 2, 71–2. On Kádár's insistence on the death penalty and later myth of Soviet pressure, cf. Gough, *Good Comrade*, 115–17. He prevented the publication of material that revealed his role: Central Committee meeting minutes, 13 October 1958: https://adatbazisokonline.mnl.gov.hu/pdfview2?file=static/documents/mszmp_mdp/HU_MNL_OL_M-KS_288_04_00190.pdf#search=&page=1, pp. 26–7.

[245] Huszár, *Kádár*, vol. 2, 64.

[246] Kádár approved the destruction of the archival material on the Rajk investigation, and his role was omitted from documents on the trial submitted to the Central Committee in 1962: ibid., 92, 98, on secrecy concerning Kádár's role, ibid., vol. 1, 149–50, vol. 2, 141–3, 149.

[247] 25 July 1958, minutes: https://adatbazisokonline.mnl.gov.hu/pdfview2?file=static/documents/mszmp_mdp/HU_MNL_OL_M-KS_288_04_00180.pdf#search=&page=1 on p. 16; Huszár, *Kádár*, vol. 2, 77.

[248] 15 October 1958 speech in Láng machine factory, in Kádár, *Tovább a lenini úton*, 19. He linked this to unwavering loyalty to communism, for which he faced death in 1944 and the early 1950s.

[249] Kádár, *Szilárd népi hatalom*, 161–2 (Central Committee report to Party conference, 27 June 1957). Similarly, a few days later at the MSZMP conference, ibid., 217; he claimed that new information about Nagy showed his role to be even more negative.

[250] Details on alleged pretence and alliance with external enemies: ibid., 164–9, 170–1 (Central Committee report to Party conference, 27 June 1957). Kádár even suggested imperialist 'enemies' sowed discord within the Party, and led Rákosi to believe in Rajk's culpability: ibid., 216 (response to comments at MSZMP conference, 29 June 1957).

STEPHEN, THE KING   109

internationally infamous traitor Nagy and his group, who dishonestly pretended to want to rectify mistakes but in fact were trying to destroy the Party; he also stated that the forces of revisionist traitors must be annihilated in order to remedy mistakes that occur during the building of socialism.[251] In an article, Kádár singled out Nagy by name to illustrate those who 'sunk into the swamp of treason'.[252] Years later, he still reproached people for having assisted Nagy's 'destructive work'.[253] The spontaneous uprising of October 1956 disappeared behind the constructed imperialist plot, reliant on Hungarian traitors, to overthrow the People's Republic.

Kádár's narrative of 1956 stabilized: grave mistakes under Rákosi and his clique created 'favourable conditions for the class enemy'.[254] 'The forces of the counter-revolution were strong and well-organised. Their men were in key positions of defence in the People's Republic. The General Staff was made up of representatives of the spy agencies of international imperialism, counter-revolutionary emigration abroad and their accomplices at home' and 'the treasonous Imre Nagy clique',[255] whose 'treason without precedent'[256] played a significant role. Armed forces were recruited from 'the remnants of the former ruling classes, Horthyist officers, former police, criminals, the lumpenproletariat, and misled youth, petit-bourgeois and intelligentsia;'[257] nationalism and 'the illusion of democracy above classes', remnants of bourgeois ideology, influenced part of the intelligentsia.[258] To camouflage its real purpose, the restoration of capitalism, counter-revolutionaries masqueraded as champions of 'democratic socialism' and 'socialism without dictatorship',[259] 'pure democracy without class content'.[260] They followed a tactic of gradual encroachment; cultural issues discussed by writers concealed the attack of bourgeois ideology to prepare the counter-revolution; the assault against the Party only emerged openly once violence erupted.[261] Thus, this narrative eliminated the acknowledgement that the uprising had legitimate aims to reform or abolish a system based on terror, and that people had wanted independence; it also cast Nagy as the arch-enemy.

---

[251] Ibid., 402–3.
[252] *Népszabadság*, 16, no. 138 (12 June 1958), in Kádár, *Szilárd népi hatalom*, 407.
[253] Letters by Kádár reproaching István Kovács for having assisted Nagy in his destructive work (21 April 1960) and writer Zoltán Vas for having 'pushed Nagy's chariot with your full force until 4 Nov. 1956' (7 December 1961), in Huszár, *Kedves, jó Kádár elvtárs!*, 156–7, at 157, and 193–4, at 194, respectively.
[254] Report of the Central Committee to the VII. Congress of MSZMP, November 1959, in Kádár, *Válogatott 1957–1973*, 129.
[255] 'From the experiences of Hungarian class struggle', *Béke és szocializmus*, February 1959, in Kádár, *Válogatott 1957–1973*, 117.
[256] Report of the Central Committee to the VII. Congress of MSZMP, November 1959, in ibid., 129.
[257] 'From the experiences of Hungarian class struggle', *Béke és szocializmus*, February 1959, in Kádár, *Válogatott 1957–1973*, 117.
[258] Ibid., 116.
[259] Ibid., 117 (similar in Report of the Central Committee to the VII. Congress of MSZMP, November 1959, ibid., 131).
[260] Ibid., 118.   [261] Ibid., 118–19.

6. Evolutions of the Kádár Regime and Interpretations of His Role

Even as he cast himself in the role of the saviour of socialism in Hungary, was Kádár saving the country from a return to Stalinist hard-liners or opportunistically grabbing power?[262] Was he a new socialist dictator who recognized the need for broader popular support to ensure his regime's longevity, or was he dedicated to creating a better life for most, while forced to recognize the constraints of the Soviet Bloc? After consolidating his power, he could espouse less heavy-handed methods. An amnesty in 1963 freed most of those who had been condemned to prison, and helped to normalize relations with the West.[263] Kádár introduced a lenient system within the Soviet Bloc, that allowed a degree of material wealth and relatively more freedom, often called 'gulyás'-communism (after goulash, a Hungarian soup) or 'the happiest barrack in the Soviet Bloc'.[264] Kádár sought to garner a wider popular base, declaring that 'he who is not against us is with us', and later 'our main method is to convince, not to dictate'[265]; he endorsed the appointment of non-communists, even priests, to certain positions and allowed a greater toleration for religious belief.[266] He set out to loosen restrictions, for example, abolishing family background checks for university admission in the early 1960s,[267] and raise the standard of living,[268] improving everyday life. The desire to ensure better living standards led to an imperative for economic reform,

---

[262] He implied the former, reportedly saying to a close friend in 1989, 'what terror there would have been if it is not me who is using it', claiming he placed the interests of the country above friendship: Huszár, *Kádár*, vol. 2, 266; similarly György Aczél, 'Közelkép Kádárról', in Rácz, *Ki volt Kádár?*, 17–25, at 20.

[263] Kádár had emphasized he would not declare an amnesty while there was international pressure for it, speech in Parliament, 21 March 1963, in Kádár, *Tovább a lenini úton*, 201–2. (Partial amnesties and abolition of internment camps earlier: Huszár, *Kádár*, vol. 2, 177; Gough, *Good Comrade*, 131.) The government also refused to publish the number of those released; 'we are not obliged to report to anyone, to any country's government...because the Hungarian People's Republic is a sovereign country': speech when U Thant, UN Secretary-General visited Hungary, 2 July 1963, in Kádár, *Tovább a lenini úton*, 222. A total of 4,123 people were released from prison, 4,629 were released from 'educative' work, 4,094 were granted amnesty from fines, and 10,044 were granted clemency; however, around 1,000 people had not been released in 1963, new criminal procedures about 1956 were still initiated, and discrimination continued: Mikó, *A terror*, 135–48, 151. Cf. Gough, *Good Comrade*, 143.

[264] Raising living standards had been his concern from as early as 1957: ibid., 111. On economic policies: Iván T. Berend, *The Hungarian Economic Reforms 1953-1988* (Cambridge—New York: Cambridge University Press, 1990). On Kádár's policies and achievements from 1957 to 1988, see Gough, *Good Comrade*, 119–240.

[265] Speech at Parliament, September 1980, in Kádár, *Szövetségi politika*, 257.

[266] Kádár discussed the appointment of a priest, Miklós Beresztóczy, to the post of one of the vice-presidents of parliament and declared 'he who is not against us is with us' in a speech at the national council of the Patriotic People's Front, 8 December 1961, in Kádár, *Tovább a lenini úton*, 36–7. Latter also in a speech at the MSZMP congress, 24 November 1962, ibid., 136–7; see also Huszár, *Kádár*, vol. 2, 86; Gough, *Good Comrade*, 143–4 ('clerical reaction' remained prohibited), 200 (rapprochement with the church).

[267] Kádár, *Tovább a lenini úton*, 60–2.

[268] E.g. interview in *Népszabadság*, 21, no. 301 (24 December 1963), in Kádár, *Tovább a lenini úton*, 285–6. The families of c. 200,000 emigrés received news about living standards in the West, which also influenced policies within the country.

STEPHEN, THE KING 111

which in turn necessitated more open relations with the West. More reform-oriented periods alternated with attempts to rein in change, however, both due to Soviet-imposed restrictions and Kádár's own conservativism.[269] The trajectory towards more openness was not unidirectional; reverses recurred, including in 1983, after Andropov (Soviet ambassador to Hungary in 1956) became General Secretary of the Communist Party in the Soviet Union.[270] Nonetheless, visits by western politicians, and economic ties to the West grew in importance in the context of an economic crisis in Hungary.[271]

As opposed to traditional Soviet models, Kádár did not foster a cult of personality, lived quite austerely, and was seen as 'extraordinarily democratic'.[272] This assessment, however, covers appearances more than the underlying structures. While his upbringing had socialized him to personal puritanism, and a plain-spoken directness in his relations to people, the regime itself was based on authoritarian rule, rather than democracy; it has been characterized as a soft dictatorship.[273] Kádár had the final say in policy as well as promotions and demotions, loyalty to him was obligatory, and the regime provided privileges for the Party elite, who were able to dispense favours to cadres.[274] Kádár prevented democratization, and tightened the reins periodically.[275] The regime's foundations rested on taboos and double-speak, with a wide discrepancy between the public and private spheres; the comparatively greater freedom was only available to those who accepted these foundations.[276] Nevertheless, the relatively better life within the Soviet Bloc led first to Kádár's widespread acceptance and then popularity in Hungary. In 1963, an interviewer from the journal L'Humanité asked Kádár how he managed to gain popularity so quickly, since in 1956 'you were not

---

[269] Huszár, Kádár, vol. 2, 181, 199–210, 233–56 (1966–8 reform, 1974–82 counter-reform); 276 (increasing conservativism); 288–93 (blocking reform); 193–5 (foreign policy towards the West); 184–8, 233–56 (Soviet constraints with Brezhnev); 210–22 (in 1968, Kádár at first supported Dubček, even challenging Soviet assessment, but finally supported military intervention).

[270] Gough, Good Comrade, 219, 223 (repression of opposition intellectuals: Rajk's home raided, Mozgó Világ editors dismissed).

[271] Ibid., 221–2 (1984, M. Thatcher visit).

[272] Ibid., 138–40, quote on 139 from Fedor Burlatsky, Khrushchev's advisor.

[273] Huszár, Kádár, vol. 2, 178.

[274] Ibid., 106–7, 258–64, example of machiavellistically ridding himself of a critic: 104–12; on his upbringing, childhood and youth, ibid., vol. 1, 7–26. Examples of elite privileges: Aczél—Méray, Tisztító vihar, 292–301.

[275] 'We do not brook action against our constitutional socialist social order from any side' and punishment of dissident 'conspiratorial groups' who had thought the amnesty of those condemned for their role in 1956 was a sign of liberalization: speech at Parliament, 11 February 1965, in Kádár, Hazafiság és internacionalizmus, 79–80. Against petit-bourgeois tendencies in culture: MSZMP IX congress, 28 November 1966, ibid., 291. In 1973, philosophers, sociologists, and economists were dismissed from their job and some were arrested.

[276] László Lengyel, A rendszerváltó elit tündöklése és bukása (Budapest: Helikon, 1996), 37–82; Huszár, Kádár, vol. 2, 257–8, 287, 335.

112 STEPHEN I, THE FIRST CHRISTIAN KING OF HUNGARY

recognized by everyone, and were not at all popular.[277] By the late 1970s, Kádár was widely seen as the guarantor of a better life compared to the rest of the bloc.[278]

The cultural sphere also experienced 'kádárization'. While keeping ultimate Party control, art and literature were to be guided by 'suitable people keeping an eye on our goals' at the head of 'independent workshops', rather than by the dictate of Party members.[279] Kádár declared that he welcomed people 'participating in public life with their opinion, recommendations and critical remarks',[280] but genuine critics of the regime were harassed: their work was not published, their passport was confiscated, or they were forced to emigrate.[281] By 1983, a great emphasis was placed on winning over youth to the socialist vision, to ward off 'opposing forces that take advantage of the political inexperience of young people'.[282] On the other hand, 'it is an important ideological and political task to overcome the palpably growing wave of nationalism', a heritage of capitalism actively fomented by imperialists.[283]

The political imperative to keep living standards high amidst increasing economic problems from the end of the 1970s led to joining the IMF (1982) and seeking more loans from the West. The need for western acceptance contributed to a cautious approach towards dissidence. Thus, during the early 1980s, 'soft' forms of dissent became increasingly possible. Prohibited books circulated, samizdat literature was widespread,[284] and critical and dissident intellectual circles formed.[285] Yet growing dissidence worried Kádár, and he encouraged harassing critics. The strengthening democratic opposition raised Kádár's fears of a new 1956,[286] against the backdrop of a state of emergency in Poland, and crisis in the Soviet Union. Moreover, no matter how permissive the state became, 1956 and the origins of the Kádár regime fell under the strictest taboo. Deviating publicly from the official version of 1956 as counter-revolution was impossible; above all, the details of the regime's establishment were repressed, obscured by silence, although rare allusions in literature and film signalled they were not entirely for-

---

[277] 6 January 1963, Hungarian tr. in Kádár, *Tovább a lenini úton*, 148 (he responded that the Party follows the best policies in the interest of the workers, based on Marxism-Leninism). The reporter also mentioned passports for travel and the existence of satirical theatres, ibid., 151.

[278] Gough, *Good Comrade*, 203.

[279] Speech at the Central Committee, April 1978, in Kádár, *Szövetségi politika*, 33. Need to support 'socialist' artistic products: Central Committee report for XII. Congress, March 1980, in ibid., 202.

[280] Central Committee report XII. Congress, March 1980, ibid., 181.

[281] Many critics were intellectuals; e.g. Iván Szelényi was forced to emigrate after the manuscript of a sociological study analysing the oppression of the working class in communist Hungary was found by the police in 1974: George Konrád—Ivan Szelényi, *The Intellectuals on the Road to Class Power*, tr. Andrew Arato and Richard E. Allen (Brighton: The Harvester Press, 1979), xiii-xix. At various times, Kádár turned against reform communists, for example, in 1972: Huszár, *Kádár*, vol. 2, 239–43.

[282] Speech at the Central Committee, April 1983, in Kádár, *A szocializmus megújulása*, 324 (see 323–5 for more detail).

[283] Speech at the Central Committee, April 1983, in ibid., 337.

[284] Tolerated since 1977: Gough, *Good Comrade*, 201.

[285] Standeisky, 'Kádár és az értelmiség'; Haraszti, 'Korai bevezetés a kádárizmusba'.

[286] Huszár, *Kádár*, vol. 2, 280–6.

gotten, as families passed on such memories. Although Kádár could mention 1956 as a 'national tragedy', sustained commemoration only emerged in a small circle of opposition intellectuals from the early 1980s in samizdat form.[287] Nagy remained a particularly neuralgic point until the end; any sign of commemoration was squashed in 1983 and even in 1986.[288]

7. The Rock Opera and 1956

In this context *István, a király*, could be read as alluding to the taboo origins of the regime, and to the most recent open expression of national feelings, the uprising of 1956. The rock opera reflects the events of 1956 in manifold ways. Stephen, as János Kádár, must accept a framework from outside, presented as necessary to ensure survival: Catholicism from Rome stands in for continued participation in the Soviet Bloc. Koppány's revolt is the doomed attempt by Imre Nagy and his government to end Hungary's membership of the Eastern Bloc, gain independence and introduce democracy. At the opening, Szörényi and Bródy sing 'who would you choose', ostensibly about Stephen and Koppány, but some of the lines as well as some of the images shown in the background in the filmed version clearly signal more modern reference points. 'Somebody has to resign from his office tomorrow' fits Nagy rather than Koppány.[289] 'Somebody has to receive the crown jewels tomorrow' is sung against the background of images of the return of the crown by the US government in 1978, the Kádár regime's great international success. 'Somebody finally has to put the weapons down tomorrow' is more apt when understood as a reference to the insurgents of 1956, rather than to Koppány's army who at that point had not taken their weapons up yet. 'Somebody has to lay down his life tomorrow' has echoes of the stories of both Koppány and Nagy. The message that Koppány's opposition was a movement for independence was reinforced by background images of a series of historical paintings: the Hungarian reformer István Széchenyi and rebels against Habsburg rule, such as Péter Zrínyi, Ferenc Rákóczi, and Lajos Kossuth, signalling a thread of 'Hungarian liberty' invariably falling victim to the triumphant oppressors.

---

[287] On repression of memory, Péter György, *Néma Hagyomány* (Budapest: Magvető, 2000); repression and early samizdat commemoration, Rainer, *Az 1956-os magyar forradalom*, 137–44. Gough, *Good Comrade*, 184.

[288] Rainer, *Nagy*, 221–3; Huszár, *Kádár*, vol. 2, 298–302 (in 1986, a poem alluding to Nagy and a thirty-year-old 'Judas tree' was published in *Tiszatáj*; Kádár demanded the suspension of the magazine and replacement of the editors, blaming the publication for preparing a new counter-revolution. Kádár claimed he was not concerned about himself, but the CIA cooperated with the enemy in Hungary). Those tending graves assumed to be those of Nagy and the others even in the 1980s were harassed, and the graves destroyed by police: Dornbach, 'A pártállami igazságszolgáltatás', 27.

[289] According to Stumpf, *Szörényi*, 156, viewers thought it referred to Kádár.

114 STEPHEN I, THE FIRST CHRISTIAN KING OF HUNGARY

After such strong hints in the introductory part, many other lines can be easily interpreted as references to 1956. Laborc's lines 'we don't need a God who doesn't speak Hungarian' and 'free Hungarians don't need such a lord' can be understood as the rejection of Soviet control. Similarly, Torda asserts that free people do not tolerate a foreign bridle—an echo of the rebels' aim of independence. In response to Koppány's song, 'shall we be captives, or shall we be free', itself a direct quotation from the 1848 poem by Sándor Petőfi instigating a revolt against the Habsburgs, the people sing 'fly free bird' 'carry the news of a new spring'. This recalls an article in the Party's daily newspaper *Szabad Nép* ('Free People') on 23 October 1956, entitled a 'new, spring muster', hailing the student movement for reform and citing a 1911 poem by Endre Ady celebrating 'eternal spring, eternal revolution'.[290] A song, later characterized as satirical by the lyricist Bródy, but understood by many as a serious expression of an alternative Hungarian history if only the road to liberty were clear, also claimed that all future defeats would turn into victories if Koppány won. Koppány's insistence on law as the basis of his rule can be read as Nagy's legitimate prime ministership versus the illegitimacy of Kádár's government in November 1956.

Koppány refuses to employ base means for a 'sacred goal', just as uncompromising Nagy refused to ask for clemency; sticking to his principles, Koppány demands a personal confrontation, while Stephen, although conflicted, relies on external force to put him on the throne, just as Kádár assumed power with the aid of Soviet tanks. Koppány's indictment of Stephen easily translates into an indictment of Kádár by Nagy: 'He calls foreigners to help him against Hungarians. They think me a pagan [a counter-revolutionary] even though I took upon myself the sign of Byzantium [a communist, but not according to the Stalinist mould]. The aim was to preserve our freedom. They think me a pagan just because I cannot tolerate the power of the priests [Soviets]. They shout "sin" when the country is defending its freedom. They think me a pagan just because I oppose the conquerors. Everyone's considered a pagan if they take my side and not Stephen's [Kádár's].'

Sarolt, Stephen's mother sings that 'rebellion and treason go hand in hand with the heroic [pagan] past'; and that rebels are committing treason—this echoes how Kádár came to present 1956 as a counter-revolution and treachery. Sarolt's 'a lot of water has flown down the old Danube, and a lot more bloody water will flow down it. There is no peace yet and you cannot know where you'll be after the battle.... You need everyone who wants you on the throne. It does not matter whether they stand by you out of self-interest or from calculation' may be seen as referring to reprisals, and then Kádár's stance that everyone not against the Party is to be accepted ('everyone not against us is with us'). 'There must be order in the land.' Sarolt insists on force and the quartering of Koppány,

---

[290] The article is reprinted in Korányi, *Egy népfelkelés*, 46–8, no. 16.

STEPHEN, THE KING   115

rejecting clemency, which recalls the reprisals and the fate of Nagy. Stephen's reluctance to shed blood matches Kádár's initial stance for a peaceful solution; Sarolt's reprimand, 'there is nothing these people understand but superior force. They don't understand the past and they cannot guess the future', is an affirmation that Hungarians can only be unified from above, so it is important that Stephen become king; it is one interpretation of Kádár's role in bloody reprisals, followed by the creation of better living standards, and a great degree of popular acceptance for the regime.

Stephen offers the kingship to Koppány on the condition that he accept the need to embrace Rome; this recalled Kádár's attempts to persuade Nagy to cease delegitimizing him, and initial public statements that Nagy was free to return and take a role in government. A story circulated in the late 1970s, claiming that Kádár had expected to gain Nagy's resignation and agreement to consolidate his government.[291] Stephen's self-torment over breaking God's law not to kill, when resorting to violence in order to protect Christianity, can be seen as matching Kádár's paradoxical decision to use terror to crush the uprising, in order to avoid a return to hard-line communism. In some readings, Stephen is even guilt-ridden.[292] Finally, Stephen's statements about loving God: 'for you [God], he would oppose even you' and 'on your side, my Lord, but without you'[293] would signal Kádár's acceptance of staying in the Soviet Bloc, while stipulating that his would not be a mere puppet government.

The rock opera therefore raised the question of choice and responsibility for the fate of the country concerning a fictional Stephen and Koppány, but also a historical Kádár and Nagy. Was Nagy a hero and Kádár a scoundrel? Was Nagy a hopeless romantic and Kádár the level-headed realist? Even the appropriate designation of what happened in 1956 has been a bone of contention both within and outside of Hungary, due partly to political motives in labelling it in particular ways, and partly to the difficulty of finding one suitable label that would cover all that happened between 23 October and roughly mid-November 1956. It has thus been called 'crisis', 'revolution', 'counter-revolution', 'war of national liberation', 'events', and 'popular uprising'.[294] In the uprising, a desire to reform the Stalinist regime, to reintroduce a multi-party political system, and to gain independence from the Soviet Union predominated, but

---

[291] György Marosán to David Irving on such expectations: Gosztonyi, *Föltámadott*, 181.

[292] E.g. Sándor, 'Megérteni a konfliktust'; Tamás Mészáros, 'Az ősi érdek', *Magyar Hírlap*, 18, no. 228 (28 September 1985), 7.

[293] 'Veled Uram, de nélküled' (literally 'with you my Lord but without you'). This text originated in the book by Miklós Boldizsár, who said it meant representing Christ's teachings, Christianity, but without ecclesiastical dogmas and bloody showdown: Magda Győri, *Egy hang Európa szívéből (portrékönyv Varga Miklósról)*, reprinted in Koltay, *István, a király 1983–2008*, 95.

[294] On interpretative framework: Rainer, *Az 1956-os magyar forradalom*, 159–72; Éva Standeisky, *Népuralom ötvenhatban* (Pozsony—Budapest: Kalligram—1956-os Intézet, 2010), 531–52; Pók, 'The year 1956', 209–10.

116 STEPHEN I, THE FIRST CHRISTIAN KING OF HUNGARY

antisemitic slogans, threats, violent attacks and lynch-mobs also appeared, with 'Jews' and 'communists' equated by many.[295]

Whether we read the rock opera as a coded message about 1956 or as the representation of the foundational paradigm that recurred throughout Hungarian history, the ambiguous presentation of Stephen and Koppány blur into the conflicting evaluations of Kádár and Nagy. János Bródy, the rock opera's lyricist, stated that Stephen is a political realist, and Koppány, the rebel, upholds a noble principle. Both in their own way are 'right': the need for cool judgement and the need for freedom are both essential. Thus, the viewer can identify emotionally with Koppány's truth, and rationally with Stephen's.[296] Such an interpretation presents Stephen/Kádár as the practical politician who acts appropriately in order to save the Hungarians. Koppány/Nagy can be seen as an idealist who follows a route of uncompromising principled action, even if he is doomed to fail, no matter what personal price he has to pay. Alternatively, he is hopelessly out of tune with the times and lacks political acumen to assess his country's possible sphere of action realistically. In any case, he is backed by traditional justice and loved by the people. At the same time, one can see emotional truth in the forced trajectory of both Stephen/Kádár and Koppány/Nagy, explicitly expressed by Koppány to both his daughter Réka and Stephen just before the final battle. The two principal political actors have no scope for independent decisions, they are swept along as outside forces determine the unfolding events: Stephen cannot decide against the battle (Kádár could not sway the Soviet decision to intervene), Koppány cannot accept Rome (Nagy could not give up the ideals by then invested in him by the population, and resign). The only potential for reconciliation exists in the realm of fantasy, with no historical basis either in 1956 or during Stephen's reign. Invented for *István, a király*, Réka, Koppány's daughter represents the voice of the people, with her songs written for traditional folk music.[297] Réka unites sincere Christian belief with an emotional understanding of her father. It is implied that she would be Stephen's true partner, with their mutual attraction manifest. Yet the possibility of reconciliation through such a union is doomed to failure: Stephen

---

[295] Lynchings of communists, real or imagined State Security Force personnel, and Jews took place in the countryside as well as Budapest: Éva Standeisky, 'Elmismásolt antiszemitizmus, elhallgatott múlt: Az 1956-os miskolci lincselés', in *OSZK 1956-os Intézet és Oral History Archívum*, http://www. rev.hu/ords/f?p=600:2:::::P2_PAGE_URI:tanulmanyok/1956/elmismasolt; on the range of behaviour, Standeisky, *Népuralom ötvenhatban*, on antisemitic slogans and deeds ibid., 433–53. See also Litván, *The Hungarian Revolution of 1956*, 124–6.

[296] János Bródy in interviews, https://zene.hu/cikkek/cikk.php?id=13351&currentPage=3; *Magyar Nemzet*, 71, no. 161 (14 June 2008), 30–1; *Magyar Nemzet*, 78, no. 193 (18 August 2015), 1. Similar views on the truth of both protagonists: Falus, 'István', 128; Péter Molnár Gál, 'Sikerrel nem vitatkozunk!', *Mozgó Világ*, 34, no. 7 (2008), 117–20, at 117–18; Koltay, *István*, 127 (Dénes Lóczy); highschool students, ibid., 133–4; Koltay in a later interview, *Új Magyarország*, 2, no. 186 (7 August 1992): 9; Sándor, 'Megérteni a konfliktust', 125; Stumpf, *Szörényi*, 155.

[297] Réka as the idealized possible future: Németh, 'István, a király', 93.

cannot escape his arranged marriage to the German Gisela (in the rock opera, the name is used in the Hungarian form Gizella).[298]

In the most positive potential reading of the rock opera from a Kádárist perspective, Stephen/Kádár is represented in a more sympathetic light than the real Kádár's actions would warrant; this is why the piece could be interpreted as an apotheosis of the regime. In the rock opera, not only does Stephen try to persuade Koppány to accept Rome until the last minute, offering him rulership; he also has no real part in Koppány's death and the fate of his body. It is Sarolt, Stephen's mother, who insists on Koppány's death and quartering. In real life, Kádár did not offer to cede leadership to Nagy (his public statements on the possibility of Nagy's return to government were insincere). Moreover, it was Kádár who was active behind the scenes to arrange Nagy's trial and death sentence; his own legitimacy was at stake.[299] Stephen does not orchestrate reprisals; Kádár did. Furthermore, the rock opera can also be read as suggesting that Koppány/Nagy's rebellion would have led to defeat and subjugation, and it was only Stephen/Kádár's compromise that ensured the conservation of a modicum of autonomy. *István* translates the real Kádár's protestation in Moscow on 3 November that his should not be a puppet government into Stephen's closing speech 'on your side, my Lord, but without you', and his programme of providing a country for the people. Stephen/ Kádár recognizes that the acceptance of Christianity (i.e. socialism) and adhesion to Christian Europe (the Soviet Bloc) is inevitable for survival, but within those constraints declares an independent government that would represent Hungarian interests, not complete subservience to the Soviet Union. In such a reading, Stephen/Kádár is a realist who understands the ways in which action is circumscribed by non-negotiable geopolitical facts. He can indeed even be seen as the true hero, who selflessly took an unpopular and difficult, but the only viable, decision in order to save the country and its inhabitants.

In cautious language, one contemporary analyst pointed out that the pagan camp is focused on freedom, while Stephen's camp is hypocritical; yet Stephen himself is different, he is motivated by concern for his people's future, and not by a desire for power; his politics are practical, clear-headed, and world-wise.[300] This may well be a veiled exoneration of Kádár. Indeed, Kádár is often credited with having been a pragmatist, giving attention to work on the ground, with a clear vision of the 'realities of power'.[301] After the fall of communism, some even branded the rock opera 'a repulsive apology of the declining Kádár regime', symptomatic of a nation that adapts to everything: although Kádár was responsible for

---

[298] Sándor, 'Megérteni a konfliktust', 124; János Bródy in interviews, *Népszabadság*, 56, no. 194 (19 August 1998), 33; *Magyar Nemzet*, 78, no. 193 (18 August 2015), 1.

[299] Levente Szörényi argued that the rock opera was not about Kádár and Nagy, as there was no equivalent: *Rendszerváltó archívum*, 2, no. 2 (June 2017), 86.

[300] Márton Koppány, 'István, a király', *Film Színház Muzsika*, 28, no. 17 (28 April 1984), 11.

[301] Gough, *Good Comrade*, 34.

118 STEPHEN I, THE FIRST CHRISTIAN KING OF HUNGARY

the execution of the revolutionaries, popular hatred against him later morphed into acceptance, just because he allowed people to say they were Hungarians.[302]

Yet this is not the only possible reading of the rock opera, especially because of the ambiguous representation of Stephen. Seemingly justifying Stephen/Kádár, is the rock opera condemning him as a traitor who is backed by external armies? Apparently struggling with his conscience, does he hypocritically allow the murder of the rebel Koppány for his own ends? He claims to have no desire for power, yet he also must know he can pretend not to want power, because others (German warriors/the Soviet army) will smooth his way to the top.

The negative interpretation is reinforced by the imbalance between the two main characters; viewers were more likely to identify emotionally with Koppány, as even a Catholic priest admitted.[303] Why is there more sympathy for Koppány? Szörényi's response was that Vikidál sung 'damned well' and the hard rock numbers make him a stronger character compared to Stephen's pop songs.[304] However, elements in the storyline of the rock opera also strengthen Koppány. He is a man with tremendous sex appeal with three devoted wives. In contrast, there is a suggestion of Stephen's impotence—or at the very least the lack of a meaningful relationship with his wife[305]—and weak-kneed inability to stand up to his mother. Koppány can control his lackeys and wants to fight face to face; Stephen leaves it to a German knight to fight him. Stephen can be construed as a weak puppet, controlled by his mother and the foreign knights in his entourage, or a pragmatist schemer who gained power without having to dirty his hands personally. Most importantly, Koppány's song with his refrain, 'shall we be captives or shall we be free', taken from the 1848 poem by Sándor Petőfi that fuelled the revolt against the Habsburgs, channels popular emotion in one determined direction.[306] Nobody could respond to that question with 'let's be captives'. A different phrasing of that question—'shall we consider the international context and make the necessary compromises, or shall we allow a stronger power to determine the course of

---

[302] Koltay, *István, a király 1983–2008*, 161 (Péter Nádori).

[303] Koltay, *István*, 125–7; Catholic priest on reaction of Christian children's groups: ibid., 126. Others on emotional identification with Koppány: ibid., 61, 106–7, 133, 140. One high school student said that this may be because revolt is more appealing than compromise: 'Ünnepi körkérdés', *Magyar Ifjúság*, 31, no. 34 (21 August 1987): 10 (János Kiss). Similar statement by István Bubik, an actor who played István in a theatre version: *Esti Hírlap*, 30, no. 300 (23 December 1985) [no page numbers]. Other performances were seen as having less imbalance between the protagonists: László Zöldi, *Népszabadság*, 42, no. 92 (19 April 1984), 7; István Takács, '"Mondd, te kit választanál?" Az István, a király a Nemzetiben', *Színház*, 19, no. 1 (1 January 1986), 5–9, at 7 and 9.

[304] *Népszabadság*, 56, no. 194 (19 August 1998), 33. Also in Jávorszky, 'István a király—Koppány a szupersztár'.

[305] In the 1984 film, Gizella is a tragic figure, full of goodwill, but unable to reach Stephen. The 2002 film's Gizella is a burlesque figure, especially because of the inclusion of the 'I am bored with politics' song, that was part of the original performance, but omitted from the first film: Falus, 'István', 125; Sándor Tóth interview with György Györffy, *Új Ember*, 40, no. 34 (19 August 1984), 3.

[306] On emotion in politics, Philippe Braud, *L'émotion en politique: problèmes d'analyse* (Paris: Presses de Sciences Po, 1996).

events completely'—may elicit a different response, but would lack emotive force. Although one could see Koppány as a reckless adventurer, or a populist manipulator, the dynamics of the rock opera force spectators to query Stephen's role much more than Koppány's.[307]

Is Stephen/Kádár's assertion that there is no other solution political pragmatism or political opportunism?[308] Did Kádár 'do the best possible, given his knowledge of the realities as they were'?[309] He had active agency, notably in the scope and target of reprisals, and was no mere pawn of Soviet decisions, despite real pressure. Did he act in the interests of the population, or did he opportunistically gain power, which he exercised for the rest of his life?

A favourite topos in Hungarian historical discourse is that realpolitik perpetually clashed with romantic emotional politics at significant crossroads of Hungarian history.[310] At the beginning of the rock opera, the audience is asked, 'Tell me, who would you choose?' Between what were people asked to choose? Political realism over idealism? The road to save the country over the road to lose it? Collaboration over freedom? An opportunist over an honest man? One form of nationalism over another? To what extent did they even have the power to choose, against the backdrop of the international framework? The rock opera also projects a less than flattering view of the masses, again with strong allusions to 1956 and its aftermath. Three fickle nobles represent the people who side now with Koppány, then with Stephen: 'we are like that and should not be ashamed of it'.[311] The unprincipled switching of sides has been described as modelling the compromise-ready stance of Hungarian citizens.[312]

No matter how stable and popular Kádár's regime became, the spectre of 1956 lurked beneath the surface. Openly questioning Kádár's responsibility was impossible; he even kept the most secret documents concerning the Nagy trial, the minutes of closed meetings, in his safe until his death.[313] If he referred to it at all, Kádár's self-justification was connected to the official narrative about 1956 as a counter-revolution and Nagy as a traitor: 'for the protection of socialist order, people's power and our national interest, we had the right and obligation to ask for international help'.[314] In 1983, openly criticizing Kádár's role in 1956 was not tolerated; hence, those who interpreted *Stephen, the king* as critical of Kádár also saw it as an example of dissidence. Creators and audiences of the rock opera could

---

[307] Later, Szörényi said, 'I was always in Koppány's camp': Stumpf, *Szörényi*, 154.

[308] Some thought only German knights, priests, and sycophantic Hungarian nobles sided with Stephen, whereas others thought that the population also did: Koltay, *István*, 127.

[309] Willy Brandt, quoted in Gough, *Good Comrade*, 250. Similarly Mihály Bihari, 'Kádár és rendszere', in Rácz, *Ki volt Kádár?*, 151–4.

[310] Criticized: Koltay, *István*, 113–15 (Ferencné Bíró).

[311] Ibid., 147.   [312] Koltay, *István, a király 1983–2008*, 161.

[313] Dornbach et al., *A per*, 110.

[314] Speech at the meeting of the commanders of the Hungarian People's Army, March 1981, in Kádár, *Szövetségi politika*, 336.

120   STEPHEN I, THE FIRST CHRISTIAN KING OF HUNGARY

not know that in a few years' time, Kádár's persona would crumble in a way that
was no pale shadow of ancient Greek tragedy or Shakespearean drama. The fates
of Kádár and Nagy were intertwined not only at Kádár's taking of power but also
at the end of his life. Nagy's rehabilitation occurred in parallel to Kádár's loss of
power, madness, and death.

8. Nagy and Kádár, 1989

In the face of mounting economic problems and desire for change, an extraordin-
ary Party conference was convened on 23–4 May 1988. The ageing and increasingly ill Kádár was no longer able to lead the country. In the run-up to the
conference, his resignation was secured (with Soviet help); he was shunted into
the newly created post of president of the Party, without effective power. At the
conference, the membership of the Party's central committee was drastically
transformed, and the old guard of Kádár loyalists was ousted. The post of General
Secretary of the Party went to Károly Grósz.[315] The Politburo also set up a historical subcommittee, to re-evaluate 1956. Imre Pozsgay in January 1989 announced
the conclusion that it was a popular uprising (népfelkelés).[316] A dialogue with
political opponents started, and the first steps towards Nagy's rehabilitation were
taken.[317] Together with his own sidelining, this clearly affected Kádár, whose
health had been deteriorating over the previous years. Grósz also wanted to demonstrate a break with the past, and thus Kádár's own role started to be queried; he
was by then an obstacle to change, but could also be used as a scapegoat.[318]

On 12 April 1989, the Central Committee of the Hungarian Socialist Party met
to ease the transition to regime change, and decided to introduce a multi-party
system and elections. Kádár appeared unscheduled at the meeting, and gave a
long, incoherent speech, querying his responsibility in the events of 1956.[319]

---

[315] Huszár, Kádár, vol. 2, 306–8; Gough, Good Comrade, 233–40.

[316] Huszár, Kádár, vol. 2, 310. The full report was published in Társadalmi Szemle, 44, Special Issue
1 (1989), 2–80; on 1956 popular uprising, see 31–4.

[317] One survivor's demand for a retrial in 1985 was rejected. A Historical Justice Committee
(Történelmi Igazságtétel Bizottsága), formed in 1988 from family members and survivors, pressured
the government to find the graves and allow reburial; this led to a judicial review in 1989: Dornbach,
'A pártállami igazságszolgáltatás', 27–9. Rainer, Nagy, 225–6. See also Csaba Békés, Malcolm Byrne,
ed., Rendszerváltozás Magyarországon 1989–1990. Dokumentumok (Budapest: National Security
Archive—1956-os Intézet, 1999).

[318] In March 1989, Kádár was interviewed with Grósz's approval, about aspects of his life he had
always refused to discuss. During the multiple sittings, Kádár's mental state deteriorated rapidly; eventually he refused to continue. Huszár suggests that Grósz may have wanted to discredit Kádár through
his own words as it became clear that 1956 had to be reappraised. Huszár, Kádár, vol. 2, 309–13;
scapegoat 316–17.

[319] Integral text: Beszélő, 1, no. 3 http://beszelo.c3.hu/cikkek/kadar-magyar-drama?utm_source=
mandiner&utm_medium=link&utm_campaign=mandiner_201803#1996-f05-11_to_8; also in Rácz,
Ki volt Kádár?, 213–16. On making the 'psychopathological' speech, Huszár, Kádár, vol. 2,

'[T]he doctor said that I cannot give a speech...But I said that on my own responsibility I will undertake it even if I make a mistake. Because I am a very old man now, and I have many kinds of illnesses, and I no longer care if anybody shoots me dead.' 'Everyone says that I am the one still alive, so I should say something.' 'Day and night my brain is spinning regarding what my responsibility is.' Mixing events from different periods of his life, he talked about having been in prison, decisions taken in the face of Soviet tanks, and 'that man [Imre Nagy] who since then has died'. He claimed to have been made a scapegoat, when what he had done was to defend the Party and the political system, at a time when the life of many people depended on him. His achievements, he pointed out, included Hungary being the first communist country visited by an English prime minister.

Intertwined with sentences about his failing health, he repeatedly returned to the question of his responsibility for the death of Imre Nagy and other members of Nagy's government:[320] 'I took responsibility for the safety of those at the embassy. But I took this on because I was naïve, I thought my request was not so very great, for two men [Imre Nagy and Géza Losonczy] to make a declaration so that [others] cannot legally refer to their rank'—a reference to the demand that Nagy resign so as not to delegitimize Kádár. '[T]he Yugoslav ambassador told me...he received their [Soviet] authorization to try to persuade those two people. And he said, I've been trying unsuccessfully for three days. And I was glad the Polish ambassador came to see me [so I could tell him], because otherwise how in God's name could I prove it?'

'[T]he first accusation against me [after '56] was that I was a Soviet agent. I wasn't..., and I can prove it.'[321] 'I did not call it a counter-revolution at all....From the 28th [of October]...because of clothing or skin-colour or I don't know what, unarmed people were killed in pogroms. And they were killed before Imre Nagy and the others...Because if I am not looking at it historically, if I look at it from the distance of 30 years, I would also easily say that I am sorry for everyone.' Whether the Kádár who spoke was a modern-day Macbeth struggling with his conscience, a Party cadre conditioned by show-trials, or a lonely old man trying to advise his Party is disputed.[322]

312–18. A thorough analysis of the speech: Lengyel, *A rendszerváltó elit*, 108–24. See also Gough, *Good Comrade*, 242–6.

[320] György Aczél claimed Kádár started to be consumed by guilt over Nagy's execution (Aczél, 'Közelkép', 25); cf. Huszár, *Kádár*, vol. 2, 275. According to Huszár, his mental deterioration evoked guilt-feelings: ibid., 314–15, 336. Lengyel argued Kádár was not beset by guilt, Nagy's execution was not a matter of conscience, because he separated action for the Party from action as a private individual: László Lengyel, 'Kádár utolsó beszéde: egy élet drámája—megközelítések' in *Ki volt Kádár?*, ed. Rácz, 208–16.

[321] He referred to 'being released', the first intimation that on 1 November 1956 he did not go voluntarily first to Carpatho-Ukraine, then Moscow: Huszár, *Kádár*, vol. 2, 315.

[322] Timothy Garton Ash, *We the People: The Revolution of '89 Witnessed in Warsaw, Budapest, Berlin and Prague* (Cambridge: Granta, 1990), 53; Lengyel, *A rendszerváltó elit*, 108–24 (Kádár saw Nagy as a traitor to an idea). Lengyel, 'Kádár utolsó beszéde', 209, analysing six interpretations of the

122 STEPHEN I, THE FIRST CHRISTIAN KING OF HUNGARY

Directly after the speech, he sent for Dezső Nyers (a senior politician, and soon to be last President of the Hungarian Socialist Workers' Party before the fall of communism), and spoke to him for twenty to twenty-five minutes; about Imre Nagy, Kádár told him, 'Believe me, the tragedy happened because he was unwilling to sign his resignation.'[323] Mentally and physically, Kádár was rapidly deteriorating. In a letter, he asked the Party's Central Committee for a judiciary investigation into his own role in the Nagy trial, to ascertain if he had interfered in the process of justice, and either declare him guilty or stop the insinuations against him.[324] Just as Imre Nagy's condemnation ushered in the Kádár regime, so his rehabilitation accompanied its end. After many months of searching for the graves during 1988–9, and disagreements over private reburial or public ceremony, finally Nagy and those executed with him were exhumed in April and solemnly reburied on 16 June 1989.[325] Kádár died on 6 July 1989, on the very day when the Supreme Court of Hungary pronounced the rehabilitation of Imre Nagy and other members of his government.[326] The reactivated memory of 1956 retrospectively delegitimized the Kádár regime, yet just as the rock opera's Hungarians were unable to choose between Stephen and Koppány, so the Hungarian population paid tribute to both Nagy and Kádár: a crowd of about 200,000 was present at Nagy's lying-in-state on 16 June, about 60,000 filed past Kádár's coffin, and about 100,000 attended his funeral on 13–14 July.[327]

9. The Rock Opera after the Fall of Communism

Despite the rich potential of political interpretations, it is impossible to tie the rock opera firmly to any one of them (be it the apotheosis or covert criticism of the Kádár regime), because its success cuts through regime change. Since the first performances, the rock opera has been in repertory continuously.[328] Shown on TV,[329] later also available on YouTube, it is thought that most Hungarians would have seen it at some point.[330] New live performances are staged every year; several were also recorded and released as films. Szörényi highlighted the changing meaning: according to him, in

---

speech. Good summing up of Kádár's achievements and responsibilities, Gough, *Good Comrade*, 249–55, including 'cold-eyed realpolitik of Nagy's execution' (250).

[323] Huszár, *Kádár*, vol. 2, 318. According to Aczél, 'Közelkép Kádárról', 21–2, Kádár made similar statements to him.

[324] Huszár, *Kedves, jó Kádár Elvtárs!*, 680, dated 26 May 1989; Huszár, *Kádár*, vol. 2, 320.

[325] Dornbach, 'A pártállami igazságszolgáltatás', 28–9; Rainer, *Nagy*, 226–33.

[326] On rehabilitation, Dornbach, 'A pártállami igazságszolgáltatás', 36–9.

[327] János M. Rainer, 'Nagy Imre újratemetése—a magyar demokratikus átalakulás szimbolikus aktusa', in *A magyar forradalom eszméi. Eltiprásuk és győzelmük (1956–1999)*, ed. Béla Király and Lee W. Congdon (Budapest: Atlanti Kutató és Kiadó Társulat-Alapítvány, 2001), 240–58; Gough, *Good Comrade*, 257.

[328] On later performances in Hungary and abroad: Koltay, *István, a király 1983–2008*, 162, 177–9, chapter 7.

[329] Watched by 15–20 million viewers: ibid., 163.   [330] Ibid., 7.

STEPHEN, THE KING 123

the 1980s the rock opera 'was the banner of independence', but by the mid-1990s, it is 'more': a reminder that national traditions and progress need to be reconciled, 'all should feel to be heirs of both Stephen and Koppány'.[331]

After 1989, nationalist readings took off.[332] For all the debate about national identity that *István* raised, instead of a resolution, old distorted grievances and nationalism were revived, to flourish more freely after 1989. The declaration by the rock opera's Stephen that he wants to be king of all Hungarians can be interpreted as an expression of national unity across political borders, in the vein of Prime Minister József Antall's declaration on 2 June 1990, shortly after forming the first post-communist elected government that 'according to the law...I wish to be head of state of every Hungarian citizen, this country of ten million, but in my soul, in feelings, the prime minister of fifteen million Hungarians [that is, including Hungarian minorities in neighbouring countries]'.[333] The Hungarian Anthem is now routinely sung by performers and audiences at the end. After initial difficulties, performances were exported to minority Hungarian communities in neighbouring countries,[334] where the rock opera can be read as a message against the treaty of Trianon. In 2003, in Şumuleu Ciuc (Csíksomlyó), Romania, at the Transylvanian premiere of the rock opera, loud cheers from the audience greeted Stephen's statement 'And I want this people to have a country'.[335] The Sekler (Székely) Anthem, a poem written in Hungarian in 1921, in the context of Hungarian territorial revisionism, and eventually adopted as a hymn of Seklerland, was also sung at the end.[336] Prohibited for decades in Romania, it includes lines asking God to save Transylvania, and for life in Hungarian Seklerland, in a free motherland.[337] Its importance for national identity ultimately invested *István* itself with cult status that, according to the political right can be 'desacralized' by performances that do not show reverence to the rock opera.

For *István, a király* did not become a monopoly of right-wing sympathizers; it has also been used to criticize current regimes, notably the performances directed by renowned director Róbert Alföldi in 2013. The SS uniforms of the Germans in Stephen's entourage and the shockingly open brutality in the murder of Koppány's envoy were suggestive of Hungarian collaboration with the Nazis during the Second

---

[331] Sebők, *Rock a vasfüggöny mögött*, 369.

[332] Povedák, 'Mitizált történelem' shows the increasingly prominent nationalistic interpretations in public discussions.

[333] Antall's speech at the third national assembly of MDF, published in Róbert Győri Szabó, *A magyar külpolitika története 1848-tól napjainkig* (Budapest: Helikon, 2011), 355. Such views were being expressed already in 1984, e.g. '16 million Hungarians' were united by the historical consciousness expressed by the rock opera: Koltay, *István*, 123.

[334] Koltay, *István, a király 1983–2008*, 231–42.

[335] https://www.youtube.com/watch?v=NbZUdUckf8E.   [336] Ibid., at 1:46:55.

[337] Ildikó Kríza, 'A székely himnusz születésének háttere', *Honismeret*, 31, no. 5 (2003), 57–68, https://epa.oszk.hu/03000/03018/00176/pdf/EPA03018_honismeret_2003_05_057-068.pdf; Ilona Erdélyi, 'A székely himnusz szerzői', *National Geographic Hungary*, 21 February 2016, https://ng.hu/kultura/2016/02/21/a-szekely-himnusz-szerzoi.

124   STEPHEN I, THE FIRST CHRISTIAN KING OF HUNGARY

World War, a part of Hungarian history that the government has been eagerly rewriting. The set was a gigantic 'Holy Crown' that snapped closed on the cast at the end like a cage, suggestive of the prison-like, restrictive nationalism that the politics of the current regime has created.[338] No wonder the performance was attacked by the political right. For journalist Zsolt Bayer, the rock opera was 'smeared with poisonous saliva.'[339] Another commentator called it a 'crime.'[340] Extreme right-wing groups demonstrated against the performance: to them, this interpretation, as well as the homosexuality of the director, was a direct attack against national identity.[341] At the same time, János Bródy celebrated the performance, calling the piece 'the conscience of the nation.'[342] Bródy also reinterpreted the Stephen—Koppány conflict to fit the present, while appealing for unity: 'St Stephen's descendants want a European Hungary, Koppány's do not want to become a colony; the interest of the country is for the two forces not to fight each other, but helping each other, realize both conceptions.'[343]

Such sentiment belongs to a minority, and even here, the most striking aspect is the idea of a country divided, a fissure, although the language aims at healing, rather than exacerbating the division. That reflects the deeply ingrained way of seeing Hungarian history as a series of recurring internal struggles, motivated by opposing views of what constitutes the right path for Hungary, such as loyalty to or independence from the Habsburgs from the early modern period, reform (István Széchenyi) or revolution for independence (Lajos Kossuth) in 1848. That dynamic is manifest in the rock opera; indeed, it even suggests that the paradigm was set by the conflict of Stephen and Koppány.

The power of myth transformed into history is revealed: Koppány may not even have existed as a historical figure, and he certainly never existed as Stephen's male relative who subscribed to a different value-system, desiring a different path for Hungary. Yet embodied in the rock opera, opposite an also mythicized Stephen, Koppány became a stand-in not just for the historical Imre Nagy, but also for a supposed 'more genuine' Hungarianness. The arguments that continue over the rock opera, that are part of the struggle over defining 'national identity', create and feed off mythicized history. However, it is exactly the story's supposed veracity that is referenced in making claims for a 'true' national identity. As early as in 1983, some claimed that the rock opera provided, instead of 'misleading history lessons, various manipulated political ideologies... an honest national identity one could experience.'[344] The fortunes of *István, a király* demonstrate how myth in the

---

[338]   Analysis of Alföldi's mise-en-scène: Sándor, 'Megérteni a konfliktust', 127–8.
[339]   http://hvg.hu/kultura/20130824_bayer_kiosztotta_szorenyit.
[340]   Kornél Bakay, 'Egy szétmállott nemzeti ikon', *Kapu*, 25, no. 9 (September 2013), 44–5, at 45.
[341]   Gyula Balogh, 'Elszabadult indulatok célkeresztjében', *Népszava*, 140, no. 200 (28 August 2013), 12; Povedák, 'Mitizált történelem', 105–6.
[342]   Balogh, 'Elszabadult indulatok', 12.
[343]   http://www.origo.hu/kultura/20150925-brody-janos-ha-en-rozsa-volnek-emberi-jogok-migrans-kerdes.html.
[344]   Gyula Vikidál in Koltay, *István*, 64.

guise of history is used in nationalist truth-claims. It also shows that supposedly driven by a wish to unify the nation, national myths are in fact divisive.[345]

Moreover, *István* demonstrates the invasive potential of myth: how a myth driven underground can survive, resurface, and grow. The rock opera's Koppány and his entourage are heirs to some of the interwar ideology, similarly to neo-paganism in many post-Soviet countries.[346] In the rock opera, there are disturbing echoes of the Turanian movement's views. The framework opposing oppression to freedom as central in the confrontation of Stephen and Koppány can be found in both. Moreover, the rock opera's line, 'we do not need a God who doesn't speak Hungarian' evokes Bencsi's book *Koppány-e vagy István*, where he writes: 'And why do Hungarians have to even forget their language? Why do Hungarians have to worship God in a foreign language?'[347] It is even possible to trace the thread from interwar myths about Koppány to the rock opera more specifically: Levente Szörényi's father, Gyula Szörényi (1916–88), painter and graphic designer, was interested in 'ancient Hungarian religion'.[348] He produced a plan for the Koppány Tower (although it was not selected for the final design), and drew the image for Bencsi's book cover: an 'ancient Hungarian warrior' with a battle-axe standing on a hill, while two hills in the background feature a church and a sun-symbol with fire.[349]

István, a király popularized the positive image of Koppány to a broad audience.[350] This followed from the decision to portray 'two truths' in the two protagonists.[351] By providing an embodied Koppány, the rock opera facilitated emotional identification. Further, it left room for the idea that Koppány was the rightful heir, and Stephen took power unlawfully.[352] Members of the public thought it was 'a historical fact' that 'Koppány remained true to his principles unto death'.[353] In the classic late communist interpretation, Koppány was elevated

---

[345] On the rock opera's long-lasting impact linking neo-nationalism and rock music, and the role of pop culture in fomenting neo-nationalism in Hungary in the twenty-first century: Margit Feischmidt—Gergő Pulay, 'Élmény és ideológia a nacionalista popkultúrában', in *Nemzet a mindennapokban: Az újnacionalizmus populáris kultúrája*, ed. Margit Feischmidt, Rita Glózer, Zoltán Ilyés, Katalin Veronika Kasznár, Ildikó Zakariás (Budapest: L'Harmattan, 2014), 249–89, at 256 on Stephen.

[346] Role of emigrants in the ideas' survival: Kaarina Aitamurto, Scott Simpson, ed., *Modern Pagan and Native Faith Movements in Central and Eastern Europe* (London: Routledge, 2013), 5–6.

[347] Bencsi, *Koppány-e vagy István?*, 8: 'És mért kell a magyarnak még a nyelvét is elfeledni? Miért kell a magyarnak idegen nyelven imádni az Istent?'

[348] Stumpf, *Szörényi*, 205.

[349] Ibid., images 19–20. Book cover also: https://antikva.hu/magyar-tortenelem/f6e470319655ad8a0b9e15adecadab6d.

[350] Povedák, 'Mitizált Történelem', 104; Attila László Hubbes, 'Ritual deliberations around mythic narratives in online ethno-pagan communities', in *Argumentor: Proceedings of the Second International Conference on Argumentation and Rhetoric*, ed. Rozália Klára Bakó et al. (Oradea: Partium Press and Debrecen: Debrecen University Press, 2012), 259–94, at 269.

[351] Koltay, *István*, 177, reprinting Gabriella Lőcsei's interview of Miklós Boldizsár, *Magyar Nemzet*, 47, no. 53 (3 March 1984), 9.

[352] Koltay, *István*, 60.

[353] Letter by Zoltán Bánáti, *Magyar Ifjúság*, 27, no. 48 (2 December 1983), 37, partly repr. Koltay, *István*, 85.

126   STEPHEN I, THE FIRST CHRISTIAN KING OF HUNGARY

to a tragic figure, who did not serve the cause of progress and had to fall, but nonetheless provided a positive example of heroism and perseverance.[354] Even those writing from a Christian perspective acknowledged Koppány was acting on principle and fighting for the people rather than out of self-interest.[355] Ecclesiastics found a justification for Koppány's 'stronger voice' in the supposed historical moment, when the fate of the country—Christian or pagan—was decided: 'both sides had to be shown to be strong', but 'Lucifer's voice is always stronger'.[356] Levente Szörényi expressed his belief that *István, a király* 'restored' Koppány to his rightful place in history, after centuries of Catholic ecclesiastical obfuscation; this can be seen as part of a broader trend, pop music serving as a vehicle of 'restoring' paganism in Europe and the USA.[357] Since taking part in composing the rock opera, Szörényi's sympathies for 'traditional' national identity have been expressed in a rock opera on Attila the Hun, in the positive portrayal of those who want to continue paganism in the eleventh century in the opera *Árpád népe*, as well as in his ongoing archaeological excavations at the site of 'the knowledge of the ancestors', which, some believed, was the burial site of Árpád.[358]

After 1989, and especially in the twenty-first century, Koppány gained prominence in alternative constructions of national identification. This is part of the burgeoning neo- (or ethno-) pagan movements in the former Soviet Bloc. While there are significant variations in their tenets and organizational forms, such movements seek to revive 'ancient religion', linking it to ethnic nationalism, and posit enemies, who try to destroy the nation, thus creating alternative discourses for national history, in significant contrast to neo-pagan movements elsewhere.[359] Based on myths, often in explicit opposition to academic history (even seeing professional history-writing as part of a conspiracy to hide the truth), these

---

[354] Bánáti, *Magyar Ifjúság*, 27, no. 48 (2 December 1983), 37, partly repr. Koltay, *István*, 85.
[355] Koltay, *István*, 35 (Zoltán Bóna, *Confessio*, 1983/4).
[356] Ibid., 98–9 (canon and titular abbot Sándor Szeles).
[357] https://zene.hu/cikkek/cikk.php?id=13351&currentPage=2. On other countries: Donna Weston, Andy Bennett, ed., *Pop Pagans: Paganism and Popular Music* (Durham: Acumen, 2013).
[358] Stumpf, *Szörényi*, 186–9 on the rock opera 'Attila the Hungarian past'; 197–8, 233–6 on excavation (236 'itt van az ősök tudása'); 214–15 on 'Árpád népe'.
[359] More generally, Victor A. Shnirelman, '"Christians! Go home!": a revival of Neo-Paganism between the Baltic Sea and Transcaucasia (an overview)', *Journal of Contemporary Religion*, 17, no. 2 (2002): 197–211; Aitamurto—Simpson, *Modern Pagan and Native Faith Movements*; overviews on Hungary: Réka Szilárdi, 'Neopaganism in Hungary: under the spell of roots', in Aitamurto—Simpson, *Modern Pagan and Native Faith Movements*, 230–48; Klára Rozália Bakó, László-Attila Hubbes, 'Religious minorities' web rhetoric: Romanian and Hungarian ethno-pagan organizations', *Journal for the Study of Religions and Ideologies*, 10, no. 30 (2011): 127–58; Ádám Kolozsi, *Social Constructions of the Native Faith: Mytho-historical Narratives and Identity-discourse in Hungarian Neo-paganism*, MA thesis Central European University—Nationalism Studies Program, 2012. On the term ethno-paganism: László-Attila Hubbes, 'A comparative investigation of Romanian and Hungarian ethno-pagan blogs' (19 December 2011), Reconect Working Papers No. 2/2011, available at https://papers.ssrn.com/sol3/papers.cfm?abstract_id=1984597. Eastern vs. Western European neopaganism: Michael F. Strmiska, 'Modern paganism in world cultures: comparative perspectives', in *Modern Paganism in World Cultures: Comparative Perspectives*, ed. Michael F. Strmiska (Santa Barbara, CA: ABC Clio, 2005), 1–53, esp. 14–22.

STEPHEN, THE KING   127

constructions encompass a wide array of national claims in Hungary, including, for example, Sumerian—Hungarian continuity.[360] With the advent of the internet, such alternative stories spread much more easily, and internet communities foster their further elaboration. Questions of origin feature prominently, as 'genuine Hungarianness' is supposed to be inherent in origins. In some ethno-pagan claims, Koppány is a martyr and symbol of the oppression of Hungarians; some leaders of ethno-pagan communities derived their ancestry from Koppány, creating cult places for him.[361] One, at the Szentesica spring, bears inscriptions expressing hope for the return of the *táltos* (a figure with supernatural power) of the Light, and the reunification of the nation; some of them call on Hungarians to awaken and return to their ancient faith. Koppány's quartering allegedly started the series of 'tragedies' for Hungarians and is symptomatic of European racism coupled to feelings of inferiority towards Hungarians.[362]

Some ethno-pagan narratives reinterpret Stephen as a traitor, who directed the Hungarians onto the wrong path; they demand a return to Koppány's heritage. Stephen features as the oppressor of shamans and of the representatives of authentic tradition.[363] The legend of the 'Turanian curse' is a key example. The curse allegedly causes Hungarians to fight against each other either until they return to their old religion or, in other versions, for a thousand years. The curse's root cause according to one version was giving up ancient religion or traditions, according to another, accepting foreign priests, and according to yet another, Stephen's usurpation of power from the rightful heir Koppány. The idea of the 'Turanian curse' originated in the early twentieth century, but this specific formulation probably dates from the 1990s; myths concerning Stephen's takeover from Koppány have been promoted on the internet by conspiracy theorists, bloggers, and seekers of right-wing national identity.[364] Analysis of such websites showed that this subculture blames Stephen for introducing a 'foreign' religion, facilitating a kind of colonization (although one strongly antisemitic variant claims that a

---

[360] Introductory summary: Szilárdi, 'Neopaganism in Hungary: under the spell of roots'. Analyses of diverse trends: Tamás Szilágyi, Réka Szilárdi, *Istenek ébredése: A neopogányság vallástudományi vizsgálata* (Szeged: JATE Press, 2007); László-Attila Hubbes, ed., *Etno-pogányok. Retorikai fogások a hálón innen és túl. Online műhelybeszélgetés a magyar etno-pogányság diskurzusairól* (Cluj: Erdélyi Múzeum-Egyesület, 2012).

[361] Kolozsi, *Social Constructions*, 73; László Koppány Csáji, 'Az egyéni és közösségi sokszínűség megragadásának vallásantropológiai nehézségei', in Hubbes, *Etno-pogányok*, 17–66, at 25; Róbert Gyula Cey-Bert, *Koppány a Fény Harcosa* (Budapest: Püski, 2014), 10. Some photos of cult places: Magyar, *Hős vagy lázadó?*, 165–6.

[362] Cey-Bert, *Koppány*, 269–81.

[363] Vilmos Voigt, ' "Nem vagyunk mink (…) Szent István szolgái" in idem, *Magyar, magyarországi és nemzetközi: Történeti folklorisztikai tanulmányok* (Budapest: Universitas Könyvkiadó, 2004), 290–308, at 295.

[364] Povedák, 'Mitizált történelem', 110–18; rock opera triggering the remythologizing of Stephen: Povedák, 'Mitizált Történelem', 101; on historical heroes between official and lived national identity, ibid., 102. Ablonczy, *Keletre, magyar!*, 26–7 on nineteenth-century roots of the 'ancient curse'; the name Turanian is from the early twentieth century.

128 STEPHEN I, THE FIRST CHRISTIAN KING OF HUNGARY

Jewish perversion of Christianity replaced 'real' Scythian-Hungarian Christianity that the Hungarians had practised prior to Stephen), and cultivates feelings of insulted national pride.[365]

Thus some versions of ethno-paganism contrast Hungarian pagan tradition with Christianity; others posit a monotheistic Hungarian paganism or an original Hungarian Christianity (the rock opera's reference to Koppány's conversion to Byzantine Christianity can even be seen as an allusion to that), or even derive 'true' Christianity (later perverted) from a Jesus who is the ancestor of the Hungarians; this true, original Christianity is destroyed by Stephen converting the country to Catholicism.[366] Yet other varieties include both Koppány and Stephen in a narrative of the sacred nation and mystical Hungarian spirituality; the ancient Scythian religion is already Christian, and Catholicism and the old faith peacefully complement each other.[367]

We have come full circle, as myth is promoted as real history, and history writing is invalidated. Medieval sources were interpreted by professional historians in ways that did not fully account for the nature of those sources. Thus, medieval myths were used as source material for history, and therefore the latter was shot through with myth, as can be seen in the story of Koppány. Academic history then enabled the creation of the rock opera, which conveyed views on current politics in a historical garb. This representation began to generate more interpretations, now entirely disconnected from professional history writing. Elaborate myths are substituted for history, while professional research is dismissed or even seen as a conspiracy to occult the truth. Thus, significant parts of the population embrace complete myth as their explanatory framework, and claim that true Hungarian identity stands on these 'origins'. Various alternative myths can coexist or underpin rival explanations. Thus, for example, pagan origins can be used to dismiss Christianity, or both paganism and Christianity can be touted as part of genuine Hungarian identity. As scholars of nation-making know, there is no content to identity claims that fits all within the supposed 'nation'. No national identity exists; assertions to the contrary are always projects of identity creation, which lead to even violent contestation. Such contestation is not a Hungarian curse, nor is it accidental; rather, it is inherent in projects of national identity that do not wish to acknowledge alternative coexisting paths, but try to define what is acceptable. Such constructs will never match reality, and will continue to foster conflict.

Stephen I, the First Christian King of Hungary: From Medieval Myth to Modern Legend. Nora Berend, Oxford University Press. © Nora Berend 2024. DOI: 10.1093/9780191995439.003.0003

---

[365] Povedák, 'Mitizált Történelem', 106–9; Hubbes, 'Ritual deliberations', 282–3.

[366] László-Attila Hubbes, 'Lázadó ősök—pogány fiatalok? Magyar újpogány közösségek kommunikációs rítusai a világhálón', in Hubbes, *Etno-pogányok*, 95–109, see 104; Szilágyi and Szilárdi, *Istenek ébredése*, 64–5. Example of monotheistic paganism of Koppány: Tamás Gönczi, *Pogány Biblia. Koppány hagyatéka. A magyar ősvallás szakrális öröksége*, 2, jav. kiad. (Budapest: Angyali Menedék, 2019).

[367] Kolozsi, *Social Constructions*, 80–2. E.g. harmonization in a novel: Cey-Bert, *Koppány*.

3
The Holy Dexter

The Holy Dexter is a mummified, tightly clenched right hand; according to modern medical experts, it belonged to a man of smaller than average stature.[1] Although some doubts have been expressed about its authenticity, the Holy Dexter is still venerated by many as a relic of St Stephen. Moreover, even sceptics who think its later story warrants suspicion have accepted that the medieval tale about its provenance is accurate in its main lines. Most recent historiography has even reasserted that the relic is genuine.[2] Not all alleged Stephen relics have fared so well.[3] Its status, however, is not merely that of an object of religious cult. Indeed, its modern, and now revived, significance is intimately tied to the alleged relic's political role, which has ensured its prominence in state-sponsored events and rhetoric, and its constant public presence. This modern function, I shall argue, mirrors the relic's original role, although current political actors are unaware of that imitation.

---

[1] Three medical exams of the hand were conducted, in 1951, 1988, and 1999; short reports were published of the first and third: Ádám Bochkor, 'A Szent Jobb orvosi szemmel', *Vigília*, 25: 8 (1960): 492–4; Miklós Réthelyi, 'Szent Jobb, az anatómus szemével', *Medikus*, 9, no. 3 (2000): 24–5. The latter states that the skin from the back of the hand is mostly missing, and a textile sewn into the palm makes it impossible to investigate the whole hand (24); an X-ray showed that the metal encasing the lower part of the hand includes the rest of the entire hand (25). The report from 1988 is unpublished, but cited in Alida Lilla Kristóf, *Paleoradiológia: non-invazív módszertani lehetőség a történeti antropológiában*. PhD dissertation, Szeged, 2015, http://doktori.bibl.u-szeged.hu/2754/1/disszert% C3%A1ci%C3%B3_12.pdf, 46–53. Kristóf observes that the conclusion about size was drawn in comparison to modern data.

[2] 'We have few relics that went through more vicissitudes than the relatively intactly preserved right hand of our first king': Antal Molnár, 'A Szent Jobb és Raguza', *Turul*, 76 (2003, nos. 1–2): 7–11, at 7.

[3] Other relics of St Stephen included a skull, subdivided into pieces, the arm, and other bones, but none can be traced back to the late eleventh century: Géza Karsai, 'Szent István király tisztelete', in *Emlékkönyv Szent István király halálának kilencszázadik évfordulóján* (Budapest, 1938), ed. Jusztinián Serédi, vol. 3, 155–256, at 166–8. Georgius Pray, *Dissertatio historico-critica de Sacra Dextera Divi Stephani primi Hungariae regis* (Vienna, 1771), 71–6 criticizes the authenticity of an alleged finger relic of Stephen. One alleged lower arm relic, supposedly sent by Sigismund of Luxemburg to his son-in-law Albert of Habsburg and kept in Vienna was subsequently revealed to be the tibia of a right leg: Konrád Szántó, 'A Szent Jobb tisztelete a középkorban', in *Szent István és kora*, ed. Ferenc Glatz, József Kardos (Budapest: MTA Történettudományi Intézet, 1988), 173–9, at 177 (a similar article, but without notes in *História*, 1988/4); Piroska Rácz, 'Szent István ereklyéi', in *Szent István király bazilikájának utóélete: A középkori romkert 1938-tól napjainkig. A Szent István Király Múzeum Közleményei B series, no. 56 (Székesfehérvár, 2016), 31–6, at 32 (the same also published as Piroska Rácz, 'Szent István ereklyéi', *Rubicon*, 24, no. 6 (2013): 20–5).

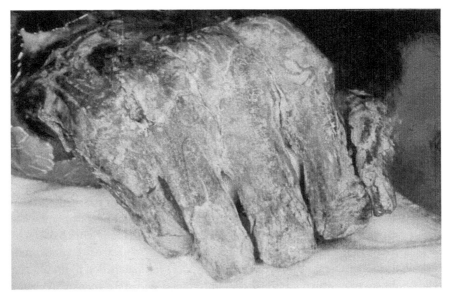

Figure 4. The Holy Dexter
https://hu.wikipedia.org/wiki/Szent_Jobb#/media/F%C3%A1jl:Hungary-0103_-_St._Stephen's_Hand_(7278347772).jpg
Dennis Jarvis from Halifax, Canada, CC BY-SA 2.0

1. The Dexter's History

The right hand has had a colourful history.[4] For a long time it was held at a monastery named after it, Szentjobb ('Holy Dexter', today Sîniob, Romania), and in the early fourteenth century the bishop of Zagreb referred to it and the monastery.[5] The relic also played a unique role for King Ladislas (Wenceslas) of Hungary in 1304. Ladislas (also king of Bohemia as Václav III and king of Poland as Wacław II in 1305–6) was elected by Hungarian nobles after the death of Andrew III. He was one of several claimants, as well as one of two crowned kings (the Angevin Charles Robert, enjoying papal support, was the other). Thus the Přemyslid youngster's position in Hungary was quite tenuous, and he hosted his father King Wenceslas II of Bohemia at Buda to boost his legitimacy. If we are to believe the *Steirische Reimchronik*, he performed a festive crown wearing ceremony to receive Wenceslas II, wearing St Stephen's crown and mantle, holding in

---

[4] Anna Farkas, *Nemzeti ereklyénk: Szent István király jobbja. Az ereklye története* (Budapest: Formatív Kiadó, 1991). This leaflet provides an uncritical history of the relic, but contains many photos of the twentieth century celebrations.
[5] Vilmos Fraknói, 'A Szent Jobb', *Századok*, 35 (1901): 880–904, at 890; Karsai 'Szent István király tisztelete', 162.

THE HOLY DEXTER 131

one hand St Stephen's sword and in his other, instead of an orb, the Holy Dexter enclosed in a gold reliquary decorated by precious stones.[6] Perhaps it was a way to create a symbolic dynastic continuity and also to exploit the double significance of the right hand as a relic and symbol of power, as suggested by J. Bak.[7]

By the mid-fifteenth century, however, the monastery fell on hard times, as shown by a series of documents describing its desolate state.[8] This was presumably due to the transfer of the relic to Fehérvár, a significant royal centre.[9] While there is no evidence about the date of the transfer, at the end of the fifteenth century, the preacher Osvát Laskai explicitly mentioned the Holy Dexter at Fehérvár.[10] No sources recorded what happened to it after that, but it surfaced in 1590 in Ragusa (modern Dubrovnik).

Its relocation was clearly linked to the Ottoman wars and Hungary's subsequent partial conquest by the Ottomans, but the details have been disputed.[11] According to one theory, it was moved to Buda before the battle of Mohács (1526), whence the conquering Ottomans took it, and the Ragusans obtained it from them; according to another, the Ottomans took it to Bosnia where Christian merchants bought it; and yet another scholar thought a renegade took the dexter from Fehérvár to the Balkans and sold it.[12] Most recently, the probable agency of Ragusan merchants has been highlighted; Ragusa, paying tribute to the Ottomans, was keen to vaunt its Catholicism, one means of which was an enormous relic collection, bought in large part by Ragusan merchants. Contemporary accounts describe how they bought various relics from the Ottomans in Hungary.[13] Several accounts depict the Ottoman destruction of the royal graves of Fehérvár and the transformation of the church into a mosque in the mid-sixteenth century, thus the relic of the right hand may have been acquired by Ragusan merchants then.[14]

In Ragusa, the relic was held in the Dominican friary, where it must have been a prized possession, as a silver reliquary was made for it in 1590. However, the

---

[6] 'sant Stephans arm, der is kluoc / in lûterm golde verwiert / und mit gesteine geziert', *Ottokars Österreichische Reimchronik*, ed. Joseph Seemüller, MGH Deutsche Chroniken V, 1–2 (Hannover: Hahn, 1891–3), vol. 2, 1091. I thank Mark Chinca for his help with the text. See János M. Bak, 'Holy Lance, Holy Crown, Holy Dexter: Sanctity of Insignia in Medieval East Central Europe', in János M. Bak, *Studying Medieval Rulers and Their Subjects: Central Europe and Beyond*, ed. Balázs Nagy and Gábor Klaniczay (Farnham: Ashgate, 2010), VI, 56–65, at 62–3; 'Sankt Stefans Armreliquie im Ornat König Wenzels von Ungarn', ibid., VII, 175–88.

[7] Bak, 'Sankt Stefans Armreliquie', 183–4.　　[8] Fraknói, 'Szent Jobb', 891.　　[9] Ibid., 891.

[10] '(Dexteram) pia devotione in civitate Albanensi [sic] positam, olim misericordiae operibus plenam, omnis populus veneratur.' Cited by ibid., 891.

[11] M. Simon erroneously argued it was Béla IV who took it with him, fleeing the Mongols, and gifted it to the Dominicans of Ragusa: Matheus Simon, *Supplementum ad Dissertationem Historico-Criticam Clar. Georgii Pray de dextra S. Stephani primi Hungariae regis cum Historia Monasterii Sz. Jog ubi olim sacra haec Dextra asservabatur* (Vác, 1797), 29–37; the dexter is clearly attested in Hungary after the Mongol invasion of the mid-thirteenth century, see Molnár, 'A Szent Jobb és Raguza', 7.

[12] Pray, *Dissertatio Historico-Critica de sacra dextera*, 50–8; Karsai, 'Szent István király tisztelete', 164; György Györffy, *István király és műve* (Budapest: Gondolat, 1977; 4th rev. edn Budapest: Balassi Kiadó, 2013), 390–1, respectively, summary in Molnár, 'A Szent Jobb és Raguza', 7.

[13] Ibid., 9–10.　　[14] Karsai, 'Szent István tisztelete', 164; Molnár, 'A Szent Jobb és Raguza', 10.

132   STEPHEN I, THE FIRST CHRISTIAN KING OF HUNGARY

Dominican chronicler from Florence, Serafino Razzi, who gave a detailed account of the Ragusan relic collection in his history of the town, published in 1595, attributed the hand relic to the Bosnian King Stephen.[15] The Dominican friars of Ragusa in 1618 included the dexter, attributed to the Hungarian king, in the list of relics held in the friary.[16]

There were various attempts in Hungary to regain the relic. Franciscans in Hungary transmitted the tradition that the Holy Dexter was in the Franciscan friary in Lemberg (today Lviv, Ukraine), and in 1639, a Hungarian noblewoman, Kata Pálffy, asked the papacy to facilitate its return. The relic in question was the alleged arm of Stephen, for which a new reliquary had been made in 1634.[17] In the late seventeenth century, news of the dexter in Ragusa reached Hungary, and Leopold I (king of Hungary as well as emperor of the Holy Roman Empire) considered acquiring it in 1684, but in the end, the relic remained in Ragusa.[18] After the defeat of the Ottomans, the Habsburg monarchy strove to legitimize its rule over Hungary and garner the loyalty of the Hungarian nobility through embracing specifically Hungarian forms of legitimation.[19] Thus, when Empress/Queen Maria Theresa found out that the Dominican friars of Ragusa guarded and venerated Stephen's right hand, she sent envoys to acquire it in 1768. After prolonged negotiations, the Ragusan republic's political need for imperial support overcame the Dominicans' initial refusal: in 1771, the Holy Dexter was put on display first in Vienna and then at Pannonhalma, and finally it was brought to Buda amidst religious festivities.[20] The reliquary contained a note authenticating the relic; this was examined by the Jesuit historian György Pray and pronounced to be similar to the charters of Stephen and Coloman.[21] Thus eighteenth-century scholarship played a significant role in a revitalized and politicized cult of the dexter.

Maria Theresa confined the relic to the royal chapel of Buda castle; she also ordered the regular celebration of the feast-day of St Stephen (20 August), as well

---

[15] Ibid., 9.

[16] Fraknói, 'Szent Jobb', 892. On its veneration in Ragusa: Pray, *Dissertatio Historico-Critica de sacra dextera*, 50–3, 59; see also an attestation of the Ragusan Dominicans from 1770, https://commons.wikimedia.org/wiki/File:Ragusa_Dominicans_certificate_10_dec_1770_of_Holy_Right_Hand_of_Saint_Stephen_-_from_Matthias_Church_IMG_0125.JPG.

[17] Pray, *Dissertatio Historico-Critica de sacra dextera*, 76–9; Fraknói, 'Szent Jobb', 892.

[18] Pray, *Dissertatio Historico-Critica de sacra dextera*, 62–4; Fraknói, 'Szent Jobb', 893.

[19] Maria Theresa's Hungarian coronation conformed to the tradition established for kings: Michael Yonan, *Empress Maria Theresa and the Politics of Habsburg Imperial Art* (University Park, PA: The Pennsylvania State University Press, 2011), 29. She founded the Order of St Stephen in 1764, and adopted other policies to gain the support of the Hungarian nobility: Charles W. Ingrao, *The Habsburg Monarchy 1618–1815*, 3rd edn (Cambridge: Cambridge University Press, 2019), 228.

[20] Pray, *Dissertatio Historico-Critica de sacra dextera*, 83–8; György Gábor, *A Szent István-napi ünnep története* (Budapest: Franklin, 1927), 31; Margit Beke, 'A Szent Jobb tisztelete az újkorban', in *Szentjeink és nagyjaink Európa kereszténységéért*, ed. Margit Beke, Miscellanea Ecclesiae Strigoniensis 1 (Budapest: Esztergom-budapesti Főegyházmegye Egyháztörténeti Bizottsága, 2001), 45–51, at 46–8.

[21] Pray, *Dissertatio Historico-Critica de sacra dextera*, 65, 81–3; Fraknói, 'Szent Jobb', 900–1. The authentication had been lost by the time of Fraknói's article. See also Bak, 'Sankt Stefans Armreliquie', 187–8.

as of other days, including coronations and the calling of the Diet, with a public display of the relic.[22] A commemorative coin was minted, and Latin, Hungarian, and German language songs and prayers were composed and printed, further spreading the cult of the dexter.[23] Even a forgery was fabricated, claiming to be a vernacular song in celebration of the dexter from the late fifteenth century.[24] In 1773, Maria Theresa also successfully lobbied the papacy to turn the 30 May celebration of the dexter into a compulsory feast in the whole of Hungary.[25] This served the purpose of the Counter-Reformation to recatholicize as well as the political aim to legitimize Habsburg rule over the country.

The dexter took on the role of protector of the country: representations of King Stephen together with the dexter multiplied from the eighteenth century onward, starting with an engraving made between 1737 and 1742, and with many more examples after the return of the dexter to Hungary.[26] Seventeenth- and eighteenth-century sermons, hymns, and drama also utilized ideas about the dexter when they represented Stephen as ensuring prosperity and abundance.[27] Eighteenth-century vernacular poetry often emphasized the dexter's protective role over the nation, and its blessings.[28] In contrast, sermons extolled the dexter as a means of punishing the sacrilegious despoiling of ecclesiastical wealth.[29] Efforts at recatholicization also led to the creation in the mid-eighteenth century of a society focused on almsgiving, called *Congregatio Sancti Stephani*, taking as its model St Stephen, whose golden age was to be restored.[30]

Enlightenment thought entailed the rejection of relics; this found expression in Hungary, too. For example, a member of the Hungarian Jacobite movement opposed to the cult of the Holy Dexter wrote a pamphlet in the form of a fictive letter by Stephen I himself, which countered the cult of the dexter in the name of rational common sense: it criticized those 'walking in so much darkness as to venerate a wizened bone.'[31] Such a view, however, was swamped by the rhetoric of incipient nationalism. Many contemporary writers celebrated the relic's return to

---

[22] Pray, *Dissertatio Historico-Critica de sacra dextera*, 88–103, Fraknói, 'Szent Jobb', 893–902, Gábor, *A Szent István-napi ünnep*, 31–3; Zsófia Szirtes, 'Jelen a múlt jövője. A Szent Jobb hazatérése', Magyar Nemzeti Levéltár, Archívum. http://mnl.gov.hu/a_het_dokumentuma/a_szent_jobb_hazater-ese.html; Beke, 'A Szent Jobb', 48–9.

[23] Fraknói, 'Szent Jobb', 901–2; Karsai, 'Szent István tisztelete', 166; Gábor, *A Szent István-napi ünnep*, 31–2, 37–43.

[24] István Harsányi, 'Volt-e az "imádság és ének Szent István király jobb kezének megtalálásáról" című nyomtatványnak 1484—iki nürnbergi kiadása?', *Magyar Könyvszemle* n.s. 20 (1912): 316–21.

[25] Karsai, 'Szent István tisztelete', 175.

[26] Éva Knapp, Gábor Tüskés, 'Szent István király és a Szent Jobb együttes ábrázolása a sokszorosított grafikában', in *Jubileumi csokor Csapodi Csaba tiszteletére: tanulmányok*, ed. Marianne Rozsondai (Budapest: Argumentum Kiadó, 2002): 103–34, at 119–28; there may have been one earlier image in the sixteenth century.

[27] Knapp—Tüskés, 'Szent István király és a Szent Jobb', 130.   [28] Ibid., 131–2.

[29] Ibid., 131.   [30] Ibid., 131.

[31] 'olly nagy homályban járni, hogy egy senyvett tsontot tiszteljetek': Pál Őz (member of Hungarian Jacobite movement, executed 1795), cited in Sándor Eckhardt, *A francia forradalom eszméi Magyarországon* (Budapest: Franklin, 1924), 77.

134   STEPHEN I, THE FIRST CHRISTIAN KING OF HUNGARY

Hungary and saw it as a significant benefit to the nation.[32] The Holy Dexter was honoured by official celebrations on St Stephen's feast day (20 August) in both Vienna and Buda; a sermon was preached in each city.[33] Under Joseph II (ruler of Hungary 1780–90), an anonymous poem promoting the cause of the Hungarian estates asked the dexter to protect the Holy Crown, as the symbol of national independence, from the Habsburg 'eagle's mauling claws'—a curious wish, given that Joseph II refused to be crowned.[34] During the Napoleonic wars in 1809, the burghers of Buda made a vow that if they were saved, they would renew Stephen's feast-day of 20 August, and the following year they petitioned the palatine to restore the festivities, including the procession in Buda castle with the Holy Dexter, which was granted.[35]

In 1819 the Palatine, Prince Joseph, regulated the 20 August procession of the Holy Dexter, turning it into a state as well as religious event by requiring secular authorities to participate as well.[36] Popular devotion is attested, for example, in a small booklet published by a chaplain from Esztergom containing devotional images, one of which is the dexter, accompanied by a prayer extolling almsgiving.[37] In the aftermath of the 1848–9 revolution against the Habsburgs, the procession of the Holy Dexter was curtailed along with many other aspects of Hungarian statehood, and only religious celebration was allowed, but the participation of secular authorities was revived in 1860.[38] In 1891, 20 August became a national holiday with a day off from work.[39] In the wake of the millennial celebrations that shifted the focus to the pre-Christian Hungarian 'land taking', the procession also emphasized the link between Catholicism and the nation, and during the First World War, it accommodated other political meanings, including lending support to the military.[40]

---

[32] Gyula Szekfű, 'Szent István a magyar történet századaiban', in Emlékkönyv Szent István király halálának kilencszázadik évfordulóján, ed. Jusztinián Serédi, 3 vols. (Budapest: Magyar Tudományos Akadémia, 1938), vol. 3, 1–80, at 48–9, 59–61; repr. Szent István Emlékkönyv (Budapest: Szent István Társulat, 1988), 529–606, at 574–5, 585–7.

[33] Szekfű, 'Szent István', Emlékkönyv, 61, repr. 587 (from 1810, the sermon at Buda was preached in the Church of the Virgin, now Matthias Church); Lajos Némethy, Szent István első és apostoli magyar királyról mondott dicsbeszédek irodalma (Budapest, 1881).

[34] Knapp—Tüskés, 'Szent István király és a Szent Jobb', 134.

[35] Beke, 'A Szent Jobb', 50. See also Károly Döme, 'Beszéd, melyet Szent István király napjára... készített', Buda, 1810, quoted in Szekfű, 'Szent István', Emlékkönyv, 64, repr. 590.

[36] Gábor, A Szent István-napi ünnep, 7–8, 33.

[37] Majer István magyar szentképei 1839–45, repr. in Szent István és kora: kiállítás az Országos Széchényi Könyvtárban 4 July–29 October 1988, ed. Györgyné Wix [no page numbers]. He offered the images for sale saying that he gave a substantial part of his income to poor but meritorious schoolboys.

[38] Gábor, A Szent István-napi ünnep, 27, 33–5; Árpád von Klimó, 'A nemzet Szent Jobbja: a nemzeti-vallási kultuszok funkciójiról', Replika, 37 (1999): 45–56, at 50; this is a revised version of 'Die Heilige Rechte des Königs. Eine Reliquie als Objekt der Zeitgeschichte', Geschichte Macht Körper—Körper Macht Geschichte, ed. Bielefelder Graduiertenkolleg Sozialgeschichte (Gütersloh: Verlag für Regionalgeschichte, 1999), 75–99.

[39] Gábor, A Szent István-napi ünnep, 36.   [40] Klimó, 'A nemzet Szent Jobbja', 50.

THE HOLY DEXTER 135

The Horthy regime, with its Christian–national ideology emphasized the significance of the dexter. Although the establishment included Calvinists (not least Regent Miklós Horthy himself), the political symbiosis with the Catholic Church meant that Catholic practices were incorporated into official state events. At the intersection of the 'sacralization of the nation' and the 'nationalization of religion', the dexter's national-religious significance solidified.[41] It continued to be carried in procession at Buda every 20 August, and the intertwining of the religious and political significance of the feast-day is well demonstrated in the celebrations of 1938. In the volume published to honour Stephen in the jubilee year of 1938, Archbishop Jusztinián Serédi, Primate of Hungary, summed up the significance and meaning of the dexter in interwar politics: 'God miraculously preserved the blessed right' because Stephen 'always governed strictly, but justly', 'drew a sword only in defence of the truth', 'folded [his hands] in prayer so many times for his nation' and 'gave alms'.[42] This echoed the contemporary regime's paternalist-authoritarian self-justification, and implicitly referred to Hungary's just cause and victimhood (as the regime saw it) after its First World War defeat, and territorial losses in the Treaty of Trianon (1920). The dexter was also taken around the country in a specially made 'golden train', starting on 30 May 1938, a modification compared to the earlier processions at Buda. In subsequent years, between 1939 and 1942, the dexter was also taken to territories that were reattached to Hungary, resulting from the country's alliance with Hitler.[43]

At the end of the Second World War, the dexter, together with the coronation regalia, was taken out of Hungary and hidden in Mattsee near Salzburg. The American military returned the relic alone to Hungary in time for the procession on 20 August 1945.[44] The hand was then entrusted to the safekeeping of the Loreto Sisters (*Institutum Beatae Mariae Virginis*) in the chapel of their monastery.[45] From 1950, it was kept in a safe in the apartment of the priest of St Stephen's Basilica, then in 1971 it was transferred to the Basilica, but was not on public view except on 20 August; public processions were no longer permitted by the Communist authorities after 1947.[46] With the liberalization of the communist regime in the 1980s, religious expression was allowed more freedom. The cult of

---

[41] Ibid., 45.

[42] Jusztinián Serédi, 'Szent István', in *Emlékkönyv Szent István király halálának kilencszázadik évfordulóján*, ed. Jusztinián Serédi, 3 vols. (Budapest: Magyar Tudományos Akadémia, 1938), vol. 1, 3–16, at 12, repr. *Szent István Emlékkönyv* (Budapest: Szent István Társulat, 1988), 9–22, at 18.

[43] Balázs Mészáros, ed., *A Szent Jobb országjárása, 1938–1942* (Budapest: Magyar Nemzeti Múzeum, 2022).

[44] Árpád von Klimó, 'The king's right hand. A Hungarian national-religious holiday and the conflict between the Communist Party and the Catholic Church (1945–48)', in *Festive Culture in Germany and Europe*, ed. Karin Friedrich (Lampeter: Edwin Mellen Press, 2000), 343–62, at 344–6.

[45] Beatrix Basics, 'A "basilica minor" és a Szent Jobb', *Budapesti Negyed*, 2, no. 1 (Spring 1994), https://epa.oszk.hu/00000/00003/00003/basics.htm.

[46] Interview with Attila Farkas, retired priest of St Stephen's Basilica, *Demokrata*, 17 August 2017, https://demokrata.hu/kultura/a-szent-jobb-kalvariaja-98058. On the conflict and communist suppression of the procession: Klimó, 'The king's right hand', 354–60; Árpád von Klimó, 'St. Stephen's

136 STEPHEN I, THE FIRST CHRISTIAN KING OF HUNGARY

St Stephen also started to creep back into public life, part of the permissiveness by the party state to shore up public support; the dexter was put on public display in St Stephen's basilica, in a chapel consecrated in 1987. The Party's attempts to find legitimacy and Catholic revival thus intertwined.[47] In 1988, when the 950th anniversary of Stephen's death was celebrated, the dexter was taken around the country again and displayed at cathedrals. The procession at Buda was also revived then, and became a yearly event from 1989 onward on Stephen's feast-day, involving not merely religious celebration but also the participation of members of the government.[48] The dexter is now seen not merely as a religious relic, but as a national one. It is carried in the 20 August procession by a military guard, as the 'nation' is openly equated with 'Christian Hungary', and state officials and public dignitaries take part in the procession.[49]

2. The Invention of the Relic

Those who have expressed doubts about the relic's authenticity, raising the possibility that it may not be Stephen's mummified right hand, have only used arguments connected to the relic's early modern fate: after a mention at Fehérvár in the fifteenth century, no information about it exists until 1590, when it appeared in Ragusa (today Dubrovnik). Thus it was queried whether the relic that appeared at the end of the sixteenth century was identical to the one previously mentioned in Hungary. Critics also pointed out the discrepancy between the representation of a right arm on the seal of the Monastery of the Holy Dexter from the second half of the fifteenth century, and the relic that returned from Ragusa, a right hand. Finally, it has been suggested that the lack of a ring on the hand means that it cannot be the same relic that existed earlier, because Hartvic, who was the first to tell the story of the dexter's discovery, mentioned a ring on the mummified hand; it would have been impossible to take the ring off the tightly clenched fingers without causing physical damage, whereas no such damage befell the ringless hand that we have today.[50] In countering these objections, various theories were offered, for example, that of the subdivision of the relic: supposedly the right arm

---

Day. Politics and religion in 20th-century Hungary', *East Central Europe = L'Europe du centre-est*, 26/2 (1999): 15–31, at 25–7; Klimó, 'A nemzet Szent Jobbja', 52–4.

[47] Chris M. Hann, 'Socialism and King Stephen's right hand', *Religion in Communist Lands*, 18/1 (1990): 4–24.

[48] Basics, 'A "basilica minor" és a Szent Jobb'; Hann, 'Socialism and King Stephen's right hand', 7–8, 15, 17–19.

[49] E.g. description of the events in 2021: 'Szent Jobb körmenet', https://infostart.hu/belfold/2021/08/20/szent-jobb-kormenet-ez-a-nap-halaadas-a-multert-nepunk-eleteert-es-konyorges-a-jovoert.

[50] Györffy, *István király*, 392 lists and discounts criticisms, although admits that the authenticity of relics cannot be absolutely ascertained.

was separated from the hand itself and donated to Poland by Louis I or at some other moment.[51] Both the objections and the responses to them are hypothetical and unverifiable. Yet in querying the provenance of the hand it is possible to go beyond merely questioning the identification of the medieval with the current relic. The earliest story about the Holy Dexter, Hartvic's account, already throws doubt on the relic's authenticity; indeed, it can be used as the basis for reconstructing how the medieval myth of the Holy Dexter was created.

The story of the relic's discovery comes from Hartvic's *Life* of Stephen, after his description of the king's canonization. At the time of the canonization, when the marble slab of the sepulchre was lifted,

> such a powerful, sweet-smelling fragrance enveloped everyone who was there, that they thought they had been carried away into the midst of the delights of the Lord's paradise. And the sepulchre itself was full of water, a little crimson as if mixed with oil, in which rested, as in some liquefied balm, the precious bones; having collected these in the finest linen cloth, they searched for a long time in that liquid for the ring that had been put on the right hand of the blessed man. When this could not be found, some people began to pour the water into silver cauldrons and large jars at the order of the king, so that having emptied the sarcophagus, the discovery of the ring would be made more certain. But, miraculously, the greater the quantity of liquid that was poured out, that much more of it kept welling up and filling the sepulchre again. Seeing this miracle, they restored the water they had drawn off to its place, and yet, although they poured it back, the grave did not overflow.

After covering the sepulchre again, miracles occurred at the tomb. Hartvic then continues:

> I have decided only to add at the end of the codex how, by a wonderful gift of God's mercy, the ring they searched for so long, but did not find, was revealed together with the right hand of the blessed man, three years after his translation. A certain monk, by the name of Mercurius, who, in the clerical order had been the guardian of the treasury of the perpetual Virgin [Fehérvár, the royal basilica where Stephen had been buried], and for the love of the heavenly homeland had renounced the world, was sent away far from there by royal order in that hour when the tomb was opened, lest he carry off something from the holy relics. As he was sitting in the choir with a sad face, a certain young man dressed in white clothes gave him a rolled up piece of cloth, saying: "I entrust this to you to preserve, and when the time comes to reveal." After the completion of the office, the

---

[51] Fraknói, 'A Szent Jobb', 904; Szántó, 'A Szent Jobb tisztelete a középkorban', 177.

monk unfolded the cloth in some corner of the building and seeing the intact hand of the man of God with the ring of marvelous craftsmanship, he got frightened; and without anyone's knowledge, he brought it with him to the monastery which had been entrusted to his governing, awaiting the time foretold to him from Christ by the youth. Here for a long time he alone undertook the guarding and watching of the treasure buried in the field, afterward he made the founders of that monastery aware of it, finally at the approach of the time when it had to be declared, he brought it to the notice of the king. The king immediately gathered the bishops and the chief lords of Hungary, obtained there many favours of miracles from Christ, and appointed the day of celebration for elevating the right hand of the man of God.[52]

Thus, according to Hartvic's narrative, when Stephen's grave was opened, King Ladislas was suspicious that Mercurius would want to steal a relic, and therefore sent him away from the grave. The unknown youth dressed in white who appeared and gave him a wrapped-up object and told him to keep it safe until the appointed time very much suggests a heavenly visitor.

3. Interpreting the Medieval Narratives

Scholars have used Hartvic's story in conjunction with an alleged charter of Stephen III (1162–72), which only exists in a much later abridged form, to 'reconstruct' the origin of Stephen's relic. The alleged charter added to Hartvic's tale that Mercurius was the father of Catapanus, provost of Fehérvár, and became the abbot of the monastery founded by Ladislas I (László, 1077–95) on the spot where the dexter had been kept by Mercurius.[53] Historians have accepted that these stories reflect in some way the genuine discovery of Stephen's relic. Building on and even adding their own fanciful interpretations to the medieval narratives, they

---

[52] 'Legenda S. Stephani Regis ab Hartvico episcopo conscripta', tr. Nora Berend and Cristian Gaşpar in *The Sanctity of the Leaders: Holy Kings, Princes, Bishops, and Abbots from Central Europe (Eleventh to Thirteenth Centuries). Sanctitas principum: sancti reges duces episcopi et abbates Europae Centralis (saec. XI–XIII)*, ed. Gábor Klaniczay, Ildikó Csepregi, Central European Medieval Texts 7 (Budapest—New York—Vienna: CEU Press, 2023), 107–75, at 166–73; SRH II, 438–9.

[53] The abridged charter is from the chartulary composed by Gregorius Gyöngyösi, prior general of the Order of St Paul the First Hermit, c. 1521–2, at the time when the monastery of Szentjobb belonged to the Order, published in Simon, *Supplementum ad Dissertationem Historico-Criticam*, 93–8, at 93. Szentpétery, *Regesta*, no. 121. There are two historically attested Catapans who were provosts of Fehérvár. One is mentioned in a charter from 1138 that survives in a transcript from 1329 (Ferdinand Knauz, *Monumenta Ecclesiae Strigoniensis*, vol. 1 (Esztergom, 1874), 97, no. 65; Szentpétery, *Regesta*, no. 63). The other is attested from 1192–8, he was chancellor of the king, and by 1198 bishop of Eger (Szentpétery, *Regesta*, nos. 152, 154, 155, 172–7). I discuss the problems relating to this charter later in this chapter.

THE HOLY DEXTER   139

created rationalizing explanations for various parts of the story.[54] These historical explanations moved within the usually unchallenged framework that Mercurius, a canon of the royal chapel of Fehérvár, appropriated Stephen's right hand either at the time of his canonization, for which the body was elevated in 1083, or during a hypothetical earlier reburial, and kept it in an equally hypothetical family monastery that was located in the village later known as Szentjobb, whence he brought it out and gave it to King Ladislas I, either on the occasion of Stephen's canonization in 1083, or thereafter.[55] According to several scholars, Hartvic's complicated story was designed to cover up the reality of Mercurius' theft, based on Mercurius' own account.[56] Hartvic's mention of the missing ring at the time of the elevation of Stephen's bones was even taken to be proof that Hartvic had known about the dexter's concealment in the monastery prior to its revelation, but remained silent.[57]

Accepting the story meant that one had to account for the preservation of the hand (or arm) only, instead of the whole body. Thus various scholars tried to fathom how it was possible for the right arm alone to have been naturally mummified. A doctor, Ádám Bochkor, who was commissioned in 1951 to examine the hand, was the first to pronounce on this, speculating that the hand was in the most elevated position, as the body was laid in the grave on its back, and was mummified in the hot air.[58] While naturally mummified bodies have been found, for example, in hot dry sand, in sub-zero temperature zones with dry air, in salt mines, crypts, and in peat bogs, natural mummification usually comprises the whole body or at least a large section of the body.[59] The conjunction of a mummified arm or hand and a decomposed body would be rather surprising. If, as Hartvic related, the tomb was full of liquid, understood by modern historians as ground-water, that would have made mummification impossible, as excavations of such burials show.[60] According to an alternative view, the hand was embalmed, suggested by the reddish-brown colour, but when this was carried out—after death, or later, in order to preserve the relic—is unclear.[61]

---

[54] A summary of the traditional view: Konrád Szántó, 'A Szent Jobb tiszteletének kezdete', Vigília (1985): 395–8.

[55] Szántó, 'A Szent Jobb tisztelete a középkorban', 173–5. Gyula Kristó remarked that it is impossible to reconstruct the true story of how the dexter was separated from the body: Szent István király (Budapest: Vince Kiadó, 2001), 133.

[56] Fraknói, 'Szent Jobb', 886–8; Györffy, István király, 389–90.

[57] Fraknói, 'Szent Jobb', 886–8.

[58] Ádám Bochkor, 'A Szent Jobb orvosi szemmel', Vigília, 25: 8 (1960): 492–4, at 493.

[59] Romedio Schmitz-Esser, The Corpse in the Middle Ages: Embalming, Cremating, and the Cultural Construction of the Dead Body, tr. Albrecht Classen and Carolin Radtke (London: Harvey Miller Publishers, 2020), 159–61. Naturally mummified bodies in a Hungarian crypt: Kristóf, Paleoradiológia, 48.

[60] Ibid., 47.

[61] Réthelyi, 'Szent Jobb, az anatómus szemével', 25 and shared by Kristóf, Paleoradiológia, 54. Bochkor and Szentágothai both wrote of embalming and natural mummification without distinction: Kristóf, Paleoradiológia, 47–8. There is evidence of even repeated embalming in some medieval cases:

140   STEPHEN I, THE FIRST CHRISTIAN KING OF HUNGARY

Bochkor's ideas became the basis for later historical speculation. According to Konrád Szántó, 'during a very hot, long and dry summer, the inner temperature of the sarcophagus, placed in the middle of the basilica, changed so much, that because of this, all moisture very quickly evaporated from the right arm, which was in contact above all with the warm air. This rapid dehydration resulted in the contraction of the arm. The forearm was bent at the elbow, and the hand clenched into a fist.'[62] György Györffy invented an episode better to explain the existence of the right hand relic, since it would come from the mummified body of the king before its reburial and thus destruction: 'the intact survival of the Holy Dexter can only be accounted for in the knowledge of the double burial. When the mummified body of King Stephen was removed from the sarcophagus during the country-wide disturbances, in order to hide it under the pavement of the basilica's floor, that is when the right arm was detached from the body.'[63] Györffy referred to the pagan rebellion of 1061, when supposedly the king's body was hidden by the canons to safeguard it, and it would have been during this secret reburial that Mercurius stole the right arm. Although this provides a more logical explanation for the existence of a mummified right hand than the supposition that the right hand (or at first arm) alone was mummified while the rest of the body was not, there is a somewhat inconvenient problem, namely that no sources ever mention such a reburial of Stephen.

Györffy's explanation is not only based on an unsubstantiated hypothesis, it is also negated by the available medieval sources. The archaeologist who excavated Stephen's tomb rejected the idea.[64] Hartvic does not mention any reburial prior to the canonization; indeed, he directly contradicts such a hypothesis by stating that the king's body rested in the same place for forty-five years without any signs of miracles,[65] and by linking the theft of the right hand to the opening of the tomb for the canonization itself. Nonetheless, Györffy's idea was also espoused by several scholars, including Attila Zsoldos, who added that the twelfth-century charter referred to Mercurius hiding the relic in his family monastery in Bihar county near the river Berettyó.[66] This seems to be a confusion between Hartvic who

---

Schmitz-Esser, *The Corpse*, 193–7. Identification of the exact method used for embalming Stephen's hand, if it was indeed embalmed, might lead to a better dating.

[62] Szántó, 'A Szent Jobb tisztelete a középkorban', 174.

[63] Györffy, *István király*, 389; see also 385 on alleged 1061 reburial of Stephen.

[64] Alán Kralovánszky, 'Szent István király székesfehérvári sírja és kultuszhelye', in *Szent István király és Székesfehérvár*, ed. Gyula Fülöp (Székesfehérvár: Szent István király Múzeum, 1996), 13–24, at 20; Alán Kralovánszky, 'Szent István király székesfehérvári sírjának és kultuszhelyének kérdése', in *Szent István és kora*, Glatz—Kardos, 166–72, at 168–70.

[65] 'Legenda S. Stephani Regis', tr. Berend—Gaşpar, 160–1; SRH, II, 432.

[66] Zoltán Lenkey [Attila Zsoldos], Attila Zsoldos, *Szent István és III. András* (Budapest: Kossuth Kiadó, 2003), 102. The theory was also accepted by e.g. Konrád Szántó, 'A Szent Jobb tisztelete a középkorban', 174. Fraknói, 'Szent Jobb', 880 pointed out that a fourth feast day of Stephen appears in a few liturgical calendars: 11 October is marked in the Pray Sacramentary as 'inventio corporis Sancti Stephani regis' and in another liturgical calendar from Esztergom, 1341 as 'translatio Sancti Stephani regis'. Based on this, Szántó, 'A Szent Jobb tisztelete a középkorban', 174 argued that this feast commemorates the reburial c. 1060, since no other elevation of Stephen's body can be dated to October;

speaks of an existing family monastery, and the charter, which describes a new royal foundation after the revelation of the Holy Dexter. The alleged charter relates that after Mercurius revealed the Holy Dexter to Ladislas, the king had a monastery built in wood and decreed that the relic should be kept there, which contradicts Hartvic, who puts Mercurius in charge of a monastery already before the relic comes into his possession.[67]

All the speculation about the relic's survival stems from the assumption that the right hand is that of Stephen. That supposition severely hampers historical analysis, setting it on only one possible trajectory: explaining how Stephen's right hand alone of all the body could have been preserved in a mummified state and how it ended up so far from Stephen's place of burial.

4. Relic, Reliquary, and the Foundation of the Abbey of the Holy Dexter

To unravel these speculations, I shall start with the hypothetical existence of a mummified arm. A range of suggestions have been offered as to the time of the relic's subdivision, when the hand was detached from the rest of the arm. According to one theory, after the Mongol invasion, when the monks of Szentjobb asked for the return of the relic they had removed for safekeeping to Ragusa, they had to acquiesce to the subdivision, so the hand remained in Ragusa, while the arm was returned to the Monastery of the Holy Dexter and later taken to Poland by those fleeing from the Ottomans.[68] There is no evidence for any of this; the early modern appearance of the relic in Ragusa is the only basis for creating this story about its supposed earlier removal. Others speculated that the subdivision happened on the order of Louis the Great, who as king of both Hungary and Poland wanted both realms to have a part of the relic;[69] or during the fifteenth century.[70] The usual problem prevents any meaningful answer: not an iota of proof exists.

---

similarly Magyar, *Szent István a magyar kultúrtörténetben,* 62. However, in 1060, Stephen had not yet been canonized and a reburial would not have been marked by a liturgical celebration. Alán Kralovánszky, 'Szent István király székesfehérvári sírjának és kultuszhelyének kérdése', in *Szent István és kora*, Glatz—Kardos, 166–72, at 171 suggests that after the elevation of Stephen's bones on 20 August 1083, they were placed on the altar of the Virgin, and then an altar for Stephen was constructed above his tomb in the basilica—a crypt and U-shaped area were excavated, interpreted as the place of the cult—and when this was ready, on 11 October his remains were transferred to this new altar. The Pray Sacramentary also included a proprium mass, which explicitly celebrates the finding of Stephen's body. This was later erased (but is still legible). It seems that there was an alternative tradition about the date of the *inventio* which eventually died out; further research may elucidate this issue. I thank Balázs Horváth for information on the mass.

[67] Fraknói, 'Szent Jobb', 888 hypothesized that Hartvic kept silent about Ladislas's foundation on purpose, due to King Coloman's hostility to the monastery.

[68] Vince Bunyitai, *A váradi püspökség története alapításától a jelenkorig*, 4 vols. (Nagyvárad, 1883), vol. 2, 336–7 and 475.

[69] Fraknói, 'Szent Jobb', 904.   [70] Karsai, 'Szent István tisztelete', 165.

142 STEPHEN I, THE FIRST CHRISTIAN KING OF HUNGARY

Various relics in the early modern period were held to be Stephen's remains, including a skull and bones. There was thus an arm relic in the Franciscan convent of Lemberg (now Lviv, Ukraine), attributed to St Stephen: according to an account from 1659, a Hungarian nobleman acquired some flesh adhering to it, which would imply some mummification, but by 1901 it consisted only of a piece of bone.[71] There is no trace of these alleged relics earlier; and the idea that Hartvic wrote of an arm, rather than a hand, is not convincing: although *manus* sometimes, and *dextera* as a separate word did mean arm as well, the expression Hartvic used, *dextera manus*, would have been a very strange choice to convey the meaning 'arm', and it is much more justified to interpret it as 'right hand'.[72]

The main alleged evidence of the existence of a mummified arm originally, however, is the image of the reliquary on monastic seals. The representation on the seal of the *locus credibilis* (place of authentication[73]) of the Benedictine abbey of Szentjobb has been interpreted as a bent arm reliquary, the faithful image of the reliquary in which Stephen's arm relic was kept, which, in turn, was made in the image of the relic itself that it contained, an arm bent at the elbow with the hand attached.[74] A reliquary in the shape of a bent arm would completely diverge from other known arm reliquaries of the period.[75] Moreover, in the Middle Ages, reliquaries usually did not mirror the exact shape of the specific relic they contained. They may signal which body-part the relic came from, but the association can be quite loose: for example, a small piece of bone that came from an arm could be kept in an arm-shaped reliquary, and a sandal was kept in a foot-shaped reliquary.[76] However, especially in the case of arm-shaped reliquaries, the container and the contents often did not correspond. It was often the function of the reliquary rather than the body-part it contained that influenced its form: arm-reliquaries were used in the performance of liturgical blessing, and often

---

[71] 'particulam notabilem carnis maceratae ex manu dextra S. Stephani regis', Simon, *Supplementum ad Dissertationem Historico-Criticam*, 48, interpreted as a piece of dried flesh by Fraknói, 'Szent Jobb' 893; on the relic in 1901, Fraknói 'Szent Jobb', 904.

[72] 'Legenda S. Stephani Regis', tr. Berend—Gaşpar, 172–3; SRH II, 439.

[73] Places of authentication were legal institutions important in legal literacy in Hungary. They were chapters and monasteries that witnessed legal transactions, issued charters under their own seal, and kept copies in their archives. See Zsolt Hunyadi, 'Administering the law: Hungary's *loca credibilia*', in *Custom and Law in Central Europe*, ed. Martyn Rady (Cambridge: Centre for European Legal Studies, Occasional Paper no. 6, Faculty of Law, University of Cambridge, 2003), 25–35.

[74] Fraknói, 'Szent Jobb', 904; Szántó, 'A Szent Jobb tisztelete a középkorban', 175. On the seals Bunyitai, *A váradi püspökség története*, vol. 2, 331–3; photo of the seal on the back of DL 65097 (1469), http://archives.hungaricana.hu/hu/charters/view/194226/?query=JELZ%3D%2865097%29&pg=2&b box=-1522%2C-2898%2C3466%2C70. I thank Mihály Kurecskó for directing my attention to the photo.

[75] Cynthia Hahn, *Strange Beauty: Issues in the Making and Meaning of Reliquaries, 400—circa 1204* (Pennsylvania: Pennsylvania State University Press, 2012), 135–41; Martina Junghans, *Die Armreliquiare in Deutschland vom 11. bis zur Mitte des 13. Jahrhunderts* (Bonn: Friedrich Wilhelms Universität, 2002).

[76] Egbert's 'foot' reliquary housed a sandal: Hahn, *Strange Beauty*, 135.

THE HOLY DEXTER   143

contained relics from diverse body-parts.[77] The iconography of the seal of the *locus credibilis* of the abbey of Szentjobb reflects this function, but the image of an arm with the hand in a gesture of blessing is no proof of a reliquary in the shape of a bent arm, nor does it prove the original existence of an arm (rather than hand) relic.

More significantly, there is absolutely no proof of the existence of the relic of the Holy Dexter prior to Hartvic's writing of the *vita* of St Stephen c. 1100. The foundation of the abbey of Szentjobb and the later text alleging to be a charter of Stephen III cannot be used to prove the existence of the relic prior to Hartvic's text, and even less prior to the canonization of Stephen (1083). The real date of the abbey's foundation is unknown, and the foundation charter does not survive.[78] The first authentic data on the Benedictine monastery of Szentjog (Szentjobb) survives from the thirteenth century, well after Hartvic wrote his hagiographical life of Stephen.[79] The *locus credibilis* of Szentjobb is first mentioned in 1239.[80] The first reliable information about an abbot of the monastery likewise comes from the first half of the thirteenth century.[81] No genuine proof has ever existed of the supposed foundation of the monastery by St Ladislas, the king who had Stephen canonized.

Those who accept as factual the story of the monastery's foundation by Ladislas rely on three much later sources, which correspond to each other in many details.[82] The first is a text included in the cartulary of the Order of St Paul the

---

[77] Caroline Walker Bynum, Paula Gerson, 'Body-part reliquaries and body parts in the Middle Ages', *Gesta*, 36, no. 1 (1997): 3–7; Cynthia Hahn, 'The spectacle of the charismatic body: patrons, artists and body-part reliquaries', in *Treasures of Heaven: Saints, Relics and Devotion in Medieval Europe*, Catalogue (London: British Museum, 2011), 163–72; Hahn, *Strange Beauty*, 136–7, 140. Arm relics were also kept in containers that were not in the shape of an arm: Junghans, *Die Armreliquiare in Deutschland*, 34–6.

[78] György Györffy, *Diplomata Hungariae antiquissima* (Budapest: Akadémiai Kiadó, 1992), 302 dates the foundation of the monastery between 1084 and 1095; Beatrix Romhányi, *Kolostorok és társaskáptalanok a középkori Magyarországon* (Budapest: Pytheas, 2000), 63 dates it between 1083 and 1193. Fraknói, 'Szent Jobb', 888 speculates that Hartvic already knew about the foundation of the monastery but did not mention it because of King Coloman's hostile feelings toward the abbey mentioned in the supposed charter of Stephen III. György Györffy, *Az Árpád-kori Magyarország Történeti Földrajza*, 1 (Budapest: Akadémiai Kiadó, 1987), 668–9 follows the dating of the alleged charter of Stephen III. Knapp—Tüskés, 'Szent István király és a Szent Jobb', 108–9 argue that the elevation of the relic to the altar of the monastic church rebuilt in stone happened on 30 May 1098, which is a hypothesis based on the alleged charter of Stephen III. Damian Fuxhoffer, *Monasteriologia Regni Hungariae*, vol. 1 *Monasteria Ord. S. Benedicti* (Vienna—Esztergom: Carolus Sartori, 1869), 232–4 merely provides excerpts from Hartvic, the charter, and Bonfini.

[79] In the early thirteenth century the abbey's name reflected that of the river Berettyó, the name 'Holy Dexter Abbey' appeared in the mid-thirteenth century: Bunyitai, *A váradi püspökség története*, vol. 2, 323; Fraknói, 'Szent Jobb', 890. If the charter by Stephen III was authentic, it would be the first to mention the abbey.

[80] Gusztáv Wenzel, *Árpádkori új okmánytár* (Pest, 1869, reprint Pápa, 2002), vol. 7, 78; Romhányi, *Kolostorok*, 63.

[81] C. 1220 (not counting Mercurius who only appears in Hartvic and the alleged charter of Stephen III): Bunyitai, *A váradi püspökség története*, vol. 2, 345.

[82] Györffy, *Diplomata*, 302–3, no. 101.

144　STEPHEN I, THE FIRST CHRISTIAN KING OF HUNGARY

First Hermit (Ordo Fratrum Sancti Pauli Primi Eremitae) by Gergely Gyöngyösi from the sixteenth century, published in the eighteenth century. He provides the abridged content of a charter of Stephen III concerning Zentyogh (Szentjog) monastery, without mentioning whether he saw the original or a later copy.[83] The second is a simple seventeenth-century transcription of a charter issued in 1326 by Charles I (also published in the eighteenth century); while relating the charter's content, the transcript explicitly mentions the uncertainty surrounding Charles's charter: 'There is an ancient letter, folded, whether it is a copy or authentic, because of its antiquity, it is not known.'[84] The third is the *Chronicle* of Antonio Bonfini from the late fifteenth century, which mentions the privileges of the monastery of the Holy Dexter, which provide an account of the invention of the relic.[85] As Fraknói noted, Bonfini misunderstood the biblical reference to buried treasure as a description of Mercurius hiding the relic by burying it in the ground, which was then repeated in some of the scholarship.[86]

How many of the details provided by these texts convey reliable information about real events, and what proportion is later invention? The similarities between them have been seen as proof of their reliability; yet they also differ in many details, and nothing precludes the possibility that they all derive from one root, which may be a late-twelfth-century or later forgery.[87] According to the eighteenth-century work by Krčelić, Charles I's charter itself was the transcript of a transcript made during the reign of King Béla (Béla IV, 1235–70) of a charter issued by Stephen III (1162–72).[88] It is probable that Gyöngyösi abridged the same source, rather than Stephen III's charter directly. Even if we accept that

---

[83] Simon, *Supplementum ad Dissertationem Historico-Criticam*, 93–8; Fraknói, 'Szent Jobb', 884–5, note 1. See also note 53 above.

[84] 'Extat antiqua littera plicata, an copia? an authentica? ob antiquitatem nescitur'. The transcription by György Marcellevich was published in [Adam Baltazar Krčelić] *Balthasaris Adami Kercselich de Corbavia Historiarum Cathedralis Ecclesiae Zagrabiensis Partis Primae* t. I (Zagreb, 1760), 127; Pray, *Dissertatio Historico-Critica de sacra dextera*, 20–2; Györffy, *Diplomata*, 302–3; see also Fraknói 'Szent Jobb', 884–5, note 1.

[85] Antonio Bonfini, *Rerum Ungaricarum Decades* (Basileae, 1543), 2. Decadis, book 1, p. 187, http://reader.digitale-sammlungen.de/de/fs1/object/display/bsb10141205_00203.html. According to this, Mercurius guards a wooden monastery at the boundary between Transylvania and Hungary. Bonfini claims to have seen the original privileges of the abbey of the Holy Dexter, shown to him by Antonius of Salona, then head of the abbey, that prove the events happened in 1078. He does not mention the restoration of privileges, nor the transcripts that we find in the charter. Both Stephen III's supposed charter and Bonfini give a much more precise description of Mercurius, naming him father of Catapan, *praepositus* of Fehérvár; this would make his son the guardian of the buried body of St Stephen according to Fraknói, 'Szent Jobb', 888.

[86] Ibid., 885. Hartvic writes about Mercurius: 'Ibi diu solus absconditi in agro thesauri custodiam et excubias decrevit': 'Legenda S. Stephani Regis', tr. Berend—Gaşpar, 172–3; SRH, II, 438–9. Matthew 13:44 ('Simile est regnum coelorum thesauro abscondito in agro quem qui invenit homo abscondit'; 'The kingdom of heaven is like treasure hidden in the field, which someone found and hid').

[87] Fraknói, 'Szent Jobb', 885 argues for authenticity; Gyula Pauler, *A magyar nemzet története az Árpádházi királyok alatt*, 2 vols. (Budapest: Athenaeum, 1899, reprint, Budapest: Állami Könyvterjesztő Vállalat, 1985), vol. 1, 444 argues that the basis is a fourteenth-century forgery that incorporates a donation of Stephen III.

[88] Krčelić calls Stephen III the *avus* of Béla, thus it could only be Béla IV.

Stephen III had issued such a charter, we could still only pursue the thread back to the second half of the twelfth century. Even this, however, is problematic; if the charter by Stephen III ever existed, new details could have been added to it during the various later transcriptions. That is evident in one detail: the text calls Ladislas I a saint, but he was canonized in 1192, so this would have been added in a later transcription rather than feature in a charter from between 1162 and 1172. Neither the supposed charter by Stephen III nor the alleged fourteenth-century transcript by Charles I is in the charter collection today.[89] Because the text we have includes a long list of possessions, the confirmation of the monastery's ownership seems to have been the paramount reason for getting such a document.

Their content renders the three versions of the text (the alleged charter of Stephen III in the two abridged versions and Bonfini's interpretation of it) truly dubious. These texts date the revelation of the Holy Dexter and the alleged foundation of the monastery to 1078, while also saying it was in the seventh year of Ladislas's reign (1077–95). This is impossible not only because 1078 was not the seventh year of Ladislas's reign but also because such an important relic, had it existed several years before the canonization of Stephen, would have been mentioned by the hagiographical *Lives* of St Stephen before Hartvic. The date may be due to scribal error, the transcription of MLXXXIII (1083) as MLXXVIII, which was then copied.[90] Further, the justification for Stephen III's alleged charter, the necessity of restoring the privileges of the monastery of Szentjobb, is typical of medieval charters that secured rights by establishing an invented past donation of privileges through forgery.

According to this supposed charter issued by Stephen III, on his deathbed King Ladislas had entrusted the monastery to Prince Almus (Álmos),[91] asking him to rebuild the monastery in stone, which he carried out. King Coloman, however, burnt Ladislas's charter of privileges to the monastery, deprived the monastery of the income Ladislas had donated to it, and transferred the monastery to the sons of Palatine Paul. King Géza II then restored the rights of the monastery, but after his death the palatine's sons, Jeronymus and Cornelius, attacked it, expelled the abbot, and robbed the monastery of its goods. They were excommunicated by Archbishop Lucas of Esztergom, and King Stephen III reissued the monastery's privileges, which included a threat that those trying to deprive the monastery of its rights will be struck down by God and the Holy Dexter. The monastery was also subordinated directly to the king and the archbishop of Esztergom, and a precise description of all its goods and lands was provided.

The hostile attitude of King Coloman is given as the root cause of the monastery's troubles. Would the very King Coloman who turned St Stephen into a real

---

[89] All the medieval charters are digitized: https://archives.hungaricana.hu/en/charters.
[90] I thank Vedran Sulovsky for this idea.
[91] Nephew of Ladislas and younger brother of Coloman, the next king.

146   STEPHEN I, THE FIRST CHRISTIAN KING OF HUNGARY

political weapon have deprived the abbey that housed Stephen's most important relic of its rights? Historians devised an explanation that linked Coloman's behaviour to the conflict between Prince Almus and the king. Almus was Coloman's younger brother and rebelled against him repeatedly, until Coloman had him blinded. According to the hypothetical explanation therefore, King Coloman even retaliated against the monastery, as it had been entrusted to Almus.[92] Some proponents of such a theory also assume that Coloman moved the Holy Dexter to another location, such as Fehérvár, though the alleged charter includes nothing of the sort.[93]

It is much more persuasive to tie the account of the supposed restitution of rights to a well-known medieval practice: institutions often resorted to invented origins and past privileges in order to secure or protect their possessions, frequently tying fictitious claims to a significant historical person retrospectively. Thus they ensured their rights to what they believed was theirs, but what, until then, lacked legal proof; the twelfth century was the heyday of such forgeries.[94] Various key protagonists cannot be identified. The list of palatines is relatively well attested, although not all palatines from the reign of Coloman are known; an alleged Palatine Paul only appears in a forged charter that purports to date from 1135.[95] Jerome (Jeronymus) and Cornelius are not attested elsewhere. The purported history of the monastery prior to the depredations the charter was intended to remedy was most likely invented to support the monastery's claims.

Thus the monastery's foundation by Ladislas I becomes questionable. It is quite possible that Ladislas I is named as the founder of the monastery as a result of a twelfth-century (or later) invention based on Hartvic's text. The fact that Stephen's canonization took place in the seventh year of Ladislas's reign may have been the reason for the dating of the alleged foundation of the monastery to that year, although it contradicts Harvic's account. Although Ladislas I cannot be completely excluded as the founder at a later date, after the relic was 'found', no evidence of this survives. When the dexter was elevated as a relic is unknown, although clearly sometime between the canonization of 1083 and Hartvic's *vita* c. 1100; it could thus theoretically still have taken place during Ladislas's reign.[96]

---

[92] Bunyitai, *A váradi püspökség története*, vol. 2, 325–6.

[93] Karsai 'Szent István király tisztelete', 162.

[94] Horst Fuhrmann, ed., *Fälschungen im Mittelalter*, 5 vols. MGH Schriften (Hannover: Hahnsche, 1988); Giles Constable, 'Forgery and plagiarism in the Middle Ages', *Archiv für Diplomatik*, 29 (1983): 1–41, at 8, 11–13.

[95] Tibor Szőcs, *Az Árpádkori nádorok és helyetteseik okleveleinek kritikai jegyzéke. Regesta palatinorum et vices gerentium tempore regum stirpis Arpadanae critico-diplomatica*, A Magyar Országos Leváltár Kiadványai II. Forráskiadványok, 51 (Budapest: Archívum, Magyar Országos Levéltár, 2012); Tibor Szőcs, *A nádori intézmény korai története 1000–1342* (Budapest: Magyar Tudományos Akadémia Támogatott Kutatócsoportok, 2014), on the forgery, see p. 30, note 143.

[96] Hartvic explicitly says that the right hand was revealed three years (trienium) after the canonization, which would mean 1086, although some manuscripts have terminum instead, which is more indeterminate: SRH II, 438. Fraknói, 'Szent Jobb', 889–90 takes the 'seventh year' of Ladislas's reign in

The feast of the dexter's elevation is 30 May; while some scholars took this as proof that the hand was detached from Stephen's body prior to the canonization, all it means is that the elevation of the relic was at a different time from the canonization, and can easily have taken place afterwards. The feast of the elevation of the right hand does not feature in a list of feasts to be celebrated in the kingdom, including the feast of King St Stephen, in 1092 in the decrees of the synod of Szabolcs.[97] When the feast was introduced is unknown; its first documentary appearance is in the calendar of the Pray Codex, a sacramentary from the end of the twelfth century (1192–5), as the 'translatio dextre S. Stephani regis'.[98] In the fourteenth and fifteenth centuries, the relic's feast became widespread under 'inventio' or 'translatio dexterae S. Stephani regis'.[99]

Therefore, there is absolutely no proof that a relic of St Stephen was kept at the monastery of Szentjobb prior to 1083, nor that Ladislas I founded the monastery. Likewise, no evidence suggests that originally an arm, rather than a hand relic was preserved; nor can we date its elevation. No evidence points to a removal of Stephen's body from his original grave decades before the elevation of the body for the canonization. In sum, there is no evidence prior to Hartvic's *Life* or independently of him, for the existence of the hand relic. The first testimony about the right hand relic was thus written by the same author who invented a number of stories, including the papal sending of Stephen's crown, and who composed his text with a view to contemporary political concerns.

5. The Meaning and Sources of Hartvic's Story and the Relic's Invention

I would suggest that the complicated story by Hartvic about the relic's discovery was necessary not because Stephen's hand indeed made its way to the river Berettyó, close to 300 kilometres in a direct line from the king's place of burial, but because, according to medieval expectations, one needed to explain how a right hand, found far away from the holy king's burial place, could be claimed as Stephen's.

It is significant that Hartvic is the first to mention the Holy Dexter, because his text is not the first to describe the canonization of Stephen. The *Legenda Minor*

---

the alleged charter of Stephen III as a precise date, combines it with the later liturgical feast-day for the dexter on 30 May, and thus dates the elevation of the dexter to 30 May 1084, a dating followed by many others. Given all the problems with the alleged charter, including the dating it provides, there is no reason to accept this.

[97] János M. Bak, György Bónis, James Ross Sweeney, ed. and tr., *The Laws of the Medieval Kingdom of Hungary 1000–1301* (Bakersfield, CA: Charles Schlacks, 1989), 60, c. 38.

[98] OSZK Mny 1, f. 31v, https://mek.oszk.hu/12800/12855/html/hu_b1_mny1_0069.html; Fraknói, 'Szent Jobb', 881, 890, suggests the feast was introduced under Stephen III.

[99] Ibid., 880–1.

148　STEPHEN I, THE FIRST CHRISTIAN KING OF HUNGARY

already relates the canonization; indeed, Hartvic cites parts of the text verbatim. It describes the elevation of the remains of Stephen, enclosing these in a silver reliquary, and the sealing of the reliquary, but it does not mention the right hand at all: 'They raised up that inestimably precious burden, giving thanks to Almighty God, and placed and sealed it in a silver casket.'[100] It is hard to imagine that the finding of an intact hand relic at the time of the body's elevation would not be mentioned in a hagiographical life. When Stephen's body was elevated in 1083, as the *Legenda Minor* implies, and Hartvic explicitly relates, only 'precious bones' were found. It was Hartvic who introduced the right hand relic. As Monique Goullet demonstrated, it is exactly the rewriting of hagiographic texts that opens a window onto their historicity: the rewritings served the purposes of the present.[101]

Hartvic explicitly draws attention to the significance of the right hand alone surviving intact:

> Why is it, brothers, that after his other limbs had become disjointed and wholly separated, once his flesh had been reduced to dust, only the right hand, its skin and sinews adhering to the bones, preserved the beauty of its wholeness? I surmise that the inscrutability of divine judgment sought to proclaim by the extraordinary nature of this fact nothing less than that the work of love and alms surpasses the measure of all other virtues.... The right hand of the blessed man was deservedly exempt from putrefaction, because, always flourishing with the flower of kindness, it never remained empty when giving gifts to nourish the poor.[102]

The praise of the right hand relic is at the very end of the *Life*. As the overall culmination of the king's *vita*, the claim that the right hand did not perish because God wanted to signal His approval for Stephen's care for the poor, however, is not particularly fitting, because according to the rest of the *vita*, it was not almsgiving and helping the poor that above all distinguished him. Almsgiving and other forms of helping the poor, widows, orphans, and pilgrims is of course present. The *Legenda Maior* already emphasized Stephen's almsgiving as part of his sanctity; following the biblical precept of 'give and it will be given to you',[103] it detailed Stephen's hospitality to pilgrims and the poor, even going incognito among the poor once to distribute alms, and always allowing a hermit to empty the royal treasury to give alms to the poor.[104] Hartvic also included these stories, just as he

---

[100] 'Assumpto inęstimabilis pretii pondere, omnipotenti deo gratias egerunt, deferentesque in thęca argentea signaverunt: Vita et actus Sancti Stephani Regis Pannoniorum (Legenda Minor),' tr. Cristian Gaşpar, in *The Sanctity of the Leaders*, ed. Klaniczay—Csepregi, 81–105, at 104–5; SRH II, 400.

[101] Monique Goullet, *Écriture et réécriture hagiographiques: Essai sur les réécritures de Vies de saints dans l'Occident latin médiéval (VIIIe–XIIIe s.)* (Turnhout: Brepols, 2005), 230.

[102] SRH II, 439. Knapp—Tüskés, 'Szent István király és a Szent Jobb', 129 suggest that the role of the Holy Dexter was linked to Stephen's role in ensuring prosperity for Hungary which was already implied in the *Legenda Maior*'s 'misericordiae et pietatis brachiis Christi pauperes, immo Christum in ipsis amblexabatur' (SRH II, 387), yet the latter is a standard way of referring to piety.

[103] Luke 6:38.　　[104] SRH II, 387–8.

THE HOLY DEXTER 149

did others relaying the usual traits of sanctity in the period;[105] yet to turn this into the be-all and end-all of Stephen's sanctity is a strange conclusion of the *Life*. Stephen's activity converting the realm to Christianity, building churches, founding monasteries, and his miraculous visions are much more central to his image as a saint, 'Hungary's apostle'.[106] (The *Illuminated Chronicle* tellingly included a sentence based on Hartvic that Stephen's almsgiving led to the dexter's preservation, but embedded this at the end of a chapter discussing the royal foundation of churches, rather than at the end of the section on Stephen.[107])

The strange fit can be explained by borrowing: Hartvic did not invent the story, but borrowed it probably from Bede. Such borrowing from earlier *vitae* of other saints was quite routine in medieval hagiography. According to Beda Venerabilis's *Historia ecclesiastica gentis Anglorum*, Oswald, a seventh-century king of Northumbria, was famous for his almost monastic life, and for his almsgiving to the poor. Once, at Easter, Oswald sat at the table together with Bishop Aidan, when he was told that many poor people were asking for alms. Thus he sent out a large silver plate full of food, and then had the plate itself broken up and given to the poor. Bishop Aidan was so impressed by such generosity that he grabbed Oswald's right hand, and cried out: 'Let this hand never decay!' And indeed this came to pass: after Oswald's death the intact arm relic proved Oswald's sanctity.[108]

Whether Hartvic borrowed directly from Bede or from another text featuring St Oswald's story is an open question. Bede was known in eleventh-century Hungary; he is, for example, cited by the author of the so-called *Admonitions* attributed to St Stephen.[109] But Bede's story, and sometimes large chunks of his text, were also incorporated into other texts on Oswald, including the Old English *Martyrologium* (ninth century), Ælfric's *Life of Oswald* in the second half of the tenth century, and Drogo of Saint-Winnoc's (d. 1084) *Life* as well as two sermons

---

[105] 'Legenda S. Stephani Regis', tr. Berend—Gaşpar, 140–3; SRH, II, 387–8.

[106] Indeed, Stephen's role spreading Christianity was the most significant aspect of his sanctity in his earliest liturgy in the St Margaret sacramentary, copied between 1083 and 1092, as well as in the twelfth century, and even in the late-thirteenth century new office: József Török, 'Szentté avatás és liturgikus tisztelet', in *Művelődéstörténeti tanulmányok a magyar középkorról*, ed. Erik Fügedi (Budapest: Gondolat, 1986), 33–47, at 35–8; László Mezey, 'Szent István XIII. századi verses históriája', in *Magyar Századok. Irodalmi műveltségünk történetéhez. Horváth János Emlékkönyv* (Budapest, 1948), 41—51; László Dobszay, *Historia Sancti Stephani Regis 1190–1270* (Ottawa: The Institute of Mediaeval Music, 2010).

[107] SRH I, 318.

[108] Venerabilis Beda, *Historia ecclesiastica gentis Anglorum*, ed. Bertram Colgrave, R. A. B. Mynors (Oxford: Clarendon Press, 1969), III.6, English translation Bede, *The Ecclesiastical History of the English People*, ed. Judith McClure, Roger Collins (Oxford—New York: Oxford University Press, 1994), 119. The relic venerated as Oswald's right hand and arm played an important role in his cult from early on: Alan Thacker, 'Membra disjecta: the division of the body and the diffusion of the cult', in *Oswald: Northumbrian King to European Saint*, ed. Clare Stancliffe, Eric Cambridge (Stamford: Paul Watkins, 1995), 97–127, at 100–1.

[109] Előd Nemerkényi, *Latin Classics in Medieval Hungary: Eleventh Century* (Debrecen—Budapest: Central European University Press, 2004), 67–8, 70–1, 86–7.

150   STEPHEN I, THE FIRST CHRISTIAN KING OF HUNGARY

on St Oswald.[110] (Many other texts also drew from Bede in the twelfth century and after, but these are too late to have served as a source for Hartvic.) Liturgical offices of St Oswald, drawing from Bede, may have been a more potent vector for the spread of the story of an uncorrupted right hand. A mid-eleventh-century liturgical office (dated by the editor to 1058–70) from the monastery of Saint-Winnoc at Bergues, Flanders included a responsory on Aidan's blessing and the survival of Oswald's hand (*manus*).[111] The English office includes an even longer section on the dexter in an antiphon, although the manuscripts are from the 1100s and later.[112]

Bede himself already mentioned the spread of Oswald's cult to the continent, including German lands (*Germania*), in the seventh century; there is evidence of the early medieval veneration of Oswald in Bavaria, and knowledge of his feast-day was widespread, found in calendars at Echternach, Mainz, Würzburg, and many other places in the Empire.[113] There was a renewed interest in St Oswald's cult in mid-tenth-century Mercia, whence it was exported to the Rhineland by Edith's marriage to Otto I.[114] Two late-twelfth-century monks at Regensburg, one from St Emmeram, made a compilation based on Bede about St Oswald.[115] Regensburg, however, may well have had texts already in the eleventh century, as cultural ties between England and Bavaria were already significant in the early Middle Ages,[116] and it seems that in 1060 there was already a church dedicated to St Oswald in the town.[117] There were ties between Regensburg and Hungary

---

[110] Karl Heinz Göller, 'König Oswald von Nordhumbrien: von der Historia Ecclesiastica bis zur Regensburger Stadtsage', in *Festschrift für Karl Schneider zum 70. Geburtstag am 18. April 1982*, ed. Ernst Siegfried Dick, Kurt R. Jankowsky (Amsterdam: John Benjamins Publishing Company, 1982), 305–23, at 308–10; David Defries, 'St Oswald's martyrdom: Drogo of Saint-Winnoc's Sermo secundus de S. Oswaldo', *The Heroic Age: A Journal of Early Medieval Northwestern Europe*, 9 (October 2006), https://www.heroicage.org/issues/9/defries.html.

[111] 'In secundo nocturno, ad cantica RESP.—Paschae die, rex esurientibus discum argenteum dividit pauperibus: reddit Aidanus benedictionem, quae permanet in hunc diem. [y.] Nunquam marcescat, manus ista nec inveterescat.—Quae permanet.' Paul Bayart, 'Les offices de Saint Winnoc et Saint Oswald', *Annals du comité flamand*, 35 (1926): 62; see also 33–4.

[112] Henning Huseby, 'Herskerens musikalske bilde': Om tekst og musikk i offisiet til St. Oswald av Northumbria, Master's thesis (Trondheim: NTNU, 2014), the relevant part of the office at 49–50: https://ntnuopen.ntnu.no/ntnu-xmlui/bitstream/handle/11250/297311/Huseby.pdf?sequence =1&isAllowed=y. I thank Roman Hankeln for drawing the liturgical texts of Oswald to my attention.

[113] Karl Heinz Göller, Jean Ritzke-Rutherford, 'St Oswald in Regensburg: a reconsideration', in *Bavarica anglica 1: A Cross-Cultural Miscellany Presented to Tom Fletcher*, ed. Otto Hietsch (Frankfurt am Main: Peter Lang, 1979), 98–118, at 99, 101; on calendars containing Oswald's feast: Thacker, 'Membra disjecta', 115–19. More broadly, Peter Clemoes, 'The cult of St Oswald on the continent', *Jarrow Lecture 1983*.

[114] Thacker, 'Membra disjecta', 120–3.

[115] Göller, 'König Oswald von Nordhumbrien', 308; Göller—Ritzke-Rutherford, 'St Oswald in Regensburg', 99–100.

[116] Ibid., 98–9.

[117] Göller, 'König Oswald von Nordhumbrien', 314. Other possible indications of an earlier knowledge of Oswald's cult in Regensburg: Göller—Ritzke-Rutherford, 'St Oswald in Regensburg', 101. A legend (whose origin is unknown) of the German knight Hans Dollinger defeating a Hungarian pagan giant, Krako, in 930 at Regensburg, was linked to St Oswald in a late thirteenth-century representation in the Dollinger house in Regensburg (in the sixteenth-century Dollinger ballad, Dollinger's opponent

THE HOLY DEXTER   151

already in the lifetime of Stephen: in 1028, Arnold of Regensburg travelled to Esztergom and taught the office of St Emmeram to the canons there.[118] Thus Bede's story about the right hand of Oswald may have arrived via the Empire.

Whatever the precise mechanisms of transmission, Bede's story of St Oswald's uncorrupted right arm served as a model for Hartvic's justification of a miraculously preserved dexter. There were other potential inspirations for the cult of a right hand: arm and hand relics were quite common since the early Middle Ages, and several could be found in the German Empire, whence information about them could reach Hungary.[119] Of these, some are particularly suggestive as possible inspiration. Rudolf of Rheinfelden (or of Schwaben), anti-king against Emperor Henry IV, died as a result of wounds received in battle against Henry in 1080, where his right hand was cut off.[120] The dying Rudolf was transferred to Merseburg, and was buried in the cathedral. He was seen as a champion of the church by the Gregorian side; his tombstone inscription called him a sacred victim of war who died for the church.[121] His right hand was preserved in a separate reliquary and a cult grew up around Rudolf.[122] Recent examination suggested that the mummified right hand still in the possession of the cathedral was cut off after death.[123] The story of Rudolf's right hand must have been known at the Hungarian court, since Ladislas I's wife was Rudolf's daughter Adelheid (d. 1090).[124]

There was another hand in the German imperial treasury from 1072, claimed to be the hand of St James the Apostle, which may have influenced the creation and later development of the cult of St Stephen's dexter. Henry IV obtained it from the possessions of Archbishop Adalbert of Hamburg-Bremen after his death, who had acquired it from Bishop Vitalis of Torcello in the 1040s. Queen Mathilda, wife of Emperor Henry V and daughter of Henry I of England, returned to England after she was widowed in 1125, with various treasures, including the hand. It ended up in Reading Abbey, probably in 1133, and its cult was developed

---

is a Turk): ibid., 103–8, see also *Geschichtliche Darstellung des Kampfes zwischen H. Dollinger und Krako im Jahre 930 zu Regensburg aus den ältesten Urkunden* (Regensburg, 1814).

[118] Nora Berend, József Laszlovszky, Béla Zsolt Szakács, 'The kingdom of Hungary', in *Christianization and the Rise of Christian Monarchy: Central Europe, Scandinavia and Rus' c. 950—c. 1200*, ed. Nora Berend (Cambridge: Cambridge University Press, 2007), 319–68, at 336.

[119] Junghans, *Die Armreliquiare in Deutschland*, 22–4 on the earliest ones, and 25–8 on hand and arm relics in the Empire up to the twelfth century.

[120] Tilman Struve, 'Das Bild des Gegenkönigs Rudolf von Schwaben in der Zeitgenössischen Historiographie', in *Ex Ipsis Rerum Documentis: Beiträge zur Medievistik. Festschrift für Harald Zimmermann zum 65. Geburtstag*, ed. Klaus Herbers, Hans Henning Kortüm, Carlo Servatius (Sigmaringen: Jan Thorbecke Verlag, 1991): 459–75, at 471.

[121] Thomas E. A. Dale, 'The individual, the resurrected body, and Romanesque portraiture: the tomb of Rudolf von Schwaben in Merseburg', *Speculum*, 77, no. 3 (July 2002): 707–43, at 715–16.

[122] Berthold Hinz, *Das Grabdenkmal Rudolfs von Schwaben: Monument der Propaganda und Paradigma der Gattung* (Frankfurt am Main: Fischer Taschenbuch Verlag, 1996), 38–9.

[123] https://www.aargauerzeitung.ch/aargau/fricktal/abgetrennte-hand-von-rudolf-von-rheinfelden-darf-nicht-untersucht-werden-ld.1801090.

[124] Marianne Sághy, 'A lovagkirály felesége, Adelheid királyné', *Rubicon*, 28, no. 9 (2017): 38–9.

152   STEPHEN I, THE FIRST CHRISTIAN KING OF HUNGARY

during the reign of Henry II.[125] The hand had been removed, but then returned to the abbey during that time, and Henry II refused Frederick Barbarossa's demand that it be returned to the imperial treasury in 1157.[126] The cult developed from 1155, helped by the grant of a fair as well as indulgences.[127] The hand came to be seen as the most important relic held by the abbey; a collection of miracles was composed around 1200, listing miracles purportedly wrought by the hand between 1127 and 1189, attesting to a cult in southern England.[128] By the 1220s, a counterseal used by the abbot and the convent depicted a right hand in blessing, and from the end of the century, the abbots' seals included the same image; whether this was an image of the hand, or the reliquary holding it, is debatable.[129]

Thus right hand relics in the Empire may have provided the template for a right hand relic of Stephen. The hand of St James may have further inspired the development of the Holy Dexter's cult. Of course, no such direct link was necessary; hand relics and reliquaries were widespread and popular, as they could be used in ceremonies of blessing.[130]

Whatever the exact route of transmission that led Hartvic to incorporate the story, it seems that he may have been instrumental in the invention of the relic, or at least wrote very soon after it was 'found'. The evidence points to the relic's invention well after the canonization, perhaps towards the end of Ladislas's or the early years of King Coloman's reign. There is nothing strange about the creation of a new relic, since in the Middle Ages the theft or sudden 'finding' of relics when they were needed was quite frequent.[131] Hartvic created a complicated smokescreen concerning the late find, not in order to protect Mercurius against the charge of theft, but to parry obvious potential objections to the authenticity of the relic due both to the location where it was found, so far from the king's burial place, and to the late date of its discovery. He also introduced the idea that those present at the time of the elevation for canonization were already looking for a ring, which is not attested in the earlier description of the canonization, to suggest that there was a sign of the miraculous already at that earlier date, a sign nobody understood at the time. The story of the divinely engineered theft was concocted to authenticate the hand that was found, rather than to exonerate a thief. Indeed, a curious reticence in Stephen's liturgical texts may indicate that the relic was not universally celebrated in Hungary as late as the late thirteenth

---

[125] Brian Kemp, 'The hand of St James at Reading Abbey', *Reading Medieval Studies*, 16 (1990): 77–98, esp. 81–3; Karl Leyser, 'Frederick Barbarossa, Henry II, and the hand of St James', in *Medieval Germany and Its Neighbours, 900–1250* (London: Hambledon Press, 1982), 215–40.

[126] Kemp, 'The hand of St James', 84.   [127] Ibid., 85.   [128] Ibid., 88–9.

[129] Ibid., 86, 88.

[130] On later medieval hand relics in other countries: Junghans, *Die Armreliquiare in Deutschland*, 29–32; Knapp—Tüskés, 'Szent István király és a Szent Jobb', 106–7.

[131] Patrick J. Geary, *Furta Sacra: Thefts of Relics in the Central Middle Ages* (Princeton: Princeton University Press, 1990); on the political use of relics: Edina Bozóky, *La politique des reliques de Constantin à Saint Louis* (Paris: Beauchesne, 2006).

THE HOLY DEXTER   153

century, but only enjoyed a local cult at Szentjobb monastery. The dexter did not feature in the office composed in the late thirteenth century for Stephen's main feast that was in use in most of Hungary for centuries; it celebrates Fehérvár, which as the burial place of the king's body deserves special respect, but makes no mention of the dexter at all.[132]

Why was it necessary to fabricate an 'authentic' relic of Stephen at some point after his canonization? I would argue that this was connected to the political significance of Stephen's sanctity. Stephen is often claimed to be unique either in the contemporary recognition of his greatness, piety, and wisdom,[133] or as a political saint who was canonized not as a martyr for the faith but for his 'performance as a ruler'.[134] In reality, Stephen was canonized not for his achievements but for his utility to King Ladislas, and his cult was fostered by the king and the Hungarian church before it became a more popular one. Stephen's canonization was itself a political act.[135] Ladislas, when he had Stephen canonized, was seeking legitimacy after gaining power through tumultuous wars: along with his brother Géza I, he had wrested the throne from the crowned King Solomon.

A Hungarian synod canonized Stephen, his son, two hermits, and the martyred bishop Gerard. Whether this was a purely local affair or papally sanctioned is debated.[136] Hartvic suggests a papal letter was sent to Hungary to canonize those who converted the population to Christianity.[137] Does this reflect papal approval or even a delegated canonization? At the time, canonization by local synods was usual; papal canonization, although it existed, only became the norm later, but papal approval was sought in some cases.[138] Delegated canonization by

---

[132] Dobszay, *Historia Sancti Stephani Regis*, 27–8. He suggests (p. xxiii) the author was from the entourage of the archbishop of Esztergom, but in light of the emphasis on Fehérvár, the question arises whether it was a cleric affiliated to the royal chapel instead. Andrew Hughes, 'The Monarch as the object of liturgical veneration', in *Kings and Kingship in Medieval Europe*, ed. Anne J. Duggan (London: King's College London, 1993), 375–424, at 404–5 also points to the difference between this chant and the others for matins, and draws a link between the characteristics of the chant and the significance of the text. Hungarian hymns did not mention it until the end of the seventeenth century: Knapp—Tüskés, 'Szent István király és a Szent Jobb', 114.

[133] The *Emlékkönyv Szent István király* contains dozens of examples.

[134] Lenkey [Zsoldos], *Szent István*, 104; similar Kristó, *Szent István*, 133.

[135] Gábor Klaniczay, 'Az 1083. Évi magyarországi szentté avatások: modellek, minták, kultúrtörténeti párhuzamok', in *Művelődéstörténeti tanulmányok a magyar középkorról*, ed. Erik Fügedi (Budapest: Gondolat, 1986), 15–32; Gábor Klaniczay, *Holy Rulers and Blessed Princesses: Dynastic Cults in Medieval Central Europe* (Cambridge: Cambridge University Press, 2002), 123–34; also accepted by Lenkey [Zsoldos], *Szent István*, 104.

[136] Klaniczay, *Holy Rulers*, 124–6; Lenkey [Zsoldos], *Szent István*, 103 also discounts Hartvic's story in this instance.

[137] 'Legenda S. Stephani Regis', tr. Berend—Gaşpar, 160–1; SRH, II, 433. Some scholars think that the *Vita* of St Gerard that dates from much later 'conserved' the papal letter, but it was likely based on Hartvic.

[138] André Vauchez, *La sainteté en Occident aux derniers siècles du Moyen Age* (Rome: École Française de Rome, 1988), 15–67; Jürgen Petersohn, 'Die Päpstliche Kanonisationsdelegation des 11. und 12. Jahrhunderts und die Heiligsprechung Karls des Grossen', in *Proceedings of the Fourth International Congress of Medieval Canon Law, Toronto 21–25 August 1972*, ed. Stephan Kuttner (Città del Vaticano: Biblioteca Apostolica Vaticana, 1976), 163–206.

154 STEPHEN I, THE FIRST CHRISTIAN KING OF HUNGARY

papal letter just started to appear; the first undoubted case is from the end of the eleventh century under Urban II.[139] However, while other papal letters to Hungary from the period survive, there is no trace of such a letter in the registers of Gregory VII. Moreover, his successors, Urban II, Paschal II, and Eugenius III, wrote about Stephen in a number of letters, without calling him a saint.[140] While the seeking of papal endorsement cannot be excluded, as it was becoming more common from the second half of the eleventh century, Hartvic could have made up this story too, in the knowledge that a lack of papal approval could be seen as dubious.

According to Hartvic, initially the stone over Stephen's grave could not be moved to elevate his body, but after Solomon was released from imprisonment on the advice of a holy woman, it was easily lifted. Hartvic's *Life* also clearly betrays the orchestrated miracles at the elevation of the body, as King Ladislas and his entourage eagerly wait: 'Thus having completed the fast and the office of Vespers on the third day, everyone expected the favours of divine mercy through the merit of the blessed man; suddenly, as Christ visited his people, the signs of miracles poured forth from heaven throughout the whole of the holy church.'[141] The *Legenda Maior* written for the canonization was already combatting Gregorian ideas about Hungary's status, emphasizing that the realm was under the protection of the Virgin Mary (and not St Peter).[142] If the dexter was 'found' during Ladislas's reign, perhaps it was to shore up the not very convincing sanctity of Stephen, as a popular cult failed to materialize.

Coloman would have had an even stronger need of such a relic. He extended Stephen's political utility quite radically: it was no longer the king's legitimacy within the realm that was at stake, but rather polemics against both papacy and empire. Stephen was weaponized to counter papal and imperial claims, and Hartvic's *Life*, commissioned by Coloman, masterfully wove an account that raised Stephen's status to that of an apostle honoured by the pope and an equal to the emperor. The new *vita* sought to protect royal rights over the church in Hungary against Gregorian ideas of separating the spiritual and temporal spheres, and set out to prove that Stephen's role and functions were equivalent to imperial ones.[143] Coloman's legislation referred to Stephen explicitly many times and

---

[139] Ibid., 173–6.

[140] János Karácsonyi, 'Kik voltak első érsekek?', II. *Századok*, 26 (1892): 131–8, at 136; József Gerics, Erzsébet Ladányi, 'A Hartvik legenda keletkezési körülményeiről', *Magyar Könyvszemle*, 120, no. 4 (2004): 317–24, at 317–19.

[141] 'Legenda S. Stephani Regis', tr. Berend—Gaşpar, 164–5; SRH, II, 435.

[142] József Gerics, 'Politikai és jogi gondolkodás Magyarországon VII. Gergely korában', in his *Egyház, állam és gondolkodás Magyarországon a középkorban* (Budapest: METEM, 1995), 144–64.

[143] Zoltán Tóth, *A Hartvik-legenda kritikájához (A Szt. Korona eredetkérdése)* (Budapest: Ranschburg Gusztáv Könyvkereskedése, 1942); József Gerics, 'A Hartvik-legenda mintáiról és forrásairól', *Magyar Könyvszemle*, 97 (1981): 175–88, at 176, 180–8; briefly on the background also Kornél Szovák, 'The image of the ideal king in twelfth-century Hungary (remarks on the legend of

distinguished between donations by him and by other kings.[144] He also named one of his sons Stephen.[145] Finally, unlike his predecessors who were all buried in churches they had preferred and often founded, Coloman stipulated Fehérvár, Stephen's burial place, as his own.[146] Such a use of sanctity, however, was more convincing buttressed by a miraculously intact relic that resisted the natural process of dissolution, rather than merely by bones (although they of course were relics themselves).[147]

Under Ladislas or Coloman, the initial lack of an intact relic that would spectacularly prove Stephen's sanctity was plugged with a right hand and a trumped-up story of its invention. The recent repoliticization of the relic follows the interwar model, but has much deeper roots. It harks back to Habsburg political legitimization in Hungary under Maria Theresa; to King Wenceslas's attempt to use it as part of the royal insignia; and ultimately, to those who invented the relic in the first place.

Stephen I, the First Christian King of Hungary: From Medieval Myth to Modern Legend. Nora Berend,
Oxford University Press. © Nora Berend 2024. DOI: 10.1093/9780191995439.003.0004

St Ladislas)', in *Kings and Kingship in Medieval Europe*, ed. Anne J. Duggan (London: King's College London, 1993), 241–64, at 241–3.

[144] Bak, *Laws*, 24–8.   [145] Lenkey [Zsoldos], *Szent István*, 108.   [146] Ibid., 109.

[147] On the significance of uncorrupted saintly bodies, Schmitz-Esser, *The Corpse*, 152–65.

4

The Hungarian Crown

The most intriguingly complex as well as the most noxious legends linked to Stephen by posterity are concentrated around his alleged crown, dubbed 'the Holy Crown'. Several independent myths originating in different centuries can be disentangled: the story about the papal sending of Stephen's own crown; the speculations about the origins of the extant medieval crown[1]; the development and meaning of the 'doctrine of the Holy Crown', which subsumed an earlier abstract notion of 'the crown'; and the symbolism with which the existing crown has been invested in modern times.[2] At their most misleading and most potent, however, the legends intertwine to the point of becoming indistinguishable, and reinforce each other. This can easily be demonstrated through a statement by the current Hungarian Prime Minister, one of many, similar in tone:

'A crown, sent to Stephen by the head of the Christian Church, to make him anointed king. King, who creates a nation and a homeland... This crown made it possible for Hungary to join Europe... This alone would be sufficient... to see it as the living symbol of the Hungarian state, the expression of national unity... This is why Hungarians still exist outside the borders of the country, and the crown of St Stephen is their inheritance too. Because a nation remains a nation, wherever the borders are drawn.'[3]

Every historical claim in this statement is false. Stephen did not receive his crown from the pope; the existing crown was never Stephen's, the crown has nothing to do with national unity, and medieval political theory was twisted out of shape to derive modern claims to territory from it. Such examples of the toxic use of

---

[1] I shall call the extant object crown, and only use 'Holy Crown' in direct quotations, and when discussing the modern doctrine of the Holy Crown.

[2] László Péter, 'The Holy Crown of Hungary, visible and invisible', *Slavonic and East European Review*, 81/3 (July 2003): 421–509 distinguished between the object (visible) and the doctrine of the holy crown (invisible), following Kantorowicz; Kees Teszelszky, *Az ismeretlen korona: jelentések, szimbólumok és nemzeti identitás* (Pannonhalma: Bencés kiadó, 2009) distinguished between the object; the crown as abstract notion; and the traditions attached to the crown.

[3] Viktor Orbán, Preface to Éva Nyáry, *A magyar Szent Korona zománcképei* (Budapest: Magyar Ház Kiadó, 2002); similar speech in 2000 when the crown was transferred to the Parliament: http://forum.index.hu/Article/showArticle?go=16016269&p=1&t=9006661.

THE HUNGARIAN CROWN   157

historical claims abound in modern politics.[4] The question, however, is why the Hungarian crown has such potential in the political field, especially in a republic.[5]

This question is the more pressing, because the existing medieval crown gained new significance in twenty-first-century political life, due to Hungary's right-wing government. After a long post-Second World War hiatus, at the turn of the new millennium the crown was instrumentalized once more to embody and symbolize the Hungarian state. It was transferred from the National History Museum to the Parliament building by legislation issued in 2000, as 'a relic embodying the continuity and independence of the Hungarian state'.[6] Trying to recreate the sacral aura so ill-suited to a modern republic, at the official celebrations of the 1100th anniversary of the Hungarian state, on 15 August 2001, a monumental copy of the crown was on display and the historical object itself was taken by ship to Esztergom, where the archbishop offered it 'again' to the Virgin Mary, reinterpreting a medieval hagiographic account, which depicts St Stephen placing himself and his kingdom under her protection.[7] Ironically, the political establishment was keener than the ecclesiastical to embrace the myth. While the Prime Minister self-confidently derived Hungary's history from the crown, the archbishop hinted that the crown 'is not certainly Stephen's'.[8]

Legislation now embeds the crown deep into the structure of the state. Since 2010, it has been the duty of the army (called 'Homeland defence force', *Honvédség*) to guard the crown, and crown guards swear to 'protect the Holy

---

[4] Among many works, see Eric Hobsbawm, *Nations and Nationalism since 1780* (Cambridge: Cambridge University Press, 1992); Patrick J. Geary, *The Myth of Nations: The Medieval Origins of Europe* (Princeton: Princeton University Press, 2003); Stefan Berger, Chris Lorenz, ed., *Nationalizing the Past: Historians as Nation Builders in Modern Europe* (Houndmills, Basingstoke: Palgrave Macmillan, 2010); R. J. W. Evans, Guy P. Marchal, ed., *The Uses of the Middle Ages in Modern European States* (Houndmills, Basingstoke: Palgrave Macmillan, 2011); Peter Steinbach, *Geschichte im politischen Kampf: Wie historische Argumente die öffentliche Meinung manipulieren* (Bonn: Verlag J. H. W. Dietz, 2012).

[5] Péter, 'The Holy Crown of Hungary', 505–10 asks a similar question.

[6] 'A Szent Korona a magyar állam folytonosságát és függetlenségét megtestesítő ereklyeként él a nemzet tudatában és a magyar közjogi hagyományban.' The text of the entire law is reprinted in László Veszprémy, ed., *Szent István és az államalapítás*, 567–8. Péter, 'The Holy Crown of Hungary', 422–4 discounted criticism of the law, even as he stated: 'The assumption of the Holy Crown "idea" frequently leads to the patently anachronistic corollary that the crown has symbolized the "Hungarian State"' (439, note 92). On the failed attempt to include the doctrine of the Holy Crown in the law, see ibid., 504.

[7] Stephen placing the kingdom under the Virgin's protection: *Legenda Maior* (there is no mention of Stephen offering his crown): *SRH* II, 385; also borrowed by Hartvic, *SRH* II, 417. The misinterpretation that Stephen offered his crown is not new; see, for example, the engraving by Jakob Gottlieb Thelot, Augsburg, from the collection of Count Ferenc Széchényi, in *Szent István és kora: kiállítás az Országos Széchényi Könyvtárban 4 July–29 October 1988*, ed. Györgyné Wix [no page numbers]. See also László Veszprémy, 'Szent István, források és mítoszok', *BBC History Magazine*, VI/3 (March 2016): 20–6, at 22. On 2001 celebrations, László Veszprémy, 'Fikció és valóság István korában: Kós Károly, Az országépítő', *Korunk* (2015, no. 8): 13–21, at 15; contemporary newspaper article: http://www.origo.hu/itthon/20010815keveseket.html. Péter, 'The Holy Crown of Hungary', 500–2 alleges the great popular significance of the crown's return in 1978 in strengthening opposition to the regime, based on one posterior account.

[8] http://www.origo.hu/itthon/20010815keveseket.html. Cf. note 3 on the Prime Minister's speech.

158   STEPHEN I, THE FIRST CHRISTIAN KING OF HUNGARY

Crown embodying Hungary's constitutional continuity'.[9] The Basic Law (*Magyarország Alaptörvénye*, a term with connotations of 'fundamental', and 'foundational'), effective from 1 January 2012, which replaced the former Constitution, stipulates that the 'Holy Crown embodies Hungary's constitutional continuity as a state and its national unity'.[10] Indeed, it now does so with renewed vigour, protected by a penal code introduced in July 2013, which has turned denigrating national symbols, including the 'Holy Crown', into an offence punishable by up to one year of imprisonment.[11]

Such instrumentalized political revival of earlier tenets entails some inconvenience. Firstly, the crown now represents a republic. The uneasy relationship between signifier and signified comes from the current government's model in the politicized use of the crown. As in so much of its rhetoric, the government of Viktor Orbán reached back to the terminology and ideology of the 1930s, when Hungary, at least nominally, was still a kingdom. Secondly, while originally the myths surrounding the crown were rooted in the long-held, though erroneous assumption that it had belonged to Stephen, today only wilful blindness to scientific research allows the political perpetuation of that idea. Thirdly, the revival, intended to create legitimation for the government, generates contestation and criticism from a significant segment of the population.[12] No wonder: the government's rhetoric is not a mere nod to venerable national sentiment, but an active revival of nationalism. Finally, as the (mythicized) pre-Christian Hungarian past is also an important building block for current conceptions of national identity, self-contradictory elements must be reconciled. Thus, the Christian symbol of the crown was coupled to supposed pre-Christian ritual in an attempt to satisfy legitimizing strategies pulling in opposing directions: in 2012, a shaman from the southern Siberian Tuva was given permission to perform a sacred dance around the crown in Parliament, accompanied by a singer who sang prayers to the Virgin Mary.[13] Another recent example of state-sponsored mythologizing integrating fictitious pre-Christian and Christian elements is the decision in 2021 to present a governmental award, the Knight's Cross of the Hungarian Order of Merit, to a self-appointed researcher of ancient Hungarian spirituality, who claimed that before their conversion to Christianity, Hungarians had horse-head shaped

---

[9] Orsolya Moravetz, *A magyar szent korona*, Országgyűlés Hivatala Nemzet Főtere Füzetek sorozat (Budapest: Országgyűlés Hivatala, 2016), 27.

[10] Accepted by Parliament in April 2011. https://net.jogtar.hu/jogszabaly?docid=A1100425.ATV, prologue '[A Szent Korona] megtestesíti Magyarország alkotmányos állami folytonosságát és a nemzet egységét'. In 1990, Parliament opted to return to the pre-Second World War form of the Hungarian coat-of-arms that includes the crown.

[11] https://net.jogtar.hu/jogszabaly?docid=A1200100.TV, 334.§.

[12] http://www.origo.hu/itthon/20010815keveseket.html on lack of interest; Péter, 'The Holy Crown of Hungary', 508 acknowledges this, despite his insistence on a popular cult.

[13] http://www.galamus.hu/index.php?option=com_content&view=article&id=127534, 27 March 2012.

THE HUNGARIAN CROWN   159

crystals to store their knowledge, and that she was able to cleanse the aura of the 'Holy Crown'.[14]

Comparing the legislation from the 1930s to that of 2000 demonstrates how the former served as the model for current government rhetoric and policy on the crown. The law of 2000 on 'The memory of the foundation of the state by St Stephen and the Holy Crown' was clearly inspired by a law issued in 1938, 'on the perpetuation of the glorious memory of St Stephen'[15] to codify the king's status in Hungarian politics. 'On the 900th anniversary of his death, Hungarian legislation, with heart-felt gratitude to divine Providence, wishes to pay homage to the immortal spirit of the great Hungarian ruler and apostle who founded the Hungarian kingdom, and led the Hungarians onto the path of their European mission'; 'the influence of Stephen's work extends until today'; he 'created the firm bases for the life and development of the Hungarian nation'—stated the law of 1938.[16] The 2000/I law looks back to 'the past 1000 years of the nation, to prepare for the next millennium'. It states that 'Hungary even today rests on the state-founding work of St Stephen', and that it was through Stephen that 'the Hungarian state and the Hungarian nation…came to be suited to the historical role they have fulfilled for a thousand years'.[17] Not only does the legislation of 2000 mimic that of the authoritarian regime of 1938; by explicitly focusing on the 'Holy Crown', joined to the state-founding activities of Stephen, the 2000/I law also enshrines a conscious distortion in legislation.

Why does the government insist on not only fostering myths but also incorporating an untruth into legislation? At this point, it is necessary to delve into the question of origins. While Marc Bloch rightly pointed out that origins never suffice as an explanation, political rationalization repeatedly claims that origins have a justificative value.[18] Thus, we need to explore how origin myths are invested with significant weight in the political sphere, because it is the alleged origin that justifies the entire structure. The compound myth of the 'Holy Crown', a tightly woven tapestry, is now used to uphold an alleged 'Hungarian identity', promoted on the political right, and to provide political legitimacy for an undemocratic, anti-liberal regime. It is also a shorthand for territorial revindication, suggesting that modern Hungary can rightfully claim all the territories detached by the Treaty of Trianon from the historical kingdom a hundred years ago. The historian, a modern-day Penelope, must separate the threads and unpick the tapestry. Therefore, I shall trace and contextualize the diverse origins of the different parts

---

[14] https://telex.hu/kult/2021/09/01/a-szent-korona-auratisztitojanak-adott-lovagkeresztet-kasler.

[15] The text of the entire law is reprinted in Veszprémy, *Szent István és az államalapítás*, 538–9.

[16] Veszprémy, *Szent István és az államalapítás*, 538.

[17] http://mkogy.jogtar.hu/?page=show&docid=A0000001.TV; Veszprémy, *Szent István és az államalapítás*, 568; Péter, 'The Holy Crown of Hungary', 423.

[18] Marc Bloch, *Apologie pour l'histoire ou métier d'historien* (Paris: Armand Colin, 1993), 86; Philippe Buc, *Holy War, Martyrdom, and Terror: Christianity, Violence, and the West* (Philadelphia, PA: University of Pennsylvania Press, 2015), 7.

Figure 5. The so-called 'Holy Crown of Hungary'
https://en.wikipedia.org/wiki/Holy_Crown_of_Hungary#/media/File:%D0%9A%D0%BE%D1%80%D0%BE%D0%BD%D0%B0_%D1%81%D0%B2._%D0%A1%D1%82%D0%B5%D1%84%D0%B0%D0%BD%D0%B0.jpg

of the current 'Holy Crown' compound, in order to demonstrate how the myth was made, and what purpose its constituent parts played originally.

This chapter thus comprises a discussion of our knowledge of Stephen's historical crown; scholarly results and questions concerning the extant crown; an analysis of the process through which the crown was identified as 'Stephen's crown' and became 'holy'; followed by a summary of the so-called 'doctrine of the Holy Crown'. This modern doctrine is contrasted to pre-modern ideas attached to the concept of the crown, which are recontextualized in their pre-modern environment. Finally, I reflect on why the object and concepts attached to it are so attractive for right-wing ideology.

1. Stephen's Historical Crown

Contemporary sources from inside and outside the Kingdom of Hungary agree that Stephen was crowned as a sign of Christian kingship.[19] The circumstances of Stephen's coronation are shrouded in contemporary silence and the one source that speaks too loudly, Hartvic, has shaped the historical narrative for a long time (despite some scholarly reservations). Stephen's coronation has been dated to 1000/1001.[20] Its location is unknown; already in the thirteenth century, it was assumed to have been Esztergom, the seat of the archbishopric.[21] (Later kings were crowned at Fehérvár.) Based on evidence for later coronations in Hungary, historians hypothesized the use of various *ordines*, but there is no testimony concerning the *ordo* used for Stephen's coronation.[22]

---

[19] 'Annales Posonienses', ed. *Emericus Madzsar SRH* I, 119–27, at 125, s. a. 1000; *Thietmari Chronicon a. 919–1018*, ed. C. I. M. Lappenberg, IV, 38, in *MGH Scriptores* [henceforth *SS*] III, 723–871, at 784; *Legenda Maior, SRH* II, 384 also includes unction.

[20] E.g. the *Annales Posonienses* dates it to 1000, *SRH* I, 125; the *Chronicon Zagrabiense* (erroneously) dates Stephen I's death to 1034, stating that he reigned thirty-three years after he 'received the name of king' ('nomen regis acciperet'), thus implying he was crowned in 1001: 'Chronicon Zagrabiense cum textu Chronici Varadiensis collatum', ed. Emericus Szentpétery, *SRH* I, 195–215, at 207; several medieval sources do not provide a date. Modern historians argue for a variety of different dates in 1000 and 1001, although 1001 is more likely: see János Karácsonyi, *Szent-István király oklevelei és a Szilveszter-bulla. Diplomatikai tanulmány* (Budapest: Magyar Tudományos Akadémia, 1891), 160–4; János Karácsonyi, 'Szent István megkoronázása', in *Szent István emlékezete*, ed. Gyula Nagy (Budapest: A Magyar Történelmi Társulat, 1901), 5–15; György Székely, 'Koronaküldések és királykreálások a 10–11. Századi Európában', *Századok*, 118, no. 5 (1984): 905–49, at 919–23; an earlier version of this was published as 'Kronensendungen und Königskreationen im Europa des 11. Jahrhunderts', in *Insignia Regni Hungariae I. Studien zur Machtsymbolik des mittelalterlichen Ungarn*, ed. Zsuzsa Lovag (Budapest: Magyar Nemzeti Múzeum, 1983), 17–28.

[21] Zoltán Lenkey [pseudonym for Attila Zsoldos], Attila Zsoldos, *Szent István és III. András* (Budapest: Kossuth Kiadó, 2003), 29; Eric Fügedi, 'Coronation in medieval Hungary', *Studies in Medieval and Renaissance History*, 3 (1980): 157–89, at 176.

[22] Lenkey [Zsoldos], *Szent István*, 29; József Gerics, 'Az úgynevezett Egbert-(Dunstan-)ordó alkalmazásáról a XI. Századi Magyarországon. (Salamon koronázásának előadása a krónikákban)', in *Eszmetörténeti tanulmányok a magyar középkorról*, ed. György Székely (Budapest: Akadémiai Kiadó, 1984), 243–54; József Gerics, Erzsébet Ladányi, 'Királyeszmény—Szent István—Európa (Szent István

162   STEPHEN I, THE FIRST CHRISTIAN KING OF HUNGARY

'The Papal Crown'

The foundational myth, that Stephen received his crown from the pope, was invented in the Middle Ages and proved tenacious, even though all the supposed evidence attesting this alleged papal crown has been dismantled, and we can trace the development of the medieval myth quite well.[23] The first text that suggests a papal sending of the crown is Hartvic's *Life of St Stephen*, c. 1100. Even though there are earlier mentions of the coronation, these do not refer to a papal crown. The contemporary Thietmar of Merseburg's chronicle entry states: 'Imperatoris autem predicti gratia et hortatu gener Heinrici, ducis Bawariorum, Waic, in regno suimet episcopales cathedras faciens, coronam et benediccionem accepit.'[24] Modern interpretations of the passage diverge: according to some, the emperor sent the crown,[25] or even made the Hungarian ruler his vassal,[26] according to others, the pope sent the crown, perhaps through imperial intercession or with imperial approval.[27] At the height of this debate in the 1930s, the key issue was Hungary's sovereignty and independence from or vassalage to the Empire, while

királlyá avatási szertartásának honi jelentősége és európai háttere', *Levéltári Szemle*, 54, no. 2 (2004): 3–14, at 6; Fügedi, 'Coronation', 175; János M. Bak, Géza Pálffy, *Crown and Coronation in Hungary 1000–1916 A. D.* (Budapest: Research Centre for the Humanities—Hungarian National Museum, 2020), 68–70.

[23] Some examples of the persistence of this myth: Hóman, *Szent István*, 119; Bálint Hóman, *Geschichte des ungarischen Mittelalters*, vol. 1 (Berlin: W. de Gruyter, 1940), 170; Bálint Hóman and Gyula Szekfű, *Magyar Történet*, 7th edn, vol. 1 (Budapest: Királyi Magyar Egyetemi Nyomda, 1941), 180; Györffy, *István király*, 140; József Kardos, *A szentkorona-tan története 1919–1944* (Budapest: Akadémiai Kiadó, 1985), 11; Endre Tóth, Károly Szelényi, *The Holy Crown of Hungary: Kings and Coronations* (Budapest: Hungarian National Museum, 1996), 6 ('the crown was sent by the Pope, which was equivalent at the time to the emperor sending it'); Kálmán Benda, Erik Fügedi, *A magyar korona regénye* (Budapest: Magvető Kiadó, 1979), 8 (the authors state that the pope's dream and the story about the crown being prepared for the Polish king is mere invention, but the papal sending of the crown to Stephen is true: ibid., 11); Éva Kovács, Zsuzsa Lovag, *The Hungarian Crown and Other Regalia*, 2nd rev. edn (Budapest: Corvina, 1980), 8, 'probable' that pope sent the crown.

[24] *Thietmari Chronicon*, C. I. M. Lappenberg, IV, 38, in *MGH SS* III, 723–871, at 784. Eng. tr. David A. Warner, *Ottonian Germany: The Chronicon of Thietmar of Merseburg* (Manchester: Manchester University Press, 2001), 193: 'With the favour and urging of the aforementioned emperor, Waik, brother-in-law of Duke Henry of the Bavarians, established bishoprics in his kingdom and received the crown and consecration.' Waik is supposed to be Stephen's pre-baptismal name.

[25] E.g. Robert Holtzmann, *Geschichte der sächsischen Kaiserzeit (900–1024)* (Berlin: Rütten & Loening, 1955), 363; József Gerics, Erzsébet Ladányi, 'Források Szent István királlyá avatásának történetéhez', *Magyar Könyvszemle*, 118, no. 3 (2002): 213–24, at 216–17.

[26] Albert Brackmann, *Kaiser Otto III und die staatliche Umgestaltung Polens und Ungarns*, Abhandlungen der Preußischen Akademie der Wissenschaften (Berlin: Akademie der Wissenschaften, 1939), 1–27, at 25–6; Hans Hirsch, 'Das Recht der Königserhebung durch Kaiser und Papst im hohen Mittelalter', in *Festschrift Ernst Heymann*, vol. 1 (Weimar: Böhlau, 1940), 209–41, at 216.

[27] E.g. Ferenc Eckhart, *Magyar alkotmány- és jogtörténet* (Budapest: Politzer, 1946), 22. Deér, 'A magyar királyság megalakulása', *A Magyar Történettudományi Intézet Évkönyve* (1942): 1–89, at 69–76 argues that the 'benedictio' mentioned by Thietmar is the same as the 'apostolica benedictio' of the *Legenda Maior* and meant papal authorization for coronation, and the crown itself was likely sent by the pope (the Hungarian version contains additional notes compared to the German version, József Deér, 'Die Entstehung des ungarischen Königtums', *Archivum Europae Centro-Orientalis*, 8, 1–2 (1942): 52–148). Arnold Ipolyi, *A magyar Szent Korona és a koronázási jelvények története és műleírása* (Budapest: Magyar Tudományos Akadémia, 1886), 56; Bónis, *István király*, 47–9.

THE HUNGARIAN CROWN   163

the underlying presentist political issue concerned Hungary's relations with Nazi Germany.[28] Others suggest Thietmar may not even have meant the sending of a physical crown at all, but the granting of the right of coronation.[29] However, if he did mean that a crown was sent, this would have been from the emperor's court; misinterpreting his text as implying papal crown-sending is only possible if one accepts Hartvic's account. The narratives of Stephen's coronation in the hagiographic *Lives* predating Hartvic avoid mentioning any imperial role, but do not suggest the presence of a papal crown either. The *Legenda Maior* stated that having received a letter of papal benediction, Stephen was anointed and crowned king.[30] According to the *Legenda Minor*, the elite and commoners raised Stephen to the throne; the text only mentions papal approval when discussing the subsequent implantation of ecclesiastical organization 'ex Romana auctoritate'.[31]

Hartvic, on the other hand, invented a complex story of how Stephen sent his envoy, Abbot Aseric (in some manuscripts Astric), to solicit a crown and blessing from the pope. A divine vision foretold the imminent arrival of the envoy of an unknown people, commanding the pope to grant what the envoy would ask, and send the crown he had ordered to be prepared for 'Mischa' of the Poles, to this new ruler instead.[32] In this account, the pope even acknowledges that while he himself is apostolic, Stephen is truly Christ's apostle for having converted so many people, and grants him temporal and spiritual rights over churches and their people.[33] This claim was so outrageous from the papal point of view that in 1201, when he authorized the use of the text for liturgical readings in the archdiocese of

---

[28] Analysis of views, including the contemporary political implications: Székely, 'Koronaküldések', 914–19; see also György Székely, 'Korona és lándzsa', in *Államalapítás, Társadalom, művelődés*, ed. Gyula Kristó (Budapest: MTA Történettudományi Intézet, 2001), 21–30, at 22–3.

[29] Bak—Pálffy, *Crown and Coronation*, 149. Péter Váczy, 'Thietmar von Merseburg über die ungarische Königskrönung', in *Insignia Regni Hungariae I*, 29–51, at 30 argued that the sentence was ambiguous on purpose. Medieval authors in the period, however, were not very interested in giving detailed accounts of coronations: Björn Weiler, *Paths to Kingship in Medieval Latin Europe, c. 950–1200* (Cambridge: Cambridge University Press, 2021), 311.

[30] *SRH* II, 384: 'benedictionis apostolice litteris allatis...Stephanus rex appellatur et unctione crismali perunctus, diademate regalis dignitatis feliciter coronatur. Post acceptum imperialis excellentiae signum...'. Székely, 'Koronaküldések', 916 argues this refers to the imperial origin of the crown, but that is unwarranted, since the crown as 'the sign of sovereign excellence' refers to the status it conferred (imperium as sovereignty, rule), rather than the emperor's involvement; the repetition is just hyperbole.

[31] *SRH* II, 394, 397.

[32] *SRH* II, 412–14. The ruler (in some manuscripts, 'Misca') is identified in scholarship as Mieszko I, who in fact died in 992; some suggest that Hartvic made a mistake regarding the name. On the broader issue of legitimacy for new rulers, Björn Weiler, 'Crown-giving and king-making in the West, ca. 1000–ca. 1250', *Viator*, 41 (2010): 57–87.

[33] *SRH* II, 414 '"ego", inquiens "sum apostolicus, ille vero merito Christi apostolus, per quem tantum sibi populum Christus convertit. Quapropter dispositioni eiusdem, prout divina ipsum gratia instruit, ecclesias simul cum populis utroque iure ordinandas relinquimus'. Utroque iure has been interpreted as canon and Roman law, or canon and secular law: Gábor Barabás, *A pápaság és Magyarország a 13. Század első felében: pápai hatás—együttműködés—érdekellentét* (Pécs: Pécsi Történettudományért Kulturális Egyesület, 2015), 196.

164 STEPHEN I, THE FIRST CHRISTIAN KING OF HUNGARY

Kalocsa, Innocent III insisted on having 'utroque iure' removed.[34] Hartvic's story of a divinely ordained crown may have been inspired by Ottonian or Byzantine precedent. The conferral of crowns by saints, Christ, and angels was often depicted in Byzantine art, especially from the later ninth century, and influenced the development of the representation of divine coronation in Ottonian art.[35]

Though doubts about the reliability of Hartvic's text surfaced early on in modern scholarship, and despite the subsequent demonstration of the constructed nature of his claim, Stephen is still often credited with political foresight and wise statesmanship in asking for a papal crown.[36] Some Protestant authors discounted the story of a papal crown already in the eighteenth century, thus arguing against papal supremacy.[37] The prevailing view, however, was to accept Hartvic's story. The papal crown sending was even explained as upholding the liberty of the Church by creating independent Christian kingdoms.[38] Until the late nineteenth century, despite some attempts to question its authenticity, an alleged bull by Pope Sylvester II addressed to Stephen and sent to accompany the crown was used as the ultimate proof of the crown's papal origin.[39] Then János Karácsonyi proved conclusively that this was a forgery made after 1576.[40] He also questioned the reliability of Hartvic's text.[41] Unequivocal evidence of papal crown-sending exists for Gregory VII and thereafter,[42] but while early historiography noted this,

[34] The claim was created in the context of the controversies of the Gregorian reform, when Hartvic wrote, rather than during Stephen's reign, József Gerics, Erzsébet Ladányi, 'A Hartvik legenda keletkezési körülményeiről', *Magyar Könyvszemle*, 120, no. 4 (2004): 317–24, at 318–20. The register of Pope Innocent III for the fourth year of his pontificate was lost (Georges Tessier, 'Les Registres d'Innocent III', *Bibliothèque de l'École des chartes*, 107, no. 2 (1947–8): 255–61, at 256), but the rubrics of the register survived in a later copy, printed in Augustinus Theiner, *Vetera Monumenta Slavorum Meridionalium historia illustrantia* (Rome, 1863), vol. 1, 57, no. 77; the phrase was omitted from subsequent manuscripts: SRH II, 369. On this episode and earlier scholarship: Barabás, *A pápaság*, 195–6.
[35] Jonathan Shepard, 'Crowns from the Basileus, crowns from heaven', in *Emergent Elites and Byzantium in the Balkans and East-Central Europe*, Jonathan Shepard (Farnham: Ashgate, 2011), IX, 145–7, and on Byzantine influence: 147–58.
[36] Even in scholarship critical of accretions around the crown, e.g. Kardos, *A szentkorona-tan*, 11.
[37] Gergely Tóth, *Szent István, Szent Korona, államalapítás a protestáns történetírásban (16–18. Század)* (Budapest: MTA Bölcsészettudományi Kutatóközpont Történettudományi Intézet, 2016), 126–31; Péter Bod (1712–69), *Historia Hungarorum ecclesiastica*, ed. L. W. E. Rauwenhoff (Leiden: Brill, 1888), vol. 1, 74–86; Szekfű, 'Szent István', *Emlékkönyv*, 54, repr. 580.
[38] Ipolyi, *A magyar Szent Korona*, 22–33 (while postulating that imperial opposition defeated the plan to send a crown to the Polish ruler: 31–2).
[39] Ibid., 34–45, with the text 34–5, note 1; doubts and their refutations at 37–42 in the note. Originally published by Menyhért Inchofer, *Annales ecclesiastici regni Hungariae* (Rome, 1644), 256. Allegedly found by Antal Verancsics in Trogir, Dalmatia in 1550, a copy was obtained through an intermediary by Rafael Levakovich, a monk and official of the Holy See, who gave it to Inchofer (Ipolyi, *A magyar Szent Korona*, 37, note 2). Tóth, *Szent István, Szent Korona*, 19–26.
[40] Karácsonyi, *Szent-István király oklevelei és a Szilveszter-bulla*, 178–216, at 182–4. Sámuel Decsy, *A' magyar szent koronának és az ahoz tartozó tárgyaknak históriája* (Vienna, 1792; reprint Budapest: Kossuth Kiadó, 2013), 133–8 already questioned authenticity.
[41] János Karácsonyi, 'Kik voltak az első érsekek?', II. *Századok*, 26 (1892): 131–8, at 133–6, although he argued that Hartvic wrote in the thirteenth century. In the 1930s, however, the doubts (until Tóth's work) disappeared: Péter, 'The Holy Crown of Hungary', 427.
[42] Székely, 'Koronaküldések', 940–3.

THE HUNGARIAN CROWN   165

it was used as an argument to enhance the significance of Stephen's 'papal' crown as the first one.[43] The earliest systematic studies that offered proof against the papal sending of the crown were published against the background of rising Nazism and the Hungarian celebrations commemorating St Stephen in 1938.[44] The new results, so contrary to tradition, were not accepted in scholarship, despite their intellectual merit; and the question of the papal crown became entangled with the debate on Hungary's independence from Germany during Stephen's reign and in the 1930s.[45] Since then, many more scholars have rejected the theory of the papal origin of the crown,[46] while, against all evidence, some continue to cling to the myth created by Hartvic.

Hartvic composed the story to fulfil contemporary aims. In one stroke, he created potent counter-arguments on all fronts. King Peter Orseolo (Stephen's successor on the throne) and King Solomon (1063–74) had relied on the help of the king of the Romans against rivals. To counter imperial pretensions, Hartvic insisted on the papal origin of the crown, demonstrating the Hungarian king's independence from the emperor, and even implying his equal status, since imperial coronation was carried out by the pope. Yet Pope Gregory VII had tried to assert his own supremacy over the Hungarian king, claiming Hungary had been offered to St Peter (see below). Hartvic thus insisted on the divinely commanded crown, with the pope merely fulfilling rather than initiating its sending; thus the crown ultimately derived from divine, rather than papal power. Against the Gregorian reform movement and the assertion that investiture needs to be independent of lay power, Hartvic also confirmed the papal (and even divine) origin of the Hungarian ruler's rights over the Church in his kingdom; he could rule by both laws.[47] Hartvic even suggested the divinely inspired priority of the Hungarian king over the Polish ruler, although there were strong ties between the two realms, particularly during Ladislas I's reign.[48] Yet the Polish court's emphasis on Emperor Otto III's journey to Gniezno (to the relics of St Adalbert) may have prompted such a counter-claim. The Polish ruler's special friendship with Otto III,

[43] Ipolyi, *A magyar Szent Korona*, 6.

[44] In part agreeing with Albert Brackmann's argument that the crown was a gift from the emperor, Zoltán Tóth, *A Hartvik-legenda kritikájához (A Szt. Korona eredetkérdése)* (Budapest: Ranschburg Gusztáv Könyvkereskedése, 1942); Tóth read the paper at the Hungarian Academy of Sciences in 1937; Zoltán Tóth, 'Történetkutatásunk mai állása' körül *(A szent korona eredetkérdéséhez)* (Budapest: Ranschburg Gusztáv Könyvkereskedése, 1943).

[45] The idea of the emperor sending a crown was thus unpalatable. On the debate, Péter, 'The Holy Crown of Hungary', 427–9.

[46] E.g. Tamás Bogyay, 'Problémák Szent István és koronája körül', *Új Látóhatár*, 13 (1970): 105–15; Váczy, 'Thietmar von Merseburg', 34–5; bibliography in Kornél Szovák, László Veszprémy, 'Krónikák, legendák, intelmek: Utószó', *SRH* II, 721–99, at 773.

[47] Lenkey [Zsoldos], *Szent István*, 30–1.

[48] The editor Bartoniek thought that Hartvic mistakenly merged two stories: Stephen asking the pope for a crown and the Polish Bolesław I (992–1025) asking for a papal crown, c. 1008–9: *SRH* II, 367.

166   STEPHEN I, THE FIRST CHRISTIAN KING OF HUNGARY

and coronation at the Gniezno meeting (1000) was soon a key part of the Gallus Anonymous' chronicle.

The Hungarian insistence on a papal crown seems to have prompted the development of a Polish tradition as well from the mid-thirteenth century, which elaborated on Hartvic's story; the latter may have reached Poland through intensified Hungarian-Polish relations during the period of Salomea of Poland's marriage to Prince Coloman of Hungary (1215–41), and Kinga's marriage to Bolesław V of Poland (1239–79).[49] According to the tale in Polish sources, Mieszko I had sent Lambert, archbishop of Cracow to Pope Sylvester II to ask for a crown. The pope ordered the making of a crown, but before he could send it, Stephen's envoy Bishop Ascherik arrived. He related that St Adalbert had baptized Stephen, the whole of Hungary had converted, and asked for a crown. The subsequent night an angel admonished the pope to give the completed crown to Stephen instead of Mieszko. The legend with various modifications then cropped up in a large number of Polish sources.[50] Whether Hartvic or the Polish versions drew on Peter Damian's *Life of St Romuald* (c. 1040) would need more research; Peter's text maintained that around 1001 Bolesław Chrobry attempted to gain a papal crown through the monks who had been sent to him on his request from Romuald's monastery. The monks, however, refused to intervene in a secular matter, and eventually the emperor ordered to have the roads guarded to capture any envoys the Polish ruler might send to the pope.[51] The text is representative of the reform movement's aims of separating the spiritual and secular spheres, and thus it would be ironic if it served as Hartvic's inspiration.

Hartvic's fabrication had such a major impact because it was reiterated for centuries. The text became the official *Life* (except the *utroque iure* passage), and thus the basis for the liturgical celebrations of Stephen. Its message was repeated in sermons, royal charters, and various later narrative accounts.[52] Later sources claiming the pope sent Stephen his crown, such as the chronicle of Henry of Mügeln, the 1233 oath of Bereg, or Pelbárt of Temesvár's sermons, based their

---

[49] First in the Krakow annals c. 1250–70: Géza Nagy, 'Szent István vérsége és a magyar kútforrások', *Turul* (1907, no. 3): 127–39. Earlier Polish sources, including Vincent Kadłubek in the early thirteenth century relate the origin of the Polish crown linked to Otto III's visit to Bolesław: ibid., 130–1.

[50] 'Annales Cracovienses compilati', [966–1291] *MGH SS* XIX, 586; 'Annales a primo christiano duce Meschone Polonorum', *Monumenta Poloniae Historica*, II, 829; 'Annales Kamenzenses', *MGH SS* XIX, 581; 'Annales minoris Poloniae', *MPH*, III, 142; 'Annales Polonorum I', *MGH SS* XIX, 618; 'Annales Polonorum III', *MGH SS* XIX, 619; 'Catalogi episcoporum Cracoviensium IV', *MPH*, III, 332; 'Rocznik Krasińskich', *MPH*, III, 129; 'Annales Silesiaci compilati', *MGH SS* XIX, 537; 'Rocznik świętokrzyskie', *MPH*, III, 60–1; 'Annales Sanctae Crucis Polonici', *MGH SS* XIX, 678; 'Zdarzenia godne pamięci', *MPH*, III, 299. Albin F. Gombos, 'Szent István a középkori külföldi történetírásban', in *Emlékkönyv*, vol. 3, 279–324, at 314–15, repr. 629–74, at 664–5. See also Weiler, *Paths to Kingship*, 78–9.

[51] 'Ex Vita S Romualdi auctore Petro Damiani', ed. G. Waitz, cap. 28–9, *MGH SS* IV, 846–54, at 852–3; Robert Folz, *Les saints rois du Moyen Âge en Occident (VIᵉ–XIIIᵉ siècles)* (Brussels: Société des Bollandistes, 1984), 83 takes this and a papal letter to Coloman as the sources of Hartvic's story.

[52] Székely, 'Korona és lándzsa', 23–4.

account on Hartvic's and do not represent independent proof of a papal crown.[53] The story also gained pictorial form, albeit in an ecclesiastical inflection: a copy of the *Liber Sextus* of Pope Boniface VIII commissioned by a Hungarian prelate, Nicholas Vásári, probably in the late 1330s or early 1340s, includes an image of the pope crowning Stephen; both the pope and the king are represented with a halo.[54]

Stephen's Crown

While Stephen certainly had one or even several crown(s), we have no verifiable information and can only make educated guesses about the form of Stephen's crown and its ultimate fate. There is a contemporary representation: on a chasuble made on the orders of the king and his wife in 1031, Stephen wears a diadem crown and holds a lance and an orb. His crown is decorated with precious stones and pinnacle decorations often understood as three lilies at the two sides and the front; however, this image is taken as a true representation of his real crown by some, and as schematic by others.[55] Similar crowns certainly existed during this period; an extant example is the small circlet crown with lilies in Essen, although it is likely to be a ritual crown created for a statue.[56] It is possible that Stephen's crown was comparable. Others interpret the image as a circlet crown with crosses rather than lilies, and that would match the silver mortuary crown of Béla III (d. 1196), which is a circlet with four crosses; however, this was not a royal crown worn in life.[57] It is equally possible that the chasuble provides a schematic, rather than authentic representation of the Hungarian regalia: Queen Gisela and various

---

[53] Székely, 'Koronaküldések', 916–17; also Innocent III, *Regesta*, XII, no. 42, PL 216, col. 50 (1209), Potthast no. 3725.

[54] Ernő Marosi, ed., *Magyarországi művészet 1300–1470 körül*, vol. 1 (Budapest: Akadémiai Kiadó, 1987), 357, 363; for the image, see Plate 12 of the colour photographs.

[55] István Bardoly, ed., *The Coronation Mantle of the Hungarian Kings* (Budapest: Hungarian National Museum, 2005), 158–9. Schematic: e.g. Tóth—Szelényi, *The Holy Crown*, 15; Iván Bertényi, *A magyar szent korona: Magyarország címere és zászlaja*, 4th edn (Budapest: Kossuth Könyvkiadó, 1996), 37, authentic: Györffy, *István király*, 154; Decsy *A' magyar*, 145–6; Benda—Fügedi, *A magyar korona*, 11–12; Szabolcs de Vajay, 'La relique Stéphanoise dans la sainte couronne de Hongrie', *Acta Historiae Artium*, 22 (1976): 3–20, at 5; Péter Váczy, 'Első királyunk koronája és a szent korona', in *Szent István és kora*, ed. Ferenc Glatz, József Kardos (Budapest: MTA Történettudományi Intézet, 1988), 95–6 (his 'proof': Queen Gisela would have been annoyed to be represented with a by then out-of-date crown, had it not been actually hers). József Gerics, Erzsébet Ladányi, 'A Szent István lándzsájára és koronájára vonatkozó források értelmezése', *Levéltári Szemle*, 40, no. 2 (1990): 3–14, at 6–7 see it as one of Stephen's crowns.

[56] It used to be called the crown of Otto III as a child; Birgitta Falk, 'Essener Krone', in *Gold vor Schwarz. Der Essener Domschatz auf Zollverein*, ed. Birgitta Falk, Exhibition Catalog (Essen: Klartext Verlag, 2009), 92–3; 11.8 cm diameter, made in the second half of the eleventh century. Cf. also the crown on St Oswald's reliquary at Hildesheim Cathedral.

[57] https://mek.oszk.hu/08800/08852/08852.pdf. The idea that the grave and thus the crown was Coloman's is not accepted in scholarship: Piroska Biczó, *Az Árpád-házi királysírok* (Budapest: Kossuth Kiadó, 2016), 24.

168 STEPHEN I, THE FIRST CHRISTIAN KING OF HUNGARY

saints appear on the chasuble with the same type of crown.[58] It has also been suggested that Stephen had a Byzantine-style crown, on the basis of eleventh- and twelfth-century Hungarian coins, which, according to this argument, represent rulers with crowns that follow the Byzantine model.[59] While this may be the case, there is no such contemporary numismatic evidence for Stephen, but only for Solomon (1063–74) and some later kings; nor does the imagery of the coins allow for any secure identification of the specific crowns worn by Hungarian kings. The so-called Liuthar evangeliary in Aachen, if Stephen is indeed one of the figures attending Otto III (which itself is hypothetical), represents a different type of crown yet again, a circlet with several parallel rows of precious stones and no lilies.[60]

Whatever crown Stephen wore, we cannot assume that it was invested with any meaning beyond being a personal symbol of power.[61] Stephen's legislation does not refer to a crown, but to the royal office: 'royal authority' and 'royal power.'[62] The *Admonitions*, written in his name during his reign, include the abstract notion of 'the crown' (*corona*) as a synonym of royal dignity (*regalis dignitas*) without reference to a physical crown.[63] Royal crowns were often made for each

---

[58] Tóth—Szelényi, *The Holy Crown*, 15; on uncertainties even concerning the much better documented Byzantine crowns, see Shepard, 'Crowns from the Basileus', 140; Albert Boeckler, 'Die "Stephanskrone"', in *Herrschaftszeichen und Staatssymbolik: Beiträge zu ihrer Geschichte vom dritten bis zum sechzehnten Jahrhundert*, 3 vols., ed. Percy Ernst Schramm, Schriften der Monumenta Germaniae Historica 13:1–3 (Stuttgart: Hiersemann Verlag, 1954–6), vol. 3, 743 concludes that there is no certainty regarding the form of Stephen's crown.

[59] László Holler, 'A magyar korona néhány alapkérdéséről', *Századok*, 130 (1996): 907–64, at 955–7, and for more detail, László Holler, 'Milyen koronája volt I. István királynak?', in *Numizmatika és társtudományok III*, ed. Péter Németh (Nyíregyháza, 1999), http://mek.oszk.hu/09800/09874/html/index.htm. This revives, in slightly different form, the argument that the *corona latina* is Stephen's crown, which must have been a closed crown: Elemér Varjú, 'A Szent Korona', *Archaeológiai Értesítő*, 39 (1920–2): 56–70, at 66.

[60] Johannes Fried, *Otto III. und Boleslaw Chrobry: Das Widmungsbild des Aachener Evangeliars, der 'Akt von Gnesen' und das frühe polnische und ungarische Königtum*, 2nd rev. edn (Stuttgart: Franz Steiner Verlag, 2001), argues that one of the figures is Stephen, but at 67 emphasizes that types, rather than individuals, are represented; Johannes Fried, 'Politik der Ottonen im Spiegel der Krönungsordnungen', in *Krönungen. Könige in Aachen—Geschichte und Mythos. Katalog der Ausstellung*, 2 vols., ed. Mario Kramp (Mainz: Verlag Philipp von Zabern, 2000), vol. 1, 252–64, image at 261, image 5, Katalog nr. 3–38, does not identify the figure as Stephen. *Krönungen* includes a very large number of representations of roughly contemporary rulers in the Empire, and these images show a great variety of crowns.

[61] Székely, 'Koronaküldések', 905–6, on the distinction between crown as symbol of state and crown as personal power symbol. On the lack of a specific object as a symbol of royal power in medieval Europe: Jürgen Petersohn, *'Echte' und 'Falsche' Insignien im deutschen Krönungsbrauch des Mittelalters? Kritik eines Forschungsstereotyps* (Stuttgart: Franz Steiner Verlag, 1993). See also Weiler, *Paths to Kingship*, 346–50.

[62] János M. Bak, György Bónis, James Ross Sweeney, ed., *The Laws of the Medieval Kingdom of Hungary*, vol. 1 (Bakersfield, CA: Charles Schlacks, 1989), 1, 3, 11 ('opus regalis dignitatis'; 'nostra regali potentia', 'ad nostram regalem dignitatem pertinet', 'contra regis...dignitatem').

[63] 'Libellus de institutione morum', ed. Iosephus Balogh, *SRH*, II, 611–27, at 621–7. For an analysis, see Josef Karpat, 'Corona regni Hungariae im Zeitalter der Arpaden', in *Corona regni: Studien über die Krone als Symbol des Staates im Späteren Mittelalter*, ed. Manfred Hellmann (Darmstadt: Wissenschaftliche Buchgesellschaft, 1961), 225–348, at 257–8.

THE HUNGARIAN CROWN   169

bearer, and many kings possessed a number of different crowns.[64] Although some examples of crowns (and other regalia) sent to a ruler's successor have been noted from the period,[65] the value of the precious objects was what made them a desirable inheritance, similar to other royal treasures, rather than their inherent importance for having belonged to a particular ruler.

It has been convincingly argued that for Stephen, the lance was in fact a much more important *insigne* of power, vested with symbolic significance.[66] Stephen is represented holding the lance on the chasuble, and the first coin minted under his rule features a hand holding a lance with the inscription LANCEA REGIS on its obverse.[67] The lance had such a symbolic charge because in all likelihood it came from the emperor and was probably similar to the extant lance that had been given to the Polish ruler Bolesław Chrobry.[68] Thus, it would have been a copy of the still existing imperial Holy Lance, believed to have belonged to St Maurice, and containing a relic of a nail from the crucifixion.[69]

The lance, unlike his crown, is also mentioned repeatedly in various sources after Stephen's death, yet it is not explicitly linked to Stephen, which strongly suggests that in these early years, objects did not gain added significance from their association to Stephen. Sections of the Annals of Altaich written around 1075 provide detailed accounts of the succession of the next three kings after Stephen.

---

[64] Jürgen Petersohn, 'Über monarchische Insignien und ihre Funktion im mittelalterlichen Reich', *Historische Zeitschrift*, 266, no. 1 (February 1998): 47–96, at 50. In the Empire, whatever crown the ruler used was considered to be royal or imperial insignia: ibid., 51. Charles V of France had twenty-one crowns: Hervé Pinoteau, *La symbolique royale Française Ve—XVIIIe siècles* (La Roche—Rigault: PSR éditions, 2003), 287.

[65] Székely, 'Koronaküldések', 906–7.

[66] László Kovács, 'A Szent István-i lándzsa', in *Koronák, koronázási jelvények. Crowns, coronation insignia*, ed. Lívia Bende, Gábor Lőrinczy (Ópusztaszer: Csongrád Megyei Múzeumok Igazgatósága, 2001), 99–136.

[67] On the reverse, an image, interpreted as a church or a crown, and the inscription REGIA CIVITAS; Lajos Huszár, *Münzkatalog Ungarn von 1000 bis Heute* (Budapest: Corvina, 1979), p. 31 no. 2. (he identifies the image on the reverse as a Carolingian Church). László Kovács, *A kora Árpád-kori magyar pénzverésről: Érmetani és régészeti tanulmányok a Kárpát-medence I. (Szent) István és II. (Vak) Béla uralkodása közötti időszakának (1000–1141) érméiről*, Varia Archaeologica Hungarica VII (Budapest: MTA Régészeti Intézete, 1997), 31–5, 51–60, 247–62 with thorough critical evaluation of all previous literature.

[68] The C version of the chronicle of Adémar de Chabannes stated that Otto III gave Géza of the Hungarians a holy lance containing relics of pieces of nails from the Crucifixion and parts of St Maurice's lance, allowing him to have the lance borne before him: *Ademari Cabannensis Chronicon*, ed. P. Bourgain, R. Landes, G. Pon, Corpus Christianorum Continuatio Mediaevalis 129 (Turnhout: Brepols, 1999), III, 31. Surviving in a twelfth-century manuscript, the C version's authenticity has been debated, but is now mostly accepted as Adémar's work: László Veszprémy, *Történetírás és történetírók az Árpád-kori Magyarországon (XI–XIII. század közepe)* (Budapest: Rerum Fides, 2019), 283–90.

[69] Székely, 'Koronaküldések', 925–6; Székely, 'Korona és lándzsa', 21, 23; Schramm, *Herrschaftszeichen*, vol. 2, 492–537; János Bak, 'Holy Lance, Holy Crown, Holy Dexter: sanctity of insignia in medieval east central Europe', in *Studying Medieval Rulers and Their Subjects: Central Europe and Beyond*, Variorum Collected Studies Series CS956 (Farnham and Burlington, VT: Ashgate, 2010), VI, 56–65, at 56–8; Fried, *Otto III. und Boleslaw Chrobry*, 136–49. The imperial lance: Kramp, *Krönungen*, vol. 1, 324, nr. 3–1.

170   STEPHEN I, THE FIRST CHRISTIAN KING OF HUNGARY

Although twice referring to the 'gilded lance' belonging to the Hungarian king (once when it was captured after Henry III defeated Samuel Aba in 1044, and once in the description of King Peter offering Hungary to his lord, Henry III), the author does not say that it had belonged to Stephen.[70] This is the case despite the quasi-certainty that the lance was the one used by Stephen. Other eleventh-century sources that mention Henry III sending the Hungarian regalia to Rome after defeating Samuel Aba do not link the regalia to Stephen either. Thus Bonizo, bishop of Sutri (c. 1045–c. 1091) remarked that the lance of the king of Hungary was sent to Rome, placed, as a sign of victory, at the Apostle Peter's tomb.[71] Pope Gregory VII in 1074 claimed that both the lance and the crown were sent to St Peter by Henry III who had subdued Hungary to the honour of St Peter. Although Gregory VII asserted that Hungary belonged to the Roman Church because Stephen had offered it to St Peter, even he did not link the regalia to Stephen.[72]

Stephen's crown (or crowns) had no special significance for his immediate successors; although it cannot be excluded that one or more of them used it, there is neither proof nor any inherent necessity for them to have done so. Nor is there any mention of Stephen's crown after his death for quite a significant period; only centuries later is a crown dubbed 'Stephen's'. Some have argued for Stephen's early, pre-canonization (1083) importance, at least as the ancestor of and founder-figure for Hungarian kings, claiming that evidence soon after his death proves that his regalia were already invested with meaning.[73] While Stephen was indeed celebrated for his role in Christianizing Hungary and making the pilgrimage route to Jerusalem across the kingdom safe, deeds that were remembered after he died, sources from the decades after his death do not mention his regalia, let alone give them a special status.[74] Two descriptions of Stephen's successors ascending the throne and of their consecration did not trigger any mention of Stephen's regalia playing a role.[75]

---

[70] 'lancea deaurata', in 'Annales Altahenses Maiores', ed. Edmundus L. B. von Oefele, *MGH Scriptores Rerum Germanicarum*, vol. 4 (Hanover: Hahn, 1891), 37, 40. Henry III is called caesar in the text; he became emperor in 1046.

[71] 'Liber ad amicum', ed. Ernestus Dümmler, in *MGH, Libelli de lite imperatorum et pontificum saeculis XI. et XII. conscripti*, vol. 1, 583–4; similar by Arnulf of Milan, *MGH SS* VIII, 18.

[72] *Gregorii Papae VII Epistolae Selectae*, ed. F.-J. Schmale, *Fontes litem de Investitura Illustrantes*, Ausgewählte Quellen zur deutschen Geschichte des Mittelalters XIIa (Darmstadt, 1978), 110, no. 33; *Das Register Gregors VII*, ed. Erich Caspar, *MGH Epistolae selectae* II,1 (Berlin: Weidmann, 1920), book 2, no. 13, 145. 'Nam … regnum Ungarię sanctę Romanę ecclesię proprium est a rege Stephano olim beato PETRO cum omni iure et potestate sua oblatum et devote traditum. Preterea Heinricus pię memorię imperator ad honorem sancti PETRI regnum illud expugnans victo rege et facta victoria ad corpus beati PETRI lanceam coronamque transmisit et pro gloria triumphi sui illuc regni direxit insignia, quo principatum dignitatis eius attinere cognovit.' These lines are omitted from his analysis of the letter by Benedict Wiedemann, *Papal Overlordship and European Princes, 1000–1270* (Oxford: Oxford University Press, 2021), 54–56.

[73] Lenkey [Zsoldos], *Szent István*, 104–6.

[74] Nor does his successors' coinage refer to Stephen; even after his canonization, it was Ladislas I rather than Stephen I who appeared on coins: Kovács, *A kora Árpád-kori magyar pénzverésről*, 62–144, 177, 183, 187, 191.

[75] 'Annales Altahenses Maiores', 37, 43.

Only according to the fourteenth-century chronicles did Henry III invest Peter with Stephen's regalia ('insignibus sancti regis Stephani') in 1044;[76] such a retrospective claim is not surprising by the fourteenth century, when 'St Stephen's crown' was a necessary part of royal coronation. King Ladislas, who had Stephen canonized, did not include in his legislation any references to Stephen's crown, although Stephen is among the saints to be celebrated in the kingdom, and people are to be punished according to Stephen's laws.[77] As to King Coloman's legislation (the king who commissioned the *Life* inventing the papal sending of the crown), Stephen became a significant reference point as the founder figure, yet there is no allusion to his crown.[78] Similarly, neither the Synod of Szabolcs (1092) nor that of Esztergom (at the start of the twelfth century, but its text includes interpolated material) mentions Stephen's crown. Therefore, at a time much closer to Stephen's lifetime, and even after his canonization, there was no interest in or knowledge of his supposed crown in Hungarian legislation.

There is one possible exception to early indifference. A passage from a text on the foundation of St Alban in Namur, written soon after 1067, has been understood to mean that Andrew I, newly enthroned in 1046, ordered a search for the regalia of Stephen (whom this text mistakenly declares to be Andrew's immediate predecessor); it has been used to argue that royal objects associated to Stephen already had special significance before his canonization in eleventh-century political thought.[79] The text does not mention Stephen's crown specifically.[80] The search for 'the accoutrement and possessions' of the king, if it happened—the author confuses or misrepresents the order of succession, and it is hard to tell whether it is more reliable concerning the search—is not described in any way as a search for regalia Andrew needed for his coronation; he had already been enthroned. At most, after tumultuous civil wars, Andrew was interested in promoting a sense of stability by relying on prototypes current during Stephen's reign. In this vein, he chose a coin-type used under Stephen as the model for his coinage, but with his own name substituted, thus not seeking to legitimize his rule by any direct reference to Stephen.[81] Further, the passage clearly details the

---

[76] *SRH* I, 333. The contemporary Annals of Altaich do not mention this when describing Peter's inauguration: Székely, 'Koronaküldések', 934.

[77] Bak et al., *Laws*, 20, 21, 22. [78] Ibid., 24–8. [79] Lenkey [Zsoldos], *Szent István*, 106.

[80] 'Qui noviter intronisatus, dum antecessoris inquireret ornamentum, supperlectilem [sic] regiam, Leuduino presuli precepit, ut breves reliquiarum legeret et, quorum lipsana essent, pro certo sciret.' 'Fundatio ecclesiae S. Albani Namucensis', *MGH SS* XV/2, 964. The author reports information from Liedvin/Leodvin, bishop of Bihar who visited Namur, in order to attest the origin of the relics Liedvin gave to Namur, which he had taken from the relics collected by King Stephen. For most recent discussion of this source, with summaries of previous scholarship: Judit Csákó, *Az Árpád-kori Magyarország a francia területen keletkezett elbeszélő kútfők tükrében*, unpublished PhD thesis (Budapest, 2015), 285–6, no. 92. I thank Vedran Sulovsky for his opinion on this text, and for drawing my attention to a similar usage of suppellex as royal possessions in the *Gesta Frederici* of Otto of Morena and his continuators: *MGH Scriptores rerum Germanicarum* n.s. 7, ed. Ferdinand Güterbock, 155.

[81] Kovács, *A kora Árpád-kori magyar pénzverésről*, 62.

172 STEPHEN I, THE FIRST CHRISTIAN KING OF HUNGARY

certification of relics while the search was conducted, and therefore a desire to inventory relics and the valuable trappings of royal power may explain the pursuit, rather than the special status of Stephen's regalia. The consistent absence of Stephen's crown in numerous near-contemporary sources strengthens the case for a lack of interest in Stephen's crown in the decades following his death.

While an argument *ex nihilo* would be weak, the point is that these sources detail events such as royal succession that would reasonably prompt a reference to Stephen's crown, had it been important at the time; yet they are silent. Finally, while some scholars hypothesize that the royal crown was stolen in the 1160s, and that this shows there was already a crown that was necessary for the royal coronation to be valid, the sole basis of this hypothesis is a miniature from the fourteenth-century *Illuminated Chronicle*.[82] The text does not refer to the stealing of the crown in the twelfth century, and the miniature, made in the second half of the fourteenth century, is no evidence for the special status of Stephen's crown earlier. There is thus no proof of the significance of Stephen's crown for his immediate successors.

Nor can we establish with any certainty what happened to Stephen's crown (or crowns). If by any chance it was still in use in 1044, then, if we are to believe the letter of Pope Gregory VII mentioned above (1074), Henry III, after his victory over Samuel Aba, sent the royal regalia, the crown, and the lance to St Peter.[83] In the late nineteenth century, it was thought that Stephen's crown had been lost after it was sent by Henry III to the pope.[84] Others, however, discounted Pope Gregory's information, because other sources do not mention the crown.[85] Some claimed that Henry III used Stephen's crown when he reinstalled Peter Orseolo (Stephen's nephew and heir) on the throne in 1044, and hypothesized that the crown was lost later.[86] According to another theory, Stephen presented his crown

---

[82] Bertényi, *A magyar szent korona*, 60–1. Image in facsimile edition in *The Hungarian Illuminated Chronicle*, ed. Dezső Dercsényi (Budapest: Corvina Press, 1969), 121.

[83] *Gregorii papae VII Epistolae Selectae*, 110, no. 33; see also József Gerics, 'A Hartvik-legenda mintáiról és forrásairól', *Magyar Könyvszemle*, 97 (1981): 175–88; Székely, 'Koronaküldések', 925–6; Péter Váczy, *A magyar történelem korai századaiból* (Budapest, 1994), 77–93.

[84] Gyula Pauler, *A magyar nemzet története az Árpádházi királyok alatt*, 2nd edn (Budapest: Athenaeum, 1899, repr. Budapest: Állami Könyvterjesztő Vállalat, 1985), vol. 1, 421–2, note 183; similar György Györffy, 'Die "corona sancti Stephani regis" zur Zeit der Arpaden', in *Insignia Regni Hungariae I*, 55–63, at 56; Benda—Fügedi, *A magyar korona regénye*, 12–14; Vajay, 'La relique Stéphanoise', 5; Kardos, *A szentkorona-tan*, 11.

[85] János Karácsonyi, 'Hogyan lett Szent István koronája a magyar Szent Korona felső részévé?', *Értekezések a történeti tudományok köréből*, 21, no. 6 (1907): 523–41; József Deér, *A magyarok szent koronája* (Budapest: Magyar Nemzeti Múzeum, Máriabesnyő—Gödöllő: Attraktor, 2005), 170 (originally published as Josef Deér, *Die Heilige Krone Ungarns*, Vienna: Österreichischen Akademie der Wissenschaften, 1966).

[86] Deér, *A magyarok szent koronája*, 170; since Gregory tried to prove papal rights, it is possible that the claim is untrue. Other theories include Deér's that Anna took it to Prague escaping from Stephen V; Váczy's that Solomon took it after the battle of Mogyoród, and it was lost. Boeckler, 'Die "Stephanskrone"', 743 simply notes the crown perished.

THE HUNGARIAN CROWN   173

to a church, as some rulers at the time did.[87] No proof of this exists; only a crown of Queen Gisela, Stephen's wife, was mentioned in 1217 in the church of Veszprém.[88] Other ideas, linking Stephen's crown to the extant 'Holy Crown' will be discussed below. While of course hypothetically we can imagine many different possible fates for Stephen's crown(s), a lack of evidence (barring some new discovery) prevents any meaningful conclusion.

2. The Extant Hungarian Crown

Believed to have been Stephen's, this crown was used for royal coronations until 1916, and kept locked away at other times apart from a few special occasions. Brief examinations from time to time, however, led to the growth of scholarly knowledge from the eighteenth century, and a scientific consensus emerged over the course of the next two centuries that invalidated the traditional identification. Research was hampered by the sacral status of the object; prior to the second half of the twentieth century, scholars were usually not allowed to touch and physically examine it, and even in the most optimal period during the 1980s not all physical examination was allowed to proceed.[89]

Books on the crown were published as early as in the seventeenth century, but the first ones consisted of panegyric. Elias Berger in 1608 wrote the first known book on the crown.[90] A royal historiographer in the service of Matthias II, he celebrated the Habsburg king for having recovered the crown, and the crown itself as holy and angelic that came from heaven. The crown was responsible for the Christianization of Hungary, and guarantor of the well-being of the country. Five years later, one of the crown guards, Péter Révay, wrote a work with the aim of fostering its veneration (although he was a Lutheran).[91] While he noted the presence of Greek letters,[92] he described the crown as given to Stephen through divine revelation (*diuina revelatione*) and through the command of an angel (*angeli iussu*), referring to the vision in which an angel instructed the pope to

---

[87] Tóth—Szelényi, *The Holy Crown*, 13. It was taken by Andrew II when he prepared for crusade: Kovács—Lovag, *Hungarian Crown*, 78.

[88] György Fejér, *Codex diplomaticus Hungariae ecclesiasticus ac civilis*, t. IX, vol. 7, 646.

[89] Zsuzsa Lovag, 'L'intégration de la couronne latine et la couronne grecque', *Acta Historiae Artium*, 43, no. 1 (2002): 62–71, at 64.

[90] Berger, Elias, D.O.M. *Jubilaeus de origine, errore et restitutione S. Coronae Hungariae Regni*, Hungarian translation in Teszelszky, *Az ismeretlen korona*, 327–41.

[91] Péter Révay, *De sacrae coronae Regni Hungariae ortu, virtute, victoria, fortuna, annos ultra DC clarissimae brevis commentarius Petri de Rewa comitis comitatus de Turocz* (Augustae Vindelicorum, 1613); he made revisions that were included in later editions; many republications listed in Ipolyi, *A magyar Szent Korona*, vi–vii. Sándor Szilágyi, *Révay Péter és a szent korona (1619–1622)*, Értekezések a történelmi tudományok köréből 5, no. 1 (Budapest: Magyar Tudományos Akadémia, 1875); Szekfű, 'Szent István', *Emlékkönyv*, 34–5, repr. 560–1. On Révay, see Tóth, *Szent István, Szent Korona*, 43–8.

[92] 'literis Graecis', Révay, *De sacrae coronae* (1613), 75.

174 STEPHEN I, THE FIRST CHRISTIAN KING OF HUNGARY

send a crown that by the time Révay wrote was thought to have been this specific crown.[93] He also claimed that the crown had secret power, and the failure to fulfil one's duty towards it was punished by God.[94]

Later, however, Révay wrote another book on the history of Hungary, focusing on issues of state and governance, published posthumously in 1659, *De monarchia et Sacra Corona Regni Hungariae centuriae septem*.[95] This was much more critical of the Habsburgs and the Catholic Church. As the title already signals, the crown played a much reduced role, and Révay also toned down the language of devotion found in his earlier work, never calling the crown 'angelic' and 'apostolic'. He also described the images of 'Greek emperors', erroneously identifying one as Constantine the Great, and drew the conclusion that the crown had been given by Constantine the Great to Pope Sylvester I, and was then sent by Sylvester II to Stephen.[96]

From then on, trends still observable today were set in motion: reverence and science pulled in opposite directions.[97] Critical analysis started to oppose centuries of tradition, but initially along the denominational divide, as Protestants challenged the Catholic narrative of the beginnings of Hungarian Christianity and statehood. In the middle of the eighteenth century, the Lutheran theologian Gottfried Schwarz argued that the crown had nothing to do with Stephen or the pope, but was a Byzantine gift bestowed on Stephen's father by Constantine VII (913–59), proving the Byzantine origins of Hungarian Christianity.[98] Other Hungarian Protestant authors followed suit in demystifying the crown, while Catholic authors refused to accept what they branded fabrications, and continued to call the crown angelic and holy.[99]

From the end of the eighteenth century, on rare occasions it became possible for a limited number of scholars to study the crown.[100] The first opportunities

[93] Ibid., 50.   [94] Ibid., 18, 50, 64.
[95] Péter Révay, *De monarchia et Sacra Corona Regni Hungariae centuriae Septem. A Magyar Királyság birodalmáról és Szent Koronájáról szóló hét század*, 2 vols., ed. and Hungarian tr. Gergely Tóth, Bernadett Benei, Rezső Jarmalov, Sára Sánta (Budapest: ELKH Bölcsészettudományi Kutatóközpont, 2022).
[96] Ibid., vol. 2, 554–67.
[97] List of publications up to 1886: Ipolyi, *A magyar Szent Korona*, vi–x. On research history: Gyula Moravcsik, 'A magyar szent korona a filológiai és történeti kutatások megvilágításában', in *Emlékkönyv Szent István király halálának kilencszázadik évfordulóján*, ed. Jusztinián Serédi (Budapest: Magyar Tudományos Akadémia, 1938), vol. 3, 425–72, repr. (Budapest: Szent István Társulat, 1988), 675–724; Thomas von Bogyay, 'Über die Forschungsgeschichte der heiligen Krone', in *Insignia Regni Hungariae I*, 65–89; Endre Tóth, *A magyar szent korona és a koronázási jelvények* (Budapest: Országház Könyvkiadó, 2018), 15–29; Eng. tr. *The Hungarian Holy Crown and the Coronation Regalia*, 2021.
[98] Gottfried Schwarz, *Initia religionis christianae inter Hungaros ecclesiae orientali adscripta* (Halle, 1739).
[99] Szekfű, 'Szent István', *Emlékkönyv*, 54–8, repr. 580–4; detailed monograph on the role of Stephen and the crown in Protestant history-writing: Tóth, *Szent István, Szent Korona*.
[100] On the various examinations see, for example, Moravcsik, 'A magyar Szent Korona', 426–30, repr. 678–82; Vajay, 'La relique Stéphanoise', 4; Bogyay, 'Über die Forschungsgeschichte', 70–2; Tóth, *A magyar szent korona*, 15–19; Bak—Pálffy, *Crown and Coronation*, 181–7.

THE HUNGARIAN CROWN   175

came in 1790 and 1792. The crown, after it had been kept under lock in the castle of Pozsony (Bratislava) for half a century after Maria Theresa's 1741 coronation, was transported from Vienna to Buda and put on public display in both years. The resulting observation that the crown was made of two separate parts, and that historical figures who lived much later than Stephen were represented on it dealt the first irrefutable blow to the centuries-long belief in St Stephen's crown.[101] Debate was stirred up by a Calvinist representative of the enlightenment, Sámuel Decsy, whose book was also the first lengthy vernacular work on the crown.[102] It argued that the crown was made in Byzantium, and was sent by Emperor Michael Doukas to Géza I, with the upper part added under the Angevins.[103] Although Decsy accepted that a crown was sent by the pope to Stephen, he argued it was not a royal crown, nor was it the same as the extant crown; he also denied that Stephen offered his country to the pope.[104]

The new findings that the crown as a whole could not have been Stephen's led to imaginative attempts to salvage the link to the first king. One hypothesis had Stephen send his father's Byzantine crown to Rome where the pope blessed it and had the upper section added.[105] Although debates continued, by the nineteenth century, the new explanation that the Greek crown was sent to Géza I by Michael Doukas, while the Latin crown was sent to St Stephen from Rome was replacing the older consensus.[106]

The Habsburg court commissioned Franz Bock to study the regalia; his work, published in 1857, maintained that the upper part of the crown went back to St Stephen.[107] Not content with a court-commissioned study, and having found that existing descriptions and images of the crown (including by Bock) were no longer up to scientific standards, the Hungarian Academy of Sciences nominated a committee in 1880 to examine the crown. This was a crucially important scrutiny, more thorough than any before, and many afterwards. It lasted for two days and included a physical examination removing the cross and the inner cap that had been added for the wearer's comfort; photos and detailed descriptions were made.[108] The most critical conclusions resulting from this, however, were only

---

[101] Josephus Koller, *De sacra regni Hungariae corona commentarius* (Pécs, 1800).

[102] Sámuel Decsy, *A' magyar szent koronának*.

[103] Ibid., 80–207, especially 166–201, and on Angevin addition, 206–7.

[104] Ibid., 95–6; 104–7 (thought that Stephen's ancestors were already kings); 138–62; 128–33, respectively. See also Teszelszky, *Az ismeretlen korona*, 41–2.

[105] Elek Horányi, *De Sacra Corona Hungariae ac de regibus eadem redimitis commentarius* (Pest, 1790), 40–67, cited in Moravcsik, 'A magyar Szent Korona', 426, repr. 678.

[106] Moravcsik, 'A magyar Szent Korona', 428, repr. 680.

[107] Franz Bock, 'Die ungarischen Reichsinsignien, VI: Die Krone des hl. Stephan', *Mittheilungen der kaiserliche königliche Central-Comission zur Erforschung und Erhaltung der Baudenkmale*, 2 (Vienna, 1857): 201–11; he repeated his opinion in *Die Kleinodien des heil. Römischen Reiches deutscher Nation nebst den Kroninsignien Böhmens, Ungarns und der Lombardei* (Vienna, 1864); he proposed that the upper bands originally formed a round circlet-crown and contained twelve apostles, as Stephen's original crown.

[108] Ipolyi, *A magyar Szent Korona*, iii–v; Deér, *A magyarok szent koronája*, 10–11.

176 STEPHEN I, THE FIRST CHRISTIAN KING OF HUNGARY

published in newspaper reports in 1880, stating that no part of the crown was Stephen's;[109] the official publication, Arnold Ipolyi's monograph on the crown in 1886, argued that the *corona latina*'s more primitive technology and artistic style compared to the Byzantine crown proved it was originally Stephen's crown.[110] Ipolyi thought it was added to the Byzantine crown—which had been gifted to Géza I in return for his chivalric behaviour to Greek captives, and was used by him on his ascension to the throne—under Géza I or Ladislas I.[111] The committee identified the enamel technique of the *pinnae* and the damage to the upper part, although this was interpreted as the result of bending the previously straight bands.[112]

During the millennial celebrations in 1896, the crown was once again examined. This led to the idea that the *corona latina*'s apostle enamels were independent of the bands and had originally been on Stephen's crown, dating from the tenth-eleventh centuries, while the bands were made in order to attach the images to the Byzantine crown in the thirteenth century.[113] Archaeologists, art historians, and historians continued to argue over the upper part. János Karácsonyi maintained that the apostle enamels had been on Stephen's circlet diadem crown, which was buried with Stephen, and found in the tomb at the time of the canonization; although four images had been damaged, the remaining eight were reused, affixed to new bands, and mounted on Géza I's crown, creating the extant crown.[114] The most critical stance was taken by Gyula Pauler: he did not believe that Stephen's crown was broken into pieces to be added to Géza I's Byzantine crown.[115]

Half an hour's examination before the coronation of 1916 led to the conclusion that the cross-bands of the upper part had been created by welding four gold bands to a central panel and two of them had been broken by some violent action, and a third half-broken. Opposing earlier opinion, scholars now maintained that the original form of the object with the apostle enamels had not been altered when it became the upper part of the extant crown.[116] Otto von Falke saw the crown briefly in 1928. The celebration of 'St Stephen's year' in 1938—the 900th anniversary of his death, but also a highly politicized undertaking in the name of the 'Christian-national idea'—drowned out some valid criticism;[117] but it also

---

[109] Ibid., 11–12.   [110] Ipolyi, *A magyar Szent Korona*, 137, 156.

[111] Ibid., 65–8; detailed description and analysis of the crown, 133–81.

[112] Tóth, *A magyar szent korona*, 16–17.

[113] Béla Czobor, *A magyar koronázási jelvények* (Budapest: Műbarátok köre, 1896), 4; Tóth, *A magyar szent korona*, 18.

[114] Karácsonyi, 'Hogyan lett Szent István koronája', thus dating the existing crown to the reign of Ladislas I.

[115] Pauler, *A magyar nemzet története*, vol. 1, 422, note 183.

[116] Varjú, 'A Szent Korona', 63–4.

[117] Z. Tóth originally tried to publish his criticism of Hartvic and the origin of the crown in the *Szent István Emlékkönyv* of 1938, but it was rejected because of the novelty of his results. He finally published the work himself in 1942, after Brackmann argued for the imperial provenance of the crown: Tóth, *A Hartvik-legenda kritikájához*, 3.

THE HUNGARIAN CROWN   177

resulted in still broadly sound scholarly advances, most notably Moravcsik's study of the *corona graeca*, detailed below.

Various art historians outside Hungary drew conclusions from drawings, without seeing the crown, about the dating of the enamels.[118] An entire book was also written by József Deér; he was unable to examine the crown physically, but advanced a novel theory about its making.[119] According to him, the Byzantine emperor Michael Doukas sent a gift with the enamel images now on the *corona graeca*; these were transferred to a crown in the late twelfth century in Hungary, to create a crown for Anne of Châtillon, wife of Béla III. He dated the apostle images to the early thirteenth century, suggesting a Venetian origin, and proposing that they were part of an object gifted to King Andrew II. He dated the creation of the current crown to the 1270s, as a replacement for St Stephen's crown taken by Anne, daughter of King Béla IV, to Prague after her father's death. Deér claimed that the new crown imitated the lost original, to keep the theft secret, and it came to be accepted as St Stephen's crown.

While earlier, apart from rare exceptions, scholars had to contend themselves with looking at the crown, making drawings and later taking photographs, after the second world war, researchers were able to handle it. First, while the crown was in the custody of the American army, scholars in Germany and then in the United States were able to examine it thoroughly, and after its return in 1978, so could those in Hungary.[120] While advances were made, several unresolved controversies and open questions remain. Art historical analysis has not been conclusive because there are so few surviving objects that can serve for comparative purposes. Many of the alterations the crown underwent cannot be dated, and some issues cannot be fully settled. Potential new avenues to gain better knowledge would entail physical examinations using modern technologies, for example on the provenance of the gold, or the technical analysis of the enamels.[121]

It is important to distinguish clearly between what can be known with certainty and hypothetical reconstructions. We also need to acknowledge the limits of scholarship; many interpretations cannot be fully proven.[122] Wishful thinking still influences some scholars; this is all the easier, because open questions are like cracks in the wall, that accommodate the hair-thin roots of speculation. As one historian

---

[118] Tóth, *A magyar szent korona*, 18–19.   [119] Deér, *A magyarok szent koronája*.

[120] Benda—Fügedi, *A magyar korona regénye*, 18–19; Kovács—Lovag, *Hungarian Crown*, 17–18; Bak—Pálffy, *Crown and Coronation*, 186–7; Éva Kovács, 'Ereignisse und Ergebnisse: ein neuer Weg der Forschung in der Geschichte der ungarischen Krönungsinsignien', in *Insignia Regni Hungariae I*, 91–7.

[121] As set out by David Buckton, 'Vorläufige Ergebnisse einer optischen Untersuchung des Emails der Krone', *Insignia Regni Hungariae I*, 129–43, at 130.

[122] Ernő Marosi, 'A magyar korona a jelenkori kutatásban és a populáris irodalomban: Megjegyzések a művészettörténet-tudomány jelenlegi helyzetéhez és megbecsüléséhez', *Művészettörténeti Értesítő*, 35, nos. 1–2 (1986): 49–55, at 49.

178 STEPHEN I, THE FIRST CHRISTIAN KING OF HUNGARY

wryly observed, especially in anniversary years, even scholars are more permissive in their hypotheses.[123] According to most scholars not in awe of national traditions, both constituent parts of the crown date from after Stephen's reign.[124] Tenacious and recently redoubled efforts by some nonetheless still try to link the crown to Stephen in some way, at least in part. These efforts spring not from truly plausible evidence, but from a desire to salvage the crown's link to the first king, frequently also resurrecting the idea of its papal donation.[125] Amateurs and conspiracy theorists, moreover, continue to elaborate unfounded alternative histories.

The crown is a composite object, consisting of two distinct parts: a lower one, the Greek crown (corona graeca), and an upper part comprising two crossed bands, the so-called Latin or Western crown (corona latina).[126] The gold used in the two parts differs, with the upper part made of softer, better quality gold, while the lower has a higher silver content.[127] The quality of the workmanship fitting the two parts together is inferior to that of either part in itself, with rudimentary riveting.[128]

The Greek crown consists of a circlet band with crest decorations (akroterioi, pinnae), and four pendilia (pendant chains) on each side and one at the back, that all end in three-lobed oval almandines.[129] The band together with the crest decorations were cut from a single sheet of thick (about 1.5 mm) gold plate and welded into a slightly elliptic circle at the back.[130] The pendilia are attached in diverse ways. The holders for five were soldered onto the lower edge of the band, which is considered the original manner of attaching the pendant chains; one of these, where the holder broke off, now hangs from a hoop suspended from the wire holding the pearls. The hoops of the two middle pendant chains on each side were suspended from holes bored into the bottom of the band, considered a later addition.[131] The pendants ending in tri-lobed palmettes are not exactly alike.[132] Whether the pendilia now on the crown include

---

[123] Veszprémy, 'Fikció és valóság', 15.

[124] E.g. Percy Ernst Schramm, 'Herrschaftszeichen: gestiftet, verschenkt, verkauft, verpfändet. Belege aus dem Mittelalter', Nachrichten der Akademie der Wissenschaften in Göttingen, Philologisch-Historische Klasse, 5 (1957): 161–219, at 174.

[125] Ernő Marosi, 'La "couronne latine"', Acta Historiae Artium, 43 (2002): 72–82, at 72. One example of the claim that recent scholarly results 'prove' that the crown dates from c. 1000: Csaba Ferencz, 'Szent István koronája', in Szentjeink és nagyjaink Európa kereszténységéért, ed. Margit Beke, Miscellanea Ecclesiae Strigoniensis 1 (Budapest: Esztergom-budapesti Főegyházmegye Egyháztörténeti Bizottsága, 2001), 37–43.

[126] The best overall introduction is Kovács—Lovag, Hungarian Crown; the most recent but biased monographic discussion is Tóth, A magyar szent korona. These two books also contain the best photographs.

[127] Tóth—Szelényi, The Holy Crown, 17.   [128] Ibid., 40.

[129] Kovács—Lovag, Hungarian Crown, 18–43; Tóth—Szelényi, The Holy Crown, 18–22; Tóth, A magyar szent korona, 111–33.

[130] József Péri, 'Időszaki jelentés a Szent Korona ötvösvizsgálatáról I', Magyar Iparművészet (1994/1): 2–6, at 2; Zsuzsa Lovag, 'Néhány technikai megfigyelés a magyar koronán', A Magyar Nemzeti Galéria Évkönyve (1991): 39–42, at 39.

[131] Lovag, 'Néhány technikai megfigyelés', 39; Péri, 'Időszaki jelentés', 4; Lovag, 'L'intégration de la couronne', 66.

[132] Kovács—Lovag, Hungarian Crown, 37.

THE HUNGARIAN CROWN   179

original ones is debated. The dowels of five of them are from the same material as other parts of the crown.[133] It has been suggested that four *pendilia* (two on each side) were added later in Hungary to the original five.[134] However, possibly four *pendilia* that were already on the crown, but in different locations, were merely transferred to the sides: drilled holes in the frame of the crest decorations, one of which still has a gold wire hook attached, may have held *pendilia* originally, and perhaps some of the pearls on the circlet, affixed in a different manner, indicate that there had been *pendilia* attached there as well.[135]

The upper and lower edge of the band is decorated by pearls strung on a gold wire; eight stones that include gemstones (almandine, sapphire, aquamarine) and green glass, chosen for size, colour harmony and their regular shape rather than their value,[136] alternate with eight cloisonné enamel portraits around the band. Over time, repairs were carried out; some stones and pearls were replaced.[137] The crest decorations are composed of alternating triangular and semicircular shapes that hold *émail de plique à jour* (also called *Fensteremail*), translucent enamel decorations; the size of these shapes diminishes towards the sides. Only rare examples of such translucent cloisonné enamels survive because of its fragility.[138] Amethysts are dowelled to the pinnacles, substituted by pearls on the two outermost ones. On the back, instead of *akroterioi* (except one), there is a row of pearls mounted on pins.[139] An enamel image of Christ Pantocrator enthroned is attached to the front crest decoration, and an image of Emperor Michael VII Doukas (1071–8) is affixed to the one at the back. The enamel images on the band include the archangels Michael and Gabriel, saints George, Demetrius, Cosmas, Damian, and two portraits at the back, underneath the emperor's. One is a youthful Byzantine ruler whose name is abbreviated as 'Kon Porphyrogenitos', who is more likely Michael's son and co-emperor Constantine, although it could designate his brother and co-emperor Constantius;[140] the other is 'Geobitzas, krales Tourkias', identified as King Géza I (1074–7) of Hungary.[141]

---

[133] Ibid., 37, photos 40–1.   [134] Tóth—Szelényi, *The Holy Crown*, 22.

[135] Lovag, 'Néhány technikai megfigyelés', 39–40; Lovag, 'L'intégration de la couronne', 66.

[136] Kovács—Lovag, *Hungarian Crown*, 37; in contrast, on the Byzantine imperial crown, gems were of high value: Paul Hetherington, 'La couronne grecque de la Sainte Couronne de Hongrie: le contexte de ses émaux et de ses bijoux', *Acta Historiae Artium*, 43 (2002): 33–8, at 36.

[137] Lovag, 'Néhány technikai megfigyelés', 40; László Papp, 'Időszaki jelentés a Szent Korona ötvösvizsgálatáról II', *Magyar Iparművészet* (1994/1): 6–9, at 8.

[138] David Buckton, 'The Holy Crown in the history of enamelling', *Acta Historiae Artium*, 43 (2002): 14–21, at 19–20.

[139] Kovács—Lovag, *Hungarian Crown*, 23.

[140] Michael's son: e.g. Moravcsik, 'A magyar szent korona', 438–42, repr. 690–4; Magda von Bárány-Oberschall, *Die Sankt Stephans-Krone und die Insignien des Königreiches Ungarn*, 2nd edn (Vienna—Munich: Verlag Herold, 1974), 41; Catherine Jolivet-Lévy, 'L'apport de l'iconographie à l'interprétation de la "corona graeca"', *Acta Historiae Artium*, 43 (2002): 22–32, at 26; Jean-Claude Cheynet, 'L'Empire Byzantin et la Hongrie dans la seconde moitié du XIe siècle', *Acta Historiae Artium*, 43 (2002): 5–13, repr. *La société byzantine: L'apport des sceaux* (Paris: Centre de recherche d'histoire et civilisation de Byzance, 2008), 609–26, at 613. Arguing for Michael's brother e.g. Szabolcs de Vajay, 'Der Kamelaukion-Character der heiligen Krone Ungarns', in *Insignia Regni Hungariae I*, 101–28, at 108.

[141] Ipolyi, *A magyar Szent Korona*, 66, 148–9; Moravcsik, 'A magyar szent korona', 442–8, repr. 694–700; Kovács—Lovag, *Hungarian Crown*, 23, photo 35.

180 STEPHEN I, THE FIRST CHRISTIAN KING OF HUNGARY

The enamel depicting Emperor Michael Doukas is roughly 8 mm larger than its mounted frame. As it does not fit inside, the mounted frame was folded out and the emperor's image is now attached to it by rivets. There is a controversy over whether the stripes welded onto the back of the enamel had been originally used to attach it to the crown, or to another object.[142] A section of the pearls strung along the upper edge of the crown's band was removed to accommodate the image, and differing views exist on whether the mounted setting was at some point moved lower than its original location.[143] The size and position of the image thus indicate that it was not originally designed for the frame on the crown. Yet both its technical and stylistic characteristics are exactly the same as those of the other enamel images of the *corona graeca* (including the cloisonné technique, colours and lettering); all were clearly made in the same workshop.[144] While no definitive explanation accounts for this discrepancy (which gave rise to the wildest conspiracy theories as mentioned below), the most plausible interpretations suggest that the image was added in Byzantium before the crown was sent to Hungary. Why the image does not fit the frame can be explained by various possibilities: the alteration of an existing crown, or the addition of actualizing political images to a half-finished crown; or damage to the intended image necessitating its quick replacement by another, existing image; or yet again, the simple reuse of an existing image of the Emperor Michael when making the crown.[145] Damage sustained later led to the reattachment of the Doukas image, which also affected the St Thomas apostle image of the cross-bands behind it; when the Doukas image was first attached to the crown cannot be proven technologically.[146]

The iconography, inscriptions, and possible context of the crown have been studied since the 1930s, relying also on comparisons to other examples of Byzantine art from the period.[147] Many researchers argue that the crown is no longer in its original form, and many different possible reconstructions of the original have been suggested.[148] Some questioned the Byzantine provenance of the band and crest decorations; an

---

[142] Péri, 'Időszaki jelentés', 4; Tóth—Szelényi, *The Holy Crown*, 19; Lovag, 'Néhány technikai megfigyelés', 41; Tóth, *A magyar szent korona*, 112, 121, 124, 126.

[143] Péri, 'Időszaki jelentés', 5; Papp, 'Időszaki jelentés', 9; Kovács—Lovag, *Hungarian Crown*, 37.

[144] Ibid., 23; Péri, 'Időszaki jelentés', 4. All flesh colours are identical: Kovács—Lovag, *Hungarian Crown*, 56.

[145] Tóth, *A magyar szent korona*, 121; Tóth—Szelényi, *The Holy Crown*, 21, existing female crown altered for Géza; Lovag, 'Néhány technikai megfigyelés', 41; Papp, 'Időszaki jelentés', 9; Hetherington, 'La couronne grecque', 36, respectively.

[146] Papp, 'Időszaki jelentés', 9.

[147] Moravcsik, 'A magyar szent korona', is still the most detailed study by a Byzantinist. See also André Grabar, *L'empereur dans l'art byzantin* (Strasbourg, 1936, repr. London: Variorum Reprints, 1971), 15–16.

[148] Useful summary: Kovács—Lovag, *Hungarian Crown*, 24; Jonathan Shepard, 'Byzantium and the steppe-nomads: the Hungarian dimension', in *Emergent Elites and Byzantium*, VIII, 73, note 58. Deér, *A magyarok szent koronája*, 53 on rearrangement of the order of the enamels. One of the arguments for such a rearrangement, that hinges on the direction of the gaze of the figures, however, is questionable, since the direction of the eyes in Byzantine art was not always consistent: H. C. Evans,

Antiochian origin of the enamels was suggested.[149] However, the enamels correspond to Byzantine and Italo-Byzantine work.[150] Deér argued that the enamels were removed from the original crown sent from Byzantium and reused on the band made in Hungary in the last quarter of the twelfth century.[151] Some others share the view that the Byzantine enamels were removed from another object.[152] The technique of making enamel meant that enamel plaques had to be attached to larger objects separately, and could indeed be detached and reused; this is neither unique for the crown, nor does it mean that plaques were necessarily changed later on.[153] Art historians, drawing on parallels from Byzantine objects, concluded that 'the *corona graeca* is an authentic Byzantine work...apart from a few minor changes, all its details are contemporary with the cloisonné enamels'.[154] The high quality of the workmanship points to a commission from a member of the court, although not necessarily the emperor himself.[155] The iconographic programme is a coherent whole, whether or not the enamels were originally made for the crown and whether or not images were rearranged.[156] There is consensus that the enamelled images represent heavenly and earthly hierarchy, although some details are disputed. Gyula Moravcsik suggested the archangels Michael and Gabriel are divine messengers linked to coronation and to the divine origin of the ruler's power, while Jolivet-Lévy sees them as companions of the enthroned Christ at the celestial court, also pointing to an analogy between celestial and terrestrial courts.[157] George and Demetrius were popular military saints and patrons of Byzantine emperors; Demetrius also featured on the seal of the Metropolitan of Tourkia (the head of the Orthodox Church in Hungary).[158] Moravcsik highlighted their association to defence against barbarians.[159] Saints Cosmas and Damian are understood to protect the ruler's health and intercede on his behalf.[160]

W. D. Wixom, ed., *The Glory of Byzantium. Art and Culture of the Middle Byzantine Era A. D. 843–1261* (New York: Metropolitan Museum of Art, 1997), 210, Catalogue no. 145.

[149] Boeckler, 'Die "Stephanskrone"', 734–8 thought the band and crest decorations were later Hungarian work; Evans—Wixom, *The Glory of Byzantium*, 188. Vajay, 'La relique Stéphanoise', 11–12, Antiochian origin (formerly on an object brought by Anna of Châtillon, Béla III's first wife).

[150] Buckton, 'The Holy Crown in the history of enamelling', 14–15.

[151] Deér, *A magyarok szent koronája*, 42.

[152] Váczy, 'Első királyunk koronája', 95–6 argued that the original crown only had gemstones and was made for Andrew I (1046–60).

[153] Hetherington, 'La couronne grecque', 35.   [154] Kovács—Lovag, *Hungarian Crown*, 37.

[155] Jolivet-Lévy, 'L'apport de l'iconographie', 28.   [156] Ibid., 22.

[157] Moravcsik, 'A magyar szent korona', 431–2, repr. 683–4; Moravcsik's conclusions accepted with more examples: Kovács—Lovag, *Hungarian Crown*, 23. Jolivet-Lévy, 'L'apport de l'iconographie', 22; similar ideas in Cecily J. Hilsdale, 'The social life of the Byzantine gift: the royal crown of Hungary reinvented', *Art History*, 31, no. 5 (2008): 603–31, at 606.

[158] Jolivet-Lévy, 'L'apport de l'iconographie', 23. For background, and their significance as imperial patrons, Monica White, *Military Saints in Byzantium and Rus, 900–1200* (Cambridge: Cambridge University Press, 2013).

[159] Moravcsik, 'A magyar szent korona', 432–3, repr. 684–5.

[160] Jolivet-Lévy, 'L'apport de l'iconographie', 23; for Moravcsik, 'A magyar szent korona', 434, repr. 686, they represent selfless divine science. Deér, adopted by Tóth—Szelényi, *The Holy Crown*, 18: guarantors of the ruler's health; Deér therefore argued that they should flank and look towards the emperor

182 STEPHEN I, THE FIRST CHRISTIAN KING OF HUNGARY

The two Byzantine emperors are represented with open *stemma* crowns with pendants and they hold the imperial military standard (*labarum*) in their right hand; in the other hand, Michael holds a sword, while the younger ruler a scroll.[161] Moravcsik established that the inscriptions identifying the two emperors match in form and content the contemporary convention and terminology of imperial signatures.[162] It has been argued that the positioning of the Michael Doukas image is in the tradition of showing the emperor's slight inferiority compared to Christ; his representation with a traditional, by that time archaizing *loros* may be a reference to Constantine the Great.[163] The emperor, although not in a military dress, holds a sword, which is rare, and Géza also holds a similar sword; this may signal their military alliance.[164]

King Géza I is represented as clearly inferior to the emperors.[165] His image is placed lower than that of Michael and he gazes towards the emperors; while they, along with the saints, have a nimbus, Géza does not; and the inscription is in dark blue rather than red. His crown and attire are more modest, he holds a sword in his left hand and a sceptre ending in a cross with ornamental foliage (a *crux florida*) in his right, a sign of 'the guarantee of the victory of the Christian ruler'.[166] The attendant inscription designates Géza as πιστός; although Moravcsik suggested a studied ambiguity, playing on the two meanings of the word 'faithful' (believer in Christ, and loyal to the Emperor),[167] since the same word is also used on the inscription for the Basileus Michael Doukas, it is more convincing to see it as merely a designation of the Christian ruler.[168]

Moravcsik contextualized the Greek crown in a Byzantine-Hungarian alliance, a thesis broadly confirmed in subsequent scholarship, although the precise date of the crown's dispatch is debated.[169] Byzantine–Hungarian relations in the period were volatile. Hostilities alternated with cooperation, due to a shared interest in the face of attacks by steppe nomads.[170] In 1071–2, the Empire was under attack simultaneously in Asia Minor, Italy and the Balkans, forcing Michael VII to seek allies; he turned to the Hungarians. King Géza's interest in a Byzantine alliance is explicable from internal affairs. After a tumultuous decade and a half, when

---

rather than Christ and considered their placement erroneous; cf. Kovács—Lovag, *Hungarian Crown*, 24.

[161] Ibid., 23–4.   [162] Moravcsik, 'A magyar szent korona', 436, repr. 688.

[163] Jolivet-Lévy, 'L'apport de l'iconographie', 23–5.   [164] Ibid., 25.

[165] Moravcsik, 'A magyar szent korona', 461–2, repr. 713–14; See also Shepard, 'Byzantium and the steppe-nomads', 74; Jolivet-Lévy, 'L'apport de l'iconographie', 27, both with further bibliography; Hilsdale, 'The social life of the Byzantine gift', 618–19.

[166] Kovács—Lovag, *Hungarian Crown*, 42; they refute that Géza is represented as ranked among the 'patricians' holding a patriarchal cross. They also suggest that this representation refers to St Stephen who received from Basil II a piece of the true cross, ibid., 42. Tóth, *A magyar szent korona*, 168.

[167] Moravcsik, 'A magyar szent korona', 456, repr. 708.

[168] Kovács—Lovag, *Hungarian Crown*, 42 with parallels to Byzantine coins.

[169] Moravcsik, 'A magyar szent korona', 448–52, repr. 700–4; Cheynet, 'L'Empire Byzantin et la Hongrie', 612–13.

[170] Shepard, 'Byzantium and the steppe-nomads', 69–72.

rivalry for the throne repeatedly caused wars between two branches of the dynasty (Andrew I and his son Solomon on the one hand, and Béla I and his sons Géza and Ladislas on the other), Géza finally defeated his nephew, the crowned King Solomon, in battle, and took power in 1074. Solomon turned to Henry IV of Germany to regain his throne, while Géza secured the goodwill of Pope Gregory VII.

Géza is widely seen as the king (*krales*) who married an unnamed member of the Synadenos family.[171] Skylitzes Continuatus recounts that Emperor Nikephoros III Botaneiates (1078–81) had given his niece, the daughter of Theodulos Synadenos, in marriage to the king of Hungary, and she returned to the Empire after her husband's death. Neither the bride's nor the king's name is provided. The Synadene's return has been hypothetically dated to 1079/80, which would indicate that her husband was King Géza, who died in 1077, although there is no absolute proof.[172] Yet such an interpretation raises some problems. Géza died before Nikephoros ascended the throne in 1078. If the text merely means that the Synadene's uncle was emperor by the time of her return, rather than at the time of her marriage,[173] then it is difficult to explain how the Synadene was entitled to an imperial crown when she married. Some suggest an early date of the marriage between 1064 and 1067, in the context of an alliance with Byzantine military leaders (including Nikephoros Botaneiates) in the northern frontier provinces of the empire; arguing that the *corona graeca* was made when the two Doukas brothers Michael and Constantius ruled jointly.[174] At that point, however, Géza was not yet king, thus the inscription on his image on the crown would be problematic.[175] Several scholars argued that the union of Géza I and the Synadene should be dated c. 1074, and is an example of Emperor Michael VII's diplomacy, which made use of marriage-alliances in the face of problems on many fronts, and that the Byzantine crown arrived in Hungary in this context.[176]

---

[171] Eric McGeer, tr., *Byzantium in the Time of Troubles: The Continuation of the Chronicle of John Skylitzes 1057–1079* (Leiden—Boston: Brill, 2020) (includes the Greek edn Of E. Th. Tsolakes), 188–9. Most detailed argument on identification, Raimund Kerbl, *Byzantinische Prinzessinnen in Ungarn zwischen 1050–1200 und ihr Einfluß auf das Arpadenkönigreich* (Vienna: Verband der wissenschaftlichen Gesellschaften Österreichs, 1979), 1–14. On debates whether Géza was the Synadene's spouse: Shepard, 'Byzantium and the steppe nomads', 74–5; Ferenc Makk, 'Rajmund Kerbl: Byzantinische Prinzessinnen in Ungarn zwischen 1050–1200 und ihr Einfluß auf das Arpaden-königreich', *Századok*, 115 (1981): 224–6, at 224–5.

[172] Kerbl, *Byzantinische Prinzessinnen in Ungarn*, 55–7; Ferenc Makk, *The Árpáds and the Comneni: Political Relations between Hungary and Byzantium in the 12th Century* (Budapest: Akadémiai Kiadó, 1989), 125.

[173] Cheynet, 'L'empire byzantin', 626.

[174] Kerbl, *Byzantinische Prinzessinnen in Ungarn*, 18–51; Vajay, 'Der Kamelaukion-Character', 108.

[175] This has been explained away as aspirational, or a sign of Byzantine support for his claim.

[176] Various hypotheses on the date of the marriage also analysed: Shepard, 'Byzantium and the steppe-nomads', 72–3, 75–82; Cheynet, 'L'empire Byzantin et la Hongrie', 613–16. Because of the military and political significance of the Synadenos family, she could have been a desirable marriage partner before her uncle acceded to the Byzantine throne: Cheynet, 'L'empire byzantin', 616. Hilsdale, 'The social life of the Byzantine gift', 619–20.

184 STEPHEN I, THE FIRST CHRISTIAN KING OF HUNGARY

Some argued the crown was sent to Géza I by Michael VII on Géza's accession to power,[177] or that, as an allied subordinate ruler, he was crowned with the Byzantine crown in 1075.[178] The crown was also interpreted as a sign of Hungary's subjection to Byzantine supremacy.[179] Research in the 1930s signalled that the crest decorations on the Hungarian crown resemble those on crowns worn by Byzantine empresses and princesses. Moravcsik took this to be part of the subtle message of subordinate status; later scholars took it as proof that it was a female crown.[180] (The idea that the original crown, destined for Géza, was subsequently transformed into a female crown in Hungary has been refuted, since the crest decorations are not later additions, but part of the original crown, made from the same single sheet of gold as the band[181]). In addition, Géza wearing his own image would be without parallel, whereas together with the imperial image, which was worn as a sign of prestige, rank, and allegiance, perhaps it could have been worn by Géza's wife.[182]

The consensus now is that the crown represents a female crown-type, thus was not intended to be Géza I's crown.[183] It has been argued that the gift of a Byzantine wife and the gift of a crown were interwoven aspects of Byzantine diplomacy, creating subordination and allegiance.[184] The possibility has also been raised that the crown was commissioned by the Synadenoi family, rather than the emperor.[185] However, since the Synadene at the time of her marriage was not yet a relative of an emperor, she would not have been eligible to wear *prependoulia* (pendants), reserved for imperial use.[186] Most commonly, the crown is seen as a diplomatic

---

[177] Györffy, 'Die "corona sancti Stephani"', 59–60; Tóth—Szelényi, *The Holy Crown*, 21. Vajay, 'La relique Stéphanoise', 7–8 argued Géza needed a crown for his coronation, since the royal crown, which Vajay claimed was the so-called 'Monomakh crown' received by Andrew I, was hidden by Solomon when he escaped.

[178] Moravcsik, 'A magyar szent korona', 462, repr. 714; Similar: Shepard, 'Crowns from the Basileus', 144–5.

[179] Robert Browning, 'A new source on Byzantine–Hungarian relations in the twelfth century: the inaugural lecture of Michael O tou Agchialou ōs ypatos tōn filosofōn', *Balkan Studies*, 2 (1961): 173–214, at 180–1.

[180] Moravcsik, 'A magyar szent korona', 461–2, repr. 713–14; Bárány-Oberschall, *Die Sankt Stephans-Krone*, 43–9; Hilsdale, 'The social life of the Byzantine gift', 614–15. However, Kovács—Lovag, *Hungarian Crown*, 37 point out that acroteria can also be found on male crowns in illustrations. In addition, not all female crowns in Byzantium conform to this model: Jolivet-Lévy, 'L'apport de l'iconographie', 28.

[181] Boeckler, 'Die "Stephanskrone"', 737–38 *pinnae* as separate and later medieval Hungarian work; Györffy, *István király*, 356; refutation Tóth—Szelényi, *The Holy Crown*, 22.

[182] Hilsdale, 'The social life of the Byzantine gift', 615–18. Yet she did not address the objection that the simultaneous presence of Byzantine and local rulers would not occur on female crowns: André Grabar, 'L'archéologie des insignes médiévaux du pouvoir', in *L'art de la fin de l'Antiquité et du Moyen Age*, André Grabar, vol. 1 (Paris: Collège de France, 1968), 81–102, at 102.

[183] Kovács—Lovag, *Hungarian Crown*, 42; Tóth—Szelényi, *The Holy Crown*, 22; Tóth, *A magyar szent korona*, 133.

[184] Hilsdale, 'The social life of the Byzantine gift', 621.

[185] Jolivet-Lévy, 'L'apport de l'iconographie', 28.

[186] Etele Kiss, 'La "Couronne grecque" dans son contexte', *Acta Historiae Artium*, 43 (2002): 39–51, at 41.

gift to mark the military alliance between Byzantium and Hungary, whether or not linked to the marriage itself; an honour for the recipient, who, however, was at the same time placed in an inferior position to the Emperor. Such an interpretation fits into the pattern of Michael VII's use of diplomatic gifts.[187] Byzantine conferral of crowns on foreign potentates was a common diplomatic practice, recognizing them 'as more or less autonomous rulers'; donor and recipient could interpret the bestowal of a crown in different ways.[188]

There are, however, other interpretations. According to one unproven hypothesis, the crown was used as part of an Eastern Orthodox marriage ceremony for Géza I's Byzantine wife, and was not intended as a royal crown.[189] Deér argued that the *corona graeca* was created in Hungary in the late twelfth century (reusing Byzantine enamels) for the wife of Béla III, Anne of Châtillon.[190] One more alternative has been mooted: that the closest parallel to the *corona graeca* is found in votive, prestige crowns that were not intended for wearing.[191] Its very large circumference (63.6 cm inner circumference, 20.9 cm diameter[192]) may be explained either by the need to wear it over an elaborate hairstyle or a cap,[193] or on the contrary, by the crown not needing to fit an actual human head. Votive crowns were often offered by kings as 'through its imperial associations the crown votive was...linked to the cross;' many head reliquaries were made in order to display such crowns, which were 'lavishly gemmed'.[194] There may be a parallel of a votive crown's transformation into a coronation crown: according to one opinion, the

---

[187] Jolivet-Lévy, 'L'apport de l'iconographie', 29; Hetherington, 'La couronne grecque', 33–8; Hilsdale, 'The social life of the Byzantine gift', 610–14, including a comparison to enamels of the Khakhuli triptych that plausibly come from similar diplomatic gifts of crowns to Georgia in the eleventh century.

[188] Shepard, 'Crowns from the Basileus', 141.   [189] Tóth, *A magyar szent korona*, 130–1.

[190] Deér, *A magyarok szent koronája*, 41–2, 45–8. (She is also known as Agnes or Anna of Antioch.)

[191] Grabar, 'L'archéologie des insignes médiévaux du pouvoir', 101–2, although he thought the original crown was a circlet without the *pinnae*; Jolivet-Lévy, 'L'apport de l'iconographie', 28. Grabar also drew a parallel to a crown in San Marco, Venice, which was the only one to feature images of a ruling emperor and saints.

[192] Kovács—Lovag, *Hungarian Crown*, 23. For comparison, the Liège crown, a reliquary crown that could be worn has a diameter of 20.5 cm, the Bamberg crown that was worn measures 20 cm, while the crown made for the reliquary head of Charlemagne, Aachen measures 20.2–22.1 cm: Schramm, *Herrshaftszeichen*, vol. 3, 871, 874, 876; Christopher Mielke, 'From her head to her toes: gender-bending regalia from the tomb of Constance of Aragon, Queen of Hungary and Sicily', *Royal Studies Journal*, 5, no, 2 (2018): 49–62, at 61, lists female funerary crowns with diameters of between 17 cm and 24 cm.

[193] Kovács—Lovag, *Hungarian Crown*, 37.

[194] Cynthia Hahn, *Strange Beauty: Issues in the Making and Meaning of Reliquaries, 400–circa 1204* (Pennsylvania: Pennsylvania State University Press, 2012), 117. Votive crowns are known from the Visigothic kingdom and were also represented in Ottonian imagery, for example the Uta Codex, an evangeliary from the abbey of Niedermünster, Regensburg, c. 1025, now in Munich, Bayerische Staatsbibliothek Clm 13601, f. 4r, https://www.digitale-sammlungen.de/en/view/bsb00075075? page=10,11; the coronation stone from 1396 in Monza cathedral also includes four hanging votive crowns: Roberto Cassanelli, 'Art and politics at the courts of the Visconti and Sforza in the 14th and 15th centuries', in *The Iron crown and Imperial Europe*, vol. 1, *The Crown, the Kingdom and the Empire: A Thousand Years of History*, ed. Graziella Buccellati (Milan: Editoriale Giorgio Mondadori, Monza: Società di Studi Monzesi, 1995), 73–115, at 93.

186 STEPHEN I, THE FIRST CHRISTIAN KING OF HUNGARY

Iron Crown of Monza (that came to be seen as the coronation crown of kings of Italy) was originally a votive crown.[195]

The so-called *corona latina* is an even more debated part of the crown. Its name derives from an earlier belief that it had been St Stephen's crown; although it is now certain that the upper part was never a crown in itself, the misnomer stuck.[196] It consists of two crossing bands decorated by the enamel images of eight apostles and a Pantocrator, and a filigree border around the enamel, studded with alternating almandines and pearls. The crossing bands were created by welding four separate gold bands to a square central panel. Then, the beaded wire border, filigree, stone and pearl settings, and the settings for the enamel were soldered in place.[197] Finally, the stones, pearls, and enamels were inserted into their settings.

Debate has been ongoing over its every aspect.[198] Was it originally an object, or part of an object in its own right, subsequently repurposed and transformed, and if so, what was it and what was its exact shape? Alternatively, was it made specifically to close the Greek crown? Were the bands and enamel images made simultaneously, or were the enamel images of the apostles removed from an earlier object and added to the newly made bands? Were there originally twelve apostles or eight? Does the Pantocrator on the top and the apostles come from the same or different workshops? The object's dating is unresolved, with a number of different arguments by experts, and its place of origin has also excited controversy. Many of these arguments are interconnected, but I shall separate them to be able to present the key controversies and their rationale.

Because enamel images had to be made separately and then affixed to an object, it is impossible to tell from that alone whether the bands and the enamels were made at the same time, or earlier enamels were reused. Those who have argued that the bands and enamels were made as one object have proposed dates between the late tenth and the early thirteenth century. Dating was not independent of the framing presumption: those who accepted that the *corona latina* was Stephen's naturally proposed the early dating, while, as this presumption fell away, scholars started to find parallels that point to a later date. Thus Otto von Falke, who examined the crown briefly in 1928, and accepted the idea that the upper part was made from Stephen's crown, suggested the bands with the images were produced

---

[195] Reinhard Elze, 'Monza und die Eiserne Krone im Mittelalter', in Buccellati, *The Iron Crown*, 45–59, at 47, Eng. tr. 307–18, at 308.

[196] Marosi characterized it as a 'fictive object': 'La "couronne latine"', 72.

[197] The setting for the uppermost apostle enamels was soldered to the central plaque's frame, therefore the top of the setting for these lack the thinner beaded wire that surrounds each enamel setting: Kovács—Lovag, *Hungarian Crown*, 43; photo: Tóth, *A magyar szent korona*, 134.

[198] Some overviews of debates: Bárány-Oberschall, *Die Sankt Stephans-Krone*, 28–40, 76–105; Marosi, 'La "couronne latine"'; 'Szent Korona', in *Korai Magyar Történeti Lexikon (9–14. Század)*, ed. Gyula Kristó (Budapest: Akadémiai Kiadó, 1994), 634 lists seven theories on the origin of the upper part; Tóth, *A magyar szent korona*, 15–29 and *passim*.

THE HUNGARIAN CROWN   187

around 1000 in Milan, based on a late tenth-century Byzantine model.[199] Ideas of an Irish origin around 1000 were advanced and refuted.[200] Some suggested it was made in Ottonian style, in Italy or the Rhineland around 1000 or the first half of the eleventh century.[201] Boeckler proposed that the similarities of the enamels to the mid-eleventh-century Monomakh crown, combined with stylistic differences, mean that the *corona latina* was made by someone who knew the Monomakh crown in Hungary in the twelfth century.[202]

Some scholars focused on a detailed technical or stylistic analysis of only the filigree or the enamels, yet this has not produced a definitive date either. The filigree technique and palmettes were used between the tenth and thirteenth centuries, making dating difficult,[203] with the added complexity that often the dating of the objects used for comparison is itself also debated.[204] Thus, the filigree frame of gems and pearls has been dated to the end of the twelfth/beginning of the thirteenth century by comparing it to the sceptre and a cross now in Salzburg;[205] between 1000 and 1300 by drawing parallels to other western analogies; and to the twelfth century by pointing to Byzantine ones.[206] It has been suggested that the bands (without the apostle images) were made in the late twelfth century to close the crown.[207] The most recent thorough art historical analysis of technique and style concluded that the closest parallels to the filigree on the band date from the second half and the end of the eleventh century, while admitting that more research is necessary and so this dating is not conclusive.[208]

Those studying the enamels argued for diverse places of origin: Hungary, or an area in southern Italy under Byzantine artistic influence, or the German Empire.

---

[199] Otto von Falke, 'A Szent Korona', *Archaeológiai Értesítő*, 43 (1929): 125–33.

[200] Deér, *A magyarok szent koronája*, 95–100; Marosi, 'La "couronne latine"', 74.

[201] Franz Bock (see note 107) argued that the apostle enamels were made at end of the tenth century in Rome, and the bands were from same period; Varjú, 'A Szent Korona', 61. Elemér Radisics, *Hungary: Pictorial Record of a Thousand Years* (Budapest: Athenaeum, 1944), plate III (between p. 4 and p. 5), upper part as Stephen's crown, the work of a goldsmith of the Benedictine abbey of Monte-Cassino. Mathilde Uhlirz, *Die Krone des Heiligen Stephan, des ersten Königs von Ungarn*, Veröffentlichungen des Instituts für Österreichische Geschichtsforschung XIV (Graz—Vienna—Munich: Verlag Stiasny G. M. B. H., 1951), 11–46, Ottonian mainly from the Rheinland. Bárány-Oberschall, *Die Sankt-Stephanskrone*, 33–9, 82–105, first half of eleventh century, German imperial lands. See Béla Zsolt Szakács, 'Remarks on the filigree of the Holy Crown of Hungary', *Acta Historiae Artium*, 43 (2002): 52–61, at 52.

[202] Boeckler, 'Die "Stephanskrone"', 740–1. Nikolaos Oikonomides, 'La couronne dite de Constantin Monomaque', *Travaux et mémoires*, 12 (1994): 241–62 raised doubts about the Monomakh crown, refuted e.g. Etele Kiss, 'Új eredmények a Monomachos-korona kutatásában?', *Folia Archaeologica*, 46 (1997): 125–64; Evans—Wixom, *The Glory of Byzantium*, Catalogue no. 145, p. 210 confirm the 1042–50 dating and parallels in Byzantine art for the supposed anomalies.

[203] Szakács, 'Remarks on the filigree', 52–3.   [204] Ibid., 59.

[205] Hermann Fillitz, cited in Bertényi, *A magyar szent korona*, 42.

[206] Kovács—Lovag, *Hungarian Crown*, 57.

[207] Lovag, 'L'intégration de la couronne', 70–1. Éva Kovács, *L'orfèvrerie romane en Hongrie* (Budapest: Corvina, 1974), 20–1, 25 argued that the filigree in itself cannot be dated as it is 'timeless', only the entirety of the piece, and dated the upper part of the crown to the end of the twelfth century.

[208] Szakács, 'Remarks on the filigree', 59.

188   STEPHEN I, THE FIRST CHRISTIAN KING OF HUNGARY

There is also no consensus on their dating.[209] The idea of their Hungarian provenance has been criticized: while art historians think the existence of a goldsmiths' workshop is plausible at the end of the twelfth and early thirteenth century, producing items for the royal court of Hungary, including filigree similar to the cross-bands, no enamel production is known in Hungary at the time.[210] The analysis of enamel colours has shown the differences from the enamel of the Greek crown (for example applying colours next to each other without cloison, and the use of a darker and a paler flesh colour).[211] The rarity of extant Romanesque cloisonné enamel, however, renders comparisons difficult.[212]

Datings of the enamels comprise twelfth-century mature Romanesque (including the gold cloisonné enamel),[213] the late twelfth century,[214] or specifically the period between 1160 and 1180.[215] The latest date, the early thirteenth century, was put forward by Deér.[216] The late twelfth-century dating was reconciled with the stylistically earlier 'look' by the suggestion of intentional archaism, the imitation of earlier forms as part of the historicism at Béla III's court.[217] A comparison to both Byzantine and Western enamels, the fact that the cloisonné enamel fields have an internal border of gold, as well as the analysis of the enamel inscriptions (outlined with a metal strip, and filled with an opaque enamel that contrasts with the background) led an expert on medieval enamels to date the apostle images to the twelfth century.[218] The enamels have also been found to be similar to the Pala d'Oro of Venice, completed in the early twelfth century.[219]

One line of argument, however, dates the enamels much earlier. This is linked to the idea that the enamels were originally on another object, and were merely reused on the cross-bands. One particular contention is that the enamels were taken from an object belonging to St Stephen. This ultimately harks back to the bid to salvage the connection between the crown and St Stephen. The apostle enamels were first deemed to be from Stephen's crown in 1896,[220] when the popular, traditional attribution of the whole crown as Stephen's was increasingly undermined by scholarship. This idea has recently been the most fully developed by Endre Tóth, especially based on epigraphic arguments. He maintained that

---

[209] Deér, *A magyarok szent koronája*, 136 (Hungary); Bárány-Oberschall, *Die Sankt Stephans-Krone*, 39 (German Empire); Boeckler, 'Die "Stephanskrone"' (western Romanesque); Kovács—Lovag, *Hungarian Crown*, 55–7 (possibly Hungarian); Tóth, *A magyar szent korona*, 156 (Italy).

[210] Marosi, 'La "couronne latine"', 76, with further discussion at 81 in notes.

[211] Kovács—Lovag, *Hungarian Crown*, 57.   [212] Ibid., 57.   [213] Ibid., 97.

[214] Buckton, 'The Holy Crown'; Éva Kovács, 'Les émaux "latins" de la couronne de Hongrie', *Atti del XXIV congresso internazionale di Storia dell'Arte*, 10 vols. (Bologna, 1982–3), vol. 2, 241–6, at 244, between 1160 and the turn of the century.

[215] Kovács—Lovag, *Hungarian Crown*, 56.   [216] Deér, *A magyarok szent koronája*, 94, 163.

[217] Marosi, 'La "couronne latine"', 77.

[218] Buckton, 'Vorläufige Ergebnisse'; Buckton, 'The Holy Crown in the history of enamelling', 15–16 (earliest example of extended inscription using this technique is the Pala d'Oro, 1105, see p. 15).

[219] H. R. Hahnloser and R. Polacco, *La pala d'oro* (Venice: Canal & Stamperia Editrice, 1994), 3, 12, 50, 51.

[220] Czobor, *A magyar koronázási jelvények*, 4.

THE HUNGARIAN CROWN   189

because the apostle enamels show both Western European Romanesque and strong Byzantine artistic influence they originate from Italy; further, that the Byzantinizing Latin script used on the enamels resembles Byzantine coinage with Latin inscriptions that ceased to be minted around 1070, and therefore the enamels can be contemporary with Stephen,[221] leaving the question open about the origin of the bands.[222] According to him, the apostle enamels were removed from a sacral object sent to Stephen by the pope or the abbot of Monte Cassino.[223] The enamels, therefore, would have been transferred to the crown because they were known to have been in the possession of the holy king.

Letterforms that resemble those on coinage that was minted up to around 1070 cannot be used to prove an early eleventh-century date. Even the coins themselves were still produced after Stephen's reign, while exemplars could have been seen even later; archaizing imitations cannot be excluded. Moreover, Tóth categorically asserted that the specific letterforms for T and U could not be dated later than the second third of the eleventh century.[224] However, similar U and T were used in an inscription on the ring of King Coloman at the end of the eleventh century, and a similar T, for example, can be found in the 1140s.[225] Moreover, the earliest example of extended inscriptions employing the technique used on the apostle enamels is from the early twelfth century.[226] Nor can one ignore several expert opinions based on other considerations detailed above. Therefore, a very late eleventh- or twelfth-century date is much more likely.

[221] Tóth, *A magyar szent korona*, 172–83. Earlier, he dated the end of the minting of the coins with such letters to the 1050s and thus the apostle enamels no later than the mid-eleventh century: Endre Tóth, 'A Szent Korona apostollemezeinek keltezéséhez', *Communicationes Archaeologicae Hungariae*, 16 (1996): 181–209, at 197; Tóth—Szelényi, *The Holy Crown*, 24. On the Byzantine coins, see Warwick Wroth, ed., *Catalogue of the Imperial Byzantine Coins in the British Museum*, 2 vols. (London: British Museum and Longmans & Co., 1908), vol. 1, cv, vol. 2, 484–6, 491–2, 498–502. Holler, 'A magyar korona néhány', 917–20 dates the apostle images to 1026–42 based on the form of the letter A: three of them on the crown have no middle bar, but do have a bar at the top. Holler argues that because only the coins of Konstantinos VIII (minted 1026–8) bear such forms of A, this dates the images securely. Yet such A features in the late eleventh century, for example: Rudolph M. Kloos, 'The paleography of the inscriptions of San Marco', in *The mosaics of San Marco in Venice, I. 11th–12th Century*, vol. 1 *text*, ed. Otto Demus (Chicago—London: University of Chicago Press, 1984), 295–307, at 297, and on an inscription dated 1151 on a metal ciborium from San Martino della Marrucina: epigraphica europea LMU, Munich, Bilddatenbank, no. 151: https://epigraphik.gwi.uni-muenchen.de.

[222] Tóth—Szelényi, *The Holy Crown*, 31.

[223] Tóth, *A magyar szent korona*, 183; Tóth, 'A Szent Korona apostollemezeinek keltezéséhez', 198; Tóth—Szelényi, *The Holy Crown*, 24. Ipolyi, *A magyar Szent Korona*, 173 already claimed the Roman origin of the enamels.

[224] Tóth, *A magyar szent korona*, 182.

[225] Béla Zsolt Szakács, 'What did Piroska see at home? Art and architecture in Hungary around 1100', in *Piroska and the Pantokrator. Dynastic Memory, Healing and Salvation in Komnenian Constantinople*, ed. Marianne Sághy, Robert Ousterhout (Budapest: Central European University Press, 2019), 39–62, at 56. A similar 'T' is used on the so-called Crosby Relief, dated to the early 1140s, representing the twelve apostles from the abbey of St Denis: Sumner McK. Crosby, *The Apostle Bas-relief at Saint-Denis* (New Haven—London: Yale University Press, 1972), 54, figures 15, 24, 29.

[226] Buckton, 'The Holy Crown in the history of enamelling', 15.

190　STEPHEN I, THE FIRST CHRISTIAN KING OF HUNGARY

Whether the Pantocrator and apostle enamels were made at the same time is also debated: the figure of Christ is enamelled, on a gold background, whereas the entire surface of each plate bearing the apostle images is enamelled, resembling *Vollschmelz*. Early research and a recent work argue for the separate origin of the Pantocrator and apostles, emphasizing enamelling and stylistic differences.[227] On the contrary, the common origin of the apostle images and the Pantocrator of the cross-bands is maintained by several experts, pointing out that they were all made with gold cloisonné enamel technique, using mostly the same palette (only yellow features on the Pantocrator alone), details, and decorative motifs.[228]

Some of the enamel images are cracked, which gave rise to different explanations: some see the damage as proof of reuse, claiming that it occurred as the images were removed from somewhere before being attached to the bands; others argued it shows that the bands were bent after assembly; while yet another line of reasoning linked it to the blow or fall that damaged the crown in modern times, also causing the crookedness of the cross on top.[229]

What was the original function of the cross-bands? One theory posits that they were made specifically in order to close the earlier Greek crown.[230] This idea can be inflected to include the entire piece, or only the cross-bands (reusing earlier apostle images). The cross-bands' similarities to the *corona graeca* are cited, including the use of enamel images on gold bands, and decoration with pearls and almandines. Whether the Pantocrator on the top is a copy of the one on the Greek crown has been disputed, as the rendition of the details is different, yet the similarities remain striking, including the cypresses on the two sides of Christ.[231] It has also been argued that the technique of the apostle plaques shows an adaptation of the technique used on the *corona graeca*'s enamels.[232]

Other scholars, on the contrary, have contended that the cross-bands had been (part of) an earlier object. Early hypotheses included bands decorating a flat object, such as a book cover, reliquary casket, or portable altar, an argument many

---

[227] Tóth, *A magyar szent korona*, 156–61.
[228] Kovács—Lovag, *Hungarian Crown*, 54. Buckton, 'Vorläufige Ergebnisse', 134; Marosi, 'La "couronne latine"', 74. On the impossibility of distinguishing between Vollschmelz and Senkschmelz (two types of cloisonné enamels): Buckton, 'Vorläufige Ergebnisse', 130.
[229] Deér, *A magyarok szent koronája*, 136 on bending originally flat cross-bands to turn them into the upper part of the crown. Tóth—Szelényi, *The Holy Crown*, 34; Péri, 'Időszaki jelentés', 5; Kovács—Lovag, *Hungarian Crown*, 43; Marosi, 'La "couronne latine"', 73–4. Damage to the bands (of the four, two are broken, one is cracked) from a later accident, rather than reuse when originally flat bands would have been bent: Varjú, 'Szent Korona', 64.
[230] Tóth, *A magyar szent korona*, 134.
[231] Boeckler, 'Die "Stephanskrone"'; Moravcsik, 'A magyar szent korona', 463, repr. 715; Péri, 'Időszaki jelentés', 5. Holler, 'A magyar korona néhány', 916–17 claimed that the *corona graeca* was made to complement the existing *corona latina*. Kovács—Lovag, *Hungarian Crown*, 56. Falke, 'A Szent Korona', 128 suggested both Pantocrator images copy a tenth-century type. Marosi, 'La "couronne latine"', 77 suggests intentional archaism in the copying.
[232] Buckton, 'The Holy Crown', 18.

THE HUNGARIAN CROWN   191

rejected on technical grounds.[233] The 1916 examination maintained that the enamel images and the bands had been created as one object in the current dome shape, but the ends of the bands were subsequently cut off, explaining the missing four apostles.[234] Numerous interpretations are based on a similar premise. Some claimed that the bands had been part of Stephen's reliquary herm, supposedly made for the canonization in 1083.[235] While this dating and attribution has been dismissed by art historians, one plausible explanation is that the bands with the images come from the upper half of a St Stephen head reliquary that was round rather than shaped as a herm, similarly to the St Elisabeth reliquary (made in the thirteenth century) that held her skull, now in Stockholm, decorated with cross-bands.[236] Some of the damage is then interpreted as signs of the existing bands being bent further to make them fit the size of *corona graeca*.[237] Yet another suggestion is that it could originally have been an asterisk used in the Orthodox liturgy, which is placed over the Eucharistic bread on the paten, so the veil covering it does not touch the bread. There are a few medieval Byzantine examples of such liturgical objects, either extant or represented in images, although they are unadorned (only later ones include decorated specimens), while patens feature the Pantocrator, Last Supper or Communion of the Apostles. With the addition of four apostle images at the bottom, the hypothetical asterisk would cover a diameter of 46 cm; an extant eleventh-century paten has a diameter of over 40 cm.[238]

Finally, whether the current eight images are the remains of the original twelve apostles or a complete set has not been definitively settled. Andrew, Peter, Thomas, James, Paul, Philip, John, and Bartholomew appear on the crown; Paul, although not one of the twelve apostles in the Bible, was often represented in the Middle Ages among the apostles.[239] It has been argued that the Thomas and Bartholomew images were swapped after the latter was severely damaged, to hide the damage behind the *corona graeca*'s Pantocrator, and that the original order of the images followed the Acts of the Apostles.[240]

One view holds that the original twelve apostles were reduced to eight as the four ends of the band were truncated.[241] Others think only eight of the twelve

---

[233] Patrick J. Kelleher, *The Holy Crown of Hungary* (Rome: American Academy in Rome, 1951); Boeckler, 'Die "Stephanskrone"'; against the idea that the bands were originally flat: Lovag, 'L'intégration de la couronne', 68.

[234] Varjú, 'A Szent Korona'. Cutting off the bands was also argued by others, either only for the cross-bands, or together with the enamels, e.g. Péri, 'Időszaki jelentés', 5.

[235] Ödön Polner, *A magyar szent korona felső részének eredetkérdése* (Kolozsvár: Ferencz-József Tudományegyetem Barátai Egyesülete, 1943); Györffy, *István király*, 357–8. Against this, Székely, 'Koronaküldések', 924.

[236] Marosi, 'La "couronne latine"', 79–80.   [237] Ibid., 73–4.

[238] Kovács—Lovag, *Hungarian Crown*, 54, based on the idea first advanced by Nicolas Kondakoff (1896).

[239] Tóth—Szelényi, *The Holy Crown*, 23; Tóth, *A magyar szent korona*, 142–3.

[240] Ibid., 142–5.

[241] Kovács, 'Les émaux "latins"'; Kovács—Lovag, *Hungarian Crown*, 43. Marosi, 'La "couronne latine"', 73–4.

192 STEPHEN I, THE FIRST CHRISTIAN KING OF HUNGARY

apostles on the object the enamels originally decorated were moved to the cross-bands, because there was space only for eight—the size was determined by the need to close the Greek crown—or the other images had been damaged.[242] While several works concluded that the pattern of the imprints of the enamels seen on the reverse of the bands indicates that the last four were cut off,[243] one author asserted that the seventy two pearls on the cross bands signify the number of Christ's disciples, and the way the beaded wire border pattern ends, indicate that the bands were not truncated.[244] However, these are the ends affixed to the Greek crown, and he did not publish photographic evidence in an otherwise richly illustrated volume.

Those who maintain there were never more than eight apostles have not advanced a convincing argument for a coherent iconographic programme.[245] Whether there were originally twelve apostles in the series, using eight on the crown was perhaps not merely dictated by lack of space. It may be linked to the number eight symbolizing Christ as the King of Heaven and the world to come;[246] Byzantine chancel screens sometimes feature eight apostles.[247]

Unless future scholarship is able to provide a more precise dating through better technical examination (for example using the research questions set out by David Buckton concerning the technical investigation of the enamels), all one can conclude is that the '*corona latina*' is likely a late eleventh- or twelfth-century object; the entire piece or just the bands, reusing existing apostle enamels, may have been made with the express purpose of closing the Greek crown, or it may have been an asterisk or decorative part of a reliquary, subsequently reused and possibly truncated to close the *corona graeca*. It is plausible that the Greek crown, which was either a previously used crown subsequently donated to a church,[248] or a votive crown, was stored in an ecclesiastical treasury (possibly the royal basilica at Fehérvár[249]), perhaps along with the object(s) that ended up as the crown's cross-bands.

---

[242] This theory holds that the object, perhaps portable altar whence the apostle images were taken, originally had all twelve apostles; Tóth, *A magyar szent korona*, 147–9.

[243] Kovács—Lovag, *Hungarian Crown*, 43; Péri, 'Időszaki jelentés', 5.

[244] Tóth, *A magyar szent korona*, 150–1, 133, respectively.

[245] József Kovács, cited by Bertényi, *A magyar szent korona*, 52 erroneously claimed those eight are on the crown who are in the Apostles' Creed. Tóth—Szelényi, *The Holy Crown*, 23 advance the weak argument: 'There is no rule to say that all must be represented.'

[246] The Iron Crown of Monza is thought to have originally consisted of eight plates for this reason: Annamaria Ambrosioni, 'The Iron Crown and the coronations: facts and speculation', in Buccellati, *The Iron Crown*, xix–xxxvi, at xxxvi. The Reichskrone is octagonal, but features images of the kings of the Hebrew Bible.

[247] I thank Jake Ransohoff for drawing my attention to this. Lawrence Nees, 'The iconographic program of decorated chancel barriers in the pre-iconoclastic period', *Zeitschrift für Kunstgeschichte*, 46 (1983): 15–26, an example at 16.

[248] Schramm, *Herrschaftszeichen*, vol. 2, 378–9.

[249] Szakács, 'What did Piroska see at home?', 55.

THE HUNGARIAN CROWN   193

The extant crown was created by attaching the gold bands to the Greek crown with rivets.[250] Questions relating to when and why the two parts were joined to produce a new crown remain unresolved. Was the crown thus assembled in order to produce a crown in the style of the Byzantine *kamelaukion*, the closed imperial crown; or a western-style closed crown (such as the crown found in Constance of Aragon's grave[251]); or to provide a base for affixing a reliquary cross on top?[252] Proposed dates range from 1075 to the fifteenth century; the arguments over form and dating are sometimes interrelated. Early on, historians thought that Géza I had the Byzantine crown altered.[253] Another theory stated that King Coloman (1095–1116) united his father Géza's Byzantine crown with Stephen's head reliquary to create a sacralized crown.[254] Yet another view is that Coloman commissioned the upper part in order to integrate it with the Greek crown.[255] Based on the mid-fourteenth-century image in the *Illuminated Chronicle* allegedly representing the theft of the crown in the 1160s, some speculate that this prompted the making of the extant crown for the coronation of Ladislas II (1162) or Stephen IV (1163). The turbulent times when different claimants from the dynasty fought against each other, one side with the support of Byzantium, and thus the need for haste would account for the technical shortcomings of joining the two pieces together.[256]

The prevalent idea, that the crown was created for Béla III (r. 1172–96), was advocated by Joseph Koller in 1800, and repeated by many since then, although with multiple rationales.[257] The simplest hypothesis refers to Béla's need to reinforce his legitimacy, taking the then-contemporary style of the closed Byzantine imperial crown as a model. This is tied to the controversy over his coronation: after Béla returned from Byzantium to ascend the Hungarian throne, the archbishop of Esztergom refused to crown him, so he was crowned by the archbishop of Kalocsa. The most complicated theory claimed Béla had the crown

---

[250] Photo of inside showing rivets: Kiss, 'La "Couronne grecque"', 41, figure 26; Tóth—Szelényi, *The Holy Crown*, 40.

[251] Whether this was her crown or Frederick's is debated: Kramp, *Krönungen*, vol. 1, 403, image 3, Katalog Nr. 5–13; 447; Mielke, 'From her head'.

[252] Vajay, 'Der Kamelaukion-Charakter', 110–12; Hilsdale, 'The social life of the Byzantine gift', 622; Marosi, 'La "couronne sainte"', 73; Kovács—Lovag, *Hungarian Crown*, 79–81. On possible models, Tóth—Szelényi, *The Holy Crown*, 30. Gerics—Ladányi, 'Források Szent István királlyá avatásának történetéhez', 223 on imperial parallel; Bertényi, *A magyar szent korona*, 62 on Byzantine model.

[253] Varjú, 'A Szent Korona', 68; Lovag, 'L'intégration de la couronne', 63.

[254] Györffy, *István király*, 359, somewhat modifying Kelleher's idea (*The Holy Crown*, 95–107) that the bands from the cover of an evangeliary belonging to Stephen and Gisela were used during the reign of King Coloman. Such hypotheses are no more than exercises in imagination, since the same evidence can be used to support diverse ideas; in an earlier work Györffy suggested that the Byzantine crown was sent to Géza as *dux*, and because Coloman abolished the duchy, he had the royal and ducal crowns united: Györffy, 'A magyar nemzetségtől a vármegyéig, a törzstől az országig (I. Rész)', *Századok*, 92 (1958): 12–87, 52–3.

[255] Szakács, 'What did Piroska see?', 56, based on similarities to Coloman's ring, József Hampel, 'Kálmán király aranygyűrűje', *Archaeologiai Értesítő*, 42 (1908): 11–12.

[256] Bertényi, *A magyar szent korona*, 59–63.   [257] Lovag, 'L'intégration de la couronne', 62.

194 STEPHEN I, THE FIRST CHRISTIAN KING OF HUNGARY

made in *kamelaukion* form to be used for his Byzantine imperial coronation when he was invited to marry the heiress to the throne of Byzantium; when that fell through, he used it as the crown of an 'Archiregnum Hungariae' that included Croatia and Dalmatia.[258] The basis of these speculations is fanciful: there is no proof Béla ever made preparations to rule in Byzantium, and no sources speak of an 'archiregnum' in this period. According to some, the assemblage of the two parts is contemporary with turning the chasuble into a coronation mantle; based on the style of the collar that was added to the chasuble at that time, this transformation has been dated to either the thirteenth[259] or the twelfth century.[260] Deér claimed the crown was made by order of Stephen V for his coronation in May 1270, to replace the crown supposedly taken by his sister Anne to Prague.[261] According to others, it would be 'futile... to pick out one or the other thirteenth-century king' who ordered it.[262] Finally, according to one theory, the *corona latina* was made from a crown that had been placed on Stephen I's head reliquary, which was used in 1440 to crown Władysław (Ulászló) I, and after Matthias Corvinus reacquired the coronation crown from Frederick III, the two were united for Matthias's coronation in March 1464.[263]

The idea that the crown was assembled during Béla III's reign is the most tenacious because it can garner the superficially most convincing conjunction of circumstances: Béla's need for legitimacy and his strong links to Byzantium, having been raised there (as a result, he made the double-barred cross part of Hungarian royal insignia); the Byzantine lower part and Byzantinizing upper part of the crown; mentions of a royal crown in Hungary in texts from the late twelfth and early thirteenth centuries; the change from the open to the closed *kamelaukion*

---

[258] Vajay, 'La relique Stéphanoise', 9–10, 14. Kovács—Lovag, *Hungarian Crown*, 79. Bárány-Oberschall, *Die Sankt Stephans-Krone*, 53–5, summary and warning about the theoretical nature of such interpretations.

[259] Kovács—Lovag, *Hungarian Crown*, 78.

[260] Tóth, *A magyar szent korona*, 281. End of the twelfth century, Deér, *A magyarok szent koronája*, 176.

[261] Deér, *A magyarok szent koronája*, 204–15; in a civil war between Béla IV and his son Stephen V, Anne took her father's side. After Béla's death Anne escaped to the Czech King Ottakar II, husband to Béla's grand-daughter. According to a contemporary Austrian chronicle—*Continuatio Vindobonensis*, ed. Wilhelmus Wattenbach ad a. 1276 *MGH SS* IX (Hanover, 1851), 708—she brought with her from the royal treasury two golden crowns, sceptres, and other golden treasures of the earliest Hungarian kings. Deér argued Anne took the coronation crown of the Hungarian kings, and Stephen had a crown made that imitated the shape of the stolen crown, hence the archaizing style, and the haste, explaining the low-quality workmanship; Stephen secretly substituted the new crown for the old, never admitting to the theft. He also suggested that a goldsmith, Matthew, who received an estate from the king in 1270 shortly after the coronation, was the maker of the crown, and that Stephen relinquished his rights to the treasures in 1271 in a peace treaty, because he had replaced the crown. Against this, Bertényi, *A magyar szent korona*, 66 argued that the coronation crown was kept at Fehérvár, not in the royal treasury and therefore Anne would not have been able to take it.

[262] Kovács—Lovag, *Hungarian Crown*, 81–2, listing the possibilities as Andrew II, Béla IV, Stephen V.

[263] Polner, *A magyar Szent Korona*, cited in Lovag, 'L'intégration de la couronne', 69; Bertényi, *A magyar szent korona*, 66–7. This is based on representations of Hungarian kings with open crowns until Matthias.

THE HUNGARIAN CROWN   195

form of the Byzantine imperial crown in the twelfth century under the Comneni; the dating of the upper part itself by many scholars to the twelfth century.[264] Yet each link in the reasoning is precarious: the textual references need not indicate the extant crown; the crown may not be imitating the *kamelaukion* form; Béla's difficulties with the coronation are relatively well documented, but there is no mention of a special crown. Finally, it is exactly Béla's familiarity with the Byzantine court that raises doubts: if he needed to compensate for his shaky legitimacy, would he have chosen a crown that through its images clearly signals the Hungarian king's subordinate status to Byzantium? A sponsor who appreciated the prestige value of a spectacular object without realizing its symbolic meaning (and the Greek crown's female type) is more likely.

Why are there so many different hypotheses? Unless future technical analysis can determine the dating of the assembly, only more-or-less plausible theories can be advanced without real proof. Most scholars created their theories by finding a historical situation in which the making of a new crown can be a feasible assumption. Of such situations, medieval Hungarian history provides many. Additionally, the nature of the workmanship, with its technologically primitive solution gave rise to the idea that it was made in haste when there was no workshop or expert available.[265] That speculation was linked to historical episodes when such haste could be justified. However, the presupposition that only haste could lead to such work has been refuted: 'in the Middle Ages such amateurish alteration and repair of even the most carefully guarded items was common, and not necessarily an indication of haste'.[266] Indeed, no care was taken to avoid damage to the Latin Pantocrator on the crown when a cross was added to the top of the crown, nor to prevent damage to the crucified Christ on the chasuble when it was transformed into a coronation mantle.[267]

If the upper part was fabricated specifically in order to close the *corona graeca*, that would also limit the possible date of the assemblage to no later than the twelfth century; however, if an existing object was used for that purpose, one could only establish the *terminus post quem*. In sum, we do not know when the crown took its current form; we can only be certain of the *terminus ante quem*. The earliest accurate representation of the extant crown is from the mid-sixteenth century (1540–50), in a history of the Habsburg dynasty, the *Ehrenspiegel des Hauses Österreich*.[268] An explicitly recorded interest in what the crown looks like

[264] Moravcsik, 'A magyar szent korona', 470–2, repr. 722–4; Kovács—Lovag, *Hungarian Crown*, 79; Bertényi, *A magyar szent korona*, 62–3; Hilsdale, 'The social life of the Byzantine gift', 622.
[265] Deér, *A magyarok szent koronája*, 208; Papp, 'Időszaki jelentés', 6.
[266] Kovács—Lovag, *Hungarian Crown*, 78.
[267] Ibid., 75.
[268] Enikő Buzási, Géza Pálffy, *Augsburg—Wien—München—Innsbruck: Die frühesten Darstellungen des Stephanskrone und die Entstehung der Exemplare des Ehrenspiegels des Hauses Österreich*, tr. Eszter Fazekas (Budapest: Institut für Geschichte des Forschungszentrums für Humanwissenschaften der Ungarischen Akademie der Wissenschaften, 2015); reproduction of the image at 8. Before this

196 STEPHEN I, THE FIRST CHRISTIAN KING OF HUNGARY

started in the second half of the fifteenth century, when the crown was ransomed from the Habsburg Frederick III by Matthias Corvinus. A delegation reportedly examined the crown to make sure the emperor returned the genuine item; they assured themselves of this through 'a certain sign' without specifying what it was.[269] Around the same time, in 1464, a crown appeared on the royal seal that resembled the extant one—albeit imperfectly.[270] Medieval depictions of the crown on coins and royal seals, whether or not schematic, definitely do not represent the object that is now in existence.[271] While on first glance it may be tempting to see a drawing, labelled the crown of Hungary, in one of Innocent III's registers from 1205, as a representation of the extant crown, we cannot even be certain it depicts the Hungarian crown in use at the time.[272] It is a circlet crown covered by an arch; three crosses decorate the sides and top and there are three pendilia. Yet such royal crowns were the norm on the seals and some other representations of Frederick I Barbarossa and Henry VI, which may have provided the prototype for the image.[273]

While a twelfth-century date for the assemblage cannot be ruled out, neither can it be proven. Because the first definite textual references to 'St Stephen's crown' are certainly datable to the end of the thirteenth century, the extant crown may have been created in that century of earlier, stylistically similar parts, found in the treasury or a church. However, 'the most honest response is to admit that we don't know' when the two parts were united.[274] Finally, the warning that 'it is erroneous to suppose that only important historical personalities can play a part in the fate of important objects' is salutary: it is not certain that a king ordered the combination of the two parts.[275] At some point, the crown sustained significant damage, and three of the cross-bands had to be mended in several places. Modern repairs were also carried out to change a damaged gem and pearls.[276]

---

discovery, early seventeenth-century coins of Matthias II were thought to be the first accurate representation: Imre Bodor, 'A magyar korona legkorábbi ábrázolásai', *Ars Hungarica* (1980, no. 1): 17–24, at 17.

[269] Antonius de Bonfinis, *Rerum ungaricarum decades*, ed. József Fógel, Béla Iványi, László Juhász (Leipzig: Teubner, 1936), vol. 3, 244–5, III:X.310–12; Teszelszky, *Az ismeretlen korona*, 39; Tamás Pálosfalvi, 'Koronázástól koronázásig: a korona elrablása és hazatérése (1440–1464)', in *A Szent Korona hazatér: a magyar korona tizenegy külföldi útja*, ed. Géza Pálffy (Budapest: MTA Bölcsészettudományi Kutatóközpont Történettudományi Intézet, 2018), 125–66, at 158.

[270] Bodor, 'A magyar korona legkorábbi ábrázolásai', 17–20.

[271] Holler, 'Milyen koronája volt I Istvánnak'; Bodor, 'A magyar korona legkorábbi ábrázolásai'; Teszelszky, *Az ismeretlen korona*, 25.

[272] Reg. Vat. 5, fol. 176; http://legalhistorysources.com/ChurchHistory220/Lecture%20Four/innociiireg.JPG; Vajay, 'Der Kamelaukion-Character', 128 thinks it is the 'Holy Crown'.

[273] József Deér, 'Die Siegel Kaiser Friedrichs I Barbarossa und Heinrichs VI in der Kunst und Politik ihrer Zeit', in *Byzanz und das abendländische Herrschertum. Ausgewählte Aufsätze*, ed. Peter Classen (Sigmaringen: Thorbecke, 1977), 196–234, e.g. images 17, 19, 21, 28, 39; Irmgard Fees, 'Die Siegel und Bullen Kaiser Friedrichs I. Barbarossa', *Archiv für Diplomatik*, 61 (2015): 95–132.

[274] Benda—Fügedi, *A magyar korona regénye*, 18.

[275] Kovács—Lovag, *Hungarian Crown*, 17. [276] Lovag, 'L'intégration de la couronne', 70.

THE HUNGARIAN CROWN 197

The current cross is a later addition, and has been dated to the sixteenth century.[277] Whether there was a cross on the crown from the beginning is unknown, but the way the current cross was fixed to the crown, by piercing the Pantocrator enamel, signals that this could not have been an originally intended location for a cross.[278] The mid-sixteenth-century *Ehrenspiegel* already depicts the crown with the cross.[279] According to one hypothesis, originally a reliquary cross was mounted on the crown, holding a fragment of the True Cross, affixed at the time when the cross-bands were attached.[280] The basis for this idea is an account that before Queen Isabella handed over the regalia to Ferdinand in 1551, she broke a piece off the crown—thought to be the cross—for her son John Sigismund; so a replacement cross had to be made. According to a contemporary Polish chronicler, John Sigismund wore this cross on his chest for the rest of his life 'because he who possesses this cross will again come into possession of the missing parts which, subjected to the power of the cross, had belonged to it'.[281] Later the cross became the property of Sigismund Báthory who then bestowed it on Rudolf II.[282] When the cross was bent cannot be dated with certainty. On representations up to 1626, it was depicted as straight, and it was known to be crooked in 1784.[283] The cross was probably pushed into its current position by the same accident that caused the cross bands to break and dented the top; it is possible that this happened in 1638, when the chest with the regalia had to be broken open by force.[284]

There is no compelling evidence for the late tenth or early eleventh-century dating of any element of the crown, and no evidence any part of it had once belonged to Stephen himself. While it is not impossible that some part of a reliquary made after his canonization in 1083 was eventually used to create the extant crown, the hypothesis cannot be proven.[285] Yet attempts to link part of the crown to Stephen continue, and have taken novel forms in every iteration. They can be explained by the unwillingness to give up the long-held myth. Indeed, one can see that while specific arguments have changed over time, the underlying logic remained the same; as one hypothesis had to be abandoned, another was put in its place.

As soon as scholars were forced by the weight of the evidence to abandon the idea that the entire crown had been Stephen's, at the end of the eighteenth century

---

[277] Péri, 'Időszaki jelentés', 6.

[278] Crossed arches surmounted by a cross became a usual part of royal crowns from the fifteenth century onwards: Alexander Gieysztor, 'Non habemus Caesarem nisi regem: La couronne fermée des rois de Pologne à la fin du XVe et au XVIe siècle', *Bibliothèque de l'École des Chartes*, 127 (1969): 5–26.

[279] Tóth—Szelényi, *The Holy Crown*, 31.   [280] Kovács—Lovag, *Hungarian Crown*, 79–81.

[281] Endre Veress, *Izabella királyné, 1519–1559* (Budapest: Magyar Történelmi Társulat, 1901), book 6, chapter 1, quoting the contemporary Annales of Stanislaw Orichovius; http://mek.niif.hu/05800/05808/html/05.htm#1228. See also Tóth, *A magyar szent korona*, 214–15.

[282] Veress, *Izabella*, note 1229 quotes the report of an Italian envoy in Prague in 1610. According to this, it was in the shape of 'a lily or something like it, a part and adornment of Hungary's crown'.

[283] Varjú, 'A Szent Korona', 69; Bak—Pálffy, *Crown and Coronation*, 155.

[284] Ibid., 156.   [285] Péri, 'Időszaki jelentés', 6; Marosi, 'La "couronne latine"', 80.

198   STEPHEN I, THE FIRST CHRISTIAN KING OF HUNGARY

the *corona latina* was 'identified' as the one sent by the pope to the king.[286] Once several researchers rejected that claim,[287] various other hypotheses tried to rescue the connection between the upper part and Stephen. Around 1900, some claimed that the original crown of Stephen was buried with him, unearthed in 1083, and, as a relic, turned into the *corona latina*.[288] This idea lacks any credible foundation: though rare late examples of such burial practice exist, even emperors were buried with imitation regalia during the eleventh century, as was the twelfth-century Hungarian king (probably Béla III) whose remains were excavated.[289] When it became obvious that the cross-bands had never been a crown, its apostle enamels were singled out to retain the association to the first king. Thus theories proliferated that they came from an object that used to belong to Stephen, or from a reliquary made for Stephen, or even from Stephen's own crown. 'Scholars were... inhibited by traditions;...they tried to maintain the plausibility of the theory that the crown, termed holy and said to be derived from St. Stephen, had actually been in contact with the person of the first Christian king of Hungary.'[290] The resurgence of nationalist history writing recently revitalized this line of argument.

The association of at least part of the crown with Stephen is also fostered by the assumption that medieval people called the crown 'St Stephen's crown' and 'holy' because they still knew of such a connection. This is a fundamental misunderstanding of medieval processes and disregards the mechanism of medieval myth making. Relics were forged just as much as charters; authenticity in the modern sense was not a requirement for the cult of saints or for legitimizing rule. Just as relics were routinely 'found' and 'identified' without the need for any real connection between the historical (or invented) person of the saint and the alleged relic, so were objects regularly associated with famous people of the past without regard to historicity: witness, for example, the objects held to have belonged to Charlemagne, including chess pieces made in the late eleventh century and a late twelfth- or early thirteenth-century Sicilian mantle.[291] How the crown became

---

[286] István Katona, *Dissertatio critica...in commentarium Alexii Horányi...de Sacra Hungariae Corona* (Buda, 1790); also Joseph Koller, *De Sacra regni Ungariae Corona commentarius* (Pécs, 1800), both cited in Lovag, 'L'intégration de la couronne', 62.

[287] Moravcsik, 'A magyar szent korona', 469, repr. 721; Eckhart, *Magyar alkotmány- és jogtörténet*, 93–4 noted the frequent criticism of the identification.

[288] Karácsonyi, 'Hogyan lett Szent István koronája' (Stephen's crown was a circlet decorated with twelve apostles; this was transformed into the *corona latina*).

[289] Emperor Henry III in 1056 was buried with a copper crown: Kramp, *Krönungen*, vol. 1, 336, nos. 3–23; crowns worn in life only used for imperial burials from the late twelfth century: Schramm, *Herrschaftszeichen*, vol. 3, 911–12; Edward I was buried in a tin crown, and while some of the clothing Henry III of England was buried in were coronation clothes, this was not the case for his crown (1272): David Carpenter, *The Reign of Henry III* (London: The Hambledon Press, 1996), 444. Přemysl Otakar II's funerary regalia were gilded silver: Kramp, *Krönungen*, vol. 1, 23, image 4, Katalog nr. 5–33; nor were French kings buried in coronation crowns: Alain Erlande-Brandenburg, *Le roi est mort: étude sur les funerailles, les sépultures et les tombeaux des rois de France jusqu'à la fin du XIIIe siècle* (Geneva: Droz, 1975), 14–15; the use of crowns at funerals started in the thirteenth century, 18–22.

[290] Kovács—Lovag, *Hungarian Crown*, 17.

[291] Danielle Gaborit-Chopin, 'Le trésor au temps de Suger', *Les Dossiers d'archéologie*, no. 158 (March 1991): 2–19, at 6; Kramp, *Krönungen*, vol. 1, 445–6, Katalog nr. 5–10.

holy demonstrates this process. Instead of hypothesizing Stephen's immediate significance for his successors, for which there is no proof, and taking into account the very precise dating of texts that start to associate a crown to Stephen only from the late thirteenth century, it is much more likely that no constituent part of the so-called *corona latina* had any real connection to Stephen.

3. The Road to 'Holy Crown'

How did the Hungarian royal crown become 'holy'? The narrative offered by scholarship with some variations proposes several possibilities. According to one view, because the extant crown was believed to have been Stephen's, and perhaps even incorporated an object (or at least parts of an object) that had been his or was associated to him, and because objects that had belonged to Stephen would also become holy after his canonization, the crown merited the designation 'sacra'.[292] According to another opinion, the crown's holiness was due to, or at least reinforced by, a reliquary cross on top that contained a piece of the True Cross, which had either been or was thought to have been in the possession of Stephen.[293] Some medieval crowns indeed included a relic.[294] The 'Holy Crown' of France contained a supposed thorn from Christ's crown of thorns,[295] as did the fourteenth-century Bohemian royal crown, 'St Wenceslas' crown'.[296] Yet another explanation claims that the idea of the royal lineage's sanctity was transferred to 'Stephen's' physical crown.[297] In addition, many scholars maintain that kings had to be crowned with 'Stephen's crown' at the latest by the beginning of the thirteenth century. It is also generally accepted that although the first attestation of the crown being called 'holy' comes from 1256, and its first explicit mention as 'St Stephen's' from the 1290s, these first textual references merely reflect long-established views.[298] A review of the sources, and their recontextualization,

---

[292] E.g. Tóth, *A magyar szent korona*, 198.

[293] Kovács—Lovag, *Hungarian Crown*, 81–2. Vajay, 'La relique Stéphanoise', 13–14 argued that Béla III had a cross that had been Stephen's removed from the orb to replace it with a double-barred cross, and the former was mounted on the crown; because of its association to the holy king, making a hole through the Pantocrator was not problematic. It was also the reason it was called the 'holy crown'.

[294] Schramm, *Herrshaftszeichen*, vol. 1, 312 (ninth and eleventh centuries); vol. 3, 852–3, 869–83 (thirteenth–fourteenth centuries). On crowns given by rulers to be placed on head reliquaries of Charlemagne and Wenceslas, and subsequent use for coronation: František Kavka, 'Karl IV. (1349–1378) und Aachen', in Kramp, *Krönungen*, vol. 2, 477–84, at 479–80; Kramp, *Krönungen*, vol. 2, 527, nos. 6–18, 531, nos. 6–29.

[295] Schramm, *Herrshaftszeichen*, vol. 3, 869–71; Pinoteau, *La symbolique royale française*, 292.

[296] Kramp, *Krönungen*, vol. 2, 531–2, nos. 6–29.

[297] Péter, 'The Holy Crown of Hungary', 431–2. Vajay, 'Der Kamelaukion-Character', 103 argued that everything belonging to the Byzantine emperor was holy, thus a kamelaukion-type crown was automatically holy. Others also link it to the papal sending of the crown and combine various reasons, Marie-Madeleine de Cevins, 'Les origines médiévales de la doctrine de la Sainte couronne', *Hungarian Studies*, 30, no. 2 (2016): 175–90, at 179.

[298] E.g. Vajay, 'Der Kamelaukion-Character', 115; Bak—Pálffy, *Crown and Coronation*, 160–1.

200 STEPHEN I, THE FIRST CHRISTIAN KING OF HUNGARY

leads to the conclusion that it was only at the very end of the thirteenth century that the crown was definitively linked to Stephen, and even later that it became 'sacra corona', with the fixed expression emerging in the fourteenth century.

While the eventual myth of a holy crown benefited from Stephen's status, it also had a separate trajectory from other objects associated with the holy king. Several elements of the coronation came to be seen as fixed in the first century or so of the existence of the Kingdom of Hungary, and many could be linked to Stephen in some way. The place of coronation was the royal basilica dedicated to the Virgin, founded by Stephen in (Székes)fehérvár. It was also the burial place of Stephen's son, who predeceased him, and of Stephen himself; therefore, from the 1083 canonization of the king and his son, the basilica of Fehérvár was the burial place of saints. From the death of King Coloman (d. 1116), many other kings were buried there.[299] The regalia were kept there as well, perhaps from the late twelfth century onwards.[300] The archbishop of Esztergom—whose archbishopric had been founded by Stephen—had the right to crown the king. This right was explicitly confirmed by the pope in 1172, after a clash between the archbishop and King Béla III. A papal letter declared that the exceptional situation, in which the archbishop of Kalocsa was allowed to crown the king after the archbishop of Esztergom refused to do so, in no way prejudiced the established prerogatives of the latter.[301]

During the thirteenth century, the coronation of Hungary's kings was sometimes explicitly associated to Stephen, other times more broadly to the 'holy ancestors'. As a Cistercian monk from Stična (Sittich) reported, who had spent a month in Sopron in 1240, Hungary's kings sat on Stephen's throne, and were adorned with his equipment (arma).[302] King Ladislas IV's charter on 27 June 1277 mentioned being clothed in 'the holy clothes of our holy ancestors on the day of our coronation'.[303] Both have been taken as references to the coronation mantle (created from the chasuble that had been made by order of Stephen I and Queen Gisela),[304] or to the royal insignia and coronation paraphernalia more generally.[305] As part of the coronation, a new king was also dressed in an array of clothes, from stockings and shoes to gloves, a girdle, and other items. Moreover, wearing the crown, sceptre, and other insignia could be referred to as 'clothed'.[306]

---

[299] Benda—Fügedi, magyar korona, 21–2. Gyula Siklósi, 'Székesfehérvár', in Medium regni: Középkori magyar királyi székhelyek, Julianna Altmann, Piroska Biczó, Gergely Buzás, István Horváth, Annamária Kovács, Gyula Siklósi, András Végh (Budapest: Nap Kiadó, 1996), 43–88.

[300] The papal letter of 1198 is the first evidence for the crown being kept there.

[301] 15 March 1209, Potthast no. 3725, PL 216, col. 50.

[302] SRH II, 607. József Deér, A magyar királyság megalakulása (Budapest: Magyar Történettudományi Intézet, 1942), 13–14 interpreted it as sword and sceptre.

[303] 'qui [Benedict, canon of Fehérvár] ipso die coronationis nostre nos beatorum progenitorum nostrorum sacris regalibus ad coronationem consecratis induit indumentis', Fejér, Codex Diplomaticus, VII/2 (Buda, 1832), 54–7, CCCXXXIX, at 55; Benda—Fügedi, magyar korona, 23.

[304] Ibid., 24.   [305] Deér, A magyarok szent koronája, 176.

[306] Petersohn, 'Über monarchische Insignien', 59.

THE HUNGARIAN CROWN   201

Clearly, Stephen's legitimizing role by then was firmly attached to at least some of the objects with which a new king was invested; however, there is no explicit mention of a specifically significant crown.[307] Moreover, some of these objects fell out of use, were given away or were lost over time, thus they were not protected by their association with the king.

When the 'Holy Crown' started to be used for coronation has been assumed rather than proven. The bold assertion that 'it cannot have been later than the mid-twelfth century'[308] cannot be substantiated. Two twelfth-century texts are traditionally used as proofs of the existence of the Holy Crown. These indicate that coronation insignia were kept at Fehérvár at the end, or perhaps starting in the latter half, of the twelfth century, but nothing warrants the interpretation that these texts refer to the now extant crown, or to the holiness of the crown. The first, Patriarch Michael Anchialus's laudation of Emperor Manuel Comnenus I, traditionally dated to 1165 or 1167, but plausibly re-dated as referring to events in 1150–1, mentions the royal diadem of the Hungarian rulers, a church where it was kept, and the metropolitanate around it, while acclaiming the Byzantine emperor's sovereignty over Hungary.[309] Scholars have suggested this church is either that in Esztergom, given that it was the seat of the archbishopric, or the basilica in Fehérvár, since the regalia were kept there according to later sources, although the town was not the seat of a bishopric.[310] It is unlikely Michael was concerned with the Catholic ecclesiastical organization of the kingdom; rather, he may well have referred to the 'metropolitanate of Tourkia', which was part of the Byzantine church, and was still included in a list of metropolitanates under the patriarch of Constantinople in the second half of the twelfth century, even though possibly there had been no bishop of Tourkia for some time.[311] We cannot thus identify which church he meant.

---

[307] Deér, *A magyarok szent koronája*, 176 argued that the crown associated to Stephen was already part of the coronation paraphernalia, assumed under these two more generic references.

[308] Tóth—Szelényi, *The Holy Crown*, 11; Tóth, *A magyar szent korona*, 198 also argued that during the twelfth-century coronation, regalia were chosen from objects associated with Stephen: the chasuble turned into a coronation mantle, the sceptre, and the crown that included an earlier object belonging to Stephen.

[309] Browning, 'A new source on Byzantine–Hungarian relations', 203, lines 569–71, 'Likewise enrolled among those subject to thy sceptre is the headband-holding (*tainiouchos*) church (*naos*) of Paionia [i.e. Hungary] and the metropolitanate (*mētropolis*) around it, so that the imperial/royal (*basileios*) crown (*stephanos*) of the Paionian rulers may be held firm/confined by thy might.' I thank Jonathan Shepard for his help with this text. Ioannis Polemis, 'Notes on the Inaugural Oration of the Patriarch Michael of Anchialos', *Byzantinoslavica: Revue Internationale des Etudes Byzantines*, 69, nos. 1–2 (2011): 162–72 on revised dating, 1150–1.

[310] Browning seems to have interpreted this as a reference to the seat of the archbishopric of Hungary, thus Esztergom.

[311] István Baán, 'Tourkia metropolitája. Újabb adalék a bizánci egyház történetéhez a középkori Magyarországon', *Századok*, 129 (1995): 1167–70; István Baán, 'The metropolitanate of Tourkia: the organization of the Byzantine church in Hungary in the Middle Ages', in *Byzanz und Ostmitteleuropa 950–1453*, ed. Günter Prinzing, Maciej Salamon (Wiesbaden: Otto Harrassowitz Verlag, 1999), 45–53; Cheynet, 'L'empire Byzantin et la Hongrie', 609–10; Nora Berend, ed., *Christianization and the Rise of*

202   STEPHEN I, THE FIRST CHRISTIAN KING OF HUNGARY

Regardless of which church it was kept in, the crown of the Hungarian ruler Michael mentioned may refer to the Byzantine crown sent to Hungary in the eleventh century (the 'Greek crown'), or to whatever crown was used in Hungary in the mid-twelfth century. The information possibly came from the Hungarian nobles from whom Michael claims to have taken oaths. This text has been interpreted as evidence that the 'coronation insignia became clearly distinct from the royal treasury' kept at Fehérvár.[312] It has also been used to argue that the Hungarian crown already had a particular importance.[313] While more research is needed to elucidate the meaning of this text fully, it does not prove the existence of the 'Holy Crown'. While it may signal Byzantine knowledge about a former gift, or the existence of a coronation crown, it may not even refer to one specific, permanent crown. Housing regalia in a church did not necessarily mean having one coronation crown. This is attested elsewhere in medieval Europe, including a case that is contemporary with Michael Anchialus's text. In France, the coronation regalia were housed at St Denis by the abbacy of Suger (d. 1151).[314] Yet there was no fixed 'royal crown'; rather, each ruler had a different crown, but the ruler's crown was always kept in the church when it was not worn.[315] Moreover, although there are cases of giving the insignia of a previous ruler to his heir,[316] the terms 'corona regni' and 'corona imperii' were also used for any crown that German rulers wore for their ecclesiastical coronation, rather than for a specific crown.[317]

The second text, a letter by Innocent III from 1198 to the provost of Fehérvár has been the basis of claims that the safety of the crown in Hungary was a major concern, and the need to guard it is proof of the crown's political significance.[318] The letter, however, discusses the provost's right to appoint a *custos*, who was an officer responsible for the safety of the church, including its archives and treasures. The *custodia* of ecclesiastical ornaments and privileges, and the royal crown

---

Christian Monarchy: Central Europe, Scandinavia and Rus' c. 950–c. 1200 (Cambridge: Cambridge University Press, 2007), 328.

[312] Tóth—Szelényi, *The Holy Crown*, 15.

[313] Kovács—Lovag, *Hungarian Crown*, 8; Tóth—Szelényi, *The Holy Crown*, 13–14 interprets this as proof of the existence of a special crown.

[314] Gaborit-Chopin, 'Le trésor au temps de Suger', 8, 10.

[315] Ibid. Similar for Norman and Angevin kings of England: Carpenter, *The Reign of Henry III*, 446.

[316] Petersohn, 'Über monarchische Insignien', 61–3.

[317] Ibid., 52; Reichskrone first c. 1200 as unmistakable according to the written sources: ibid., 57; on items within regalia changed until the fifteenth century: ibid., 56–7. The terms also denoted royal/imperial dignity.

[318] 'Innotuit apostolatui nostro per petitionem nobis ex tua parte porrectam, quod, cum in Albensi ecclesia quedam dignitas, que custodia dicitur, ad tuam donationem pertinens habeatur, cuius cure ac sollicitudini ornamenta et privilegia ipsius ecclesie et diadema etiam regium committuntur, eam persone idonee conferri desideras; ne forte per imperitiam aut infidelitatem vel negligentiam custodis ipsius, ecclesia incurrat aliquod detrimentum aut honor patrie de corona aliquam lesionem sustineat. Volentes igitur indempnitati ecclesie precavere, et tibi tuam iusticiam conservare, ut custodiam ipsam, sicut tui iuris existit, idonee persone nullius appellatione obstante conferas et assignes, liberam tibi damus auctoritate apostolica facultatem.' 21 December 1198, in *Die Register Innocenz' III*, vol. 1, *Pontifikatsjahr 1, 1198/99*, ed. Othmar Hageneder, Anton Haidacher (Graz—Cologne: Böhlau, 1964), 708; Potthast no. 494; Péter, 'The Holy Crown of Hungary', 433–4.

THE HUNGARIAN CROWN   203

('diadem of the kings') in the church of Fehérvár are mentioned together. Liturgical equipment included precious objects; written ecclesiastical privileges were also prized possessions of churches. When justifying the need to appoint an appropriate custodian, the potential detriment to the church from the custodian's negligence is mentioned along with the possibility that the honour of the *patria* sustain some injury because of the crown. While perhaps one particular crown used for coronations was meant in this letter—although that is far from certain— there are also significant issues we should not overlook. Stephen is not mentioned at all, the crown is not called his.[319] Additionally, the crown of the kingdom was linked to the *patria* in France as well, without reference to a specific crown, and the dignity, injury, shame and honour of the crown all appeared in expressions.[320] In sum, these sources are no proof of the existence of a 'holy crown'. The fact that royal regalia were kept in a specific church and guarded is usual for the period. Whether the same physical object is meant by both twelfth-century sources cannot be ascertained. It is equally possible that the royal crown kept at Fehérvár was not the same crown over the decades, but rather the crown used by any particular ruler at the time.

According to several scholars, a text from the continuation of the Annals of Admont provides proof that by the early thirteenth century, the validity of coronation depended on using a specific crown, or even the now extant crown; that is why Andrew threatened the Duke of Austria with war in 1205 unless it was returned.[321] However, on closer examination of the context and the text, such an interpretation cannot be substantiated. After King Emeric (Imre) died, his infant son Ladislas III, who had been crowned in his father's lifetime, inherited the throne. Yet the aspirations of Andrew, Emeric's brother, went beyond governing in his nephew's name, and the widowed queen escaped to Austria along with the child-king, and 'with treasures and great riches'.[322] The chronicler writes that Andrew mounted an army to regain the 'treasure, that is crown', but the issue was

---

[319] The term *diadema* may suggest a band (or circlet) crown, rather than the now existing crown, but the terminology is too ambiguous to provide certainty. In 1309, the Hungarian bishops also use *diadema* to refer to the coronation crown, while in 1317, Charles I uses *diadema* and *corona* interchangeably; see below.

[320] Ernst H. Kantorowicz, *The King's Two Bodies: A Study in Medieval Political Theology* (Princeton, NJ: Princeton University Press, 1981), 341; Yves Sassier, 'La *Corona regni*: émergence d'une *persona ficta* dans la France du XIIe siècle', in *La puissance royale: Image et pouvoir de l'antiquité au Moyen Âge*, ed. Christian-Georges Schwentzel, Emmanuelle Santinelli-Foltz (Rennes: Presses Universitaires de Rennes, 2012), 99–110. The honour of the king's estate was linked to the crown in an Icelandic saga as well: Erich Hoffmann, 'Coronation and coronation ordines in medieval Scandinavia', in *Coronations: Medieval and Early Modern Monarchic Ritual*, ed. János M. Bak (Berkeley: University of California Press, 1990), 125–51, at 127.

[321] Deér, *A magyarok szent koronája*, 174; Tóth—Szelényi, *The Holy Crown*, 9; Kovács—Lovag, *Hungarian Crown*, 8; Attila Zsoldos, 'Az Árpádok koronája először külföldön (Bécs, 1205)', in *A Szent Korona hazatér*, 49–70.

[322] 'cum thesauris et divitiis magnis', 'Continuatio Admuntensis', *MGH SS* IX, 591.

204　STEPHEN I, THE FIRST CHRISTIAN KING OF HUNGARY

resolved because Ladislas III died.[323] The text relates that Ladislas' body was returned to Hungary to be interred in Fehérvár; while the treasure and crown may have accompanied the corpse back to Hungary, the author says nothing about this. There is no indication that the crown in question was the same object as the 'Holy Crown'. Any crown used in Ladislas' coronation would have been a symbol of rulership; while Ladislas was alive, a potential threat was harboured in neighbouring Austria, so Andrew would have wanted the crown to delegitimize Ladislas as king. Therefore, Ladislas' death alone would have been sufficient, without the need to return the crown, to re-establish peace with the Duke of Austria. Had possession of the crown itself been Andrew's objective, the text's silence on its return would be curious.

Moreover, had the validity of his coronation been dependent on a specific crown, one could assume that Andrew II, in a charter donating money to the Archbishopric of Esztergom to commemorate his coronation, would have put some emphasis on having obtained that crown. Yet he says nothing about a specific crown at all, and does not even single out Stephen, but just refers to being 'on the throne of our fathers' bearing the royal insignia of his ancestors.[324] There is another logical problem with assuming that Andrew wanted the crown while Ladislas was still alive because coronation with that specific crown was necessary to be a legitimate king: had Ladislas not died or renounced the throne, simply taking the crown from Ladislas and crowning Andrew would not have nullified the legitimacy of the earlier coronation.

That royal regalia were kept at Fehérvár is thus clear; whether the same crown appears in all the sources is less so, since the crown used for coronation may have changed over time. None of the sources mentions that the coronation crown was thought to be St Stephen's crown. A general continuity with royal 'ancestors' is emphasized, but there is nothing peculiar about this, as it was a phenomenon broadly consistent with medieval custom.[325] It did not even necessarily mean that the same crown was a permanent part of the regalia, let alone that a 'holy crown' existed. While a contemporary source described how at the time of the Mongol invasion in 1241, King Béla IV had the remains of St Stephen and ecclesiastical treasures from many churches (together with his wife and son) conveyed to safety,

---

[323] Ibid. 'Sicque [with the death of Ladislas] sedata est controversia grandis, que inter ducem et Andream regem orta fuerat, pro repetenda tam regina, quam thesauris seu corona quam simul asportaverat, in tantum ut contratis utrimque exercituum copiis inter se dimicaturi residerent.'

[324] 'Sane miserationum domini... in solio patrum nostrorum sedimus, recordantes ecclesiae beati Adalberti martyris, quam matrem regni esse et metropolim, quamque patribus et predecessoribus nostris cum insignibus fidei sacramenta regalibus, administrasse constat, in nostrae coronationis memoriam, quam de sursum capiti nostro per manus venerabilis patris Ioannis Archiepiscopi Strigoniensis, Deus imponere est dignatus, has donorum nostrorum primitias... attribuimus... centum marcae argenti . . .' Fejér, CD, III/1 (Buda, 1829), 32.

[325] Robert Bartlett, *Blood Royal: Dynastic Politics in Medieval Europe* (Cambridge: Cambridge University Press, 2020), 283–339.

THE HUNGARIAN CROWN   205

there is no mention of a crown, let alone holy crown.[326] A forged charter purporting to renew the privileges of the church of Fehérvár in 1254, in the name of Béla IV, states what had, by the thirteenth century, become standard reference-points: that the throne of the kingdom and crown are kept in the church, which is where Hungary's kings are anointed (as part of the coronation), and buried.[327] None of this is remarkable or unique, as medieval monarchies had similar ritual centres: Aachen, St-Denis, or, later on, Prague.[328]

According to traditional scholarship, however, just two years later the term 'sacra corona' appeared.[329] In a charter confirming the privileges of St Adalbert's Cathedral in Esztergom on 16 December 1256, the king recalled all the benefits he and Hungary's kings received from the archbishop: coronation and unction, the remission of sins, and ecclesiastical backing to compel those disloyal to the king. In this context, for the first time, the term 'sacra corona' is used: those unfaithful to the king and to the holy crown would be compelled by ecclesiastical censure (excommunication) to the obedience of the king and the holy crown.[330]

[326] 'susceptis...multarum ecclesiarum thesauris'; Queen Mary 'cum omnibus regalibus gazis' then takes up residence in the castle of Klis: *Thomae archidiaconi Spalatensis Historia Salonitanorum atque Spalatinorum pontificum. Archdeacon Thomas of Split: History of the Bishops of Salona and Split*, ed., tr. Olga Perić, Damir Karbić, Mirjana Matijević Sokol and James Ross Sweeney (Budapest: Central European University Press, 2006), 286–7. Although Zsoldos argues that the holy crown must have been among these treasures, such a hypothesis is only possible by the assumption that the holy crown already existed; and there is no proof of that before and during the invasion: Attila Zsoldos, 'A magyar korona menekítése a tatárjárás idején (1241–1242)', in *A Szent Korona hazatér*, 73–88, especially 76. Two other mentions of taking 'royal treasures' to safety in the second half of the thirteenth century make no specific reference to a crown: T. Smičiklas, ed., *Codex Diplomaticus Regni Croatiae, Dalmatiae et Slavoniae*, 15 vols. (Zagreb, 1904–34), vol. 6, 52 (1262); Magyar Nemzeti Levéltár Országos Levéltára, Budapest, DL 70621 (1282), both quoted in Zsoldos, ibid., 85.

[327] Fejér, CD, IV/2, 231: 'vbi solium regni et corona conseruatur; et vbi reges Hungariae sacro consecrationis munere perunguntur, vbi nostrorum etiam Antecessorum sacra corpora requiescunt...'. Imre Szentpétery, Iván Borsa, *Regesta regum stirpis critico-diplomatica. Az Árpád-házi királyok okleveleinek kritikai jegyzéke*. 3 vols (Budapest: MTA, 1923–1987), no. 1012; Deér, *A magyarok szent koronája*, 187.

[328] On royal thrones, Schramm, *Herrschaftszeichen*, vol. 1, 316–69, vol. 2, 707–13; although the throne was not part of royal insignia in medieval terminology, ritual enthronement on 'Charlemagne's throne' in Aachen was part of German royal coronation from the tenth century: Petersohn, 'Über monarchische Insignien', 55, 65.

[329] This is repeated in all the literature, e.g. Tóth—Szelényi, *The Holy Crown*, 15; Bak—Pálffy, *Crowns and Coronation*, 160. Györffy, 'Die "corona sancti Stephani regis"', 62 argued that a forged charter purportedly dated 1057, but forged between 1228 and 1247, is the first to mention the holy crown ('prouincia Sancte Corone'); Fejér, CD, I, 394–7, at 395. However, the alleged transcript from the thirteenth century is also a forgery: Szentpétery, *Regesta*, no. 544, and the text is only securely attested from 1404: Tibor Szőcs, ed., *Regesta Palatinorum et vices gerentium tempore regum stirpis Arpadianae critico-diplomatica. Az Árpád-kori nádorok és helyetteseik okleveleinek kritikai jegyzéke* (Budapest: Magyar Országos Levéltár, 2012), 23–4, no. 1.

[330] Fejér, CD, IV/2, 385–7, at 386–7; Szentpétery, *Regesta*, no. 1122: 'consideratis etiam iustis petitionibus praefati Patris B. Archiepiscopi Strigoniensis, fidelis nostri, pro eadem ecclesia, sancta matre nostra, a qua nos sumus, ac nostri Progenitores fuerunt coronati et vncti, et regium honorem consecuti, et adepti; quae etiam nobis et nostris successoribus corde humiliatis, transgressis diuina mandata, absolutionis beneficium, et remissionem peccatorum vice Dei impertitur; ac infideles nostros, et sacrae coronae per censuram Ecclesiasticam arcet et compellit ad nobis et sacrae coronae obediendum'.

206 STEPHEN I, THE FIRST CHRISTIAN KING OF HUNGARY

The charter was written by Master Smaragdus, the king's vice-chancellor, provost of Fehérvár (later archbishop of Kalocsa), who returned the previous year after becoming *doctor decretorum* (thus a canon lawyer) at an unspecified university.[331] It is usually assumed that he merely made explicit what had already been self-evident; that St Stephen's crown was sacred, and the only crown that could be used for coronations to be valid.[332] Some even think this was an early expression of the 'doctrine of the Holy Crown' (see below).

This oft-repeated assertion, however, rests on multiple errors. The charter only survives in a transcript made in 1332.[333] The abbreviated word that appears is 'sancta', rather than 'sacra', contrary to the old edition that has been the basis of this argument.[334] The expressions 'infidelity to us and the crown' and 'obedience to us and the crown', that appear in the charter were frequent ones in the period, and do not refer to a physical object, but to the concept of monarchical power. During the thirteenth century, the crown as a metaphor for royal dignity, a more abstract concept of rule (distinct from the individual king who embodied it) became customary, especially in constructs such as loyalty and service to the crown;[335] yet that was not a uniquely Hungarian phenomenon and had nothing to do with any special physical crown, but rather, it was a common European development.[336] It is quite plausible that the word 'sancta' is an interpolation, inserted before the original 'corona' in 1332 when the charter was copied, in order to fit the by then more usual terminology. That would account for the sudden appearance of 'sancta corona' in this charter, with no precedent and no follow-up for a long time. Even Béla's own charters did not continue to use the term.[337] If, however, 'sancta' appeared in the original charter, while it is hypothetically possible that Smaragdus, provost of Fehérvár, would have tried to elevate the object

---

[331] 'Datum per manus dilecti nostri et fidelis Magistri Smaragdi, Albensis Ecclesiae Praepositi, aulae nostrae Vice-Cancellarii.' On Smaragdus: László Fejérpataky, *A Királyi kanczellária az Árpádok korában* (Budapest: A Magyar Tudományos Akadémia, 1885), 105–6; Endre Veress, *Olasz egyetemeken járt Magyarországi tanulók anyakönyve és iratai 1221–1864* (Budapest: Magyar Tudományos Akadémia, 1941), 391.

[332] Benda—Fügedi, *magyar korona*, 26–7, explaining the term *sacra corona* through its attribution to St Stephen.

[333] The original is in the archives of the Archbishopric of Esztergom, digitalized: MOL DF 248074: https://archives.hungaricana.hu/hu/charters/view/4645/?pg=4&bbox=-365%2C-2243%2C3293%2C-440.

[334] On the abbreviation: Adriano Cappelli, *Dizionario di Abbreviature Latine ed Italiane* (Milan: U. Hoepli, 1990), 343. I thank Tessa Webber for the confirmation.

[335] The same charter used 'corona' in the meaning of royal power, Fejér, CD, IV/2, 385–7, at 385: 'Et si petitiones iustas singulorum ex officio Celsitudinis regiae tenemur admittere; maxime tamen eorum debemus precibus inclinari, per quos praecipue Coronae nostrae insignia extolluntur.' Karpat, 'Corona regni Hungariae', 303–40 provides a thorough list of the occurrence of such expressions in Hungary. See below for other examples.

[336] Kantorowicz, *The King's Two Bodies*. See also below.

[337] The stop and start nature of the usage would not in itself invalidate a 1256 date, as seen with 'sacrum imperium'; however, the sole use for decades in a much later copy is a strong indication of interpolation.

THE HUNGARIAN CROWN   207

held at his church at Fehérvár,[338] it is more likely that it referred to the abstract concept of the crown—that is, royal power, and not a particular physical crown, along the lines of the 'sacrum imperium', the Holy Roman Empire.[339]

There are only two instances of 'sancta corona' certainly appearing in charters in the thirteenth century: in 1272 and 1291. Both refer to service to the crown (called *sancta* in one case, *sanctissima* in the other), and both crop up in circumstances where royal power was weak, in the first case, because a child inherited the throne, and in the second, because of the king's doubtful legitimacy.[340] Because of the formula used, which was widespread in Europe at this time, it is likely that not a physical object, but the abstract concept was meant in these charters.[341] Thus, an emphasis on the sanctity of royal dignity was intended to counterbalance the personal weakness of the king. Ladislas IV's charter of 1272 was written by Magister Nicolas, provost of the church of Alba Iulia in Transylvania, the king's vice-chancellor, who was deeply embroiled in royal politics, repeatedly receiving ecclesiastical appointments from Queen Elizabeth, Ladislas IV's mother, only to be deprived of them by the pope;[342] and Queen Fenenna's by her chancellor, Benedict, bishop of Veszprém. 'Sacra corona' did not appear, only in faulty modern editions.[343]

The first references to the crown having been St Stephen's come from the years 1292 and 1293: two charters of King Andrew (András) III (1290–1301) stated that he had been crowned with St Stephen's crown according to custom.[344] It has

[338] Smaragdus would have then coined the term in a charter confirming privileges for the cathedral whose archbishop crowned the king, and was, in a sense, a rival.

[339] On the development of the latter, Vedran Sulovsky, *Making the Holy Roman Empire Holy: Frederick Barbarossa, Saint Charlemagne and the sacrum imperium* (Cambridge: Cambridge University Press, forthcoming). Karpat, 'Corona regni Hungariae', 346 concluded that 'corona' was mostly used in the abstract sense in Hungarian sources in the period.

[340] The first is Ladislas IV's donation to Magister Sixtus and his brother 'pro eorum seruitiis meritoriis fideliter sancte corone impensis', 20 November 1272, Szentpétery, *Regesta*, no. 2325, MOL DF 248143; https://archives.hungaricana.hu/hu/charters/view/7896/?pg=4&bbox=-399%2C-2593% 2C3795%2C-173; Fejér, CD, V/2, 47 based on a charter, erroneously has 'sacrae coronae'; the transcript doubtless conformed to later usage. The second is Queen Fenenna rewarding the Archbishop of Esztergom in 1291, for services 'domino regi, sanctissimeque per consequens corone regie, nobis et toti regno', Imre Szentpétery, *Az Árpád-házi hercegek, hercegnők, és a királynék okleveleinek kritikai jegyzéke* (Budapest: Magyar Országos Levéltár, 2008), no. 267, MOL DF237875: https://archives.hungaricana.hu/hu/charters/view/12229/?pg=0&bbox=1902%2C-1962%2C3665%2C-945. Fejér, CD, VI/1, 91 omits 'sanctissimeque'.

[341] Karpat, 'Corona regni Hungariae', 288–9.   [342] Fejérpataky, *A Királyi kanczellária*, 41–5.

[343] Still the most thorough investigation, Karpat, 'Corona regni Hungariae', 298–9 lists several instances; however, he worked from editions, not the originals, and these are all either later transcripts or forgeries: the alleged charter of 1267 is a fourteenth-century transcript, those of 1274 and 1283 are forgeries: Szentpétery, *Regesta*, nos. 1519, 2500, 2846 (János Karácsonyi, *A hamis, hibáskeltű és keltezetlen oklevelek jegyzéke 1400-ig* (Budapest: Magyar Tudományos Akadémia, 1902), 29), 3238, respectively. The 1272 charter analysed above also has a faulty edition that uses 'sacra' instead of 'sancta': Fejér, CD, V/2, 47.

[344] 26 June 1292, MOL DF 256 331: https://archives.hungaricana.hu/hu/charters/view/12773/?pg= 0&bbox=-429%2C-2889%2C4559%2C-107; Joannes Bapt. Tkalčić, ed., *Monumenta historica episcopatus Zagrabiensis saec. XII et XIII*, vol. 1 (Zagreb, 1873), 228–9, no. 232; Szentpétery, *Regesta*, no. 3880. 10 January 1293, MOL DL 49684, https://archives.hungaricana.hu/hu/charters/view/12902/

208 STEPHEN I, THE FIRST CHRISTIAN KING OF HUNGARY

long been taken for granted that both the custom, and the belief that the royal crown of Hungary had belonged to Stephen, had existed much earlier and these merely happen to be the earliest extant mentions of a well-established custom.[345] At most, it has been pointed out that Andrew III's insistence on wearing Stephen I's crown can be explained by his dire need for legitimacy.[346] However, we need to pay more attention to the context, since Andrew III's charters referred to the royal crown earlier (1290–1), both in the sense of a physical crown, and in the construct 'service to the crown', without linking it to St Stephen.[347] Moreover, several earlier charters of Andrew III refer to his coronation without mentioning St Stephen's crown. One charter, dated 8 September 1290 and addressed to his relative King James of Sicily, mentions gaining the throne and crown by right and the order of birth.[348] Another, confirming trading privileges for inhabitants of the lands of the archbishopric of Esztergom, refers to ascending the throne, and receiving the crown of the kingdom of Hungary from the archbishop of Esztergom.[349] Thus, a closer examination of the first charters that associated the crown to Stephen and their context is in order.

The first charter was issued at the request of the cathedral chapter of Zagreb, about the royal donation of the right to collect toll from a market. The cathedral was dedicated to St Stephen, and the charter mentions Andrew's coronation 'with the diadem of the most holy King Stephen', and states that the chapter entreated Andrew 'for love of St Stephen'. In turn, the king indeed accedes to their request partly out of devotion to St Stephen, whose merits and prayers would preserve Andrew's throne and crown, or so the king hopes.[350] The second charter was issued after Magister Theodore, provost of Fehérvár and the king's vice-chancellor, had asked the king for an estate. Fulfilling his request, the king enumerates Theodore's merits in justification of the donation, among them in first place securing the physical crown for Andrew: 'as the custom is, we wanted to be crowned at Fehérvár with the crown and diadem of the most holy king Stephen;

?pg=4&bbox=151%2C-4218%2C8542%2C-81, Fejér, CD, VI/1, 236–40, at 237; Szentpétery, Regesta, no. 3900. Péter, 'The Holy Crown of Hungary', 433 argues this was the extant crown.

[345] Deér, A magyarok szent koronája, 171–7.   [346] Benda—Fügedi, magyar korona, 27–8.

[347] Fejér, CD, VI/1, 136; Szentpétery, Regesta, no. 3782 (9 August 1291): 'pro adeptione coronae nostrae diadematis, seu solio regiminis regni Hungariae'; 'pro fidelitate coronae regiae debita'. Ibid., no. 3784 (10 August 1291): 'pro...fidelitate coronae regiae debita'. Fejér, CD, VI/1, 139; Szentpétery, Regesta, no. 3820 (4 October 1291): 'nostrae coronationis insignia'.

[348] Ibid., no. 3662: 'successimus...in totius regni Hungarie gubernaculum, solium et coronam iure et ordine geniture', 'nostre...coronationis insignia vestre celsitudini nuntiantes'.

[349] Fejér, CD, VI/1, 55–8, at 56; Szentpétery, Regesta, no. 3668. Dated 22 September 1290, near Zólyom, there is no mention of who issued the charter.

[350] Coronation: 'preordinacio divine clemencie,...nos...ad tronum et coronam regalis fastigii sublimasset iure et ordine geniture et sanctissimi regis Stephani dyademate ex inmensa clemencia et misericordia ipsius beati regis Stephani fuissemus coronati'. Chapter asking for donation: 'pro salute nostra et amore divini nominis et ipsius beati regis Stephani'. King giving donation: 'Nos itaque ob reverenciam et devocionem, quam in ipso beato rege Stephano gerimus et habemus, cuius meritis et precibus tronum nostri regiminis pariter et nostram coronam conservari nutu divino indubitanter credimus et speramus, ac pro anime nostre remedio...'

THE HUNGARIAN CROWN 209

and certain rivals of our rule and coronation set up plots at first secretly, and then in the open, so that he would not be able to give us the crown of the holy king at the time of our coronation'; nonetheless, Theodore prevailed and 'gave us the same crown of King St Stephen at the necessary day and time'.[351] Both charters were issued by Master Theodore as vice-chancellor.

Was it genuinely long-standing custom to see the crown as St Stephen's? Alternatively, did Theodore elaborate on the usual idea of kings referring to 'our (holy) predecessors' and innovate by calling the crown St Stephen's, perhaps in the wake of Andrew's renewed problems with legitimacy as king of Hungary? The chancery was not a faceless bureaucracy; the ecclesiastics producing the charters had significant input into formulating them. That during Andrew's reign the supposed crown of St Stephen played a newly invented or at least newly emphasized role is confirmed by Ottokar of Horneck's early fourteenth-century *Steirische Reimchronik*. According to Ottokar, King Andrew III was clothed in garments that had been worn by St Stephen and crowned with 'St Stephen's crown'. Moreover, according to him, Hungarian nobles told Andrew that they did not have to swear loyalty to him until he swore to uphold the peace, obey the papacy, protect widows and orphans, regain lost Hungarian lands, and give just judgements. The king accordingly swore on 'St Stephen's crown' and other relics.[352] The existence of a coronation oath itself is confirmed by Andrew's charter, surviving in a contemporary transcript by the chapter of Alba Iulia (Gyulafehérvár), Transylvania; it states that the king took an oath after his coronation at a general congregation (the forerunner of Parliament) and lists the articles of the oath.[353] However, while several articles mention the 'Holy Kings' his predecessors, there is no mention of taking an oath on Stephen's crown; indeed there is no mention of Stephen's crown at all. The protection of the rights of the church of Fehérvár, however, features prominently, and the original charter had been issued by Master Theodore.

The available evidence thus, while it can never be fully conclusive, points in one direction: that Stephen's crown was not a reference point initially, but started

---

[351] MOL DL 49684, https://archives.hungaricana.hu/hu/charters/view/12902/?pg=4&bbox=151%2C-4218%2C8542%2C2C-81, Fejér, CD VI/1, 237: 'et coronari apud Albam Regalem, prout moris est, corona et dyademate Sanctissimi regis Stephani voluissemus; et quidam regiminis et coronationis nostrae aemuli, primitus insidias latenter, et demum in patulo, ne ipsa corona Sancti regis tempore coronationis nostrae dari nobis possit, et vt nostri regiminis auctoritas et salutis exordium regnicolarum differretur, posuissent; idem Magister Th. Praepositus cum summae fidelitatis feruore, subtiliter et caute, et vbi debuit potenter, et viribus laborans, omni casui fortunae se exponens, ipsam coronam Sancti Stephani Regis, nobis dedit et statuit die et tempore debito, ac placito coronationis nostrae.'
[352] 'dô krônet er si schône/ mit Sant Stephans krône', 'daz swuor er behalten schône/ ûf Sant Stephanes krône/ und ûf ander heiltum'. *Ottokars Österreichische Reimchronik*, part 1, ed. Joseph Seemüller (Hanover, 1890), *MGH, Deutsche Chroniken*, 5/1, 535–6.
[353] MOL DL 30586: https://archives.hungaricana.hu/hu/charters/view/310603/?pg=15&bbox=-2255%2C-5640%2C9611%2C212, Fejér, CD, VII/2, 139–47, no. 402 (1291); Szentpétery, *Regesta*, no. 3705.

210 STEPHEN I, THE FIRST CHRISTIAN KING OF HUNGARY

to be specifically mentioned from 1292. Were these merely the first explicit references, or was something new invented? While it is not impossible that the idea was older, there is contextual evidence that it was not; instead, joining elements that until then had been disparate, something new emerged. I would argue that it is no mere accident that Stephen's crown is mentioned from 1292 rather than from Andrew III's coronation in 1290. A novel regrouping of former ideas resulted in a new formulation through the active agency of the vice-chancellor Master Theodore, at a time when Andrew's succession had a new challenger. Thus claiming that a legitimate ruler had to be crowned by Stephen's crown and Andrew had been crowned in such a way could have been a new response to a new challenge. This would fit the pragmatic approach to the sacrality of kingship emphasized by Björn Weiler.[354] At the same time, Theodore, as provost of Fehérvár, whose church by then housed the coronation insignia for more than a century, was personally interested in augmenting the significance of the crown, as it enhanced the prestige of the church and its provost. Ecclesiastics played such a role elsewhere: the monks of St-Denis apparently quietly substituted the queen's crown as a coronation crown when 'Charlemagne's crown' was lost, while the dean and canons of Monza were instrumental in promoting Monza as the coronation site.[355]

What new threat could have prompted this change? Andrew's legitimacy had always been questionable.[356] His father had been a posthumous son of King Andrew II, and Andrew II's other sons, Béla IV of Hungary and Duke Coloman, considered him a bastard. Andrew's mother was a member of the Venetian Morosini family and he grew up in Venice. Initial attempts by some oligarchs to put Andrew on the Hungarian throne bore no fruit; yet as the reigning king Ladislas IV died assassinated without heirs in 1290, Archbishop Lodomer and some of the aristocracy backed Andrew. Other claimants, including Albert of Austria were frustrated in their hopes as Archbishop Lodomer crowned Andrew III king of Hungary on 23 July 1290.

The Angevin King Charles II of Naples, however, whose wife Mary was daughter of King Stephen V of Hungary, started a new campaign to put her on the throne in 1291.[357] He did not recognize Andrew's right to the throne and called on the Hungarian nobility to abandon Andrew and back Mary. By the start of 1292, Charles had an important ally in the baronial Kőszegi family in Hungary, especially John Kőszegi. They gained the right from Charles to wage war against

[354] Weiler, *Paths to Kingship*, 344–5.
[355] Danielle Gaborit-Chopin, 'Les couronnes du sacre des rois et des reines au trésor de Saint-Denis', *Bulletin Monumental*, 133, no. 2 (1975): 165–74, at 172; Elze, 'Monza und die Eiserne Krone'.
[356] For a biography and details of these events: Zsoldos, *III. András*, especially 178–80.
[357] Vinni Lucherini, 'The Hungarian *Constitutiones synodales* of 1309 and the "Holy Crown": the theological use of an art object as political symbol', in *Political Theology in Medieval and Early Modern Europe: Discourses, Rites, and Representations*, ed. Montserrat Herrero, Jaume Aurell, Angela C. Miceli Stout (Turnhout: Brepols, 2017), 267–83, at 269–70 on events.

THE HUNGARIAN CROWN   211

Andrew's followers; at the same time, Mary transferred her claim to the throne to her son, Charles Martell. The Angevins were also building their system of alliance in Croatia and Slavonia. From April 1292, Charles Martell started to use the Hungarian royal title. Archbishop Lodomer excommunicated John Kőszegi, and Andrew tried to reinforce the loyalty of some baronial families, but in the spring of 1292, the Kőszegi started a military revolt against the king. This was only suppressed by July. Therefore, the appearance of the first mention of 'St Stephen's crown' on 26 June 1292 fits into this sequence of events rather too well to be a coincidence. In June, Andrew was also rewarding those who distinguished themselves in the fight against the Kőszegi.

It is thus plausible that the Angevin-instigated revolt triggered the formation of the idea that Hungarian kings must be crowned with 'St Stephen's crown' and Andrew had been thus crowned. In this, we can see a new claim born from the amalgamation and logical extension of earlier ideas: that of a papal crown invented by Hartvic and echoed in thirteenth-century papal documents, and the association of kingship and coronation with St Stephen. These elements led to a new interpretation, with a keen focus now on the crown. Such retrospective attribution of a crown is not surprising; the *Reichskrone* started to be thought of as the former crown of Charlemagne from the fourteenth century.[358] Moreover, a novel focus on the crown for legitimization exactly when political fragility threatened can also be seen in France: the crown first appeared as sole indicator of sovereign power on the seal Louis IX's had made for the regents in 1270, who were to govern during the king's absence on crusade.[359] In 1300, 'sacro dyademate coronati' occurs in one of Andrew's charters, when he describes the services of someone prior to, as well as after, his royal coronation.[360] The expression could have been borrowed from antiquity or a medieval author.[361]

The crown's new identity and function were reinforced in the early fourteenth century due to a change in dynasty. Upon Andrew III's death, with the extinction of the Árpáds, several pretenders with an equally good claim to the throne appeared. The succession was decided by military means, and eventually, the Angevin Charles Robert won. Yet he had to be crowned three times.[362] The first time, directly after his victory in 1301, a newly made crown was used; he was re-crowned in 1309 with a crown blessed by a papal legate, and finally a third time in 1310 with the recovered 'Holy Crown',[363] which had earlier been held by his rivals,

---

[358] See below.   [359] Pinoteau, *La symbolique royale Française*, 283.
[360] 9 April 1300, MOL DL 102890: https://archives.hungaricana.hu/en/charters/view/14752/?pg=0 &bbox=433%2C-2843%2C2896%2C-1608; Szentpétery, *Regesta*, 4296.
[361] The charter was written by Stephen, vice-chancellor of the king, who may have been a *doctor decretorum*: Fejérpataky, *A királyi kanczellária*, 146. On 'sacrum diadema', *Thesaurus Linguae Latinae*, vol. 5, pt. 1 (Leipzig: Teubner, 1909–14), 945–6; I thank Vedran Sulovsky for this reference.
[362] János M. Bak, *Königtum und Stände in Ungarn im 14.–16. Jahrhundert* (Wiesbaden: Franz Steiner Verlag, 1973), 13–22.
[363] 'cum sancta corona': *SRH* I, 486.

212 STEPHEN I, THE FIRST CHRISTIAN KING OF HUNGARY

first the Czech Wenceslas, crowned king of Hungary in 1301; and then Otto of Wittelsbach, crowned king in 1305. In this context, it was stated that 'St Stephen's crown' must be used for coronation to be valid.[364] The Hungarian bishops signalled how the inhabitants of the realm invested royal rights in the crown.[365] Thus in the context of rivalry for the throne, the function of the crown as an indispensable tool of political legitimation was fixed.[366] One may question whether the crown was so essential because its meaning had already been fixed, or whether those opposed to Charles Robert used the excuse of the missing crown to refuse to acknowledge him and thereby contributed to set such a requirement. From then, coronation with 'St Stephen's crown' remained constitutionally essential until the end of the monarchy.[367]

This was also when 'sacra corona' emerged. The papal legate Cardinal Gentilis held a synod at Buda between 8 May and 14 July 1309, where he decreed that if

[364] Charles' charter from 1315 described this; Gyula Kristó, ed., *Anjou-kori oklevéltár*, vol. 4, *1315–1317* (Budapest—Szeged: Szegedi Középkorász Műhely, 1996), 56, no. 131, transcribed in 1317, 200, no. 530; Ferdinand Knauz, ed., *Monumenta Ecclesiae Strigoniensis*, vol. 2 (Esztergom, 1882), 709–11, no. 806, at 710–11 (transcription of 1317 at 734, no. 838): 'primo videlicet tempore domini Gentilis, tituli Sancti Martini in montibus presbiteri Cardinalis, apostolice sedis legati de latere missi, quia corona Sancti regis Stephani, progenitoris nostri, qua de more gentis Vngarice reges Vngarie solent coronari, per infideles illicitos detentores rapta detinebatur, noua corona, specialiter pro nobis fabricata, per eundem dominum Legatum benedicta, et auctorizata, per ipsum dominum Thomam Archiepiscopum iuxta consuetudinem regni nostri approbatam, et constitucionem, ab ipso domino Legato tunc de nouo editam, que habet, vt nonnisi honorem nostre coronacionis nos et nostri successores per ipsum archiepiscopum sumpmeremus, quemadmodum ceteri reges, nostri antecessores habuerunt solium regale conscendentes, ipso nouo dyademate extitimus coronati, et licet huiusmodi coronacionis modus sufficiens exstitisset; tamen vt opinioni gentis Vngarice satis fieret, et vt scandalum de medio vulgi tolleretur, recuperata et rehabita per sollicitam curam eiusdem domini archiepiscopi ipsa sancta corona ab illicitis detentoribus, rursum in loco debito, videlicet in Alba regali, vbi solitum est ab antiquo reges Vngarie coronari, facta conuocacione vniuersorum prelatorum, Barronum fidelium Regni nostri, obseruataque sollempnitate consueta, et a progenitoribus nostris constituta, solium nostri regiminis conscendimus, et de manibus eiusdem domini Thome Archiepiscopi dyademate regio, videlicet eadem sancta corona denuo extitimus coronati.' See also Benda—Fügedi, *magyar korona*, 30; Emma Bartoniek, 'A magyar királyválasztási jog', *Századok*, 70 (1936): 359–406, at 388; Pál Engel, *The Realm of St Stephen: A History of Medieval Hungary 895–1526* (London: I.B. Tauris, 2001), 128–30. It should be noted that repeated coronations were known in medieval Europe: Carpenter, *The Reign of Henry III*, 445; Johanna Dale, *Inauguration and Liturgical Kingship in the Long Twelfth Century* (York: York Medieval Press, 2019), 136–41.

[365] Gentilis 'cernens, quod ob ipsius carentiam, cui multum reverentie atque auctoritatis ex dicti regni incolarum opinione defertur, quasi in eo sit ius regium constitutum unde et detentores ipsius audacia cresccere et regie dignitati poterit plurimum derogari...idem diadema, donec sic occupatum existeret, ne cum eo reges coronarentur aut possent coronari, penitus interdixit'. Letter of the Hungarian archbishops and bishops to the Pope, 29(?) June 1309, Buda in *Acta legationis cardinalis Gentilis, 1307–1311* Monumenta Vaticana historiam Regni Hungariae illustrantia, Series I, vol. 2 (Budapest, 1885; a reprint edition also exists, Budapest: METEM, 2000), 352–4, no. LXVII, at 353 (also describes making of a new crown, blessed by the legate, and the coronation); Emma Bartoniek, 'Corona és regnum', *Századok*, 68 (1934): 314–31, at 321.

[366] The crown gaining a new legal significance with the extinction of St Stephen's dynasty: Szekfű, 'Szent István', *Emlékkönyv*, 12, repr. 538; Péter, 'The Holy Crown of Hungary', 434–5; Teszelszky, *Az ismeretlen korona*, 40.

[367] Péter, 'The Holy Crown of Hungary', 437.

'St Stephen's crown', the 'sacra corona' that had been a gift from the pope, could not be recovered from Ladislas, voyvode of Transylvania, who at the time had it in his possession, until a deadline, then 'pro interdicta, profana et reproba tamdiu ab omnibus habeatur'—that is, it should be held by all to be banned, profane and rejected, until it is returned. Instead, a crown the legate had ordered to be made would be solemnly blessed by him or through his authority and could be used for coronations henceforth. Should this, too, be wrongfully appropriated, the archbishops should ban its use until it is returned, have a new one made and bless it. Finally, the synod decreed that if anyone in the future had the temerity to steal by stealth or seize by violence the 'sacra corona', or that or those that had been substituted for it, they should be excommunicated.[368] Therefore, the term 'sacra' referred to the consecrated (rather than 'holy') crown;[369] otherwise, it would have been impossible to deprive it of its status and put another crown in its place. The legate also took this opportunity to assert in a document signed by papal notaries that the popes and the Roman church had the right to confirm and crown Hungary's kings.[370]

Thus, the idea that Hungary's kings had to be crowned by St Stephen's crown merged with the idea of a consecrated crown, but the distinctions between 'sacra' and 'sancta', and between *corona* as physical crown and royal dignity were soon blurred, as seen in Charles I's letter of 1315, turning the physical crown 'holy'.[371] As research has shown for both medieval and more modern times, traditions could develop very fast; thus, it is not surprising that within two decades, a new idea could become embedded.[372] This also jibes with the Angevins' cult of the Arpadian dynastic saints: the theme of the 'three holy kings' (Stephen, Emeric,

---

[368] Canon III. De corona regis, in *Acta legationis cardinalis Gentilis*, 273–5: the pope 'sacram destinavit coronam' to Stephen; 'per nos seu auctoritate nostra benedicatur sollemniter qua in locum succedente prioris, dictus rex successoresque sui coronentur'. 'Statuimus, ut si quis deinceps in eam temeritatem proruperit, quod prefatam sacram coronam, vel eas, quas illius loco subrogari contigerit... furtive subripiat vel per violentiam occupet... sententiam excommunicationis incurrat.' The original does not survive, only two fifteenth-century copies, on which the edition is based. Lucherini, 'The Hungarian *Constitutiones synodales* of 1309', 272–80.

[369] Hans-Werner Goetz, '*Sacer* und *sanctus*. Sakralität und Heiligkeit im frühmittelalterlichen Verständnis', in *Heilige: Bücher—Leiber—Orte*, ed. Daniela Wagner, Hanna Wimmer (Berlin: Reimer, 2018), 11–25, although these distinctions were not universal.

[370] *Acta legationis cardinalis Gentilis*, 115–19, no. XXXIX, Pest, 27 November 1308, Publicum instrumentum de electione Caroli, praesente et interveniente cardinale Gentili. He states that St Stephen 'coronam a Romano pontifice consecratam acceperit', and against the nobles who do not want to accept a king confirmed by a papal legate, asserts 'quod etiam perpetuis futuris temporibus veri summi pontifices et ipse Romana ecclesia haberet ius confirmandi et coronandi reges Ungarie'.

[371] See note 364.

[372] The tradition of 'St Edward's crown' was established very fast: initiated by Henry III, it was 'custom' under his successor: Martin Holmes, 'New light on St Edward's crown', *Archaeologia*, 97 (1959): 213–23, at 215; so were 'traditions' at St Denis: Spiegel, 'The cult of St Denis', 63–4. More broadly, Eric Hobsbawm, Terence Ranger, ed., *The Invention of Tradition* (Cambridge: Cambridge University Press, 1983).

214   STEPHEN I, THE FIRST CHRISTIAN KING OF HUNGARY

and Ladislas) in art took off under their patronage to reinforce continuity and thus legitimacy.[373]

It does not seem coincidence that two other developments date from this time. First, colourful stories started to multiply about stealing or hiding the crown in order to achieve (or prevent) legitimate coronation. In contrast to the earlier putative allusions, whose significance depends on modern historians' interpretation, from the fourteenth century onwards, texts are explicit about the link between a specific 'holy crown' and legitimate coronation, hence the need to secure the physical object. Second, the terms 'sancta corona' and 'sacra corona' to designate royal power independent of the person of the king, as well as the physical crown needed for coronation, occur in numerous charters from the fourteenth century onwards.[374] Such continuity from this time and the strength of the evidence also bolsters the case that instead of being the accidental first explicit expressions of age-old ideas, it was only from the end of the thirteenth century that the crown became 'St Stephen's' and only from the fourteenth that people saw it as the 'Holy Crown'. By the end of the fifteenth century, the 'Holy Crown' was so deeply ingrained in political thought in Hungary that people could even joke about it. The Italian humanist Antonio Bonfini, King Matthias's court historian, writing in 1495 recorded that 'whoever you see crowned with the holy crown, even if it were an ox, must be worshipped and treated as a sacrosanct king'.[375]

Therefore, while the notion of a holy crown did not develop in a vacuum, it was also much more specifically tied to the particular context of the late thirteenth and early fourteenth centuries than hitherto assumed.[376] Although pre-existing ideas about Stephen's significance conditioned the invention of 'St Stephen's crown', they were not in themselves sufficient to produce the 'Holy Crown'. Celebrated as the first Christian king who converted the Hungarians, Stephen was

---

[373] Tünde Wehli, 'Az 1083-ban kanonizált szentek kultusza középkori művészetünkben', in Művelődéstörténeti tanulmányok a magyar középkorról, ed. Erik Fügedi (Budapest: Gondolat, 1986), 54–60; Terézia Kerny, 'A magyar szent királyok tisztelete és ikonográfiája a XIII. századtól a XVII. századig', in Uralkodók, királyi szentek: Válogatott ikonográfiai és kultusztörténeti tanulmányok, Terézia Kerny (Budapest: MTA Bölcsészettudományi Kutatóközpont Művészettörténeti Intézet, 2018), 9–63. Emeric was never king, but the type is called thus.

[374] From the first two decades, for example: Imre Nagy, Anjou-kori okmánytár, vol. 1, 1301–1321 (Budapest, 1878), 289–91, no. 265; 515–17, no. 465; Gyula Kristó, ed., Anjou-kori Oklevéltár, vol. 3, 1311–1314 (Budapest—Szeged: Szegedi Középkorász Műhely, 1994), 219, no. 487; vol. 5, 1318–1320 (Budapest—Szeged: Szegedi Középkorász Műhely, 1998), 180, no. 454; László Blazovich, ed., Anjou-kori Oklevéltár, vol. 8, 1324 (Budapest—Szeged: Szegedi Középkorász Műhely, 1993), 108, no. 203. In just one year, 1339, there are six occurrences: Ferenc Piti, ed., Anjou-kori Oklevéltár, vol. 23, 1339 (Budapest—Szeged: Szegedi Középkorász Műhely, 1999), nos. 340, 563, 576, 717, 740, 747. Methodical research on the fourteenth-century usage of sancta/sacra corona may reveal more details about the development of the notion.

[375] 'Quencunque sacra corona coronatum videris, etiamsi bos fuerit, adorato et pro sacrosancto rege ducito et observato.' Antonius de Bonfinis Rerum Ungaricarum Decades, vol. 4, 41, IV:III.8–9. This was probably aimed at King Vladislav (Ulászló) II. György Szerémi, who was chaplain to Kings Louis II and John, in his memoirs written c. 1545–7, calls Vladislav II an ox and discusses how this sobriquet started: György Szerémi, A mohácsi vész kora (Szeged, 1941), 27, 30.

[376] On the gradual process of emergence: Tóth, A Hartvik-legenda kritikájához, 126.

THE HUNGARIAN CROWN   215

soon regarded as the holy predecessor of Hungary's kings. His laws and his donations acquired a different standing from those of other kings; annual law-days
were held on his feast day in Fehérvár where he was buried. Ecclesiastical texts
from the thirteenth century derived the king's right to the throne from being the
heir of St Stephen, even though he had no direct heir when he died.[377] Andrew II
in 1233 in the oath of Bereg dictated by a papal legate, then Ladislas IV, also
swearing according to the stipulations of a legate, emphasized that, as the second
text put it, 'we, along with the other most serene kings of Hungary, who descended
from the same shining seed, gained our... crown in our ancestor King St Stephen
from the Roman Church'.[378]

Thus, legitimation was tied to Stephen, which prepared the ground for identifying the coronation crown as his. By the thirteenth century, political rights were
also derived from Stephen. Therefore, linking valid coronation to 'Stephen's
crown' was a logical extension of the thought embodied in the Golden Bull of
1222, for example. Nobles demanded that 'the liberty of the nobles and others of
our kingdom established by King St Stephen' be restored, and so at their request
King Andrew II granted to them in the Golden Bull 'the liberty conceded by the
holy king'.[379] Further, the church of Fehérvár founded by Stephen that became the
place of coronation and burial, housed the regalia and throne, also enabled the
association of that key attribute of kingship, a physical crown, to Stephen.

Hartvic's story about a papal crown sent to Stephen, and Stephen's very name
may have played into the notion of his 'Holy Crown'. The *Legenda Maior*, in line
with etymological explanations that were very popular in the Middle Ages, stated
that the Greek *stephanos* means 'crowned' in Latin (Hartvic corrected this to
'crown'), and the etymology was used to suggest that Stephen was predestined to
both earthly and heavenly crowns—that is, to royal power and eternal glory
through the crown of salvation.[380] None of this led inevitably to 'Holy Crown', but
prepared the ground. It is debatable if emerging ideas about an angelic crown

---

[377] Szekfű, 'Szent István', *Emlékkönyv*, 9, repr. 535.

[378] Bartoniek, 'A magyar királyválasztási jog', 363. 'Stephani...huius sancti regis hereditario iure,
per Dei gratiam, regni solium obtinemus, cupientes predicti Sancti Stephani...vestigia imitare...'
(1233). (Augustin Theiner, *Vetera Monumenta Historia Hungaricam Sacram Illustrantia*, vol. 1 (Rome,
1859), 116; Szentpétery: *Regesta*, 501.) 'In progenitore nostro sancto rege Stephano...una cum reli-
quis serenissimis regibus Hungariae claro germine descendentibus ab eadem [Romana Ecclesia] regni
gubernaculum suscepimus et coronam...' (Theiner, *Vetera Monumenta*, vol. 1, 339; Szentpétery:
Regesta, 2962).

[379] Bak et al., *Laws*, 34.

[380] 'Nomen sibi impositus est Stephanus, quod alienum a consilio dei non credimus, Stephanus
quippe Grece, coronatus sonat Latine. Ipsum quod et in hoc seculo deus voluit ad regni potentiam, et
in futuro corona beatitudinis semper permanentis redimere decrevit ad percipiendum iugis indeficientem gloriam.' *SRH* II, 380–1. Incorporated with slight changes by Hartvic, who emphasized the
crown even more by adding 'coronare' between 'seculo' and 'deus': 'Stephanus quippe Grece corona
sonat Latine. Ipsum quidem et in hoc seculo coronare deus voluit ad regni potentiam, et in futuro
corona beatitudinis semper manentis redimere decrevit ad percipiendam vite iugiter indeficientem
gloriam.' *SRH* II, 406–7. On crown of heavenly life and royal insignia, see Schramm, *Herrschaftszeichen*,
vol. 2, 378.

216 STEPHEN I, THE FIRST CHRISTIAN KING OF HUNGARY

contributed to this identification as well, or, on the contrary, the notion of an angelic crown developed due to the existing 'Holy Crown'. The first appearance of the angelic crown comes from the illustrations of the fourteenth-century *Illuminated Chronicle*, but according to some, the idea was older.[381] The images show Kings Géza (r. 1074–7) and Ladislas (r. 1077–95), crowned by angels, although the text only mentions that Ladislas had a vision of an angel crowning Géza prior to the battle with Solomon, while Ladislas did not want to be crowned.[382] In a different episode, linked to Otto of Wittelsbach, the fourteenth-century chronicles also claimed that Pannonia cannot be deprived of the crown given by an angel, blurring the distinction between the coronation crown, by then believed to be St Stephen's, and the crown brought by an angel.[383] Eventually, the idea of an angelic coronation was transferred to St Stephen (possibly facilitated by Hartvic's story of an angel admonishing the pope to give the crown to Stephen's envoy), with the first known visual representation from between 1460 and 1470; the belief was widely held later.[384]

Having a holy crown was not unique to Hungary, despite numerous assertions to the contrary. Crowns elsewhere rose to similar prominence: St Edward's crown, the *Reichskrone*, several crowns of 'Charlemagne', and the Iron Crown of Lombardy (or Monza) all had similar legitimizing status, and some were called holy. What is unusual in the Hungarian case was not the medieval or even modern use of the crown, but its twentieth- and twenty-first-century fate,[385] as some of the other crowns were destroyed, and the remaining ones lost their legitimizing function. A brief comparison demonstrates this. A variety of crowns were used for the coronation of English kings, until King Henry III in the twelfth century promoted 'St Edward's crown', which subsequently became the coronation crown; in the fourteenth century there was even an attempt to turn it into 'Alfred's crown'.[386] Royal insignia including a crown were referred to as 'Charlemagne's' in

---

[381] Images in facsimile: *The Hungarian Illuminated Chronicle*, 83, 92. Byzantine iconographic influence is usually assumed. Terézia Kerny, 'Az angyali koronázás motívuma Szt. István ikonográfiájában', in *Uralkodók, királyi szentek*, 64–86, at 67 (German tr. Terézia Kerny, 'Das Engelskrönungsmotiv in der Ikonographie der König Stephans des Heiligen', *Acta Ethnographica Hungarica*, 49, nos. 3–4 (2004): 313–42). Péter Váczy, 'Az angyal hozta korona', in *A magyar történelem korai századaiból*, Péter Váczy (Budapest: MTA Történettudományi Intézet, 1994), 94–102, at 98–9 and 'Thietmar', 40–1, hypothesizes that a crown from heaven was an old Hungarian popular belief, and the basis of the crown's holiness, with no evidence. Edina Eszenyi, 'Corona Angelica Pannoniae:… "ecce Angelus Domini"', *Arts*, 8, no. 4 (2019): 141, https://doi.org/10.3390/arts8040141.

[382] *SRH* I, 388, 405. [383] Ibid., 484. Péter, 'The Holy Crown of Hungary', 434–5.

[384] Kerny, 'Az angyali koronázás', 70. It was reported by the seventeenth-century traveller, Edward Brown: László Veszprémy, 'The Holy Crown of Saint Stephen', in *Saint Stephen and His Country: A Newborn Kingdom in Central Europe—Hungary*, ed. Attila Zsoldos (Budapest: Lucidus Kiadó, 2001), 95–109, at 109.

[385] Thus, I only agree with the second part of the observation by Péter, Holy Crown, 432, that the 'Holy Crown tradition went deeper and lasted much longer' than elsewhere.

[386] Carpenter, *The Reign of Henry III*, 448–55; on Alfred's crown, 448; Holmes, 'New Light on St Edward's Crown'.

THE HUNGARIAN CROWN   217

France at the latest from the fourteenth century.[387] 'Charlemagne's crown' was used for the coronations of French kings until it was melted down in 1590; then another, smaller, but in many ways similar crown until then used for the queen was substituted to disguise the loss and called 'Charlemagne's'.[388] The transformations of another French crown that included supposed relics from the Crucifixion (a nail and a thorn from the Crown of Thorns) also signal how a crown could accumulate diverse identifications over time: it was variously called 'Holy Crown' (*sancta corona*) and crown of the Lord by the end of the thirteenth century, and St Louis's crown by 1350; later authors used one or the other of these names.[389] Exceptionally, it was even used for royal coronation.[390]

French kings were not the only ones to lay claim to Charlemagne's crown: another crown, also called Charlemagne's, was employed in crowning kings of the Romans in the late medieval and early modern period.[391] The *Reichskrone* (dated to the second half of the tenth century with eleventh-century additions of the arch and cross, or to the early twelfth century), although it was not seen as necessary for royal coronation for a long time, because the *sine qua non* of legitimate coronation was enthronement on the throne in Aachen, was nonetheless called 'holy' from the thirteenth century and 'Charlemagne's' at the latest by the fourteenth.[392] It also demonstrates how new objects could be retrospectively attributed to famous kings through association. The link between the throne in Aachen and Charlemagne was extended to the crown centuries later. From the early fourteenth century, the Polish crown was considered to have belonged to Bolesław I the Brave (r. 992–1025), and in modern times the misfortunes of some kings were blamed on using another crown.[393] The 'St Wenceslas crown', a circlet crown with lilies closed with crossed bands displaying a cross on top, was made for Charles IV in 1346 and the abstract concept of *corona* as monarchical power was soon linked to this crown.[394]

---

[387] Hervé Pinoteau, 'Les deux couronnes françaises dites "de Charlemagne"', *Bulletin de la Société nationale des Antiquaires de France 1972* (1974): 22–9, at 22, and Pinoteau, *La symbolique royale Française*, 293–5 argues the crowns are identical to those made under Philippe Auguste and given to St-Denis by Louis IX. Gaborit-Chopin, 'Les couronnes', 165–74, at 168 argues that Philippe Auguste's are not the same crowns as those later called 'Charlemagne's', and dates the latter crowns to the second half of the thirteenth century.

[388] Ibid., 168–72; Pinoteau, *La symbolique royale Française*, 278–9, 368.

[389] Ibid., 278. There is disagreement over the origin of the crown, regarding whether a reliquary crown existed in the eleventh century, or was made under Suger in the twelfth century, or in the thirteenth century.

[390] Ibid., 293.   [391] Petersohn, 'Über monarchische Insignien', 90–1.

[392] Jürgen Petersohn, 'Die Reichsinsignien im Krönungsbrauch und Herrscherzeremoniell des Mittelalters', in Kramp, *Krönungen*, vol. 1, 151–60, at 158 (on throne); Nikolaus Gussone, 'Ritus, Recht und Geschichtsbewußtsein. Thron und Krone in der Tradition Karls des Großen', in Kramp, *Krönungen*, vol. 1, 35–47, at 39–40.

[393] Aleksander Gieysztor, 'Gesture in the coronation ceremonies of medieval Poland', in *Coronations: Medieval and Early Modern Monarchic Ritual*, 152–64, at 159.

[394] Alexander Bělohlávek, 'Die böhmischen Krönungsinsignien', *Zeitschrift für Kunstgeschichte*, 53 (1990): 209–15.

218   STEPHEN I, THE FIRST CHRISTIAN KING OF HUNGARY

Scholars disagree about the Iron Crown of Monza's rise to become the crown of Italy: some believe that Conrad II's coronation as King of Italy in 1026 set the scene for Monza as the location, while, according to another view, the 1026 coronation is a later myth.[395] While no evidence exists that kings were crowned with the Iron Crown up until the fourteenth century, from then it was common knowledge that kings of the *regnum Italiae* had to be crowned with the iron crown.[396] Thereafter, some rulers went to great lengths to secure their coronation with it.[397] Matteo Villani referred to it as 'santa corona del ferro' in his description of the coronation of Charles IV at Monza.[398] It was also credited with multiple significance: that it held a nail from the Crucifixion, and was worn by Constantine, and that it was necessary for the coronation of a legitimate king of the Kingdom of Italy or Lombardy. Myth was also connected to an object retroactively: the legend of an iron crown significantly pre-dated the identification of a particular object as the iron crown.[399]

Further myths were woven around these crowns, such as the belief that the Iron Crown of Monza was miraculously protected against theft.[400] It was also deployed for modern legitimation, and we can observe a snowball effect, with the crown gathering importance in this regard in the modern period, without having such a role earlier. Although the Iron Crown 'of the ancient Lombards' had no part in political legitimation for roughly 250 years between c. 1550 and 1800, yet Napoleon saw coronation with the crown as essential for legitimizing his rule in Italy; he also created the Order of the Iron Crown to reward his Italian followers.[401] The crown continued to be necessary for coronation in the kingdom of Lombardy-Veneto.[402] The Habsburgs kept it in Vienna after 1848 as a supreme symbol of their power over Italy.[403] For the House of Savoy, the Iron Crown came to symbolize the nation, the kings deriving their power from popular will.[404]

---

[395] Carlo Paganini, 'Monza and the Royal Coronations of Lombardy', in Buccellati, *The Iron Crown*, vol. 1, 11–44, at 18; Reinhard Elze, 'Monza und die Eiserne Krone im Mittelalter', ibid., 45–59, English tr. 307–18.

[396] Elze, 'Monza und die Eiserne Krone', 59, English tr. 316–17.

[397] Felipe Ruiz Martín, 'Coronación de Carlos V en Bolonia', in Buccellati, *The Iron Crown*, vol. 1, 117–56, English tr. 319–34.

[398] Diverse versions of this text exist, some of which do not include 'santa' but 'seconda corona', but the most recent critical edition, Matteo Villani, *Cronica: Con la continuazione di Filippo Villani*, ed. Giuseppe Porta (Parma: Ugo Guanda Editore, 1995), vol. 1, 532 has 'santa corona'. See also Elena Abramov-van Rijk, 'The Italian experience of the Holy Roman Emperor Charles IV: musical and literary aspects', *Early Music History*, 37 (2018): 1–44, at 43, doi: 10.1017/S0261127918000025; Cassanelli, 'Art and politics', 73–115, at 92.

[399] Elze, 'Monza und die Eiserne Krone'.

[400] Peter Burke, 'Myth and history', in Buccellati, *The Iron Crown*, vol. 1, 3–8, at 3.

[401] Alain Pillepich, 'Napoléon Ier et la couronne de fer', in Buccellati, *The Iron Crown*, vol. 1, 197–212, English tr. 335–43.

[402] Henrike Mraz, 'Die Eiserne Krone und das Lombardo-venetianische Königreich im Vormärz', in Buccellati, *The Iron Crown*, vol. 1, 225–50, English tr. 344–52.

[403] Giorgio Rumi, 'The Iron Crown between Austria and Italy', in Buccellati, *The Iron Crown*, vol. 1, 251–72, at 272.

[404] Giorgio Rumi, 'The Savoy', in Buccellati, *The Iron Crown*, vol. 1, 287–96.

THE HUNGARIAN CROWN   219

Finally, royal thrones, swords and other objects could also fulfil a similar legit-imizing function to crowns, many of them retrospectively attributed to a putative first possessor, such as Charlemagne's throne in Aachen (necessary for legitimate coronation[405]), 'Charlemagne's sword' used for girding the king of the Romans at the coronation in Aachen;[406] the coronation sword in France from the late twelfth century (called Charlemagne's Joyeuse in the thirteenth century) and the stand-ard of St-Denis, later called oriflamme, also attributed to Charlemagne from the early thirteenth century;[407] 'St Edward's sword' in thirteenth-century England;[408] 'St Wenceslas's sword' in fourteenth-century Bohemia;[409] and Szczerbiec, the Polish coronation sword believed to have belonged to Bolesław I from the second half of the fourteenth century.[410]

Thus using a legitimizing object as part of the regalia, including the ascription of a crown to an earlier ruler who is seen as particularly significant, turning it into the coronation crown and using it for legitimation is not uniquely Hungarian. Moreover, clearly no historical link was needed to the supposed first owner of the crown for the rise of such myths. Myths could be quickly established and their great antiquity taken for granted, when in fact there was no historical basis for the claims.

New research may throw more light on the issue, but at present, it seems that the notion of a holy crown that had been Stephen's developed piecemeal over more than a decade. The very occasional references to 'sancta corona', perhaps in 1256 and certainly in 1272 and 1291, were due to circumstances where shaky and contested royal power was innovatively buttressed by clerics, perhaps combining the king's right to the throne from descent from 'holy kings' with the abstract notion of the crown as monarchical power, creating 'sancta corona'. This, however, by no means became standard; indeed, it was the exception, and referred to royal dignity rather than to the physical crown. Andrew III's dire need for legitimacy gave rise to the idea that kings had to be crowned with St Stephen's crown. In the fourteenth century, in the context of rivalry for succession, this was quickly blurred with 'sacra corona' in the sense of the consecrated coronation crown. The distinctions were forgotten, creating 'Holy Crown', the physical coronation crown. Stephen's alleged holy crown played a key role in royal legitimacy from this time

---

[405] Mario Kramp, 'Krönungen und Könige in der Nachfolge Karls des Großen: Eine Geschichte und ihre Bilder', in Kramp, *Krönungen*, vol. 1, 2–18, at 5–8; Petersohn, 'Die Reichsinsignien', in Kramp, *Krönungen*, vol. 1, 157–8; Rolf Große, 'Parallele und Kontrast: Reims und Aachen', in Kramp, *Krönungen*, vol. 1, 407–15, at 411–13.

[406] Kramp, *Krönungen*, vol. 1, 329, no. 3–6.

[407] Pinoteau, *La symbolique royale Française*, 318–20, 618–26; image of the sword in Kramp, *Krönungen*, vol. 1, 380, no. 4–1; Gabrielle M. Spiegel, 'The cult of St Denis and Capetian kingship', *Journal of Medieval History*, 1 (1975): 43–69, at 58–9.

[408] Carpenter, *The Reign of Henry III*, 452.   [409] Kramp, *Krönungen*, vol. 2, 533–4, no. 6–32.

[410] Jan Dąbrowski, 'Corona regni Poloniae au XIVe s.', *Bulletin International de l'Académie Polonaise des Sciences et Lettres*, Classe de Philologie—classe d'Histoire et de Philosophie, no. supplémentaire 7 (1953): 41–64, at 46.

220 STEPHEN I, THE FIRST CHRISTIAN KING OF HUNGARY

on; the equation of the royal crown with St Stephen's crown and the requirement that it be used for a coronation to be valid persisted. Hartvic's story of the pope sending a crown to Stephen was also attached to the 'Holy Crown'.

In addition to being essential for legitimacy, the 'Holy Crown' came to be seen as the guarantor of the fate of the kingdom. A shift in its meaning also turned the crown into a tool of the estates, representing the nobles as the community of the realm.[411] This allowed governance even in opposition to the king by the estates, who imprisoned King Sigismund in 1401 and issued decrees 'auctoritate iurisdictionis sacrae Coronae regni'.[412] In practice, kings were able to rule without it, although they could not donate lands in perpetuity; yet they endeavoured to get it back. Thus in 1440, Władysław was crowned with a crown taken from St Stephen's head reliquary, with the estates depriving the coronation crown, in the hands of Frederick III of Habsburg, of its validity (as with Cardinal Gentilis in the previous century), but making several attempts to have the crown returned; Matthias Corvinus had already been ruling for five years when he was able to redeem the crown from Frederick III, in 1463 for an enormous sum, eighty thousand gold florins, and various concessions; even then, he waited with the coronation.[413] Perhaps it was this absence of the coronation crown, as well as his lack of royal blood that made Matthias particularly interested in the theme of angelic coronation.[414] The crown continued to play a role in wars and anti-Habsburg rebellions.[415] Much later, the 'doctrine of the Holy Crown' was woven around the object.

4. The Doctrine of the Holy Crown

The 'doctrine of the Holy Crown', 'a historicized political ideology'[416] made the crown the central piece in constitutional and political thought. At its very centre, and providing its potent force, is the claim that the doctrine had existed, unchanged, since the beginnings of the Hungarian realm. Its basic definition consists of public authority vested in the Holy Crown, whose members, the king and 'nation' (a concept that itself underwent significant redefinitions), divide the exercise of that public authority. Even the basic definition, however, is slippery, as details change in the writings of different authors; for example the king may or may not be explicitly designated as the head in the organicist imagery. The alleged

---

[411] de Cevins, 'Les origines médiévales de la doctrine de la Sainte couronne', 183–6.
[412] Bartoniek, 'Corona és regnum', 324.
[413] Emma Bartoniek, *A magyar királykoronázások története* (Budapest, 1939 repr. Budapest: Akadémiai Kiadó, 1987), 64–5; Bak—Pálffy, *Crown and Coronation*, 169–70; Pálosfalvi, 'Koronázástól koronázásig', 136–59.
[414] Kerny, 'Az angyali koronázás', 71–3.   [415] Teszelszky, *Az ismeretlen korona*, 83–158.
[416] Kardos, *A szentkorona-tan története*, 7.

THE HUNGARIAN CROWN   221

doctrine ties together arguments about the political system, rights, and territory, and offers historical justification centred on Stephen I and a claim to uniqueness. The doctrine is making a comeback, propagating the nationalist myth of a unique Hungarian constitutionalism.[417]

The doctrine in fact is a markedly modern creation, although its inventors used elements from earlier political thought that they misinterpreted and distorted. However, the claim about its centuries-long existence grew so embedded not only in political discourse but also in Hungarian scientific culture within decades of its creation, that when a scholar, Ferenc Eckhart, dared to challenge it in 1931, it nearly destroyed his career. In a volume on new trends in Hungarian historiography, he argued that the idea of a 'thousand-year old constitution' rooted in uniquely Hungarian soil and more ancient than any in Europe was untenable. He drew attention to parallels both in Polish and Czech history, and highlighted the chronological development (rather than eternity) of Hungarian constitutional thought.[418]

In the ensuing wave of criticism, which included parliamentary interpellations, supposedly scientific counter-claims, and the demand that he be fired from his university position, Eckhart was accused of having given offense against the doctrine of the Holy Crown.[419] As he pointed out, traditional theses without scholarly foundation were merely repeated in the arguments against him.[420] Subsequently, Eckhart was the first to undertake a serious study of the historical development of the doctrine of the Holy Crown, 'one of the key tenets of public law'.[421] Although Eckhart—understandably after the furore that had greeted his essay and in the context of the oppressive political climate at the time—was

---

[417] E.g. István Kocsis, *A Szent Korona tana: múltja, jelene, jövője* (Budapest: Püski, 1995), 5: 'The Holy Crown lives, both as a personality and as a public law concept...the Holy Crown doctrine...is a public law doctrine with binding validity.' József Zoltán Tóth, *Megmaradásunk alkotmánya: A Szent Korona-eszme a magyar történelemben és közjogban* (Budapest: HUN-idea, 2007); József Zoltán Tóth, ed., *A Szent Korona-eszme időszerűsége* (Budapest: Szent István Társulat, 2004) also approaches the doctrine as 'unique' (7) and dating from the beginnings of the state (8). A whole industry of pseudo-scientific book production now exists on the 'Holy Crown' and the 'doctrine of the Holy Crown'.

[418] Ferenc Eckhart, 'Jog- és alkotmánytörténet', in *A magyar történetírás új útjai*, ed. Bálint Hóman (Budapest: Magyar Szemle Társaság, 1931, 2nd edn 1932), 269–320, at 304–9, explicitly stating that false constitutional history is transmitted in schoolbooks (309). He also drew parallels between Hungarian, Czech, and Polish concepts of the crown (301–3), and refuted the parallels to English parliamentary developments (297–300). Overall, he argued in the chapter that law can only be understood in its historical context and was historically changing, giving many examples from Hungarian laws, including on servitude and witch-trials.

[419] Eckhart, *Magyar alkotmány- és jogtörténet*, 3; József Kardos, 'Az Eckhart-vita és a Szentkorona-tan', *Századok*, 103, nos. 5–6 (1969): 1104–17; Kardos, *A szentkorona-tan*, 154–72; Bertényi, *A magyar szent korona*, 161–4. Eckhart didn't give a detailed analysis of the doctrine of the Holy Crown in his first piece, but critics saw his remarks on Hungarian constitutional development as an attack against that doctrine. See also Péter, 'The Holy Crown of Hungary', 495–500 (also on criticism in 1950s).

[420] Ferenc Eckhart, 'A magyar alkotmányfejlődés', *Magyar Jogi Szemle*, 12, no. 5 (1931): 201–15 (where he still accepted Werbőczy as the originator of the doctrine of the Holy Crown).

[421] 'A közjog egyik legfontosabb tétele.' Ferenc Eckhart, *A Szentkorona-eszme története* (Budapest: Magyar Tudományos Akadémia, 1941), 3; Kardos, 'Az Eckhart-vita'.

222 STEPHEN I, THE FIRST CHRISTIAN KING OF HUNGARY

cautious in his formulations to the point where he was often misunderstood or misrepresented, his book is still fundamental in demolishing the myth of the doctrine of the Holy Crown.[422]

Analyses tend to include the earlier political thinking on the crown as a prelude to the fully fledged doctrine, even when they are critical of the doctrine's central tenet concerning its own timelessness.[423] Earlier political ideas, however, were not forerunners of the 'doctrine'; they were turned into precursors only by their modern interpreters. Service and loyalty, just as much as injury to the crown, the abstract concept of 'the crown' as representing royal dignity independent of any individual king; the conceptualization of the realm as crown lands, thus territories belonging to the crown, the fiscal meaning of the *corona regni*, and the crown as possessor of rights, as well as organicist imagery, including 'members' of the crown, were all standard expressions in medieval and early modern thought, starting at the end of the eleventh century.[424] Despite routinely seeing these as early stages in the development of the uniquely Hungarian doctrine of the Holy Crown, they were instead, as demonstrated by Eckhart, common in medieval and early modern European political thought.[425] What was Hungarian was their distortion: nineteenth-century thinkers lifted elements from medieval and early modern thought and changed their meaning; the process was more invention than incorporation.[426] We must distinguish clearly between the modern political ideology expressed as the basis of Hungarian public law and earlier European

---

[422] His personal bravery in even such cautious formulations is perhaps hard to appreciate by those who never experienced authoritarian oppression. On the potential for being misunderstood, and sensitive to the context of contemporary politics on why Eckhart used ambiguous terms: Teszelszky, *Az ismeretlen korona*, 54–6. In his book on the Hungarian legal system in 1946, Eckhart, *Magyar alkotmány- és jogtörténet*, 114–20, although he summarized the medieval and early modern legal significance of the crown as representing royal power and then the state, citing English and Czech parallels, he entitled the section 'The doctrine of the holy crown' (A szentkorona-eszme).

[423] Kardos, *A szentkorona-tan*, 11–37 on the 'development of the doctrine of the Holy Crown' covers the eleventh to the nineteenth centuries. Péter, 'The Holy Crown of Hungary', 439 points out the multivocal nature of the 'crown' and goes on to distinguish its different uses. Teszelszky, *Az ismeretlen korona*, 40 argued that the 'early modern crown concept greatly influenced modern national political thought from the nineteenth-century'. Bertényi, *A magyar Szent Korona*, 142–51, on 'the development of the doctrine of the Holy Crown prior to Werbőczy'. De Cevins, 'Les origines médiévales de la doctrine de la Sainte couronne', 175–90 recapitulates the medieval evidence.

[424] Kantorowicz, *The King's Two Bodies*; Eckhart, *A Szentkorona-eszme*, 19–33; Fritz Hartung, 'Die Krone als Symbol der Monarchischen Herrschaft im ausgehenden Mittelalter', in *Corona regni*, 1–69; Karpat, 'Corona Regni Hungariae', 227–39; Sassier, 'La corona regni' (the earliest example is 1092); Weiler, *Paths to Kingship*, 347; Lenka Bobková, 'Corona regni Bohemiae und ihre visuelle Repräsentation unter Karl IV', in *Kunst als Herrschaftsinstrument: Böhmen und das Heilige Römische Reich unter den Luxemburgen im europäischen Kontext*, ed. Jiří Fajt, Andrea Langerde (Berlin—Munich: Deutscher Kunstverlag, 2009), 120–35; de Cevins, 'Les origines médiévales de la doctrine de la Sainte couronne', 176, provides Hungarian examples from the thirteenth century at 183–4.

[425] Reaffirmed in ibid.

[426] Josef Karpat, 'Die Idee der Heiligen Krone Ungarns in neuer Beleuchtung', in *Corona regni*, 349–98. The fiction of an 'ancient constitution' also developed in England: Janelle Greenberg, *The Radical Face of the Ancient Constitution: St Edward's 'Laws' in Early Modern Political Thought* (Cambridge: Cambridge University Press, 2001).

THE HUNGARIAN CROWN   223

ideas attached to the crown, for not to do so means unwittingly buying into the doctrine. Additionally, the modern doctrine is distinct in its strong appeal to nationalist emotions, not just in political rhetoric, but also in jurisprudence.[427]

While earlier legal writing dated the doctrine of the Holy Crown from Werbőczy in the early sixteenth century, or the thirteenth—fourteenth centuries or even earlier,[428] Eckhart's thorough study demonstrated that the doctrine of the Holy Crown emerged in jurisprudence in the late nineteenth century, and was developed fully at the end of the nineteenth, beginning of the twentieth century. Its real roots lay in turn-of-the-century nationalism, rather than in a thousand-year-old constitution; and it gained a key role in the self-justification of the authoritarian Horthy regime between the two world wars.

Whether 1867 or the early 1890s should be seen as the date of the first expression of the doctrine is a matter for legal scholarship; in any case, the doctrine came to be entrenched between the 1890s and 1902. Eckhart traced its roots to the work of Imre Hajnik (1867), but also signalled that the fully fledged doctrine was the result of the contributions of several jurists in the late nineteenth century.[429] Hajnik took the formula of service to the crown in royal donation charters to mean that the territory of the country was possessed by king and nation—that is, by the Holy Crown.[430] Elsewhere, he also wrote about the Holy Crown as an entity in public law (the body of the Holy Crown being present in Parliament).[431] This differed from the merely territorial use of the Hungarian crown that had been in existence from a few decades earlier, which was also expressed in the official name of the Hungarian part of the Austro-Hungarian monarchy—the dual structure that was created through the Compromise (Ausgleich) of 1867—'Lands of the Crown of Saint Stephen'.

---

[427] Kardos, *A szentkorona-tan*, 247; also true of recent work, e.g. 'The history of Hungarian public law is also the history of Hungarian destiny, election and persecution. The abolition of the historical constitution, in existence until 1944/49...aimed at abolishing Hungarian statehood and Hungarian self-consciousness, because the Hungarian Holy Crown and the attached doctrine of the Holy Crown...was a part and guarantee of Hungarian national consciousness.' Tóth, *Megmaradásunk alkotmánya*, 9.

[428] Hajnik in the fourteenth century: Kardos, *A szentkorona-tan*, 27; Ákos Timon, *Magyar alkotmány- és jogtörténet tekintettel a nyugati államok jogfejlődésére* (Budapest: Politzer Zsigmond és fia, 1902), 464–8 saw the roots of this in thirteenth-century changes of the power structure, and social and economic systems.

[429] Eckhart, *A Szentkorona-eszme*, 316–17; Imre Hajnik, *Magyarország az Árpád-királyoktól az ősiségnek megállapításáig a hűbéri Európa* (Pest, 1867) exaggerated and connected random medieval mentions into a 'theory': Kardos, *A szentkorona-tan*, 27. On Eckhart's book: ibid., 230–2. Péter, 'The Holy Crown of Hungary', 481 gave credit instead to Győző Concha, 'Közjog és magyar közjog. Viszonválasz Nagy Ernőnek', *Magyar Igazságügy*, 36, no. 1 (1892): 46–113, repr. in *Hatvan év tudományos mozgalmai között. Concha Győző igazgató és tiszteleti tagnak összegyűjtött értekezései és bírálatai*, 2 vols. (Budapest: MTA, 1928–35), vol. 1, 568–618. Eckhart signalled Concha's role in the triumph of the doctrine in legal writing: *A Szentkorona-eszme*, 320.

[430] Ibid., 316–17.

[431] Ibid., 317–20 on Hajnik's *Egyetemes európai jogtörténet* (1875); Péter, 'The Holy Crown of Hungary', 477.

224   STEPHEN I, THE FIRST CHRISTIAN KING OF HUNGARY

Hajnik's work did not have an immediate impact on legal writing; subsequent jurists ignored or barely mentioned it, until 1891, when Győző Concha turned the doctrine of the Holy Crown into a basic tenet of Hungarian public law.[432] He not only claimed that royal rights belonged to the Holy Crown but also created a venerable past for the legal tenet that the king and diet were joint possessors of legislative sovereignty in Hungary, mistakenly linking its formulation to the legal scholar István Werbőczy (c. 1458–1541).[433] Thereafter, Ákos Timon, Károly Kmety, and Artúr Balogh developed the doctrine of the Holy Crown fully by around 1901.[434] Timon's textbook in 1902 enshrined the doctrine as the central tenet of Hungarian constitutional history, and as a specifically Hungarian institution.[435] Timon defined the doctrine of the Holy Crown as 'a division of public authority between the king and the members of the Holy Crown', meaning that supreme authority belongs to the crown rather than the king; the crown is the fount of all power and rights, the territory of the realm is the territory of the Holy Crown, and the members of the Holy Crown are the political nation (nobles, ecclesiastics, and the towns in Parliament).[436]

This fully fledged version includes several key assertions. The doctrine's basis becomes an innate principle in the soul of the Hungarian people, forever present, and finally embodied at the end of the thirteenth century in the doctrine of the Holy Crown.[437] According to Timon, king and nation (at that point meaning the estates[438]) together possessed public authority, which constitutionally limited royal power; legislation and the exercise of public power in general gained a constitutional form in the doctrine in the Middle Ages. Further, nation and king (crowned by the Holy Crown) together formed the living body of the Holy Crown; this organic theory excluded the possibility of conflict within society. Members of the Holy Crown shared all public authority, including legislative, judicial, and executive power.

The doctrine was invented and elaborated in the late nineteenth, beginning of the twentieth century in the context of debates on relations to Austria and to national minorities. The doctrine provided the legal fiction to reconcile the lack of independent statehood within the Austro-Hungarian Monarchy with Hungarian nationalism and a sense of superiority. The Holy Crown in this conceptualization embodied independent national life, and provided the illusion of

---

[432] Eckhart, *A Szentkorona-eszme*, 320–3; Kardos, *A szentkorona-tan*, 27–8.

[433] Péter, 'The Holy Crown of Hungary', 481–4.

[434] Eckhart, *A Szentkorona-eszme*, 323–33; Bertényi, *A magyar szent korona*, 159–60.

[435] Péter, 'The Holy Crown of Hungary', 485.

[436] Timon, *Magyar alkotmány- és jogtörténet*, 477, 472–4.

[437] According to Timon, *Magyar alkotmány- és jogtörténet*, 469–80 with the rise of noble power, the notion of public authority belonging to the king and nation together, a public law idea rooted in the nation and brought from the *Urheimat*, came to the fore; the doctrine of the Holy Crown put an end to personal royal power and created the system of estates. See also Kardos, *A szentkorona-tan*, 29.

[438] Later writers added that in 1848, non-nobles were also included in the nation.

sovereignty, through the tenet that the crowned king was a member of the Holy Crown just as much as the nation; the Hungarian elite insisted that the emperor of the Austro-Hungarian Monarchy in his capacity as king of Hungary was an independent legal entity and had to be crowned separately. Sovereign power, therefore, belonged to the Holy Crown, not to the king, and since the Holy Crown was separate from the imperial crown even if the person of the emperor and the Hungarian king was the same, the illusion of sovereignty and the national state within the Monarchy could be safeguarded.

The doctrine also provided 'proof' of Hungarian superiority over other nationalities in the Monarchy, and a 'historical' argument for their subjection, although in reality the Monarchy was the basis for Hungarian rule over the nationalities. Ákos Timon militated for the uniqueness of the Hungarian legal system (derived from the Hungarians' sense of public law, 'közjogi érzék', brought from their *Urheimat*) in the region and even in the whole of Europe.[439] Because of their sense of public law, Hungarians were also supposedly the strongest state-creating force, thus having the right to rule over other nationalities. In addition, the Holy Crown since the time of St Stephen allegedly provided the legal unity of the realm, as all territories were members of the Holy Crown. Thus, Croatia-Slavonia, for example, was an integral part of the political nation of Hungary.[440] Political rhetoric also started using the doctrine, to prove Hungarian exceptionalism, and the superiority and early nature of the Hungarian constitution.[441] While some jurists and other critics refused to accept the doctrine—one publication even bearing the title 'The lies of the doctrine of the Holy Crown'[442]—it became entrenched in legal thought.

Indeed, its heyday—with some changes—came after the disintegration of the Austro-Hungarian Monarchy in the wake of the First World War.[443] This was linked to the rapid and dramatic change of the political landscape. The doctrine of the Holy Crown started to play a significant role in constitutional debate soon after the end of the war. During the 1918–19 revolutions, Hungary gained independence and transformed, after centuries of monarchy, into a republic. After the

---

[439] Timon, *Magyar alkotmány- és jogtörténet*, 469, 472 (through the doctrine, Hungarians reached an abstract concept of the state earlier than all western peoples), 476–7; Ákos Timon, *A Szent Korona elmélete és a koronázás* (1920, repr. Nemzeti Örökség Kiadó no place, no date), 10–11; Kardos, *A szentkorona-tan*, 29–31, 156–8.

[440] Ibid., 28–33 links it especially to nationalism, on 28–9 citing Concha who in 1890 'proved' that the nationalities were too immature to have independent states, whereas Hungarians could build a strong state because of their unique doctrine of the Holy Crown.

[441] Péter, 'The Holy Crown of Hungary', 486–9; 492–5 on the doctrine's use in the late nineteenth and early twentieth centuries.

[442] Ibid., 491, 495–6. Oszkár Gellért, *A szent korona tan hazugságai: alkotmányjogi tanulmány* (Budapest: Légrády Testvérek, 1908), argued the need for a constitutional monarchy, where the national will was the source of law and wrote that the doctrine hindered the development of a new constitution for popular sovereignty.

[443] Péter, 'The Holy Crown of Hungary', 496.

226 STEPHEN I, THE FIRST CHRISTIAN KING OF HUNGARY

fall of the Republic of Councils, so-called legitimists desired Habsburg restoration, while advocates of free elections wished to restore kingship by electing a new Hungarian king. Both legitimists and champions of elective kingship justified their view by reference to the doctrine of the Holy Crown, seeing it as the guarantee of legal continuity. In this discourse, king, Parliament, and nation were constitutive parts of the Holy Crown, which embodied the Hungarian state. Strong polemics surrounded the specifics: while the Holy Crown's fundamental significance to constitutional law was not questioned, the legal consequences following from its status were. Some legitimists argued that the doctrine of the Holy Crown meant the nation could not unilaterally sever the bond between itself and its king; a king, once crowned, was only responsible to God and it was illegal to legislate against him. According to those championing elective kingship, however, the doctrine ensured that sovereignty lay in the nation, represented at the time in the national assembly.[444]

The constitutional status of the country had to be resolved without the Habsburgs; their return, even as kings of Hungary exclusively, was unacceptable to the Allied Powers and Hungary's neighbours. The national assembly desired to avoid negative repercussions in advance of the peace treaty, and legislated on the form of government in an ambiguous manner, creating a kingdom without a king. The parliamentary debate referred to the Holy Crown as the embodiment of the nation, and not simply a representative sign (the analogy was drawn with the consecrated host truly being the body and blood of Christ), legitimizing the national assembly. The 1920/I law made provision only for the temporary exercise of power through instituting Miklós Horthy as Regent to govern Hungary. It declared the national assembly to be the exclusive representative of national sovereignty, and stated that the exercise of royal power ceased on 13 November 1918; the consequences of this would be drawn by the assembly after the peace treaty.[445] The law, therefore, did not abolish monarchy in Hungary. Three weeks later a ministerial decree (2394/1920) confirmed that Hungary was a kingdom, reflected in the names of institutions of state, such as the royal Hungarian army, and royal Hungarian government.[446]

After two failed attempts at Habsburg restoration, legislation to dethrone the Habsburgs was accepted by the national assembly despite legitimist protest (1921/XLVII), both sides invoking the doctrine of the Holy Crown.[447] The law retained monarchy as Hungary's form of government, but postponed filling the throne. In the end, until after the Second World War, Hungary remained a monarchy without a king, with the Horthy regime's hold on power excluding any real possibility

---

[444] József Kardos, *A Szent Korona és a szentkorona-eszme története* (Budapest: IKVA, 1992), 55–60; Kardos, *A szentkorona-tan*, 39–45, and on continued debate from 1920, 52–9; Bertényi, *A magyar szent korona*, 160–1.

[445] Kardos, *A szentkorona-tan*, 45–52.   [446] Ibid., 50–2.

[447] Ibid., 52–71, 95–9, also 129–34.

for a royal election.[448] In 1926, a two-house Parliament was created, with the new legal structure both criticized and legitimized by calling on the notion of legal continuity.[449]

Those writing on public law in the interwar years all gave central place to the doctrine of the Holy Crown, although details of what it meant exactly varied.[450] For example, while one author saw the national will, in Parliament, as the actualization of the Holy Crown's sovereignty,[451] a hard-line legitimist maintained that legislation could only be issued by king and Parliament together, implicitly invalidating the state legislation of the time.[452] Whether king and nation separately formed the members of the Holy Crown or merged as head (caput sacrae regni coronae) and members (membra sacrae regni coronae) in the body (corpus sacrae regni coronae) of the Holy Crown was a matter for debate.[453] The doctrine was strongly historicizing, alleged to derive from the ancient Hungarians, and laid claim to a unique Hungarian constitutional public authority, that provided equality before the law for all, and equal political rights. The existence of this thousand-year-old 'historical constitution' obviated the need for a written constitution. The doctrine in this reincarnation also emphasized legal continuity.[454] It was celebrated in jurisprudence, and in historical and literary works until the end of the Second World War.[455]

Ákos Timon in 1920 wrote a work to popularize the doctrine, congratulating himself on making its significance central in national consciousness.[456] He emphasized that through the mystery of the Holy Crown Hungarians developed public authority and a state earlier than western Europe.[457] With its roots in the *Urheimat*, there was no parallel anywhere on the continent to this ancient constitutional development, allowing the free members of the nation to participate in public affairs.[458] He claimed that twelfth-century charters mentioning service and loyalty to the crown indicated a theoretical entity above the king, the Holy Crown, which comprised the king and nation together.[459] The legal personhood of the Holy Crown, and the state organization built on this was not invented by any lawyer, but was the outcome of the Hungarian constitution's centuries-long development; it also allowed people of different ethnicities and languages to be

---

[448] On the tensions around trying to turn a supposedly temporary situation created by necessity into a permanent legal structure, especially contestation by legitimists of the 1920/I law: ibid., 112–19.

[449] Ibid., 134–9.   [450] Ibid., 244.   [451] Móric Tomcsányi, quoted in ibid., 81–2.

[452] Kálmán Molnár, quoted in ibid., 82–3.   [453] Ibid., 82–3.

[454] Ibid., 84–7. On blurring of public law and legal history, ibid., 242.

[455] Ibid., 232–7; e.g. Radisics, *Hungary*, 5 emphasized that 'the doctrine of the Holy Crown of Hungary' meant that the crown belonged to 'the whole country', uniting king and nation, 'the Holy Crown is the source of all power and the basis of sovereignty'. 'The territory of the State is the territory of the Crown; and any territory lost must be recovered by the Holy Crown.'

[456] Timon, *A Szent Korona elmélete*, 6 (on 5, he claimed the doctrine's significance waned in the nineteenth century due to the influx of western legal theories).

[457] Ibid., 10.   [458] Ibid., 11.   [459] Ibid., 19.

228 STEPHEN I, THE FIRST CHRISTIAN KING OF HUNGARY

encompassed in an organic unity through public law.[460] 'The essence of the doctrine of the holy crown is concentrated in the public law concept that supreme power in the state, sovereignty, belongs to the Holy Crown, which unites the king and the nation in an organic unity, and that royal power originates from the Holy Crown and is transferred by the nation.'[461] This conveniently also meant that if one was 'impeded', the other part of the Holy Crown could exercise power; thus, if there is no king, Parliament can govern.[462]

The doctrine became so important because it served the interwar regime's key political agendas. In the wake of the Treaty of Trianon (1920), which drastically reallocated territory, roughly 30 per cent of Hungarian speakers became minorities in the surrounding countries: Romania (in Transylvania), Czechoslovakia (both in today's Slovakia and Ukraine), and Yugoslavia (in Serbia and Croatia).[463] The interwar Hungarian political establishment never accepted that status quo and territorial revisionism became a main driving-force in Hungarian politics.[464] Territorial rights over the realm had already been attached to the 'Hungarian (Holy) Crown';[465] this could now be marshalled to claim that all earlier parts of the kingdom of Hungary regardless of ethnic composition (Croatia, Slavonia, Dalmatia, Transylvania) by right belong to Hungary.

Additionally, the 'St Stephen concept' (*szent istváni gondolat*), alleging that Hungarians always integrated nationalities peacefully in one realm, linked to the assertion that according to the doctrine of the Holy Crown, all former nationalities were members of the Holy Crown, now served as a justification for the demand to reunite all the lands of the 'Holy Crown' under the allegedly tolerant aegis of a multinational kingdom.[466] The old 'cultural superiority' thesis, still part and parcel of the doctrine of the Holy Crown, which asserted the Hungarians' superior sense of public law (creating an early and unique constitution) and state-forming ability as well as mission in the region, merged with the demand for territorial revision.[467] Jurisprudence described the Treaty of Trianon as 'having torn apart the body of the Holy Crown', but foretold the reuniting of all territories under St Stephen's crown, through continued fidelity to the doctrine of the Holy Crown.[468] References to the entire territory of the Holy Crown, coupled to the Hungarian will to live, cropped up in debates on public law.[469] The nation was to find historical power in the Holy Crown, which would restore its vocation in the

---

[460] Ibid., 25–7.   [461] Ibid., 33.   [462] Ibid., 33–4.

[463] Miklós Zeidler, 'Trianon, Treaty of', https://encyclopedia.1914-1918-online.net/article/trianon_treaty_of.

[464] Miklós Zeidler, *Ideas on Territorial Revision in Hungary: 1920–1945* (Boulder, CO: Social Science Monographs, 2007).

[465] Péter, 'The Holy Crown of Hungary', 458–60; in 1916: Kardos, *A szentkorona-tan*, 32.

[466] Kardos, *A szentkorona-tan*, 219–29, 243–4. From 1933, this was increasingly used in arguments against the government and its German orientation: ibid., 212–13, 215, 217–18.

[467] Ibid., 164.   [468] Ibid., 87, 221, 228.   [469] Ibid., 146, 150.

region.[470] As an author in 1938 put it, 'If our nation remains faithful to its holy ideals that live in the doctrine of the holy crown,…it will prove to be stronger than even Trianon.'[471] As some territories were reattached to Hungary through Hitler's gift, legislation celebrated their 'return to the body of the Hungarian Holy Crown' as a victory of the doctrine.[472]

Similarly, the authoritarian Horthy regime used the pseudo-scientific pretence of 'unbroken' constitutional continuity vested in the doctrine of the Holy Crown to legitimize itself, and maintain the kingdom without a king, despite repeated challenges by legitimists who wanted to restore Habsburg kingship. The doctrine also provided the illusion that as a member of the Holy Crown, the entire nation shared in state power.[473] Ancient Hungarian constitutionalism supposedly guaranteed political rights and freedoms when in reality a limited parliamentary system ensured the exclusion of real democracy. The claim of legal continuity (in spite of very real rupture) and the inadmissibility of revolution or constitutional change in the name of the doctrine of the Holy Crown were equally important parts of self-legitimization.[474]

When the sphere of Horthy's authority was expanded in 1933, some even demanding that as regent, he should possess all royal rights, this extension of the regent's powers was labelled a return to ancient Hungarian constitutionalism, and alleged to be in line with the doctrine of the Holy Crown.[475] When the regent's power was extended again in 1937, the reasoning carefully emphasized the rights that, in line with the doctrine of the Holy Crown, only a coronation could confer and that therefore were not granted to the regent.[476] Horthy himself affirmed that 'every authority belongs to the Holy Crown, every right derives from it'.[477] Legitimists also insisted that the essence of the constitution was the doctrine of the Holy Crown, in which, they maintained, royal power and the rights of the people are knit together. They presented legitimism as not simply loyalty to the king, but also to constitutional continuity and the people's rights.[478]

Clearly, 'the doctrine of the Holy Crown' had no precise legal meaning, and could be used to prop up many claims. As Kantorowicz pointed out in another context, 'The indefiniteness itself of the symbol [the invisible Crown] may have

---

[470] Ibid., 213.

[471] Miklós Nagy, 'A Szent Korona Eszméje', in *Emlékkönyv Szent István király halálának kilencszázadik évfordulóján*, vol. 2, ed. Jusztinián Serédi (Budapest: Magyar Tudományos Akadémia, 1938), 267–307, at 305.

[472] Péter, 'The Holy Crown of Hungary', 460–1; Kardos, *A szentkorona-tan*, 229, 233, 237; Bertényi, *A magyar szent korona*, 164.

[473] Kardos, *A szentkorona-tan*, 242–4; The legitimist Kálmán Molnár denied this continuity; his views on public law were strongly contested: ibid., 99–107.

[474] Ibid., 88–93, 162–3. [475] Ibid., 173–80, 183–5.

[476] Ibid., 187–93. Further extension in 1942, ibid., 193–7. [477] Quoted in ibid., 193.

[478] Ibid., 202–11. A more detailed study: József Kardos, *A Szent Korona-tan és a legitimizmus* (Budapest: Gondolat, 2012).

been its greatest value, and haziness the true strength of the symbolic attraction.'[479] The doctrine was an unstable compound 'of several, often contradictory ideas' which gained a semblance of coherence from being attached to the physical object of the crown.[480] The doctrine's fundamental position in constitutional thought and political rhetoric thus reinforced the status of the physical crown.

It is not enough to point out that various ideas that changed over time were attached to the physical crown.[481] While in itself this is true, there is a crucial caesura between using the crown in order to legitimize particular claims on the one hand, and attaching the essence of Hungarian identity and statehood to the crown, increasingly divorced from any reality of kingship, on the other hand. It is also misleading to classify the 'doctrine of the Holy Crown' as a 'reinterpretation' of earlier political ideas: distortion is much closer to real processes.

5. The 'Holy Crown' as a National Symbol

With the shift to a kingless kingdom, the importance of the physical crown increased rather than decreased, replacing its significance in crowning the king of Hungary, since there was no king, with being the embodiment of the state. The layers of myth that had accrued to the crown over time also helped make it so desirable as a political symbol and an anchor of legitimate rule; the doctrine of the Holy Crown itself in its many variations invested the crown with a new meaning, in a radical shift from its earlier role in legitimizing kingship. It now stood for historical statehood and territory, and continuity amidst drastic change, with a particular ideological bent. Therefore, the physical 'Holy Crown' became embedded in discourses of national identity.

Holy Crown alliances formed by legitimists from 1926 to 1944 perpetuated the idea of 'historical Hungary based on a thousand-year-old legal continuity'.[482] They saw themselves as guardians of the angelic Holy Crown, the Hungarian constitution, national honour, historical traditions, and loyalty.[483] The protection of the physical crown itself was the centre of legislation (1928/25), nominally proposed by a crown guard. The explicit justification included the crown's constitutional status and its role as a signifier of national continuity and unity. The crown also stood in for the absent king in legitimizing the political structures, as possessor and fount of all public authority. The crown and regalia were to be kept under

---

[479] Kantorowicz, *The King's Two Bodies*, 340.   [480] Péter, 'The Holy Crown of Hungary', 506.
[481] ibid., 439, 509; Teszelszky, *Az ismeretlen korona*, 20–9, 40. Eckhart had traced such changes in his book.
[482] Kardos, *A Szent Korona*, 69.   [483] Kardos, *A szentkorona-tan*, 120–9, especially 124.

armed guard in a strongroom, with specially designated Keepers of the Crown and the Prime Minister each keeping one of the keys.[484]

Following on from the demand of the National Association of Judges and Prosecutors in 1928, the law of 1930/34 decreed that all judgements were to be issued in the name of the Holy Crown, since 'according to public law developed during the centuries, the Hungarian Holy Crown embodies the thousand-year-old Hungarian statehood....Juridical power is one of the rights belonging to supreme authority and therefore its root is the Holy Crown.' Although the proposal was criticized out of respect for the Holy Crown, it passed into law.[485] How important the crown became to statehood can be seen from the fact that the last Hungarian government at the end of the Second World War, formed by the Arrow Cross Party (the Hungarian Nazi party) under its own 'nation-leader' (the Hungarian version of the Führer), tried to secure the crown by hiding it as the country faced defeat.

The current focus on the 'Holy Crown' and its reinsertion into the legislation is a direct revival and extension of the distinct interwar sanctification of the crown as an embodiment of the state. Indeed, there was an attempt to revive the doctrine of the Holy Crown as well, especially championed by the extreme right, that failed because of strong opposition.[486] Government rhetoric in the end invested the crown with the doctrine's political significance, turning the crown into the carrier of sovereignty, legal continuity, and territorial revisionism, without openly embracing the doctrine itself.

The reason for the resurrection of the crown's political significance in the twenty-first century is clear. It provides pseudo-historical legitimizing rhetoric for the government, and serves for covert revisionist allusions.[487] In the last decades, an emphasis on the unity of all Hungarians has returned to the Hungarian political agenda. Thus the symbolism of 'Stephen's crown', as the representative of the political nation of all Hungarian-speakers, is embraced once again in political rhetoric. The 'Basic Law' maintains that all Hungarian speakers are part of the nation and Hungary has a responsibility for Hungarians living outside its borders;[488] effective from 2011, the government gave the right to apply for Hungarian citizenship (and the ability to vote in Hungarian elections) without

---

[484] Ibid., 140–5; on laws about the protection of the Holy Crown and keepers of the crown, 1464–1928: Tamás Katona, *A Korona kilenc évszázada: történelmi források a magyar koronáról* (Budapest: Magyar Helikon, 1979), 569–87.

[485] Kardos, *A szentkorona-tan*, 145–50, quotation on 145.

[486] Péter, 'The Holy Crown of Hungary', 423, note 7.

[487] In this, I disagree with Péter, 'The Holy Crown of Hungary', 424, who identified independent statehood and entry into Europe as the key points. He thought it was too early to tell whether the crown will have significance beyond the millennial celebrations; now it is obvious that was only the start. While he acknowledged revisionism as a motivating factor (502), he claimed it was marginal.

[488] https://net.jogtar.hu/jogszabaly?docid=A1100425.ATV, paragraph D, p. 10657.

232   STEPHEN I, THE FIRST CHRISTIAN KING OF HUNGARY

moving to Hungary to all ethnic Hungarians who are the citizens of neighbouring states.

Attempts to implant the cult of the crown into the consciousness of all citizens include a recent proposal by an MP to create a national holiday to celebrate the Holy Crown, and on-going efforts to rewrite history. The government directly sponsors work written by people who had no formal academic training in medieval history, for example giving a substantial subsidy for a book about the origin of the 'Holy Crown' in 2016.[489] A booklet on 'The Hungarian Holy Crown' was published by the Office of the National Assembly in 2016; the Office of the National Assembly, 'supports Parliament organisationally' and employs professionals in order to do so.[490] Its title indicates that this is no neutral statement, as the booklet's reverent tone and the emphasis on the 'unique', 'matchless' nature of the crown further demonstrate. (The 'proof' of uniqueness is comical; forced to admit to the existence of the medieval *Reichskrone* which predates the Hungarian crown, this difficulty is sidestepped by arguing that the Holy Roman Empire no longer exists, therefore the Hungarian crown is the oldest crown that was in active use for coronations.)

The booklet suggests that some part(s) of the crown would have come from an object in Stephen's possession. It also states that 'the Holy Crown' has been a sacral symbol since the Middle Ages, 'surrounded by a special set of notions', whose essence, despite changes over time, has survived. The crown's sacrality, the booklet states, is based on the tradition around St Stephen.[491] The supposed historical development of the 'doctrine of the Holy Crown' is then presented starting in the Middle Ages, paying no heed to the fact that this myth has been thoroughly debunked.[492] The 'Holy Crown', it further states, 'became a determinant part of national consciousness' after the First World War because of Hungary's 'mutilation' in the Treaty of Trianon.[493] The content is presented in a misleadingly 'balanced' way, as if summarizing scholarly research. Thus the author claims there is a debate about the origin of the crown, with the majority of researchers arguing for the construction of the crown from two separate parts, but 'some researchers think that the Holy Crown is a unified sacral object, made during the period of St Stephen, or earlier under Charlemagne'.[494] This is about as objective as saying that most researchers argue the Earth moves around the Sun, but some researchers think it is the Sun that moves around the Earth. The reader can freely decide who is right.

---

[489] Zsolt Kácsor, 'Többet ad az NKA a Szent Koronára, mint a szépíróknak', *Népszabadság*, 74, no. 194 (17 August 2016), 11.
[490] http://www.parlament.hu/web/house-of-the-national-assembly/office1.
[491] Moravetz, *A magyar szent korona*, 28 (including quotation).   [492] Ibid., 29–30.
[493] Ibid., 30.   [494] Ibid., 9.

THE HUNGARIAN CROWN   233

Contemporary political discourse not only revives the myths actively but also contributes in major ways to their entanglement. This is no accident. The claim of historical continuity is just as central to modern uses of the crown, as they had been to the interwar doctrine of the Holy Crown. This continuity is artificially constructed from the many layers of myth, which hide significant ruptures. Thus the earlier history of the crown, when it was important for legitimizing royal power, is not distinguished from its history as a 'national symbol', merging its old significance as a coronation crown with its new, national identity one. This is helped by the colourful history of the crown.

The crown was repeatedly stolen, hidden, taken away and always returned, facilitating the creation of modern myths about its special national significance. The need to be crowned with this specific crown from the early fourteenth century for a valid royal coronation repeatedly caused claimants to secure possession of the crown by any means. According to a fourteenth-century story, Otto, the Wittelsbach duke of Bavaria, one of the contenders for the Hungarian throne in 1305, hung the crown in a container from his saddle when he rode into Hungary; it fell off unheeded, and when hours later he and his retinue returned to look for it, they found it in the middle of the road, as it remained miraculously invisible to everyone else on the busy road.[495] This story may be a mere literary invention; subsequently, however, reality often surpassed the most imaginative storyteller.[496]

The crown was stolen several times; the most celebrated episode concerns a theft by a lady-in-waiting, Helene Kottanner (c. 1400–after 1458), who smuggled it out sewn into a pillowcase, which she recounted in an autobiographical text. The daughter of a lesser nobleman, she served Queen Elizabeth (c. 1409–42), the wife of the Habsburg Albert II, King of the Romans (thus emperor-elect) (r. 1438–9) and King of Hungary (r. 1437–9). When Albert died on 27 October 1439, Elizabeth was five months pregnant. A powerful party of nobles wanted her to marry King Władysław III of Poland (1424–44), who was only sixteen years old. Elizabeth refused, hoping she would have a son and planning to have him crowned.

To secure a valid coronation, the queen asked her lady-in-waiting Helene Kottanner to steal the crown from the royal stronghold of Visegrád. On 20 February 1440, Helene and a Hungarian nobleman managed to lay hold of the crown, and they took it to the queen and her newborn son. They then went to Székesfehérvár, the coronation city of the Hungarian kings. On 15 May 1440, the Archbishop of Esztergom crowned the baby boy king of Hungary. Elizabeth

---

[495] *SRH* I, 484; image in facsimile: *The Hungarian Illuminated Chronicle*, 135.
[496] These events have been reported many times, e.g. Decsy, *A' magyar szent koronának*, 216–50; Ipolyi, *A magyar Szent Korona*, 85–129; Benda—Fügedi, *A magyar korona regénye*; Bertényi, *A magyar szent korona*, 72–141, 167–82, Bak—Pálffy, *Crown and Coronation*, 168–90.

234 STEPHEN I, THE FIRST CHRISTIAN KING OF HUNGARY

subsequently took the crown with her, and it was held by Emperor Frederick III for more than twenty years.

Some of the other notable 'adventures' of the crown included being in the hands of the Ottomans briefly in 1529. It spent time in a variety of towns, including Prague. It was repeatedly hidden to protect it or to deny legitimacy to a ruler during wars and revolts, including in a hole dug near the Hungarian border by the revolutionaries escaping from Hungary in 1849. It remained there until 1853, when its location was revealed by a spy to the Habsburg court. At the beginning of 1945, members of the Arrow Cross government, fleeing from the Red Army liberating Hungary from Nazi rule, took the crown with them to Mattsee, and ended up hiding it in a hole dug on the lakeshore. Arrested by the American Army, one of those overseeing this operation confessed, and the crown ended up first in Frankfurt, then in the United States; it was returned to Hungary in 1978.

Thus securing the coronation crown eventually segued into securing governmental legitimacy, unconnected to kingship. This can be seen clearly in the controversy over the return of the crown from the US, with some émigré circles opposed to returning it to the communist regime:[497] it was seen as legitimizing the Kádár government. The motif that the crown always returned and survived adversity also blurred into the notion that the crown had special significance as the miraculously surviving symbol of the nation. Thus, Elias Berger already linked its fate to that of Hungary: when it was in danger, so was the country, and it was a sign of divine providence that the crown survived.[498] Peter Révay wrote of its 'miraculous' conservation amidst wars and internal tumult.[499] In 1830, Kölcsey celebrated the crown's glory, sanctity, and inviolability.[500] Ipolyi in 1886 hailed the crown for its protective holiness, which both had legal significance and made it the object of popular piety.[501] Twentieth- and twenty-first-century nationalism, especially after the drastic political and territorial changes in the wake of the First World War transformed these ideas into a victimhood narrative, where the crown's continued existence was a source of pride, and a sign of survival against the odds. This has been perpetuated in right-wing discourse. It is the modern political will that keeps the significance of the crown alive that is unusual, although not unprecedented. However, Hitler's brief revival of the imperial insignia's significance had no follow-up, unlike the Hungarian case.[502]

While earlier popular interest focused on the crookedness of the cross, explaining it with a pagan attack against Stephen, his refusal to be crowned, or the Treaty of Trianon,[503] an entire book could be dedicated to the fantasist ideas woven

---

[497] Hilsdale, 'The social life of the Byzantine gift', 603–4.
[498] Teszelszky, Az ismeretlen korona, 329.   [499] Révay, De sacrae coronae Regni Hungariae, 6.
[500] Quoted in Kardos, A szentkorona-tan, 19.   [501] Ipolyi, A magyar Szent Korona, iii.
[502] Hans-Ulrich Thamer, 'Mittelalterliche Reichs- und Königstraditionen in den Geschichtsbildern der NS-Zeit', in Kramp, Krönungen, vol. 2, 829–37.
[503] Zoltán Magyar, Szent István a magyar kultúrtörténetben (Budapest: Helikon Kiadó, 1996), 124.

THE HUNGARIAN CROWN   235

around the crown since the twentieth century, trying to enhance its nationalist significance.[504] One of the main triggers of pseudo-scientific new 'results', leading to a growing number of publications, was the study of the crown by goldsmiths in 1983.[505] While their physical examination of the crown proved to be useful on technical points such as the size of the Michael Doukas image, some of their arguments and the fanciful theories based on their conclusions include the claim that the extant crown was made as a unified whole in the Avar Kaganate around 796;[506] that the cross is the original one and its angle matches the earth's axis, bestowing a universal importance on the crown;[507] that the crown reflects ancient cosmology through its proportions, and through numerology portrays apocalyptic visions.[508] For some, it is not sufficient to uphold the idea that the crown was Stephen's. Thus, it was Charlemagne's crown or even Attila the Hun's originally, made in Armenia or in 'Sabir-Hungary' in the fourth century, before it became Stephen's crown.[509] It has also been claimed that 'Geobitzas, krales Tourkias' cannot refer to Géza I of Hungary, because by the eleventh century Tourkia was not used in Byzantine sources as a name for Hungary, but for an otherwise unknown kingdom between Bulgaria, Serbia, Croatia and Hungary.[510] Conspiracy theories abound as well, on how academic historians made up the story of the two parts and the Byzantine crown in order to conceal the fact that the crown had belonged to Stephen. Targeting the crown is allegedly part of the warfare against the Scythian—Hun—Hungarian continuity.[511] Machinations allegedly hid the

[504] Excellent articles, containing refutations of many specific allegations: Zsuzsa Lovag, 'A koronakutatás vadhajtásai', *Művészettörténeti Értesítő*, 35, nos. 1–2 (1986): 35–48; Ernő Marosi, 'A magyar korona a jelenkori kutatásban és a populáris irodalomban: Megjegyzések a művészettörténettudomány jelenlegi helyzetéhez és megbecsüléséhez', *Művészettörténeti Értesítő*, 35, nos. 1–2 (1986): 49–55; Ernő Marosi, 'A létező Szent Korona mitizálása', in *Mítoszaink nyomában*, ed. Gyöngy Kiss Kovács (Cluj—Napoca: Komp-Press, 2013), 37–55.

[505] The reports written in 1983 were not published, but the authors subsequently published their opinion. Lajos Csomor, Béla Lantos, Rezső Ludvigh, Magdolna Poór, 'A Magyar Korona aranyműves vizsgálatáról', *Fizikai Szemle*, 34, no. 1 (1984): 36–41; Lajos Csomor, Béla Lantos, Rezső Ludvig, Magdolna Poór, 'A Magyar korona. Az aranyműves vizsgálat eredményei', *Életünk*, 22, no. 8 (1985): 727–40.

[506] Lajos Csomor, *Magyarország szent koronája*, 3rd edn (Vaja: Vay Ádám Múzeum Baráti Köre, 1988), 157.

[507] Csomor, *Magyarország szent koronája*, 63; Mihály Beöthy, András Fehér, Ilona Árkos Ferenczné, Csaba Ferencz, 'Egy régi kor kozmológiájának emlékei: a magyar korona', *Fizikai Szemle*, 31, no. 12 (1981): 473–82, at 476; see also Bertényi, *A magyar szent korona*, 44–5. The idea that the cross reflects the earth's axis appears in Sándor Bosnyák, 'Aranyalma, bot, suba...Koronázási jelvényeink a néphagyományok tükrében', *Művészet*, 16, no. 6 (1975): 5–7, at 7.

[508] Beöthy et al., 'Egy régi kor kozmológiájának emlékei', 479.

[509] Csomor himself put the crown's origins ever earlier. Lajos Csomor, *Szent István koronája nyomában* (Budapest: Panoráma, 1987); views quoted in *Történelmi érdekességek*, ed. Károly Kocsis, vol. 1, *A magyar szent korona* (Sepsiszentgyörgy: Európai Idő Kiadó, 1993), 10; István Szigeti, *A Szent Korona titka* (Aachen: Antológia Nyomda, 1996).

[510] Holler, 'A magyar korona néhány', 923–51; the author dismisses the evidence of Skylitzes and the seals of the bishops of Tourkia to the contrary.

[511] Lajos Csomor, 'A Szent Korona egy ötvös szemével', in *1100 éves értékekre építkezünk*, ed. Iván Kas (Budapest: Albertfalvi Keresztény Társas Kör, Karolina Egyesület, Szentimrevárosi Egyesület, 1997), 51–70, at 51.

236 STEPHEN I, THE FIRST CHRISTIAN KING OF HUNGARY

crown's true origins: a key element of that theory is that the Doukas image was affixed later, replacing an image of the Virgin Mary, which had been on the crown, because it was described by Révay in 1613; the change is linked to Habsburg scheming, stating that before Joseph II allowed the return of the crown to Hungary he had the images changed.[512] The inability of scholarship to resolve fully many questions facilitates the propagation of 'alternative' histories.

*   *   *

The more deeply the crown is entangled in discourses of national identity, the more convoluted and toxic the fantastic allegations become to hold it in that place. Reverence and rigorous scientific inquiry cannot be reconciled; we either ditch scientific reasoning and learning in order to keep myths, or we must relinquish ideas, however dearly held, that do not stand up to scholarly scrutiny.

Stephen I, the First Christian King of Hungary. From Medieval Myth to Modern Legend. Nora Berend, Oxford University Press. © Nora Berend 2024. DOI: 10.1093/9780191995439.003.0005

---

[512] Gábor Pap's views summarized in András Zsuppán, 'Politikai okkultizmus Magyarországon, 5. Alternatív Szent Korona-elméletek: István antennája', *Magyar Narancs*, 24 February 2005. Révay also described three Byzantine emperors in his *De monarchia*, vol. 2, 558–9, 566–7, and Révay's claim about an image of the Virgin on the crown has been thoroughly refuted: Tóth, *Szent István, Szent Korona*, 50, 54; https://telex.hu/tudomany/2021/10/26/szent-korona-hamisitas-habsburg-revay-peter-altudomany.

Epilogue

Humankind craves meaning. We need to find or invent a rationale even for the most terrible events to be able to live. 'There is nothing in the world...that would so effectively help one survive even the worst conditions as the knowledge that there is a meaning in one's life.'[1] We also need stories to give meaning to the existence of communities. Medieval origin stories of a *gens*, a people, were one iteration of such community construction, for example; they were made-up stories of migration based on the biblical model of the Israelites. Stories about the origin of kingship were another way to provide coherence to a group in the medieval period. Human communities' desire for meaning also gave birth to narratives of nationhood and continues to influence the ways in which we try to create and narratively construct community. Beginnings and national heroes take pride of place in such accounts. These stories cannot admit grey zones; even when historical analyses are more nuanced, they tend to lose those nuances in the popular retelling, and even more so in political usage. We are witnessing today the proliferation of palpably untrue stories: the mobilization of people via conspiracy theories, and barefaced lies about what a nation should be. As Eric Hobsbawm famously quipped, 'Historians are to nationalism what poppy-growers in Pakistan are to heroin-addicts: we supply the essential raw material for the market.'[2] He continued: 'What makes the nation *is* the past....The history that nationalists want is not the history that professional academic historians, even ideologically committed ones, ought to supply. It is retrospective myth.'[3] As I hope to have demonstrated, it is particularly easy to supply medieval myths as history, since they have served as our primary sources. Different generations of historians possess different sensibilities; we are now much more alert to the constructed nature of all types of sources. I am under no illusion that this knowledge will prevent old and new nationalisms from exploiting mythistory. But perhaps we can show those who care to listen that it is infinitely more interesting to look at how and why the stories were woven in the first place, instead of perpetuating fake certainties.

Stephen I, the First Christian King of Hungary: From Medieval Myth to Modern Legend. Nora Berend, Oxford University Press. © Nora Berend 2024. DOI: 10.1093/9780191995439.003.0006

---

[1] Viktor E. Frankl, *Man's Search for Meaning* (London: Rider, 2004), 109.
[2] E. J. Hobsbawm, 'Ethnicity and nationalism in Europe today', *Anthropology Today*, 8, no. 1 (February 1992): 3.
[3] Ibid.

Selected Bibliography

Abbreviations

MGH   *Monumenta Germaniae Historica*. Edited by Gregorius Pertz et al. (1826–)
SRH   *Scriptores Rerum Hungaricarum*. Edited by Imre Szentpétery, 2 vols (Budapest: MTA, 1937–1938, reprint Budapest: Nap Kiadó, 1999).

Primary sources

Budapest, Magyar Országos Levéltár (MOL) (Hungarian National Archives) https://archives.hungaricana.hu/en/charters/
  Diplomáciai Levéltár (DL)
  30586
  49684
  65097
  102890

  Diplomáciai Filmtár (DF)
  237875
  248074
  248143
  256331

Budapest, Országos Széchényi Könyvtár
  Mny 1, https://mek.oszk.hu/12800/12855/html/index.html
Cambridge University Library
  Johannes de Thurocz. *Chronica Hungarorum*. (Augsburg, 1488) Inc.5.A.6.18.

Adémar de Chabannes. *Ademari Cabannensis Chronicon*, edited by P. Bourgain, R. Landes, and G. Pon. Corpus Christianorum Continuatio Mediaevalis 129 (Turnhout: Brepols, 1999).
'Annales Altahenses maiores'. Edited by Wilhem von Giesebrecht and Edmund L. B. von Oefele. *MGH Scriptores Rerum Germanicarum* vol. 4 (Hanover: Hahn, 1891).
'Annales Posonienses'. Edited by Imre Madzsar. *SRH*, vol. 1, 119–127.
Antonio Bonfini, *Rerum ungaricarum decades* (Basileae, 1543) https://www.digitale-sammlungen.de/de/view/bsb10141205?page=1
Antonius de Bonfinis Rerum Ungaricarum Decades, edited by József Fógel, Béla Iványi, László Juhász. 4 vols. (Leipzig: Teubner, 1936–Budapest: Egyetemi Nyomda, 1941).
A turáni egyistenhívők egyszerű istentiszteletének szertartása. Composed and partly written by Batu (Budapest: Turáni Roham Kiadóhivatal, 1936).
Bak, János M., György Bónis, and James Ross Sweeney. ed., tr. *The Laws of the Medieval Kingdom of Hungary 1000–1301* (Bakersfield, CA: Charles Schlacks, 1989).

240   SELECTED BIBLIOGRAPHY

Békés, Csaba and Malcolm Byrne. ed. *Rendszerváltozás Magyarországon 1989-1990. Dokumentumok* (Budapest: National Security Archive – 1956-os Intézet, 1999).

Bencsi, Zoltán. 'Koppány és Vattha nyomában...'. *Turáni roham* 1, no. 4 (7 February 1935): p. 1.

Bencsi, Zoltán. *Koppány-e vagy István (Történelmi korrajz)* (Budapest: author's edition, Gyarmati Ferenc könyvnyomda [1938]).

'Chronici Hungarici compositio saeculi XIV'. Edited by Sándor Domanovszky. *SRH*, vol. 1, pp. 217–505.

'Chronicon Zagrabiense cum textu Chronici Varadiensis collatum'. Edited by Emericus Szentpétery. SRH, vol. 1, 195–215.

Constantine Porphyrogenitus. *De administrando imperio*, edited by Gyula Moravcsik, translated by R. J. H. Jenkins, rev. edn. (Washington DC: Dumbarton Oaks Center for Byzantine Studies, 1967).

Decsy, Sámuel. *A' magyar szent koronának és az ahoz tartozó tárgyaknak historiája* (Vienna, 1792; reprint Budapest: Kossuth Kiadó 2013).

Dercsényi, Dezső. ed. *The Hungarian Illuminated Chronicle* (Budapest: Corvina Press, 1969).

Dobszay, László. *Historia Sancti Stephani Regis 1190-1270* (Ottawa: The Institute of Mediaeval Music, 2010).

Fejér, György. *Codex diplomaticus Hungariae ecclesiasticus ac civilis*. 11 vols. (Buda, 1829–1844).

'Fundatio ecclesiae S. Albani Namucensis'. Edited by O. Holder-Egger. *MGH Scriptores* XV/2 (Hanover: Hahn, 1888), pp. 962–964.

Gombos, Albinus Franciscus. *Catalogus Fontium Historiae Hungaricae*. 4 vols. (Budapest: Szent István Akadémia 1937–1943, repr. Budapest: Nap Kiadó, 2011).

Gregory VII, *Gregorii papae VII Epistolae Selectae. Fontes litem de investitura illustrantes*, edited by Franz-Josef Schmale. Ausgewählte Quellen zur deutschen Geschichte des Mittelalters XIIa (Darmstadt: wbg-Verlag, 1978).

Györffy, György. ed. *Diplomata Hungariae antiquissima* (Budapest: Akadémiai Kiadó, 1992).

Hageneder, Othmar and Anton Haidacher. ed. *Die Register Innocenz' III*, vol. 1, *Pontifikatsjahr 1, 1198/99* (Graz and Cologne: Böhlau, 1964).

Horváth, Mihály. *A kereszténység első százada Magyarországon* (Budapest: Ráth Mór, 1878).

Huszár, Tibor. ed. *Kedves, jó Kádár elvtárs! Válogatás Kádár János levelezéséből* (Budapest: Osiris, 2002).

Johannes de Thurocz, Chronica Hungarorum. vol. 1, *Textus*, edited by Elisabeth Galántai and Julius Kristó (Budapest: Akadémiai Kiadó, 1985), vol. 2, *Commentarii*, 1. *Ab initiis usque ad annum 1301*, (Budapest: Akadémiai Kiadó, 1988). Elemér Mályusz and Julius Kristó.

John Skylitzes. *Byzantium in the Time of Troubles: The Continuation of the Chronicle of John Skylitzes 1057-1079*, translated by Eric McGeer (Leiden and Boston: Brill, 2020).

Kádár, János. *Szilárd népi hatalom: független Magyarország* (Budapest: Kossuth Könyvkiadó, 1959).

Kádár, János. *Tovább a lenini úton* (Budapest: Kossuth Könyvkiadó, 1964).

Kádár, János. *Hazafiság és internacionalizmus* (Budapest: Kossuth Könyvkiadó, 1968).

Kádár, János. *Szövetségi politika – nemzeti egység: beszédek és cikkek, 1978–1981* (Budapest: Kossuth Könyvkiadó, 1981).

Kádár, János. *A szocializmus megújulása Magyarországon: Válogatott beszédek és cikkek 1957-1986* (Budapest: Kossuth Könyvkiadó, 1986).

SELECTED BIBLIOGRAPHY   241

Kádár, János. *Válogatott beszédek és cikkek 1957–1973* (Budapest: Kossuth Könyvkiadó, 1974).

Katona, István. *Historia critica regum Hungariae*. 42 vols (Pest, 1779–1817).

Knauz, Ferdinand. *Monumenta Ecclesiae Strigoniensis*, vol. 1 (Esztergom, 1874).

Koltay, Gábor. *István, a király* (Budapest: Ifjúsági Lap- és Könyvkiadó Vállalat, 1984).

Krčelić, Adam Baltazar. *Balthasaris Adami Kercselich de Corbavia Historiarum Cathedralis Ecclesiae Zagrabiensis Partis Primae*, vol. 1 (Zagreb, 1760).

Kristó, Gyula et al. ed. *Anjou-kori oklevéltár*, 52 vols to date (Budapest and Szeged: Szegedi Középkorász Műhely, 1990–).

'Legenda Sancti Stephani regis maior et minor, atque legenda ab Hartvico episcopo conscripta'. Edited by Emma Bartoniek SRH, vol. 2, pp. 363–440. English translations with introduction 'Saint Stephen of Hungary'. Gábor Thorockay, Nora Berend and Cristian Gaşpar. In *The Sanctity of the Leaders: Holy Kings, Princes, Bishops, and Abbots from Central Europe (eleventh to thirteenth centuries). Sanctitas principum: sancti reges duces episcopi et abbates Europae Centralis (saec. XI-XIII)*, edited by Gábor Klaniczay and Ildikó Csepregi. Central European Medieval Texts 7 (Budapest, New York and Vienna: CEU Press, 2023), pp. 19–175.

Moravetz, Orsolya. *A magyar szent korona*. Országgyűlés Hivatala Nemzet Főtere Füzetek sorozat (Budapest: Országgyűlés Hivatala, 2016).

Nagy, Imre. *Snagovi jegyzetek: Gondolatok, emlékezések 1956–1957*, edited by István Vida (Budapest: Gondolat Kiadó – Nagy Imre Alapitvány, 2006).

Ottokar von Steiermark. *Ottokars Österreichische Reimchronik*, edited by Joseph Seemüller MGH, *Deutsche Chroniken* 5, 1–2. 2 vols (Hannover: Hahn, 1890).

Pór, Antal and László Fejérpataky. ed. *Acta legationis cardinalis Gentilis, 1307–1311* Monumenta Vaticana historiam Regni Hungariae illustrantia, Series I, vol. 2 (Budapest, 1885; reprint Budapest: METEM, 2000).

Pray, Georgius. *Dissertatio historico-critica de Sacra Dextera Divi Stephani primi Hungariae regis* (Vienna, 1771).

Révay, Péter. *De sacrae coronae Regni Hungariae ortu, virtute, victoria, fortuna, annos ultra DC clarissimae brevis commentarius Petri de Rewa comitis comitatus de Turocz* (Augustae Vindelicorum, 1613).

Révay, Péter. *De monarchia et Sacra Corona Regni Hungariae centuriae Septem. A Magyar Királyság birodalmáról és Szent Koronájáról szóló hét század*, edited and translated by Gergely Tóth, Bernadett Benei, Rezső Jarmalov, and Sára Sánta. 2 vols. (Budapest: ELKH Bölcsészettudományi Kutatóközpont, 2022).

Sámuel, Alajos. *Szent István első és apostoli magyar király mint népe szent hite- 's nemzetiségének megalapítója* (Pest, 1845).

Sándor, István. *Sokféle írás egybeszedése, 1. darab* (Győr, 1791).

Simon of Kéza. *Simonis de Kéza, Gesta Hungarorum. Simon of Kéza, The Deeds of the Hungarians*, edited by László Veszprémy (Budapest: CEU Press, 1999).

Simon, Matheus. *Supplementum ad Dissertationem Historico-Criticam Clar. Georgii Pray de dextra S. Stephani primi Hungariae regis cum Historia Monasterii Sz. Jog ubi olim sacra haec Dextra asservabatur* (Vác, 1797).

Szentpétery, Imre and Iván Borsa. *Regesta regum stirpis critico-diplomatica. Az Árpád-házi királyok okleveleinek kritikai jegyzéke*. 3 vols (Budapest: MTA, 1923–1987).

Szentpétery, Imre and Attila Zsoldos, *Az Árpád-házi hercegek, hercegnők, és a királynék okleveleinek kritikai jegyzéke. Regesta Ducum Ducissarum stirpis Arpadianae necnon reginarum Hungariae critico-diplomatica. A Magyar Országos Levéltár Kiadványai II. Forráskiadványok* 45 (Budapest: Magyar Országos Levéltár, 2008).

242 SELECTED BIBLIOGRAPHY

Szereda, Vjacseszlav and János M. Rainer. ed. *Döntés a Kremlben, 1956. A szovjet pártel-nökség vitái Magyarországról* (Budapest: 1956-os intézet, 1996).

Szőcs, Tibor. *Az Árpádkori nádorok és helyetteseik okleveleinek kritikai jegyzéke. Regesta palatinorum et vices gerentium tempore regum stirpis Arpadanae critico-diplomatica.* A Magyar Országos Leváltár Kiadványai II. Forráskiadványok 51. (Budapest: Archívum, Magyar Országos Levéltár, 2012).

Theiner, Augustinus. *Vetera Monumenta Historia Hungaricam Sacram Illustrantia*, vol. 1 *1216–1352* (Rome, 1859).

Thietmar of Merseburg, *Thietmari Chronicon a. 919–1018*, edited by C. I. M. Lappenberg. *MGH Scriptores*, vol. 3 (Hannover: Hahn, 1839), pp. 723–871.

Thomas of Split. *Thomae archidiaconi Spalatensis Historia Salonitanorum atque Spalatinorum pontificum. Archdeacon Thomas of Split: History of the Bishops of Salona and Split*, edited and translated by Olga Perić, Damir Karbić, Mirjana Matijević Sokol and James Ross Sweeney (Budapest: Central European University Press, 2006).

Timon, Ákos. *Magyar alkotmány- és jogtörténet tekintettel a nyugati államok jogfejlődésére* (Budapest: Politzer Zsigmond és fia, 1902).

Timon, Ákos. *A Szent Korona elmélete és a koronázás* (1920, repr. Nemzeti Örökség Kiadó no place, no date).

Tkalčić, Joannes Bapt. ed. *Monumenta historica episcopatus Zagrabiensis saec. XII et XIII*, vol. 1 (Zagreb, 1873).

Varga, László. ed. *A forradalom hangja. Magyarországi rádióadások 1956 október 23. – november 9.* (Budapest: Századvég Kiadó – Nyilvánosság Klub, 1989).

Secondary sources

Ablonczy, Balázs. *Keletre, magyar! A magyar turanizmus története* (Budapest: Jaffa Kiadó, 2016).

Aczél, Tamás and Tibor Méray, *Tisztító vihar* (Szeged: JATE Kiadó, 1989).

Bagnoli, Martina, Holger A. Klein, C. Griffith Mann, and James Robinson. ed. *Treasures of heaven: Saints, relics and devotion in medieval Europe*, Catalogue (London: British Museum, 2011).

Bak, János M. *Studying Medieval Rulers and Their Subjects: Central Europe and Beyond*, edited by Balázs Nagy and Gábor Klaniczay (Farnham: Ashgate, 2010).

Bak, János M. and Géza Pálffy. *Crown and coronation in Hungary 1000-1916 A. D.* (Budapest: Research Centre for the Humanities – Hungarian National Museum, 2020).

Bárány-Oberschall, Magda von. *Die Sankt Stephans-Krone und die Insignien des Königreiches Ungarn*, 2nd ed (Vienna – Munich: Verlag Herold, 1974).

Bardoly, István. ed. *The Coronation Mantle of the Hungarian Kings* (Budapest: Hungarian National Museum, 2005).

Bartoniek, Emma. 'Corona és regnum'. *Századok* 68 (1934): pp. 314–331.

Bartoniek, Emma. *A magyar királykoronázások története* (Budapest, 1939, reprint Budapest: Akadémiai Kiadó, 1987).

Beke, Margit. 'A Szent Jobb tisztelete az újkorban'. In *Szentjeink és nagyjaink Európa kereszténységéért*, edited by Margit Beke. Miscellanea Ecclesiae Strigoniensis 1 (Budapest: Esztergom-budapesti Főegyházmegye Egyháztörténeti Bizottsága, 2001), pp. 45–51.

Benda, Kálmán and Erik Fügedi. *A magyar korona regénye* (Budapest: Magvető Kiadó, 1979).

SELECTED BIBLIOGRAPHY   243

Benei, Bernadett. *A magyar krónika Árpád-kori szakaszának latin nyelve* (Budapest: Bölcsészettudományi Kutatóközpont Történettudományi Intézet, 2022).

Berend, Nora, József Laszlovszky and Béla Zsolt Szakács. 'The Kingdom of Hungary'. In *Christianization and the rise of Christian monarchy: Central Europe, Scandinavia and Rus' c. 950 – c. 1200*, edited by Nora Berend (Cambridge: Cambridge University Press, 2007), ch. 8.

Berend, Nora, Przemysław Urbańczyk and Przemysław Wiszewski. *Central Europe in the High Middle Ages, c. 900-c.1300* (Cambridge: Cambridge University Press, 2013).

Bertényi, Iván. *A magyar szent korona: Magyarország címere és zászlaja*, 4th ed. (Budapest: Kossuth Könyvkiadó, 1996).

Bochkor, Ádám. 'A Szent Jobb orvosi szemmel'. *Vigilia* 25, no. 8 (1960): pp. 492–494.

Bock, Franz. 'Die ungarischen Reichsinsignien, VI: Die Krone des hl. Stephan'. *Mittheilungen der kaiserliche königliche Central-Comission zur Erforschung und Erhaltung der Baudenkmale* 2 (Vienna, 1857): pp. 201–211.

Bock, Franz. *Die Kleinodien des Heiligen Römischen Reiches deutscher Nation nebts den Kroninsignien Böhmens, Ungarns und der Lombardei*. 3 vols (Vienna, 1864).

Bogyay, Tamás. *Stephanus Rex* (Budapest: Ecclesia Kiadó, 1988).

Bónis, György. *István király* (Budapest: "Művelt Nép" Tudományos és Ismeretterjesztő Kiadó, 1956).

Browning, Robert. 'A new source on Byzantine - Hungarian relations in the twelfth century: The inaugural lecture of Michael O tou Agchialou ōs ypatos tōn filosofōn'. *Balkan Studies*, 2 (1961): pp. 173–214.

Buccellati, Graziella. ed. *The Iron Crown and Imperial Europe*, vol. 1, *The Crown, the Kingdom and the Empire: A thousand years of history* (Milan: Editoriale Giorgio Mondadori, Monza: Società di Studi Monzesi, 1995).

Buckton, David. 'The Holy Crown in the History of Enamelling'. *Acta Historiae Artium* 43 (2002): pp. 14–21.

Bunyitai, Vince. *A váradi püspökség története alapításától a jelenkorig*. 4 vols (Nagyvárad, 1883).

Cevins, Marie-Madeleine de. 'Les origines médiévales de la doctrine de la Sainte Couronne'. *Hungarian Studies* 30, no. 2 (2016): pp. 175–190.

Cheynet, Jean-Claude. 'L'Empire Byzantin et la Hongrie dans la seconde moitié du XIe siècle'. *Acta Historiae Artium* 43 (2002): pp. 5–13, reprint Jean-Claude Cheynet. *La société byzantine: L'apport des sceaux* (Paris: Centre de recherche d'histoire et civilisation de Byzance, 2008), pp. 609–626.

Csatári, Bence. *A Kádár rendszer könnyűzenei politikája*. PhD dissertation (Budapest: ELTE, 2008) http://doktori.btk.elte.hu/hist/csatari/disszert.pdf

Csepeli, György. *National identity in contemporary Hungary*, translated by Mario D. Fenyo (Boulder, Co: Social Science Monographs – Highland Lakes, NJ: Atlantic Research and Publications, Inc, 1997).

Csóka, Lajos J. *A latin nyelvű történeti irodalom kialakulása Magyarországon a XI-XIV. században* (Budapest: Akadémiai Kiadó, 1967).

Deér, Josef. *Die Heilige Krone Ungarns* (Vienna: Österreichischen Akademie der Wissenschaften, 1966; Hungarian tr. Deér, József. *A magyarok szent koronája* (Budapest: Magyar Nemzeti Múzeum, Máriabesnyő – Gödöllő: Attraktor, 2005).

Dobszay, László. 'From "crudelitas" to "credulitas": Comments on Saint Stephen's Historia Rhythmica'. In *Political plainchant? Music, Text and Historical Context of Medieval Saints' Offices*, edited by Roman Hankeln (Ottawa: The Institute of Mediaeval Music, 2009), pp. 93– 106.

244 SELECTED BIBLIOGRAPHY

Dornbach, Alajos, Péter Kende, János M. Rainer, and Katalin Somlai. ed. *A per: Nagy Imre és társai* (Budapest: 1956-os Intézet – Nagy Imre Alapítvány, 2008).

Duggan, Anne J. ed. *Kings and Kingship in Medieval Europe* (London: King's College London, 1993).

Eckhart, Ferenc. 'Jog- és alkotmánytörténet'. In *A magyar történetírás új útjai*, edited by Bálint Hóman (Budapest: Magyar Szemle Társaság, 1931, 2nd ed. 1932), 269–320.

Eckhart, Ferenc. *A Szentkorona-eszme története* (Budapest: Magyar Tudományos Akadémia, 1941).

Érszegi, Géza. 'Szent István pannonhalmi oklevele (Oklevéltani-filológiai tanulmány)'. In *Mons Sacer, 996-1996, Pannonhalma ezer éve*, edited by Imre Takács. 3 vols., vol 1 (Pannonhalma: Pannonhalmi Bencés Apátság, 1996), pp. 47–89.

Evans, H. C. and W. D. Wixom. ed. *The Glory of Byzantium. Art and Culture of the Middle Byzantine Era A. D. 843–1261* (New York: Metropolitan Museum of Art, 1997).

Fehértói, Katalin. *Árpád-kori személynévtár (1000–1301)* (Budapest: Akadémiai Kiadó, 2004).

Feischmidt, Margit, Rita Glózer, Zoltán Ilyés, Katalin Veronika Kasznár, and Ildikó Zakariás. ed. *Nemzet a mindennapokban: Az újnacionalizmus populáris kultúrája* (Budapest: L'Harmattan, 2014).

Fejérpataky, László. *A Királyi kanczellária az Árpádok korában* (Budapest: A Magyar Tudományos Akadémia, 1885).

Folz, Robert. *Les saints rois du Moyen Âge en Occident (VIe–XIIIe siècles)* (Brussels: Société des Bollandistes, 1984).

Fügedi, Erik. ed. *Művelődéstörténeti tanulmányok a magyar középkorról* (Budapest: Gondolat, 1986).

Fraknói, Vilmos. 'A Szent Jobb'. *Századok* 35 (1901): pp. 880–904.

Fried, Johannes. *Otto III. Und Boleslaw Chrobry: Das Widmungsbild des Aachener Evangeliars, der "Akt von Gnesen" und das frühe polnische und ungarische Königtum. Eine Bildanalyse und ihre historischen Folgen*, 2nd edn (Stuttgart: Franz Steiner Verlag, 2001).

Gábor, György. *A Szent István-napi ünnep története* (Budapest: Franklin, 1927).

Gaborit-Chopin, Danielle. 'Les couronnes du sacre des rois et des reines au trésor de Saint-Denis'. *Bulletin Monumental* 133, no. 2 (1975): pp. 165–174.

Gerics, József. *Legkorábbi Gesta-szerkesztéseink keletkezésrendjének problémái* (Budapest: Akadémiai Kiadó, 1961).

Gerics, József. 'A Hartvik-legenda mintáiról és forrásairól'. *Magyar Könyvszemle* 97 (1981): pp. 175–188.

Gerics, József. *Egyház, állam és gondolkodás Magyarországon a középkorban* (Budapest: METEM, 1995).

Gerics, József and Erzsébet Ladányi, 'A Hartvik legenda keletkezési körülményeiről'. *Magyar Könyvszemle* 120, no. 4 (2004): pp. 317–324.

Glatz, Ferenc and József Kardos. ed. *Szent István és kora* (Budapest: MTA Történettudományi Intézet, 1988).

Gough, Roger. *A Good Comrade: János Kádár, Communism and Hungary* (London and New York: I.B. Tauris, 2006).

Goullet, Monique. *Écriture et réécriture hagiographiques: Essai sur les réécritures de Vies de saints dans l'Occident latin médiéval (VIIIe–XIIIe s.)* (Turnhout: Brepols, 2005).

Grévin, Benoît. 'Nationalisme et médiévalisme'. In *Middle Ages without borders: a conversation on medievalism. Medioevo senza frontiere: una conversazione sul medievalismo. Moyen Âge sans frontières: une conversation sur le médiévalisme*, edited by Tommaso di

SELECTED BIBLIOGRAPHY 245

Carpegna Falconieri, Pierre Savy, and Lila Yawn. Collection de l'École française de Rome 586 (Rome: École française de Rome, 2021), pp. 155–183.

Györffy, György. 'Koppány lázadása'. *Somogy megye múltjából. Levéltári évkönyv 1* (Kaposvár, 1970), pp. 5–30.

Györffy, György. *István király és műve* (Budapest: Gondolat, 1977; 4th rev edn Budapest: Balassi Kiadó, 2013).

Hahn, Cynthia. *Strange beauty: Issues in the Making and Meaning of Reliquaries, 400 – circa 1204* (Pennsylvania: Pennsylvania State University Press, 2012).

Hann, Chris M. 'Socialism and King Stephen's Right Hand'. *Religion in Communist Lands* 18, no. 1 (1990): pp. 4–24.

Hajdu, Tibor. 'A Rajk-per háttere és fázisai'. *Társadalmi Szemle* 11 (1992): pp. 17–36.

Halmágyi, Miklós. '"boldog István törvénye szerint" – A Szent István királyra való hivatkozás példái a középkori jogi és társadalmi gondolkodásban'. In *Urbs, civitas, universitas: ünnepi tanulmányok Petrovics István 65. születésnapja tiszteletére*, edited by Sándor Papp, Zoltán Kordé, and László Sándor Tóth (Szeged: Szegedi Tudományegyetem, 2018), pp. 152–158.

Hetherington, Paul. 'La couronne grecque de la Sainte Couronne de Hongrie: le contexte de ses émaux et de ses bijoux'. *Acta Historiae Artium* 43 (2002): pp. 33–38.

Hilsdale, Cecily J. 'The Social Life of the Byzantine Gift: The Royal Crown of Hungary Reinvented'. *Art History* 31, no. 5 (2008): pp. 603–631.

Hóman, Bálint. *A Szent-László kori Gesta Ungarorum és XII-XIII. századi leszármazói (Forrástanulmány)* (Budapest: Magyar Tudományos Akadémia, 1925).

Horváth, János. *Árpád-kori latin nyelvű irodalmunk stílusproblémái* (Budapest: Akadémiai Kiadó, 1954).

Huszár, Lajos. *Münzkatalog Ungarn von 1000 bis Heute* (Budapest: Corvina, 1979).

Huszár, Tibor. *Kádár János politikai életrajza*. 2 vols (Budapest: Szabad Tér Kiadó – Kossuth Kiadó, 2001–2003).

Huszár, Tibor and János Szabó. ed. *Restauráció vagy kiigazítás: A kádári represszió intézményesülése 1956–1962* (Budapest: Zrínyi Kiadó, 1999).

Ipolyi, Arnold, *A Magyar Szent korona és a koronázási jelvények története és műleírása* (Budapest: Magyar Tudományos Akadémia, 1886).

Jolivet-Lévy, Catherine. 'L'apport de l'iconographie à l'interprétation de la "corona graeca"'. *Acta Historiae Artium* 43 (2002): pp. 22–32.

Junghans, Martina. *Die Armreliquiare in Deutschland vom 11. bis zur Mitte des 13. Jahrhunderts* (Bonn: Friedrich Wilhelms Universität, 2002).

Kantorowicz, Ernst H. *The King's Two Bodies: A Study in Medieval Political Theology* (Princeton, NJ: Princeton University Press, 1981).

Karácsonyi, János. *Szent István oklevelei és a Szilveszterbulla. Diplomatikai tanulmány* (Budapest: Magyar Tudományos Akadémia, 1891).

Karácsonyi, János. *A hamis, hibáskeltű és keltezetlen oklevelek jegyzéke 1400-ig* (Budapest: Magyar Tudományos Akadémia, 1902).

Karácsonyi, János. *Szent István király élete* (Budapest: Szent István Társulat, 1904).

Kardos, József. 'Az Eckhart-vita és a Szentkorona-tan'. *Századok* 103, nos. 5-6 (1969): pp. 1104–1117.

Kardos, József. *A szentkorona-tan története 1919–1944* (Budapest: Akadémiai Kiadó, 1985).

Kardos, József. *A Szent Korona és a szentkorona-eszme története* (Budapest: IKVA, 1992).

Karpat, Josef. 'Corona regni Hungariae im Zeitalter der Arpaden'. In *Corona regni: Studien über die Krone als Symbol des Staates im Späteren Mittelalter*, edited by Manfred Hellmann (Darmstadt: Wissenschaftliche Buchgesellschaft, 1961), pp. 225–348.

246 SELECTED BIBLIOGRAPHY

Kerbl, Raimund. *Byzantinische Prinzessinnen in Ungarn zwischen 1050–1200 und ihr Einfluß auf das Arpadenkönigreich* (Vienna: Verband der wissenschaftlichen Gesellschaften Österreichs, 1979).

Kerny, Terézia. *Uralkodók, királyi szentek: Válogatott ikonográfiai és kultusztörténeti tanulmányok* (Budapest: MTA Bölcsészettudományi Kutatóközpont Művészettörténeti Intézet, 2018).

Kiss, Etele. 'La "Couronne grecque" dans son contexte'. *Acta Historiae Artium* 43 (2002): pp. 39–51.

Klaniczay, Gábor. *Holy Rulers and Blessed Princesses: Dynastic Cults in Medieval Central Europe*, translated by Éva Pálmai (Cambridge: Cambridge University Press, 2002).

Klimó, Árpád von. 'A nemzet Szent Jobbja: a nemzeti-vallási kultuszok funkcióiról'. *Replika* 37 (1999): pp. 45–56.

Klimó, Árpád von. 'St. Stephen's Day. Politics and Religion in 20th-Century Hungary'. *East Central Europe = L'Europe du centre-est* 26. no. 2 (1999): pp. 15–31.

Klimó, Árpád von. 'The King's Right Hand. A Hungarian National-Religious Holiday and the Conflict between the Communist Party and the Catholic Church (1945–48)'. In *Festive Culture in Germany and Europe*, edited by Karin Friedrich (Lampeter: Edwin Mellen Press, 2000), pp. 343–362.

Knapp, Éva and Gábor Tüskés. 'Szent István király és a Szent Jobb együttes ábrázolása a sokszorosított grafikában'. In *Jubileumi csokor Csapodi Csaba tiszteletére: tanulmányok*, edited by Marianne Rozsondai (Budapest: Argumentum Kiadó, 2002).

Koltay, Gábor. ed. *István, a király, 1983–2008: Emlékkönyv az ősbemutató 25. évfordulójára* (Budapest: Szabad Tér, 2008).

Korányi, Tamás G. ed. *Egy népfelkelés dokumentumai 1956* (Budapest: Tudósítások Kiadó, 1989).

Kovács, Éva. 'Les émaux "latins" de la couronne de Hongrie'. *Atti del XXIV congresso internazionale di Storia dell'Arte*, edited by A. A. Schmid et al. 11 vols (Bologna: CLUEB, 1981–1984), vol. 2, 241–246.

Kovács, Éva and Zsuzsa Lovag, *The Hungarian Crown and Other Regalia.* 2nd rev. ed. (Budapest: Corvina, 1980).

Lovag, Zsuzsa. 'L'intégration de la couronne latine et la couronne grecque'. *Acta Historiae Artium* 43, no. 1 (2002): pp. 62–71.

Kovács, László. *A kora Árpád-kori magyar pénzverésről: Érmetani és régészeti tanulmányok a Kárpát-medence I. (Szent) István és II. (Vak) Béla uralkodása közötti időszakának (1000-1141) érméiről.* Varia Archaeologica Hungarica VII (Budapest: MTA Régészeti Intézete, 1997).

Kovács, László. 'A Szent István-i lándzsa'. In *Koronák, koronázási jelvények. Crowns, coronation insignia*, edited by Lívia Bende and Gábor Lőrinczy (Ópusztaszer: Csongrád Megyei Múzeumok Igazgatósága, 2001), pp. 99–136.

Kralovánszky, Alán. 'Szent István király székesfehérvári sírja és kultuszhelye'. In *Szent István király és Székesfehérvár*, edited by Gyula Fülöp (Székesfehérvár: Szent István király Múzeum, 1996), pp. 13–24.

Kramp, Mario. ed. *Krönungen. Könige in Aachen – Geschichte und Mythos. Katalog der Ausstellung.* 2 vols (Mainz: Verlag Philipp von Zabern, 2000).

Kristó, Gyula. 'Szempontok korai helyneveink történeti tipológiájához'. *Acta Universitatis Szegediensis de Attila József Nominatae: Acta Historica* 55 (1976): pp. 1–101.

Kristó, Gyula. *Levedi törzsszövetségétől Szent István államáig* (Budapest: Magvető Könyvkiadó, 1980).

Kristó, Gyula. *A történeti irodalom Magyarországon a kezdetektől 1241-ig* (Budapest: Argumentum Kiadó, 1994).

SELECTED BIBLIOGRAPHY 247

Kristó, Gyula. *Írások Szent Istvánról és koráról* (Szeged: Szegedi Középkorász Műhely, 2000).

Kristó, Gyula. *Szent István király* (Budapest: Vince Kiadó, 2001).

Kristó, Gyula. *Árpád fejedelemtől Géza fejedelemig: 20 tanulmány a 10. századi magyar történelemről* (Budapest: Akadémiai Kiadó, 2002).

Kristó, Gyula. *Magyar Historiográfia I. Történetírás a középkori Magyarországon* (Budapest: Osiris Kiadó, 2002).

Kristó, Gyula, Ferenc Makk, and László Szegfű, 'Adatok korai helyneveink ismeretéhez [part 1]'. *Acta Universitatis Szegediensis de Attila József Nominatae: Acta Historica* 44 (1973): pp. 1–96.

Kristóf, Alida Lilla. *Paleoradiológia: non-invazív módszertani lehetőség a történeti antropológiában.* PhD dissertation (Szeged, 2015) http://doktori.bibl.u-szeged. hu/2754/1/disszert%C3%A1ci%C3%B3_12.pdf.

Lengyel, László. *A rendszerváltó elit tündöklése és bukása* (Budapest: Helikon, 1996).

Lenkey, Zoltán and Attila Zsoldos, *Szent István és III. András* (Budapest: Kossuth Kiadó, 2003).

Lovag, Zsuzsa. 'A korona-kutatás vadhajtásai'. *Művészettörténeti Értesítő* 35, nos 1–2 (1986): pp. 35–48.

Lovag, Zsuzsa. ed. *Insignia Regni Hungariae I. Studien zur Machtsymbolik des mittelalterlichen Ungarn* (Budapest: Magyar Nemzeti Múzeum, 1983).

Magyar, Kálmán. *Szent István államszervezésének régészeti emlékei* (Kaposvár – Segesd: Segesd Önkormányzat Kiadása, 2001).

Magyar, Zoltán. *Szent István a magyar kultúrtörténetben* (Budapest: Helikon Kiadó, 1996).

Magyar, Zoltán. *Hős vagy lázadó? Koppány alakja a folklórban és a kultúrtörténetben* (Budapest: Magyarságkutató Intézet, 2020).

Makk, Ferenc. *The Árpáds and the Comneni: Political Relations between Hungary and Byzantium in the 12th century* (Budapest: Akadémiai Kiadó, 1989).

Mályusz, Elemér. 'Az Eckhart-vita'. *Századok* 65 (1931): pp. 406–419.

Marczali, Henrik. *Szent István királysága* (1896, reprint Budapest: Kassák Könyv és Lapkiadó Kft, 2000).

Marosi, Ernő. 'A magyar korona a jelenkori kutatásban és a populáris irodalomban: Megjegyzések a művészettörténet-tudomány jelenlegi helyzetéhez és megbecsüléséhez'. *Művészettörténeti Értesítő* 35, nos 1–2 (1986): pp. 49–55.

Marosi, Ernő. ed. *Magyarországi Művészet 1300–1470 körül* (Budapest: Akadémiai Kiadó, 1987).

Marosi, Ernő. 'La "couronne latine"'. *Acta Historiae Artium* 43 (2002): pp. 72–82.

Marosi, Ernő. 'A létező Szent Korona mitizálása'. In *Mítoszaink nyomában*, edited by Gyöngy Kiss Kovács (Cluj-Napoca: Komp-Press, 2013), pp. 37–55.

Mészáros, Balázs. ed. *A Szent Jobb országjárása, 1938–1942* (Budapest: Magyar Nemzeti Múzeum, 2022).

Mezey, László. 'Szent István XIII. századi verses históriája'. In *Magyar Századok. Irodalmi műveltségünk történetéhez. Horváth János Emlékkönyv*, Dezső Pais et al. (Budapest: Egyetemi Nyomda, 1948), pp. 41–51.

Molnár, Antal. 'A Szent Jobb és Raguza'. *Turul* 76, nos. 1-2 (2003): pp. 7–11.

Nemerkényi, Előd. *Latin Classics in Medieval Hungary: Eleventh Century* (Debrecen-Budapest: CEU Press, 2004).

Pálffy, Géza. ed. *A Szent Korona hazatér: a magyar korona tizenegy külföldi útja* (Budapest: MTA Bölcsészettudományi Kutatóközpont Történettudományi Intézet, 2018).

Pauler, Gyula. *A magyar nemzet története az Árpádházi királyok alatt*. 2 vols (Budapest: Athenaeum, 1899, reprint, Budapest: Állami Könyvterjesztő Vállalat, 1985).

248 SELECTED BIBLIOGRAPHY

Péter, László. 'The Holy Crown of Hungary, visible and invisible'. *Slavonic and East European Review* 81, no. 3 (July 2003): pp. 421–509.

Petersohn, Jürgen. 'Über monarchische Insignien und ihre Funktion im mittelalterlichen Reich'. *Historische Zeitschrift* 266, no. 1 (February 1998): pp. 47–96.

Pinoteau, Hervé. *La symbolique royale Française Ve – XVIIIe siècles* (La Roche-Rigault: PSR éditions 2003).

Polemis, Ioannis. 'Notes on the Inaugural Oration of the Patriarch Michael of Anchialos'. *Byzantinoslavica: Revue Internationale des Etudes Byzantines* 69, no. 1–2 (2011): pp. 162–172.

Povedák, István. 'Mitizált Történelem. Szent István dekonstruált – rekonstruált legendáriuma'. In *Már a múlt sem a régi… Az új magyar mitológia multidiszciplináris elemzése*, edited by László Hubbes and István Povedák (Szeged: MTA-SZTE: Vallási Kultúrakutató Csoport, 2015), pp. 100–121. English tr. 'Mythicised history: the deconstructed – reconstructed legend of Saint Stephen'. *Religion, Culture, Society* 2, Yearbook of the MTA-SZTE Research Group for the Study of Religious Culture (Szeged, 2015), pp. 100–116.

Rácz, Árpád. ed. *Ki volt Kádár? Harag és részrehajlás nélkül a Kádár-életútról* (Budapest: Rubicon-Aquila, 2001).

Rácz, Piroska. 'Szent István ereklyéi'. In *Szent István király bazilikájának utóélete: A középkori romkert 1938-tól napjainkig*, edited by Petra Gärtner. A Szent István Király Múzeum Közleményei B series no. 56 (Székesfehérvár, 2016), pp. 31–36.

Rainer, János M. *Nagy Imre* 2nd corr. enlarged edn (Budapest: Nagy Imre Alapítvány, 2016); English translation of first edition, *Imre Nagy. A biography*, translated by Lyman H. Legters (London–New York: Tauris, 2009).

Rainer, János M. *Az 1956-os magyar forradalom* (Budapest: Osiris, 2016).

Réthelyi, Miklós. 'Szent Jobb, az anatómus szemével'. *Medikus* 9, no. 3 (2000): pp. 24–25.

Sassier, Yves. 'La *Corona regni*: émergence d'une *persona ficta* dans la France du XIIe siècle'. In *La puissance royale: Image et pouvoir de l'antiquité au Moyen Âge*, edited by Christian-Georges Schwentzel and Emmanuelle Santinelli-Foltz (Rennes: Presses Universitaires de Rennes, 2012), pp. 99–110.

Schramm, Percy Ernst. ed. *Herrschaftszeichen und Staatssymbolik: Beiträge zu ihrer Geschichte vom dritten bis zum sechzehnten Jahrhundert*. 3 vols. Schriften der Monumenta Germaniae Historica 13, no. 1–3 (Stuttgart: Hiersemann Verlag, 1954–1956).

Sebők, János. *Rock a vasfüggöny mögött: hatalom és ifjúsági zene a Kádár korszakban* (Budapest: GM & Társai Kiadó, 2002).

Serédi, Jusztinián. ed. *Emlékkönyv Szent István király halálának kilencszázadik évfordulóján*. 3 vols (Budapest: Magyar Tudományos Akadémia, 1938), partial reprint in *Szent István Emlékkönyv* (Budapest: Szent István Társulat, 1988).

Shepard, Jonathan. *Emergent Elites and Byzantium in the Balkans and East-Central Europe* (Farnham: Ashgate, 2011).

Simpson, Scott and Kaarina Aitamurto. ed. *Modern Pagan and Native Faith Movements in Central and Eastern Europe* (London: Routledge, 2013).

Solymosi, László. *Írásbeliség és társadalom az Árpád-korban: diplomatikai és pecséttani tanulmányok* (Budapest: Argumentum, 2006).

Standeisky, Éva. *Népuralom ötvenhatban* (Pozsony – Budapest: Kalligram – 1956-os Intézet, 2010).

Szabados, György. *Magyar államalapítások a IX-XI. században: Előtanulmány a korai magyar állam történelmének fordulópontjairól* (Szeged: Szegedi Középkorász Műhely, 2011).

Szakács, Béla Zsolt. 'Remarks on the filigree of the Holy Crown of Hungary'. *Acta Historiae Artium* 43 (2002): pp. 52–61.

SELECTED BIBLIOGRAPHY   249

Szakács, Béla Zsolt. *The Visual World of the Hungarian Angevin Legendary* (Budapest: Central European University Press, 2016).

Szakács, Béla Zsolt. 'What did Piroska see at home? Art and architecture in Hungary around 1100'. In *Piroska and the Pantokrator. Dynastic Memory, Healing and Salvation in Komnenian Constantinople*, edited by Marianne Sághy and Robert Ousterhout (Budapest: Central European University Press, 2019), pp. 39–62.

Szántó, Konrád. 'A Szent Jobb tiszteletének kezdete'. *Vigília* (1985): pp. 395–398.

Székely, György. ed. *Magyarország története: Előzmények és magyar történet 1242-ig* (Budapest: Akadémiai Kiadó, 1984).

Szendrei, Janka. 'Commune pro missionariis? Die ältesten Offiziumsgesänge für König Stephan, den Heiligen'. In *Political plainchant? Music, Text and Historical Context of Medieval Saints' Offices*, edited by Roman Hankeln (Ottawa: The Institute of Mediaeval Music, 2009), pp. 81–92.

Székely, György. 'Koronaküldések és királykreálások a 10-11. századi Európában'. *Századok* 118, no. 5 (1984): pp. 905–949.

Szendrei, László. *Turanizmus: Definíciók és értelmezések 1910-től a II. Világháborúig* (Máriabesnyő and Gödöllő: Attraktor, 2010).

Teszelszky, Kees. *Az ismeretlen korona: jelentések, szimbólumok és nemzeti identitás* (Pannonhalma: Bencés kiadó, 2009).

Thoroczkay, Gábor. *Írások az Árpád-korról: történeti és historiográfiai tanulmányok* (Budapest: L'Harmattan, 2009).

Tóth, Endre and Károly Szelényi. *The Holy Crown of Hungary: kings and coronations* (Budapest: Hungarian National Museum, 1996).

Tóth, Endre. *A magyar szent korona és a koronázási jelvények* (Budapest: Országház Könyvkiadó, 2018; English tr. *The Hungarian Holy Crown and the Coronation Regalia*, 2021).

Tóth, Gergely. *Szent István, Szent Korona, államalapítás a protestáns történetírásban (16-18. század)* (Budapest: MTA Bölcsészettudományi Kutatóközpont Történettudományi Intézet, 2016).

Tóth, Zoltán. *A Hartvik-legenda kritikájához (A Szt. Korona eredetkérdése)* (Budapest: Ranschburg Gusztáv Könyvkereskedése, 1942).

Tóth, Zoltán „Történetkutatásunk mai állása" körül (A szent korona eredetkérdéséhez) (Budapest: Ranschburg Gusztáv Könyvkereskedése, 1943).

Török, József. 'Szentté avatás és liturgikus tisztelet'. In *Művelődéstörténeti tanulmányok a magyar középkorról*, edited by Erik Fügedi (Budapest: Gondolat, 1986), pp. 33–47.

Török, József. ed. *Doctor et apostol: Szent István tanulmányok* (Budapest: Márton Áron Kiadó, 1994).

Uhlirz, Mathilde. *Die Krone des Heiligen Stephan, des ersten Königs von Ungarn.* Veröffentlichungen des Instituts für Österreichische Geschichtsforschung XIV (Graz, Vienna and Munich: Verlag Stiasny G. M. B. H., 1951).

Váczy, Péter. *A magyar történelem korai századaiból* (Budapest: História–MTA Történettudományi Intézet, 1994).

Varga, László. *Kádár János bírái előtt. Egyszer fent, egyszer lent. 1949-1956* (Budapest: Osiris – Budapest Főváros Levéltára, 2001).

Veszprémy, László. 'The Invented 11th Century of Hungary'. In *The Neighbours of Poland in the 11th Century*, edited by Przemysław Urbańczyk (Warsaw: DIG, 2002), pp. 137–154.

Veszprémy, László. ed. *Szent István és az államalapítás* (Budapest: Osiris, 2002).

Veszprémy, László. 'Megjegyzések korai elbeszélő forrásaink történetéhez'. *Századok* 138 (2004): pp. 325–347.

250   SELECTED BIBLIOGRAPHY

Veszprémy, László. 'Fikció és valóság István korában: Kós Károly, Az országépítő'. *Korunk* 26, no. 8 (2015): pp. 13–21.

Veszprémy, László, Tünde Wehli, and József Hapák, *The Book of the Illuminated Chronicle* (Budapest: Kossuth Publishing House, 2009).

Voigt, Vilmos. "'Nem vagyunk mink (…) Szent István szolgái'". In *Magyar, magyarországi és nemzetközi: Történeti folklorisztikai tanulmányok*, Vilmos Voigt (Budapest: Universitas Könyvkiadó, 2004), pp. 290–308.

Weiler, Björn. *Paths to Kingship in Medieval Latin Europe, c.950–1200* (Cambridge: Cambridge University Press, 2021).

Wix, Györgyné. ed. *Szent István és kora: kiállítás az Országos Széchényi Könyvtárban 4 July–29 October 1988* (Budapest: Országos Széchényi Könyvtár, 1988).

Zeidler, Miklós. *Ideas on Territorial Revision in Hungary: 1920–1945* (Boulder, CO: Social Science Monographs, 2007).

Zinner, Tibor. *A kádári megtorlás rendszere* (Budapest: Hamvas Intézet, 2001).

Zinner, Tibor. *"A nagy politikai affér": a Rajk-Brankov ügy*. 2 vols (Budapest: Saxum Kiadó, 2013–2014).

Zsoldos, Attila. ed. *Saint Stephen and His Country: A Newborn Kingdom in Central Europe – Hungary* (Budapest: Lucidus Kiadó, 2001).

Index

Since the index has been created to work across multiple formats, indexed terms for which a page range is given (e.g., 52–53, 66–70, etc.) may occasionally appear only on some, but not all of the pages within the range.

Aachen 168, 205, 217, 219
Admonitions (*Libellus de institutione morum*) 7, 149, 168
Almus, prince 145–6
Andrew I, king of Hungary (1046–60) 34, 171
Andrew II, king of Hungary (1205–35) 18, 177, 203–4, 215
Andrew III, king of Hungary (1290–1301) 207–10
  coronation of 207–10
  war against 210–11
Andropov, Yuri 95, 111
Angevin dynasty 43, 68, 210–14
Anne of Châtillon 177, 185
Anne, princess, daughter of Béla IV 177, 194
Árpád 21, 53–4, 62, 126
Árpád dynasty 7, 18, 52–3
Arrowcross Party 97, 231, 234
Attila the Hun 18–19, 21, 62–3, 126, 235

Beda Venerabilis 149–51
Béla III, king of Hungary (1172–96) 167, 177, 185, 188, 193–5, 200
Béla IV, king of Hungary (1235–70) 131 n.11, 144, 177, 204–6
Bencsi, Zoltán 62–3, 125
Berger, Elias 173, 234
Bolesław I the Brave (Chrobry) 166, 169, 217
  alleged crown of 217
Bonfini, Antonio 49, 51–2, 55, 58, 60, 144–5, 214
Bródy, János 72, 84–8, 113–14, 116–17, 124
Buda 131–6
Byzantine–Hungarian relations 7, 64–5, 174–5, 182–5

'Charlemagne's crown' 210–11, 216–17, 234–5
Charles Robert (Charles I), king of Hungary (1308–42) 130, 144–5, 211–14
Chronicle of Buda. See Chronicles, fourteenth-century

Chronicles, fourteenth-century 2, 30–1, 34, 44–5, 52, 57, 60
Coloman, king of Hungary (1095–1116) 6, 14, 34–5, 56, 132, 145–6, 152–5, 171, 189, 193, 200
Constantine VII Porphyrogenitus 53–4, 174
corona graeca 175–86
'*corona latina*' 175–8, 186–92, 197–8
coronation mantle (chasuble) 1, 130, 167–8, 194–5, 200–1
coronation oath 209
counter-reformation 8, 132–3
crown, abstract concept of 168, 206–8, 218–19, 222
crown of Hungary 12–13, 113, 124, 130, 134. *See also* Stephen, crown of; Holy Crown; *corona graeca*, '*corona latina*'
  angelic 173–4, 215–16, 220
  apostle images on 176–7, 186–92
  as coronation crown 199–200, 211–13
  as 'St Stephen's' 198–9, 207–12, 219–20
  assemblage of 178–9, 193–6
  conspiracy theories about 158–9, 177–8, 234–6
  cross on 197, 234–6
  damage to 176–7, 190–1, 195–7
  depictions of 167–8, 195–6
  enamel images on 176, 179–82, 186–92, 197
  examination of 173–7, 191
  folk traditions about 50, 234
  guards of 157–8, 173–4, 230–1
  in Parliament 157–8
  in US custody 177, 234
  kamelaukion form of 193–5
  legislation about 157–9
  political use of 156–9
  Protestant views on 164, 174
  stealing of 172, 214, 233
  wearing of 130
'crown of St Louis' 217

252 INDEX

'crown of St Wenceslas' 217
Cupan (Kupa, Koppány) 27–66, 68–70, 86,
    113–19, 122, 124–8
  conversion of 64–5, 114, 128
  incest by 30, 42, 51, 54
  folk traditions about 48–9
  national identity and 27, 57–65, 124–8
  nationalist interpretation of 65, 68
  neo- (ethno-)paganism and 62–4, 125–8
  quartering of 30, 40–3, 51–2, 60, 68,
    117, 127
  toponyms and 46–7, 49–50
Cupan, bishop 39, 56, 57 n.156
Cupan, chaplain 57
Cupan, great-grandson of Vecellinus 56, 68
Cupan, son of Cund 57

Decsy, Sámuel 175
Deér, József 177, 188, 194
Dexter, holy
  Enlightenment criticism of 133
  examination of 129 n.1, 139
  feast day of 132–3, 146–7
  folk traditions about 49–50
  inventio of 136–9, 144, 146–53, 155
  monastery of 130–1, 136–41, 143–7. See also
    Stephen III, charter of
  mummification of 139–40
  political role of 129, 134–5, 153, 155
  procession of 134–6
  reliquary of 131–2, 142–3
  representation of 12, 133–4
  ring and 136–9, 152
  seal of monastery of 142–3
  sermons on 133–4
  doctrine of the Holy Crown 220–31, 233
  ducatus, dux 30, 52

Eckhart, Ferenc 221–3
Esztergom 5, 18, 30, 41, 157, 161, 201, 205–6
  archbishop of 18, 135, 145, 157, 193, 200,
    204–8, 233

Fehérvár 1, 5, 18, 40–1, 131, 136–9, 146, 192
  burial of kings at 131, 153–5, 161, 200, 215
  coronation at 200, 208–9, 215, 233
  law-days at 215
  regalia kept at 41, 161, 201–4, 209–10, 215

Gerő, Ernő 90, 93, 99
Géza, Stephen's father 4–7, 19, 31, 53–4, 60, 174
Géza I, king of Hungary (1074–7) 16, 153,
    175–6, 179, 182–5, 193, 216, 235
Géza II, king of Hungary (1141–62) 145

Gisela, Stephen's wife 1, 5–6, 63, 117–18, 167,
    173, 200
Gregory VII, pope 153–4, 164–6, 170, 172, 183
Gyöngyösi, Gergely 144
Györffy, György 41, 52, 73, 140
Győr 5, 30, 41

'hand of St James' 151–2
Hartvic, Life of St Stephen 29–30, 40, 43–4, 51,
    136–43, 146–54, 162–7, 211
Henry III, emperor (1046–56) 170–72
'Holy Crown' 12, 159–61, 173–4,
    199–216, 219–20
  as national symbol 157–8, 230–3, 236
'holy kings' of Hungary 3, 200, 213–14
Hóman, Bálint 9–10, 61
Horthy, Miklós 12, 79, 135, 226, 229
Hungarian Socialist Workers' Party 71–121
Hunt and Paznan 30–1, 44–6, 55

Illuminated Chronicle 43, 55–6, 149, 172,
    193, 216. See also Chronicles,
    fourteenth-century
Innocent III, pope 163–4, 196, 202–3
Iron crown of Monza 185–6, 216–18
István a király, rock opera 65, 68–88, 113–19,
    122–6
  financing of 83
  justification for János Kádár and 83–4
  national identity and 71–80, 87, 123–8
  success of 70–1

Ják family 31, 45–6, 48
Joseph II, Holy Roman Emperor and king of
    Hungary (1780–90) 134, 236

Kádár, János 72–3, 81–4, 88, 92–122
  regime of 80–4, 87–8, 100–13, 119–20, 234
Karácsonyi, János 9, 26, 165, 176
Khrushchev, Nikita 90–1, 94–5,
    97 n.167–8, 99, 105
Koltay, Gábor 71, 77, 83–4
Koppány, See Cupan
Kottanner, Helene 233
Kristó, Gyula 40
Kupa, See Cupan

Ladislas I, king of Hungary (1077–95) 6, 14–16,
    34, 49, 138–41, 143–7, 151–5, 165, 171, 176,
    183, 216
Ladislas IV, king of Hungary (1272–90) 18,
    200, 207, 215
Lalli 66–8
Laskai, Osvát 48, 131

INDEX   253

Lemberg (Lviv) 132, 142
Leopold I, Holy Roman Emperor and king of
 Hungary (1657–1705) 132
Louis I, king of Hungary (1342–82) 137, 141

Maria Theresa, Holy Roman Empress and
 Queen of Hungary (1740–80) 8, 132–3,
 155, 175
Mary (Virgin Mary) 1, 8, 154, 157–8, 236
Matthias Corvinus, king of Hungary
 (1458–90) 49, 194–6, 220
Mattsee 135, 234
Mercurius 137–41, 144, 152
Michael VII Doukas 175, 177, 179–80, 182–5
Mohács, battle of 131
Mongol invasion of Hungary 131 n.11, 141, 204
Moravcsik, Gyula 177, 181–4

Nagy, Imre 72, 87–99, 103–9, 113–17, 119–20
 trial and execution of 106–7
 rehabilitation of 120–22

Orbán, Viktor 156–8
Oswald, king of Northumbria 149–51
 arm relic of 149–51
Otto of Wittelsbach 212, 216, 233
Otto III (996–1002) 5, 7, 28 n.4, 165–8
Ottomans 8, 49, 131–2, 141, 234

pagans, pagan beliefs 6, 27, 35–7, 51, 54–6,
 58–64, 66–8, 158–9
pagan revolt 29–31, 44–5, 48, 51, 55
Pannonhalma, Abbey of St Martin 5, 29–30,
 58, 132
 charter of privileges of 31–2, 44
 child tithe and 29–30, 40
Pauler, Gyula 61, 176
Peter Orseolo, king of Hungary (1038–41) 7,
 165, 170–72
Pray Codex 147

Ragusa (Dubrovnik) 131–2, 136, 141
Rajk, László 90–2, 108
Rajk, László junior 111 n.270
Rákosi, Mátyás 64, 88–93, 98–100
Regensburg 150–1
Reichskrone 216–17, 232
Révay, Péter 173–4, 234–6
revolution of 1848–9 13, 114, 118, 124, 134, 234
Rudolf of Rheinfelden, hand relic of 151

Saint-Denis 202, 205, 210, 219
Samuel Aba, king of Hungary (1041–4)
 170, 172

Sarolt, Stephen's mother 30, 42, 51, 70,
 114–15, 117
Simon of Kéza 31, 38–9, 43–6, 55–6
Solomon, king of Hungary (1063–74) 15,
 34, 153–4, 165–8, 183
Somogy, county 27, 30–2, 43, 47–8, 50, 57,
 57 n.154, 64
Somogyvár 49
'St Edward's crown' 216
Stephen I, king of Hungary (997–1038)
 almsgiving by 135, 148–9
 arm relic of 132, 136–7, 141–2, 147.
  See also dexter
 Basilica of 135–6
 birth date 2–4
 canonization of (1083) 1, 2 n.11, 138–9,
  146–8, 152–4, 171
 Christianization and 4–6, 19, 69–70, 115,
  117, 149, 166, 170
 coinage of 7, 169, 171
 Communist interpretation of 9–12, 64
 condemnation of 13–14, 60, 62, 75,
  127–8
 coronation of 161
 crown of 156–7, 161, 167–73
 cult of 17–18. See also Dexter
 depictions of 1–2, 19, 167
 feast days of 1, 132–6
 historiography on 7–11, 69
 inventio of 140 n.66
 jubilee year (1938) of 11–12, 135, 165,
  176–7
 lance of 7, 167–70, 172
 laws of 6, 42, 168, 215
 Legenda Maior of 29, 148, 154, 162–3, 215.
  See also Vitae
 Legenda Minor of 29, 38, 39, 147–8, 163.
  See also Vitae
 liturgy of 18–19, 152–3
 pagan revolt against. See pagan revolt
 papal crown of 156, 162–7, 174–5, 178,
  211, 215–16, 220
 political uses of 11–14, 20–4, 159
 reburial hypothesis and 139–41, 147
 relics of 129, 142. See also arm relic of; dexter
 rights and 19–20, 215
 royal legitimacy and 14–18
 rulership of 6–7
 Vitae (Lives) of 2–4, 29–30, 43–4, 55, 57,
  60, 145. See also Hartvic
Stephen the king, rock opera, See István
 a király
Stephen III, king of Hungary (1162–72), charter
 of 138–41, 143–6

254 INDEX

Stephen V, king of Hungary (1270–2) 194
Sylvester II, pope 28 n.4, 164–6, 174
Szekfű, Gyula 4, 9, 63–4
Szentjobb (Sîniob). *See* Dexter, monastery of
Szörényi, Gyula 125
Szörényi, Levente 72–5, 84–8, 113, 118–19, 122–3, 126

Thietmar of Merseburg 162–3
Thuróczy, John 51, 56, 58
Tóth, Endre 188–9
Transylvania 30, 41, 51–2, 123
Trianon, Treaty of 11–12, 60, 62, 76–79, 123, 135, 159, 228–9, 232, 234
Turanism 61–4, 125

uprising of 1956 72, 87–100
designations of 115–16, 120
narratives about 102–6, 108–9
reprisals for 100–1

Ur-chronicle 34–40. *See also* Chronicles, fourteenth-century

Vecellinus 30–1, 39, 45–6, 48, 56
descendants of 56
Veszprém 5, 29–30, 41, 173
Veszprémy, László 14
Vienna 132–4
Vikidál, Gyula 72, 84, 118
Visegrád 233

Waik (pre-baptismal name of Stephen) 162
Wenceslas (Ladislas), king of Hungary (1301–5) 130–1, 155
Werbőczy, István 223–4
Władysław III (Ulászló I), king of Hungary (1440–4) 194, 220

Zala, county 47–8